EDEXCEL GCSE (9–1) RELIGIOUS

Catholic Christianity

Faith and Practice in the 21st Century

Victor W. Watton
Assisted by Kevin O'Donnell

Specification A

DYNAMIC LEARNING

HODDER EDUCATION
AN HACHETTE UK COMPANY

In order to ensure that this resource offers high-quality support for the associated Pearson qualification, it has been through a review process by the awarding body. This process confirms that this resource fully covers the teaching and learning content of the specification or part of a specification at which it is aimed. It also confirms that it demonstrates an appropriate balance between the development of subject skills, knowledge and understanding, in addition to preparation for assessment.

Endorsement does not cover any guidance on assessment activities or processes (e.g. practice questions or advice on how to answer assessment questions), included in the resource nor does it prescribe any particular approach to the teaching or delivery of a related course.

While the publishers have made every attempt to ensure that advice on the qualification and its assessment is accurate, the official specification and associated assessment guidance materials are the only authoritative source of information and should always be referred to for definitive guidance.

Pearson examiners have not contributed to any sections in this resource relevant to examination papers for which they have responsibility. Examiners will not use endorsed resources as a source of material for any assessment set by Pearson.

Endorsement of a resource does not mean that the resource is required to achieve this Pearson qualification, nor does it mean that it is the only suitable material available to support the qualification, and any resource lists produced by the awarding body shall include this and other appropriate resources.

In loving memory of
Abby Watton 1974–2015
A wonderful daughter, mummy, sister, friend and RS teacher

Photo credits: are listed on page 370.

Acknowledgements: Bible quotations are from The Holy Bible, New International Version®, NIV® Copyright © 1973, 1978, 1984, 2011 by Biblica, Inc.® Used by permission. All rights reserved worldwide. Qur'an quotations are from The Holy Qur'an translated by Abdullah Yusuf Ali. CAFOD, Linda Jones. Hodder, Yves Dubois, quoted in Christians in Britain Today by Denise Crush, Carol Miles and Margaret Stylianides, 1991. Pennsylvania Catholic Conference.

Every effort has been made to trace all copyright holders, but if any have been inadvertently overlooked, the Publishers will be pleased to make the necessary arrangements at the first opportunity.

Although every effort has been made to ensure that website addresses are correct at time of going to press, Hodder Education cannot be held responsible for the content of any website mentioned in this book. It is sometimes possible to find a relocated web page by typing in the address of the home page for a website in the URL window of your browser.

Orders: please contact Bookpoint Ltd, 130 Milton Park, Abingdon, Oxon OX14 4SE. Telephone: +44 (0)1235 827720. Fax: +44 (0)1235 400454. Email education@bookpoint.co.uk Lines are open from 9 a.m. to 5 p.m., Monday to Saturday, with a 24-hour message answering service. You can also order through our website: www.hoddereducation.co.uk

ISBN: 978 1 4718 6654 8

© Victor W. Watton and Kevin O'Donnell 2016

First published in 2016 by
Hodder Education,
An Hachette UK Company
Carmelite House
50 Victoria Embankment
London EC4Y 0DZ
www.hoddereducation.co.uk

Impression number	10 9 8 7 6 5 4 3 2
Year	2020 2019 2018 2017

All rights reserved. Apart from any use permitted under UK copyright law, no part of this publication may be reproduced or transmitted in any form or by any means, electronic or mechanical, including photocopying and recording, or held within any information storage and retrieval system, without permission in writing from the publisher or under licence from the Copyright Licensing Agency Limited. Further details of such licences (for reprographic reproduction) may be obtained from the Copyright Licensing Agency Limited, Saffron House, 6–10 Kirby Street, London EC1N 8TS.

Cover photo: © Shaunl/istockphoto.com; © Getty Images/iStockphoto/Thinkstock
Produced and typeset in 10/12pt DIN by Gray Publishing, Tunbridge Wells, Kent
Printed in Dubai

A catalogue record for this title is available from the British Library

Contents

Preface — vi

Area of study 1: Study of Catholic Christianity

Section 1: Beliefs and teachings — 1

Topic 1.1.1 The Trinity — 2
Topic 1.1.2 Biblical understandings of God as a Trinity — 7
Topic 1.1.3 Creation — 11
Topic 1.1.4 The nature of humanity — 16
Topic 1.1.5 The incarnation — 19
Topic 1.1.6 The events of the Paschal mystery — 23
Topic 1.1.7 The nature of salvation and grace — 29
Topic 1.1.8 Eschatology — 33

Section 2: Practices — 41

Topic 1.2.1 The sacramental nature of reality — 42
Topic 1.2.2 Catholic liturgical worship — 50
Topic 1.2.3 The Catholic funeral rite — 54
Topic 1.2.4 Prayer — 57
Topic 1.2.5 Forms of popular piety — 61
Topic 1.2.6 Pilgrimage — 66
Topic 1.2.7 Catholic social teaching — 72
Topic 1.2.8 Catholic mission and evangelisation — 77

Section 3: Sources of wisdom and authority — 85

Topic 1.3.1 The Bible — 86
Topic 1.3.2 Interpretation of the Bible — 92
Topic 1.3.3 Scripture, tradition and the magisterium — 95
Topic 1.3.4 The Second Vatican Council — 100
Topic 1.3.5 The Church as the Body of Christ and the People of God — 105
Topic 1.3.6 The four marks of the Church — 108
Topic 1.3.7 Mary as a model of the Church — 112
Topic 1.3.8 Sources of personal and ethical decision-making — 115

Contents

Section 4: Forms of expression and ways of life — 121

Topic 1.4.1 The architecture, design and decoration of Catholic churches — 122
Topic 1.4.2 The different internal features of a Catholic church — 127
Topic 1.4.3 The meaning and significance of sacred objects within Catholicism — 132
Topic 1.4.4 The meaning and significance of paintings, frescos and drawings within Catholicism — 135
Topic 1.4.5 The meaning and significance of sculptures and statues — 140
Topic 1.4.6 The purpose and use of symbolism and imagery in religious art — 143
Topic 1.4.7 The meaning and significance of drama: mystery plays and passion plays — 147
Topic 1.4.8 The nature and use of traditional and contemporary styles of music in worship — 151

Area of study 2: Study of second religion, either Islam or Judaism

Section 1a: Beliefs and teachings — 157

Area of study 2: Introduction (Islam) — 158
Topic 2.1a.1 The six beliefs of Islam — 160
Topic 2.1a.2 The five roots in Shi'a Islam — 163
Topic 2.1a.3 The nature of Allah — 165
Topic 2.1a.4 *Risalah* (prophets) — 170
Topic 2.1a.5 Muslim holy books — 175
Topic 2.1a.6 *Malaikah* (angels) — 180
Topic 2.1a.7 *Al-Qadr* (fate) — 183
Topic 2.1a.8 *Akirah* (Muslim beliefs about life after death) — 185

Section 2a: Practices — 191

Topic 2.2a.1 The Ten Obligatory Acts — 192
Topic 2.2a.2 *Shahadah* — 194
Topic 2.2a.3 *Salah* — 196
Topic 2.2a.4 *Sawm* — 200
Topic 2.2a.5 *Zakah* and *khums* — 205
Topic 2.2a.6 *Hajj* — 209
Topic 2.2a.7 *Jihad* — 214
Topic 2.2a.8 The celebration/commemoration of Id-ul-Adha — 218

Section 1b: Beliefs and teachings — 223

Area of study 2: Introduction (Judaism) — 224
Topic 2.1b.1 The nature of the Almighty — 226
Topic 2.1b.2 *Shekhinah* — 231
Topic 2.1b.3 Messiah — 234
Topic 2.1b.4 The covenant at Sinai — 237
Topic 2.1b.5 The covenant with Abraham — 240

Topic 2.1b.6 Sanctity of life	244
Topic 2.1b.7 Moral principles and the *mitzvot*	246
Topic 2.1b.8 Jewish beliefs about life after death	249

Section 2b: Practices — 255

Topic 2.2b.1 Public acts of worship	256
Topic 2.2b.2 The Tenakh and Talmud	259
Topic 2.2b.3 Prayer	263
Topic 2.2b.4 *Shema* and *amidah*	266
Topic 2.2b.5 Rituals and ceremonies	270
Topic 2.2b.6 *Shabbat*	278
Topic 2.2b.7 Festivals	281
Topic 2.2b.8 Features of the synagogue	289

Area of study 3: Philosophy and ethics based on Catholic Christianity

Section 1: Arguments for the existence of God — 293

Topic 3.1.1 Revelation as proof of the existence of God	294
Topic 3.1.2 Visions	298
Topic 3.1.3 Miracles as proof of the existence of God	302
Topic 3.1.4 Catholic attitudes to religious experience	306
Topic 3.1.5 The design argument	310
Topic 3.1.6 The cosmological argument	314
Topic 3.1.7 The problem of evil and suffering	317
Topic 3.1.8 Solutions to the problem of evil and suffering	320

Section 2: Religious teachings on relationships and families in the twenty-first century — 325

Topic 3.2.1 Marriage	326
Topic 3.2.2 Sexual relationships	330
Topic 3.2.3 Families	334
Topic 3.2.4 Support for the family in the local parish	339
Topic 3.2.5 Contraception	342
Topic 3.2.6 Divorce and remarriage	346
Topic 3.2.7 Equality of men and women in the family	350
Topic 3.2.8 Gender prejudice and discrimination	353

Glossary — *359*

Index — *368*

Preface

This book covers all aspects of the Edexcel GCSE Religious Studies A:

- Area of Study 1: Study of Catholic Christianity
- Area of Study 2: Study of second religion, either Islam or Judaism
- Area of Study 3: Philosophy and ethics based on Catholic Christianity.

Each chapter of the book covers one of the sections in each of the areas, and each of the eight sub-topics in each section is covered as a separate topic.

You will have to take a separate examination for each area, when you will have to do:

- a one-hour and 45-minute paper on Area 1 where you will have to answer one question on each of the four sections
- a 50-minute paper on Area 2 where you will have to answer one question on each of the two sections
- a 50-minute paper on Area 3 where you will have to answer one question on each of the two sections.

To help you understand how to relate the information in the book to the exam questions, a high mark answer to a specimen question is given at the end of each section.

How to use the book

- Work through each topic. Words which you might want to use to show you can use specialist vocabulary (6 marks are available for this in each exam) are in boldface type and defined in a useful words box in the margin.
- Pay special attention to quotations from the Bible, Creeds, Catechism, the Qur'an and hadith, the Tenakh, Talmud and Mishneh as these are sources of wisdom and authority which you may have to refer to in the examination.
- Answer the practice questions at the end of each topic. The 'How to answer questions' at the end of each section gives you hints as to the approach which will gain you full marks.
- You should study all the topics in Areas 1 and 3, but in Area 2 you have a choice of religions (Islam or Judaism). You only need to study one of these (your teacher will tell you which you are studying), and so wherever there is a choice, you should only work through the topic relevant to your religion.

We hope you enjoy your study of Religion, Philosophy and Ethics. Remember! Religious Studies is not about making you religious, it is about enabling you to think for yourself about religious and moral issues so that you become a responsible citizen of a multiethnic and multifaith society free from the ignorance which causes prejudice, hatred and violence.

We wish you the best of luck with your studies.

Victor Watton and Kevin O'Donnell

1 Beliefs and teachings

Area of study 1: Study of Catholic Christianity

Section 1: Beliefs and teachings

Topic 1.1.1 The Trinity

> **Thinking points**
>
> In this topic, you need to:
> - think about the nature and significance of:
>   - the Trinity as shown in the Nicene Creed
>   - the oneness of God
>   - God as the Father
>   - God as the Son
>   - God as the Holy Spirit
> - be able to evaluate how this is reflected in worship and belief, and in the life of a Catholic today.

The nature of the Trinity as expressed in the Nicene Creed

Christians believe that there is only one God. Believing in one God is called **monotheism**. Also, Christians believe that although God is one, he is also a Trinity: Father, Son and Holy Spirit.

Beliefs about God, the Holy Trinity, are clearly stated in the Nicene **Creed**:

> We believe in one God, the Father, the Almighty ... We believe in one Lord Jesus Christ, the only Son of God, eternally begotten of the Father, God from God ... begotten not made, of one Being with the Father ... We believe in the Holy Spirit, the Lord and giver of life, who proceeds from the Father and the Son. With the Father and the Son he is worshipped and glorified. *(Nicene Creed)*

The Nicene Creed explains that there is one Being – God is one being who exists in three persons or relationships, the Father, the Son and the Holy Spirit, who are all equal and all eternal. The explanation that the Son was 'eternally begotten not made' means that there never was a time when the Son did not exist. This shows that there was a Father/Son relationship, one coming from the other, but that this always existed, from eternity. It never began and will never end.

The nature and significance of the oneness of God

Christians worship only one God. The Trinity is not three gods, it is a unity. It is important for Christians to believe in the oneness of God because:

- The teachings of the Bible in both Old and New Testaments show very clearly that there is only one God.
- God's unity was taught by Jesus as the greatest commandment, and Christians must believe and follow the teachings of Jesus, God's Son.
- God's unity is the teaching of the magisterium, as seen in the Creeds, the **Catholic Catechism** and the writings of the saints, and Catholic Christians must believe and follow the teachings of the Church.
- Christians believe that God is omnipotent; if there were other gods, then they would have some power and so the Christian God would not be all-powerful. Only if God is a unity can God be all-powerful, which is why it is so important.

The nature and significance of God the Father

Believing that God is the Father means that:

- The father–child relationship known in human life should be the same as a Christian's relationship with God.
- God creates human life like a father does. God is not a creator who creates and then leaves his creation to get on with things, he has a relationship of love and care with his creation.

> **Useful words**
>
> **Monotheism** – belief that there is only one God
> **Creed** – statement of Christian beliefs
> **Catholic Catechism** – a compendium of the official teaching of the Catholic Church

> **Activity**
>
> Why are the persons of the Trinity important for Christians?

Painting of the Trinity from the Holy Sepulchre Basilica, Jerusalem.

- As seen in the Lord's Prayer or 'Our Father', God will provide people with daily bread and protect them from evil precisely because he is 'our Father'.

Catholics believe that God is their Father because the Bible shows very clearly that Jesus referred to God as his Father, and Jesus told his disciples to call God Father. Also the Catechism teaches Catholics to call God Father, showing how important this belief is.

> *I will be a Father to you, and you will be my sons and daughters, says the Lord Almighty.* (2 Corinthians 6:18)

> *By calling God 'Father', the language of faith indicates two main things: that God is the first origin of everything and transcendent authority; and that he is at the same time goodness and loving care for all his children.* (Catechism of the Catholic Church 239)

The nature and significance of God the Son

Catholics believe that Jesus is the Son of God, the second person of the Trinity. They believe that:

- Jesus is God incarnated. This means that Jesus is God who has become a human being, experiencing everything that human beings experience in their daily lives.
- As the Son of God, Christians believe that Jesus was both fully human and fully divine. The Catechism says 'Jesus Christ possesses two natures, one divine and the other human, not confused, but united in the one person of God's Son' (481).
- It means Christians can worship Jesus because he is God, the second person of the Trinity. The Bible teaches that only God should be worshipped and that idolatry is a sin. However, worshipping Jesus is not idolatry because Jesus is God who has become a human being.

Activity

Look at the painting above and explain how it illustrates Christian beliefs about the Trinity.

Section 1: Beliefs and teachings

- Jesus is the Son of God. He was conceived by the action of the Holy Spirit and not by sex. This is an important part of Catholic belief which is known as the virgin birth.

- Only the Son of God could bring salvation from sin. Sin prevented people from having a full relationship with God. The sacrifice of God the Son brought forgiveness of sins and reconciliation to God, which also gave people the chance to enter heaven.

- Believing that Jesus is the Son of God is important because only God's Son could institute the Mass – God comes into people's lives as Jesus becomes present in the bread and wine at Mass.

> The title 'Son of God' signifies the unique and eternal relationship of Jesus Christ to God his Father: he is the only Son of the Father, he is God himself. To be a Christian, one must believe that Jesus Christ is the Son of God. (Catechism of the Catholic Church 454)

The nature and significance of God the Holy Spirit

The Holy Spirit is the third person of the Trinity who, with the Father and the Son, is to be worshipped. Catholics believe that:

- The Holy Spirit is the means by which God communicates with humans, revealing God's presence in the world. In the Old Testament, the Spirit is called *ruah*, meaning breath, air, wind; that is, a presence which can only be felt, not seen.

- The Holy Spirit inspired the Bible by encouraging the writers of the Bible and guiding their writing to reveal the nature and will of God.

- The Holy Spirit is the means by which God assists the Church in its task of preserving the Apostolic Tradition and in helping the magisterium to formulate teaching.

- The Holy Spirit is the means by which all the sacraments of the Church put believers into communion with Christ.

- The Holy Spirit enables Catholics to live lives full of charity, joy, peace, patience, kindness, goodness, generosity, gentleness, faithfulness, modesty, self-control and chastity.

> The Holy Spirit, who has led the chosen people by inspiring the authors of the Sacred Scriptures, opens the hearts of believers to understand their meaning. This same Spirit is actively present in the Eucharistic celebration. (Pope Benedict XVI on World Youth Day, April 2006)

> The seven gifts of the Holy Spirit are wisdom, understanding, counsel, fortitude, knowledge, piety, and fear of the Lord. They belong in their fullness to Christ. (Catechism of the Catholic Church 1831)

Belief in the Trinity as explained in the Nicene Creed is a central Catholic belief that is shared by the vast majority of other Christians. The current official teaching of the Church is in the *Catechism of the Catholic Church*, which declares that, 'The mystery of the Most Holy Trinity is the central mystery of the Christian faith and of Christian life' (Catechism 262).

Topic 1.1.1 The Trinity

How the Trinity is reflected in worship

Such an important belief is expressed in all forms of Christian worship:

- Catholic worshippers remind themselves of the Trinity as soon as they enter a church when they cross themselves in the name of the Trinity with the holy water.
- At the beginning of every Mass, the celebrant greets the worshippers with the words, 'In the name of the Father, and of the Son, and of the Holy Spirit', to which the worshippers reply 'Amen' and make the sign of the cross again.
- In every Mass, worshippers repeat the Nicene Creed, which states Catholic belief in the Trinity, so expressing and reaffirming their belief in the Holy Trinity.
- The priest blesses the worshippers at the end of Mass with the words, 'May almighty God bless you, the Father, and the Son and the Holy Spirit. Amen.'
- All **sacraments** such as baptisms and marriages are performed in the name of the Trinity.

How the Trinity is reflected in belief

Catholic Christians feel that belief in the Trinity helps them to understand the different ways that God has shown his presence in the world:

- God the Father helps Christians to understand the power and creativity and his care for the world and its people. It also shows that God creates human life like a father does, and has a relationship of love and care with his creation. In the Lord's Prayer or 'Our Father', Christians learn that God will provide their daily bread and protect them from evil precisely because he is 'our Father'. Because God is the Father, Christians can turn to God as they would to a human father when they are in need.
- God the Son helps Christians to understand the love of God in action as 'God with us', entering creation and walking in our shoes, feeling human joys and sorrows.
- The Holy Spirit helps Christians to understand the presence of God in the world. Christians believe that the Holy Spirit is the means by which God communicates with humans, revealing God's presence in the world. Catholic Christians believe that the Holy Spirit is the means by which God assists the Church in its task of preserving the **Apostolic Tradition** – the faith taught by Jesus and the apostles – and in helping the Pope and the bishops today to formulate teaching. The Holy Spirit is the means by which all the sacraments of the Church put believers into communion with Christ.

It should never be forgotten that the Christian belief in God as the Holy Trinity is also belief in God's unity: Christians only believe in one God. As the Catechism of the Catholic Church says: 'The Christian faith confesses that God is one in nature, substance and essence' (Catechism 200).

Activities

1. Why is the oneness of God significant for Catholics?
2. What is the significance for Catholics of each of the persons of Father, Son and Holy Spirit?
3. Look at how the Trinity is reflected in Catholic worship today. Can you think of any other ways in which belief in the Trinity is reflected in worship?

Useful words

Sacraments – outward signs of an inward blessing through which invisible grace is given to a person

Apostolic Tradition – the faith taught by Jesus and the apostles

Section 1: Beliefs and teachings

Catholics believe that God is vast and bigger than the universe, but as close as a father; God was at work in Christ; the Holy Spirit is felt by Catholics and other Christians today. This drawing from a thirteenth-century parchment shows God as the universe's architect.

How belief in the Trinity is reflected in the life of a Catholic today

The doctrine of the Trinity is not just an idea; for Catholics it is deeply spiritual and practical. For example:

- It emphasises the role and value of relationships that Catholics are not alone with God as believers but are part of a family, a community, and they need to listen to and help others.
- Just as the Father, Son and Holy Spirit work together as three persons in one substance, so Catholics, as parts of the family of the Church, need to work together to bring God's love into the world.
- The Trinity also gives a Catholic the sense that God is not only an infinite mysterious being far greater than humanity, but also a creative being active and present in the world as Father, Son and Holy Spirit.
- For Catholics in their prayer and worship, the Trinity gives a great spiritual sense. All Christians believe that they pray to the Father, through the Son, by the power of the Holy Spirit. It is a sense of God as 'beyond us, with us and in us', as some believers would express it.

Practice questions

c Explain two things Catholics believe about the Trinity. In your answer you must refer to a source of wisdom and authority.

d 'You either believe in one God or three Gods, you can't have three in one.' Evaluate this statement considering arguments for and against. In your answer you should:
- refer to Catholic points of view
- refer to different Christian or non-religious points of view
- reach a justified conclusion.

Summary

Catholics believe that there is one God active in the world as three persons: the Father who created and sustains the world, the Son who revealed God and saved people from their sins, and the Spirit who brings God into people's lives. The Trinity is revealed in worship, especially the Mass, and in belief because it helps Catholics to understand how God works in the world. Catholics find that belief in the Trinity helps them to become more spiritual and to work for God in the world.

Topic 1.1.2 Biblical understandings of God as a Trinity

God as a Trinity

Belief in the Trinity comes from the Bible; for example, when asked what was the greatest commandment, Jesus replied in Mark 12:29, 'The most important one is this, "Hear O Israel, the Lord our God, the Lord is one".' and Jesus' final words in Matthew 28:19 were, 'All authority in heaven and on earth has been given to me. Therefore go and make disciples of all nations, baptising them in the name of the Father and of the Son and of the Holy Spirit'. As Christians believe that the Bible is the Word of God, then they must believe in one God who is revealed as, and experienced in the world as, the Holy Trinity.

How belief in the Trinity is shown in the Bible

Christian belief in the oneness of God is clearly shown throughout the Bible:

- The Ten Commandments are summarised in Deuteronomy 6:4 with the words, 'Hear O Israel, the Lord our God, the Lord is one'.
- In Isaiah 45:22 God says, 'For I am God, there is no other'.
- Saint Paul said in 1 Corinthians 8:6, 'Yet for us there is but one God'.

However, the Old Testament hints at a threefold nature of God:

- God speaks the Word and the Spirit hovers over creation in Genesis 1:1–3.
- Some Christians see the three mysterious, angelic visitors to Abraham as a representation of the Trinity (Genesis 18:1–2).
- God sends his Word and Spirit to create and guide (Isaiah 59:21).

The New Testament makes plain that the one God is a Trinity:

- St Paul said in 2 Corinthians 13:14, 'May the grace of the Lord Jesus Christ, and the love of God, and the fellowship of the Holy Spirit be with you all'.
- In Ephesians, St Paul said, 'There is one body and one Spirit, just as you were called to one hope when you were called; one Lord, one faith, one baptism; one God and Father of all, who is over all and through all and in all'.
- St Peter said at the beginning of his first letter, 'To God's elect … who have been chosen according to the foreknowledge of God the Father, through the sanctifying work of the Spirit, for obedience to Jesus Christ and sprinkling by his blood' (1 Peter 1:1–2).

> **Thinking points**
>
> In this topic, you need to:
> - think about biblical understandings of God as a Trinity of persons
> - consider the nature and significance of God as a Trinity of persons
> - think about biblical understandings of the baptism of Jesus
> - understand the historical development of the doctrine of the Trinity, including the First Council of Nicaea and the First Council of Constantinople.
> - be able to evaluate the importance of the Trinity for Christians today.

Activities

1. Explain how the greatest commandment and Jesus' final command show that Christians believe in God as one and as the Holy Trinity.
2. Do you think the Old Testament shows belief in the Trinity?
3. Do you think the New Testament shows belief in the Trinity?

Section 1: Beliefs and teachings

The significance of belief in God as a Trinity of persons

As discussed in Topic 1.1.1, belief in God as a Trinity of persons is significant for Catholics because the Trinity helps Catholics to understand the different ways that God has shown his presence in the world:

- God the Father helps Catholics to understand God's power and creativity and his care for the world and its peoples.
- God the Son helps Catholics to understand the love of God, the sacrifice of God leading to salvation from sin and the promise of eternal life.
- God the Holy Spirit helps Catholics to understand the presence of God in the world and the strength that it brings to Catholics.

Believing in God as a Trinity of persons reminds the believer that God is inter-relational and dynamic. There is self-giving love and sharing within the existence of God which human beings cannot understand.

How belief in the Trinity is shown in the Gospel accounts of Jesus' baptism

The baptism of Jesus, as recorded in the Gospel descriptions, clearly shows that God is the Trinity:

> *Then Jesus came from Galilee to the Jordan to be baptised by John. But John tried to deter him, saying, 'I need to be baptised by you, and do you come to me?' Jesus replied, 'Let it be so now; it is proper for us to do this to fulfil all righteousness.' Then John consented.*
>
> *As soon as Jesus was baptised, he went up out of the water. At that moment heaven was opened, and he saw the Spirit of God descending like a dove and alighting on him. And a voice from heaven said, 'This is my Son, whom I love; with him I am well pleased.'* [Matthew 3:13–17]

God is seen as three things working together here:

- It is the Father who speaks from heaven declaring that Jesus is God's Son, that the Father loves the Son and that the Son is doing the will of the Father.
- It is Jesus the Son who is baptised.
- It is God, the Holy Spirit, who descends on Jesus in the form of a dove and who sends Jesus out into the wilderness to prepare for his task.

So at the very beginning of the **ministry of Jesus** – his teaching and his miracles – there is a statement that the Father, the Son and the Holy Spirit are at work as the one God in his ministry.

Andrei Rublev's **icon** symbolises the persons of the Trinity as the three angelic visitors in the Genesis story. They sit at a table which is open for all to join in with them.

Useful words

Icon – a devotional painting of Christ or other holy figures
Ministry of Jesus – the teaching and public activity of Jesus

Activity

Look at the icon of the Trinity by Andrei Rublev above. What do you think Rublev is trying to say about the nature of the Trinity?

Topic 1.1.2 Biblical understandings of God as a Trinity

Activity
Look at the painting of the baptism of Jesus. How does it show the Trinity?

Baptism of Jesus. A modern painting by Davezelenka.

Historical development of the doctrine of the Trinity

In the early years of the Church, believers had many debates about the nature of the Trinity. Several **heresies** arose from these debates, most of which were about the nature of Jesus and the relationship of the persons of the Trinity.

The major heresies were:

- **Adoptionism**: the belief that Jesus was an ordinary man, born of Joseph and Mary, who became the Christ and Son of God at his baptism when he was 'adopted' by God.
- **Arianism** (from the priest Arius): the belief that the Father existed before the Son who was made Son of God when he was created at the beginning of the universe. The Son is therefore a god, but not God.

As a result, the Church summoned **Church Councils** – meetings of bishops representing all areas of the Church – to make a final declaration of Christian beliefs on these matters. Catholics believe that the Holy Spirit guides the bishops when they meet together to arrive at the truth. The Councils of Nicaea (325CE) and Constantinople (381CE) explained the doctrine of the Trinity and formulated the Nicene Creed as a statement of Christian belief. To deal with the heresies, it described Christ as 'God of God, Light from Light, true God from true God, begotten, not made, being **consubstantial** with the Father'.

In 381CE, the bishops meeting in Constantinople refined the Nicene Creed to its present form, adding these words:

> *I believe in the Holy Spirit, the Lord, the giver of life, who proceeds from the Father, who with the Father and the Son together is adored and glorified, who has spoken by the prophets ...*

Useful words

Heresies – religious opinions which contradict official Church teaching

Adoptionism – the heresy that the Son of God was adopted by God and not begotten of God

Arianism – the heresy that the son of God was created by God after the creation

Church Councils – assemblies of bishops authorised to make decisions on theological issues

Consubstantial – of one substance

Section 1: Beliefs and teachings

Activities

1. Why do you think the Church needed to call a Council about the Trinity?
2. Do you think that the differences between the Western and Eastern Christian Churches matter?

This asserted that the Holy Spirit was also part of God and not a separate force or lesser god. The current form of the Nicene Creed is slightly different from that agreed at the Council of Constantinople as that form simply said that the Holy Spirit proceeds from the Father, unlike the present form (believed by both Protestants and Catholics) which states 'who proceeds from the Father and the Son'. These additional words, 'and the Son', are rejected by the Orthodox Churches because they claim these words make the Holy Spirit subservient to the Son and so take away from the equality of the persons of the Trinity. The Western Churches (Catholic and Protestant) believe that the present words represent the views of the early leaders of the Church and make plain the fact that the Father and the Son are of one Being. This dispute was closely connected with beliefs about the Pope's power to decide on doctrine and resulted in the split between the Eastern (Orthodox) and Western (Catholic) Churches in the Great Schism of 1054.

All Catholics accept the Councils of Nicaea and Constantinople, as do other Christians.

Practice questions

c. Explain two reasons why belief in the Trinity is important for Catholics. In your answer you must refer to a source of wisdom and authority.

d. 'The decisions of Church Council 1500 years ago have nothing to do with life in the twenty-first century.' Evaluate this statement considering arguments for and against. In your answer you should:
- refer to Catholic points of view
- refer to different Christian or non-religious points of view
- reach a justified conclusion.

Summary

Belief in the Trinity is hinted at in the Old Testament, but is clearly stated in the New Testament and shown in what happened at the baptism of Jesus. The doctrine of the Persons of the Trinity developed in the first three centuries. After heresies arose, the Church called a Council of Bishops in Nicaea and Constantinople, and these made a final declaration about the nature of God in the Nicene Creed, which is accepted by all Christians.

Topic 1.1.3 Creation

The biblical creation

The account of creation in Genesis 1

According to Genesis chapter 1, God created the whole universe in six days:

- he created heaven and earth, light and dark on day 1.
- he separated the earth from the sky on day 2
- he created the dry land, plants and trees on day 3
- he created the sun, moon and stars on day 4
- he created fish and birds on day 5
- he created animals and humans on day 6.

Each part of the creation came about because of God's words: 'God said, "Let there be light," and there was light' (Genesis 1:3). Male and female were made at the same time and were made in the image of God. Humans were also made to have authority over the world: 'Let us make man in our image, in our likeness, and let them rule over the fish of the sea and the birds of the air, over the livestock, over all the earth' (Genesis 1:26). When God had finished the creation, it was perfect: 'God saw all that he had made and it was very good' (Genesis 1:31).

> **Thinking points**
>
> In this topic, you need to:
> - think about the nature and significance of the biblical account of creation
> - consider how the biblical account of creation can be understood in different ways
> - think about its significance for understanding the nature and characteristics of God
> - be able to evaluate the importance of creation for Catholic Christians today.

Woodcut from Miles Coverdale's Bible, 1535, depicting the six days of creation from the Book of Genesis.

> **Activity**
>
> Do you think it is possible for us to know that God created the universe?

Section 1: Beliefs and teachings

The account of creation in Genesis 2–3

According to Genesis chapter 2, creation happened in the following way:

- God created the heavens and the earth.
- God formed man (Adam) from the dust of the earth and breathed life into him.
- God made trees grow out of the ground and formed the Garden of Eden.
- God placed Adam in the Garden of Eden.
- God thought Adam would be lonely, so he created birds and animals which Adam named.
- The birds and animals were not suitable helpers for Adam, so God put Adam to sleep, removed one of his ribs, and from the rib he created woman, Eve.
- Adam and Eve lived in innocence in the Garden of Eden until the serpent tempted them to eat the fruit of the tree that God had forbidden them to eat, telling them that if they ate they would become like God and know good and evil. Eve ate the fruit and gave some to Adam. As a result of this first (original) sin they were banished from the Garden. Eve was condemned to bearing children in pain and to be ruled over by her husband. Adam was condemned to working hard for his living 'until you return to the ground, since from it you were taken for dust you are and to dust you shall return' (Genesis 3:19).

The nature and significance of the creation account

The extent to which the creation stories in Genesis 1–3 can be viewed literally is a subject of debate among Catholics and other Christians. The creation stories in Genesis 1–3 use images and symbols relevant at the time in the ancient Near East, with order coming from primeval chaos. This was traditionally pictured as a battle between God and a monster, and from the body of the beast the world was formed, and human beings in the process. Gardens and trees were sacred places and images of blessing. Serpents were feared and were often used as symbols of evil and death. The stories in Genesis take these elements and use them, but use them more sublimely and intelligently. God created everything from nothing, and the Spirit brings order out of the chaos at the start of time. Human beings are the pinnacle of creation and are made in God's image as special, not just as servants. These stories are full of spiritual insights and ideas about the purpose of the universe and of the significance of human life within it. The universe is not seen as a random event but as carefully planned and guided. Human life is not an accident of evolution, but designed and intended to relate to the 'Creator' – God.

Catholic and divergent Christian understandings of Genesis

The Catholic view

The Catholic Church believes that the Bible is the Word of God expressed through the writers of the time. The writers were inspired, but used their own ideas sometimes to make sense of what God was saying through them. Catholics see the Bible as using symbols and stories at times as well as historical details, particularly in the story of creation. The creation story of Genesis 1 and 2 is not regarded as absolute scientific fact. If the Bible taught exact science, it would not have been understandable for thousands of years. It has stories with true meanings, based on the first human beings and their knowledge of God and then their rejection of his commandments (**original sin**), whoever they were exactly and whenever they lived. There are two versions of the creation story, written at different times, set alongside each other as they both have different angles on the truth about God and humanity. They communicate eternal, spiritual truths about God's purpose and human sinfulness, taking into account the theory of evolution and the idea of the Big Bang. (Interestingly, the basic sequence of events in Genesis 1 follows that of modern science, if you interpret 'days' as vast ages of time. The sudden beginning from chaos could be thought of as the Big Bang.)

Useful words

Original sin – the sin of the first humans (symbolised by Adam and Eve) inherited by humans as mortality and selfishness

Fundamentalist Protestants – those who believe that statements in the Bible are the literal truth

> *Among all the Scriptural texts about creation, the first three chapters of Genesis occupy a unique place. From a literary standpoint these texts may have had diverse sources. The inspired authors have placed them at the beginning of Scripture to express in their solemn language the truths of creation – its origin and its end in God, its order and goodness, the vocation of man, and finally the drama of sin and the hope of salvation. (Catechism of the Catholic Church 289)*

Divergent Christian views

Fundamentalist Protestants believe that the Bible is not only the Word of God, but also the words of God. That is they think that the Bible was written by people who acted as dictaphonists for God, that is they simply wrote down what God dictated to them. This means that every word in the Bible is the Word of God and so must be true. As far as Genesis 1 and 2 are concerned, such Christians believe that both accounts are correct and do not contradict each other. Genesis 1 gives the overall broad picture of creation, whereas Genesis 2 zooms in on Day 6 of creation and gives details of exactly how God created male and female and animals. They believe Adam and Eve were the first people and that their sin has been inherited by all humans (original sin) until people are saved by the atoning death of Jesus. They do not accept the Big Bang and evolution.

Mainstream Protestants believe that the Bible is the Word of God, but not his actual words. This means that they think the writers of the Bible were inspired by God, and guided by God in what they wrote, but they used their own ideas. These Protestants see Genesis chapter 2 as a commentary on chapter 1 rather than a different story, especially as Genesis chapter 2 carries on into chapter 3, which explains how Adam and Eve sinned and were thrown out of the Garden so that evil and suffering came into the

Activities

1. What are the main differences and similarities between the two biblical accounts of creation?
2. Why do you think Christians interpret the biblical accounts in different ways?
3. Do you think the Catholic interpretation makes sense of these stories?
4. Look at the statement from the Catechism above. What do you think it means?

Section 1: Beliefs and teachings

world. So they tend to regard Genesis 1 as fairly factual (although they would see the days as eras lasting millions, or billions, of years rather than 24 hours), whereas Genesis 2 and 3 are poetic explanations of such things as how suffering and evil came to the world. Such Christians accept the Big Bang and evolution.

Liberal Protestants believe that the Bible is words about God rather than the words of God. They feel that the Bible writers were people who had special insights or experiences of God which they wrote in their own way. This means that there may well be mistakes and contradictions in the Bible, but what matters are the great truths about God which the Bible contains. Such Christians regard Genesis 1 as a story about creation where what is important is the truth that the universe was created by God, and that that creation was good. They see Genesis 2 and 3 as written by a different person, and so give a different story of creation expressing some other truths, such as that evil in the world comes from human misuse of free will. They accept the Big Bang and evolution.

The significance of creation for understanding the nature and characteristics of God

God the Creator

The Bible begins with the words, 'In the beginning God created the heaven and the earth' (Genesis 1:1). Genesis 1 records that at the beginning of creation, 'The Spirit of God was hovering over the waters'. God created the universe, showing that God is all-powerful and is the cause of everything in existence (which is why the Christian Creeds teach that God is the Father Almighty). The believer sees God as the origin of the Big Bang and everything that exists within the universe.

God the **Creator** is God the Father and Christians believe that he continues to be 'creator' because he holds everything in existence at each moment – he is the source of all existence, at all times, not just at the beginning. Christians believe that God's work did not stop with the creation of humans; he continues to care for the world and used his creative power to show his love for the world in the life, death and resurrection of Jesus, which brought salvation.

Useful words

Creator – used with a capital C to describe God as the Creator of the universe

Compassion and care help us to make sense of a world where things can go wrong and people suffer.

God the benevolent

The major significance of Christian beliefs about creation is that they show God's goodness (**benevolence**). The key teaching of the Bible is that God's creation is good. Genesis 1 states after each day of creation, 'and God saw that it was good', and at the completion of creation, 'God saw all he had made and indeed it was very good' (Genesis 1:31).

The God who created a good world must himself be good. Furthermore, God showed his love for humans in the creation. God created the world for humans, made it a good place for them to live with all the sustenance they need, and gave them their purpose in living.

God the omnipotent

Genesis teaches that God created the universe out of nothing (*ex nihilo*): 'In the beginning God created the heavens and the earth' (Genesis 1:1). There was nothing before God created everything. This shows God's **omnipotence**: only an all-powerful God could create the universe out of nothing.

God's omnipotence as creator means that life is sacred because God is its creator. Those things which God creates must be like him, holy, so humans need to treat creation carefully and with respect.

God the eternal

If God created the universe 'in the beginning' out of nothing, then he must exist outside of time. God had no beginning because he existed before the beginning of time. This is backed up by the statement at the beginning of John's Gospel: 'In the beginning was the Word, and the Word was with God, and the Word was God' (John 1:1).

The biblical story of creation teaches that God is the eternal creator who has no beginning and will never come to an end. For Catholics, God is therefore a wonderful mystery to be worshipped and adored.

Useful words

Benevolence – being all-good, all-loving
Ex nihilo – Latin words meaning from nothing
Omnipotence – the quality of being all-powerful

Summary

There are two biblical accounts of creation. Genesis 1 says that God created everything in six days, beginning with light and ending with creating humans. Genesis 2 says that God created the heavens and earth, then created man (Adam), then vegetation, then animals and finally woman. Catholics believe that the biblical accounts are not science; they are stories communicating eternal truths about God's purposes in creating the world. Other Christians have different views. Fundamentalist Protestants believe that the Bible is the literal Word of God. They reject the scientific view and believe that Genesis is the truth. Mainstream Protestants have similar views to Catholics. Liberal Protestants accept science and believe that Genesis 1–3 is just stories giving the important truth that everything was created by God.

The creation story has implications for how Catholics see God. Catholics believe that it shows God as a benevolent, omnipotent and eternal creator.

Practice questions

c Explain two reasons why the creation stories are important for Catholics. In your answer you must refer to a source of wisdom and authority.

d 'It's hard to believe the biblical accounts of creation.' Evaluate this statement considering arguments for and against. In your answer you should:
- refer to Catholic points of view
- refer to different Christian or non-religious points of view
- reach a justified conclusion.

Section 1: Beliefs and teachings

Topic 1.1.4 The nature of humanity

> **Thinking points**
>
> In this topic you need to:
> - consider the nature and significance of humanity as created in the image of God
> - think about humanity's relationship with the creation (stewardship and dominion), including divergent understandings
> - consider the implications of these beliefs for Catholics today
> - be able to evaluate Catholic and other views about the nature of humanity.

Useful words

Self-knowledge – knowing who you are and why you are here
Human dignity – the belief that humans are persons, not things, and that they have self-knowledge and free will

The nature and significance of humanity being created in God's image

Genesis teaches that God created human beings in his image, meaning that humans occupy a unique place in creation. They are the only creatures who are able to know and to love their creator. The Catechism of the Catholic Church states that being in the image of God means that humans have dignity because they are not a thing, they are persons. It does not mean that they look like God but that they have free will, reason and a conscience. They are capable of **self-knowledge** (knowing who they are, and why they are here), and have free will, meaning that God has given them the freedom to choose between good and evil.

It is this freedom which reflects how humans have been made in the image of God, but it also reflects the huge responsibility they have been given. Part of **human dignity** is to have responsibility for God's creation: to care for the planet God has made rather than spoil it.

This teaching is significant because it reminds Catholics that each human being is special, unique and sacred in God's sight. Humans are more than animals and are not to be used as objects but have fundamental human rights such as freedom of conscience and expression, and a right to food, shelter and health care.

> *Then God said, 'Let us make humankind in our image, according to our likeness; and let them have dominion over the fish of the sea, and over the birds of the air, and over the cattle, and over the wild animals of the earth, and over every creeping thing that creeps upon the earth.' So God created humankind in his image, in the image of God he created them, male and female he created them. God blessed them, and God said to them 'Be fruitful and multiply, and fill the earth and subdue it; and have dominion over the fish of the sea and over the birds of the air and over every living thing that moves upon the earth.' God said, 'See, I have given you every plant yielding seed that is upon the face of all the earth, and every tree with seed in its fruit; you shall have them for food. And to every beast of the earth, and to every bird of the air, and to everything that creeps on the earth, everything that has the breath of life, I have given every green plant for food.' And it was so. God saw everything that he had made, and indeed it was very good. And there was evening and there was morning, the sixth day. (Genesis 1:26–31)*

> **Activity**
>
> Look at the quotation from Genesis 1:26–31. What does this say about the importance of stewardship for Catholics and other Christian denominations?

Humanity's relationship with creation

The Bible account teaches that God created the universe and everything in it and, when it was created, it was good. This means that Christians should regard the whole of creation as a gift from God to be used by humans in the way in which God intended.

Topic 1.1.4 The nature of humanity

In Genesis 1:28, God commanded humans, 'Fill the earth and subdue it. Rule over the fish of the sea and the birds of the air and over every living creature that moves on the ground.' From this Christians believe that God has given humans control of the earth and its resources. However, this control brings responsibilities. Christians believe that God has created humans to share in the task of making his creation fair and harmonious. As the Catechism of the Catholic Church says:

> *God thus enables men to be intelligent and free ... to complete the work of creation, to perfect its harmony for their own good and that of their neighbours. (Catechism of the Catholic Church 307)*

Christians believe that when God created humans he gave them **dominion** over the rest of creation, but not to do as they please with creation, rather to look after God's creation in the way God wants it.

It is a basic facet of Christian belief that God gave humans dominion and **stewardship** of the earth and its resources. Dominion speaks of power and control. With our skills and intelligence we can try to control nature, inventing technology and changing our surroundings. Stewardship means looking after something so that it can be passed on to the next generation. The Catholic Church teaches that stewardship not only means looking after the earth's resources, but also means making sure that the earth's resources are shared out fairly.

The responsibility is, however, great. Human beings have free will, and can exploit nature and pollute the environment through carelessness and greed just as easily as they can help it. This is why Catholics are at the forefront of efforts to protect the environment and to reduce the effects of climate change. As Pope Benedict XVI said,

> *In nature, the believer recognises the wonderful result of God's creative activity ... The environment is God's gift to everyone, and in our use of it we have a responsibility ... We should respect 'the intrinsic balance of creation'. In other words, we should not engage in 'reckless exploitation' of the air, water or land or needless disruption of the natural world. (Caritas in Veritate 48)*

In the same way, the Catechism tells Catholics:

> *Use of the mineral, vegetable and animal resources of the universe cannot be divorced from **moral imperatives**. Man's dominion over inanimate and other living beings granted by the Creator is not absolute; it is limited by concern for the quality of life of his neighbour, including generations to come; it requires a religious respect for the integrity of nature. (Catechism of the Catholic Church 2415)*

Useful words

Dominion – power and authority over the earth
Stewardship – looking after something so it can be passed on to the next generation
Moral imperatives – things people feel they must do because they are the right things to do

Christians launching a campaign for climate justice.

Activities

1. Look at the photo above. Why do Catholics work for such things as climate justice?
2. When Catholics state that humans have been given dominion over the world, does this mean that they are free to do whatever they please?
3. Look at the Catechism quotation opposite. Put it into your own words.

Section 1: Beliefs and teachings

Activities

1. Why is it important for Catholics and other Christian denominations to be good stewards of the earth?
2. Do you think that Catholics should be prepared to give up things like cars so that future generations will not suffer the effects of climate change?

Divergent understandings of humanity's relationship with creation

Although most non-Catholic Christians have a similar attitude to their relationship with creation as Catholics, other people have different understandings:

- Humanists trust the scientific method to understand how the universe works and they completely reject the idea of the supernatural, so are therefore atheists or agnostics. They do not believe in an afterlife or in any purpose to the universe, so they believe that the nature of humanity is to work to give their own lives meaning by seeking happiness in this life and helping others to do the same. However, the moral principles they believe have developed from living in communities (such as utilitarianism – doing whatever ensures the greatest happiness of the greatest number) mean that they feel that humans have a responsibility to the environment to ensure the future of humanity. They believe that people should work together to improve the quality of life for all and make it more fair for everyone.

- Non-religious people (a term used to describe both those who are uninterested in religion and those who reject religion) believe that the nature of humanity is to get on with life, making life as pleasant and enjoyable as possible for their family and community. Some will feel they need to preserve the environment for the future, but others may feel it is more important to enjoy the present.

Practice questions

c) Explain two reasons why Catholics should look after the environment. In your answer you must refer to a source of wisdom and authority.

d) 'Climate change would not be a problem if everyone was a Catholic.' Evaluate this statement considering arguments for and against. In your answer you should:
   - refer to Catholic points of view
   - refer to different Christian or non-religious points of view
   - reach a justified conclusion.

Summary

Genesis teaches Catholics that God created human beings in his image, meaning that humans occupy a unique place in creation: capable of self-knowledge and free will. They believe that God wants them to be good stewards of the earth and its resources, and will judge them accordingly. Most other Christians have a similar view, but some non-religious people think it is more important to have a good life now.

Topic 1.1.5 The incarnation

Jesus, the incarnate Son of God

The **incarnation** is the Christian belief that God became a human being in Jesus. Christians believe that before the incarnation, it was only possible to have a partial relationship with God because of the effects of sin. However, through the incarnation (which led to the life, death and resurrection of Jesus), the power of sin was cancelled so that it became possible for humans to have a full relationship with God and go to heaven after death.

Catholics see Jesus as showing what God is like in a human life. God is involved in the pain of the world and went beyond it in the resurrection.

As the only Son of God, Catholics believe that Jesus did not have a normal conception, but he did have a normal birth. They believe that Jesus was God incarnate. His mother, Mary, was a virgin when Jesus was born. Catholics believe that being born of a virgin was the way God became man, to reveal his power and that the birth of Jesus was a new beginning for humanity.

The virgin birth is important to all Christians because it shows that Jesus was the Son of God. Christians believe that all human beings are children of God, but by giving Jesus the title, the only Son of God, they express their belief that Jesus was not just a human being chosen and sent by God, but God was in him and he was in God. Christians believe that this means that Jesus had two natures. In his human nature he was a human being, but in his divine nature he was God. So Christians believe that Jesus, the only Son of God, was both fully human and fully divine. This is shown by the virgin birth.

The importance of Jesus being both fully human and fully divine is explained in Catechism 464: 'The unique and altogether singular event of the Incarnation of the Son of God does not mean that Jesus Christ is part God and part man, nor does it imply that he is the result of a confused mixture of the divine and the human. He became truly man while remaining truly God. Jesus Christ is true God and true man.'

Thinking points

In this topic you need to:
- think about the nature and importance of the person of Jesus Christ as:
  - the incarnate Son of God both fully human and fully divine
  - the divine Word as seen in John 1
  - the biblical origins of this belief
- be able to evaluate the importance of the incarnation for Catholics today.

Useful words

Incarnation – the belief that God became a human being as Jesus

Activity

Look at the photo. How did Christ bring a new beginning?

In Christ, Catholics see a new beginning for the world.

Section 1: Beliefs and teachings

The wise men from the East: a lithograph from Germany, c.1898.

Catechism 470 explains this further:

> The Son of God therefore communicates to his humanity his own personal mode of existence in the Trinity. In his soul as in his body, Christ thus expresses humanly the divine ways of the Trinity.

Jesus the Divine Word (John chapter 1)

John's Gospel records the incarnation in a theological rather than story form. He identifies Jesus as the Word of God and begins his Gospel at the beginning of the universe: 'In the beginning was the Word, and the Word was with God, and the Word was God' (John 1:1). John then goes on to say that the Word made everything that is and is the light and life of the world. After this clear description of the second person of the Trinity, John continues, 'The Word became flesh and made his dwelling among us. We have seen his glory, the glory of the One and Only (or Only Begotten) who came from the Father full of grace and truth' (John 1:14). This is the basis of the incarnation: that Jesus was God in human form.

John sums this up by saying that, 'No one has ever seen God, but the one and only Son, who is himself God and is in closest relationship with the Father, has made him known' (John 1:18). So Jesus, the Divine Word, made God known to humans.

Activity

Look at the picture of the wise men. Why do Catholics see the baby Jesus as God incarnate?

The biblical basis for the incarnation

Our knowledge of Jesus and his incarnation comes from the four gospels of Matthew, Mark, Luke and John.

Mark's Gospel

Mark's Gospel has no account of the incarnation, but does recognise Jesus as 'Son of God'. He begins his Gospel with John the Baptist baptising Jesus.

Matthew's Gospel

Matthew's Gospel tells how Mary became pregnant while engaged to Joseph and how Joseph was told by an angel that this was a virgin conceiving by the Holy Spirit and that the child was to be called Jesus because he would save the people from their sins. Matthew records that the birth took place in Bethlehem in the time of King Herod and that wise men came from the East to worship Jesus. Matthew says that when Herod's plan to kill the baby (he didn't want any claimants to his throne) was foiled, he organised the slaughter of all babies under the age of two in Bethlehem, but being warned by an angel, Joseph escaped with his family to Egypt and did not return to Bethlehem until Herod was dead. This gospel seems to suggest that the family settled in Nazareth only because they were afraid to return to Bethlehem. Luke has them living in Nazareth at first.

Luke's Gospel

Luke's Gospel begins with the miraculous birth of John the Baptist (his mother Elizabeth, a relative of Mary, was old and infertile). The Angel Gabriel then appears to Mary and tells her she will be made pregnant by the Holy Spirit and give birth to a child who will be called 'the Son of the Most High'. Mary and Joseph travel from Nazareth to Bethlehem because of a Roman census and Jesus is born in Bethlehem. Shepherds are told of this by angels and they come to worship Jesus. After the birth, the family go to the Temple in Jerusalem for the afterbirth purification ceremony and then return to live in Nazareth.

There are references to the incarnation throughout the rest of the New Testament. For example, St Paul says in Colossians 1:15, 'the Son is the image of the invisible God, the firstborn over all creation.' He also says in 1 Timothy 3:16, 'Beyond all question, the mystery from which true godliness springs is great: He [Jesus] appeared in the flesh, was vindicated by the Spirit, was seen by angels, was preached among the nations, was believed on in the world, was taken up in glory.'

The **virgin birth** is important to all Christians because it shows that Jesus was the Son of God. It shows that Jesus was conceived by the Holy Spirit and not by Joseph. This is important for Catholics because if Jesus was not conceived of the Holy Spirit, but was brought into the world by sex in a normal way, he would not be God incarnate, but just a man.

The importance of Jesus being both fully human and fully divine is explained in the following Catechism:

> *The unique and altogether singular event of the Incarnation of the Son of God does not mean that Jesus Christ is part God and part man, nor does it imply that he is the result of a confused mixture of the divine and the human. He became truly man while remaining truly God. Jesus Christ is true God and true man. (Catechism 464)*

Activity

What are the similarities and differences between the accounts of the incarnation in Matthew, Luke and John?

Useful words

Virgin birth – the belief that Jesus was not conceived through sex

Section 1: Beliefs and teachings

Why the incarnation is important for Christians

The incarnation is important for Catholics because:

- It shows people that God cared so much about the world that he came in Jesus to show humans what God is like, to teach them how to live and to save them from their sins.

- In Jesus, the incarnate Word of God, humans can see what God is like. It is hard for humans to understand an infinite, non-material, omnipotent being, but an incarnate God brings God closer to human understanding.

- Through the incarnation, God began the process of **salvation** from sin, so making it possible for humans to have a full relationship with him and go to heaven after death.

> At Christmas, the Almighty becomes a child and asks for our help and protection. His way of showing that he is God challenges our way of being human. By knocking at our door, he challenges us and our freedom; he calls us to examine how we understand and live our lives. (Urbi et Orbi, Pope Benedict XVI, Christmas 2005)

Catholics do not think of God and humanity mixed together in Jesus, or as totally separate, but united in a single person in a mysterious way.

Useful words

Salvation – deliverance from sin and its consequences

Activities

1. Look at Pope Benedict's *Urbi et Orbi* message from 2005. What do you think it means?
2. Look at the photo. Do you think this makes the incarnation easier to understand?

Practice questions

c. Explain two reasons why the incarnation is important for Catholics. In your answer you must refer to a source of wisdom and authority.

d. 'Jesus was God incarnate.' Evaluate this statement considering arguments for and against. In your answer you should:
   - refer to Catholic points of view
   - refer to different Christian or non-religious points of view
   - reach a justified conclusion.

Summary

Catholics believe that Jesus is the incarnate Son of God, fully human and fully divine. He came to earth to reveal the nature of God and to save humans from sin. John's Gospel teaches that he is the Word made flesh. There are stories of the birth of Jesus in the Gospels of Matthew and Luke, and the incarnation is explained elsewhere in the New Testament and in the Catechism.

Topic 1.1.6 The events of the Paschal mystery

The Paschal mystery

The Paschal mystery is the term the Church uses to refer to the death and resurrection of Jesus and their effects on salvation.

> The **Paschal** mystery of Christ's cross and Resurrection stands at the centre of the Good News that the apostles, and the Church following them, are to proclaim to the world. God's saving plan was accomplished once for all by the redemptive death of his Son, Jesus Christ. (Catechism of the Catholic Church 571)

The Catholic Church teaches that there are some things which are beyond human understanding and which can only be revealed by God. The key events of the Paschal mystery are:

The last days of Jesus

The Last Supper

The night before his crucifixion, called Holy Thursday (sometimes known as **Maundy Thursday**), Jesus shared a final meal with his disciples, which is known as the Last Supper.

According to Matthew, Mark and Luke, the meal took place in the Upper Room in Jerusalem and Jesus **prophesied** that one of the disciples would betray him. Then at the end of the meal, Jesus 'took bread, gave thanks and broke it, and gave it to them, saying, "This is my body given for you, do this in remembrance of me"' (Luke 22:19).

> Then he took the cup, gave thanks and offered it to them, saying, 'Drink from it, all of you. This is my blood of the covenant which is poured out for many for the forgiveness of sins.' (Matthew 26:27–28)

Jesus offering the disciples wine at the Last Supper.

Thinking points

In this topic you need to:
- think about the events in the Paschal mystery:
  - Catholic teachings about the life, death, resurrection and ascension of Jesus (Luke 24)
  - Catholic teaching about the redemptive power of these events
- be able to evaluate the implications and significance of these events for Catholic practice today.

Useful words

Paschal – relating to Easter: the death and resurrection of Jesus
Maundy Thursday – the day before Good Friday
Prophesied – predicted events in the future

Activity

Why do you think the Last Supper is important?

23

Section 1: Beliefs and teachings

The betrayal and arrest

Jesus then went out into the Garden of Gethsemane with his disciples to pray.

All four gospels record that Judas Iscariot, one of the twelve disciples, had already agreed to betray Jesus to the chief priests.

In Matthew, Mark and Luke, Jesus left the disciples to watch while he prayed asking God to save him from death – 'Father, if you are willing, take this cup from me; yet not my will, but yours be done' (Luke 22:42) – and the disciples fell asleep. When Jesus came to wake them, soldiers arrived and Judas betrayed Jesus with a kiss.

The trial

Jesus was then taken for trial by the Jewish Council known as the **Sanhedrin**, who condemned him for claiming to be 'the Christ, the Son of God', which they regarded as **blasphemy**. Early the next morning, Jesus was taken before the Roman governor, Pontius Pilate, and accused by the Sanhedrin leaders of claiming to be the King of the Jews. Pilate then tried him for **treason** but could not find him guilty of the charges and so Pilate offered to release either Jesus or a Jewish freedom fighter, Barabbas. The crowd chose Barabbas and Jesus was condemned to crucifixion. The soldiers guarding Jesus put a crown of thorns on his head and mocked him as a pretend king, although in Luke's Gospel it is the soldiers of the Sanhedrin who mock Jesus before he is taken to Pilate.

All four gospels agree that the disciples ran away; only Jesus' women followers stayed with him and stood by while he was crucified.

The above description is a harmonisation of what the gospels say. They are each distinctive in their details:

- *Matthew*: Jesus holds the Last Supper at Passover. Judas leads the guards to arrest him in Gethsemane. He is taken before the High Priest and accused of blasphemy for claiming to be the Son of Man, a heavenly figure whom the prophet Daniel said would be sent by God. Peter denies Jesus. Judas hangs himself. Jesus is before Pilate and the people want Barabbas released. Pilate's wife is troubled, asking for Jesus' release. Pilate washes his hands, sends Jesus to be crucified after having him flogged, and the soldiers mock him with the robe and crown of thorns. Simon of Cyrene helps to carry the cross. Jesus is on the cross with two thieves as the crowd mock him, but Mary and other women stand nearby. His final words are 'My God, my God, why have you forsaken me?' and he dies. The curtain of the Temple tears in two. An earthquake also strikes Jerusalem. Joseph of Arimathea donates his **tomb** for the burial.

- *Mark*: follows Matthew very closely, omitting Pilate washing his hands and his wife's concerns. There is no earthquake and Judas' suicide is not mentioned.

- *Luke*: also follows Matthew closely but adds a cup of wine in the Last Supper which Jesus shares before taking the usual bread and wine. Jesus is blindfolded and beaten by the Temple guards and later mocked by King Herod's men with the robe and thorns. The Sanhedrin accuse him of being the 'Son of God', not the 'Son of Man' figure. Pilate has Jesus sent to Herod, who sends him back. There is no mention of Pilate's wife and Pilate has Jesus flogged and wants to release him

Useful words

Sanhedrin – the supreme religious authority in Israel in biblical times
Blasphemy – speaking sacrilegiously about God or sacred things
Treason – attempting to overthrow one's government or state
Tomb – an underground burial place

Activities

1. Why do you think Judas Iscariot betrayed Jesus? Perhaps have a jury that looks at various ideas. Was he evil or selfish, or did he have other possible motives?
2. What evidence is there to say that Pilate was troubled by judging Jesus?
3. Why would Pontius Pilate have thought claiming to be the King of the Jews was worse than claiming to be the Son of God?
4. Can you find any changes in the story that might be symbolic or deliberate to bring out the meaning?

Topic 1.1.6 **The events of the Paschal mystery**

but the people demand Barabbas. The detail of the weeping women of Jerusalem is added on the journey to the cross. One of the two thieves crucified with him repents. Jesus' final words are 'Father into your hands I commend my spirit.' There is no earthquake mentioned. The suicide of Judas is not mentioned (although it is in Acts, later).

- *John*: the basic story is the same but some details are quite different. The disciples meet in the Upper Room but the Last Supper is never mentioned. Instead, Jesus washes his disciples' feet. There are sections of lengthy teaching from Jesus. This is before the Passover, which is on the day of the crucifixion in John. Pilate is anxious to release Jesus, having him flogged and then brought before the people again, who demand Barabbas. Pilate also argues that the inscription on the cross, 'This is the King of the Jews', has to stay after people complain. Judas' suicide is not mentioned. The detail is added about not tearing the seamless tunic Jesus wore. Jesus' final words are, 'It is finished'. The side of Jesus is pierced with a lance to prove he is dead.

The Gospels have much in common but add or leave out various details. Sometimes theology might be at work, such as in John, where he might have changed the actual day of the Passover to make a point that Jesus was the Lamb of God, offering himself as the lambs were sacrificed in the Jerusalem Temple. Some details might be interpretation or symbolic rather than factual history.

The crucifixion

All four gospels record that Jesus was crucified on the day before the Sabbath (now known as **Good Friday** in the Church) on Golgotha and that Simon of Cyrene carried the cross for him because Jesus had been flogged and was too weak to carry the cross himself. They agree that two robbers were crucified on either side of him, that a sign above him said he was the King of the Jews, and that the bystanders mocked Jesus and challenged him to come down from the cross. The crucifixion lasted just over three hours before Jesus spoke his last words.

> **Activity**
>
> Look at the painting of the crucifixion below. Why do you think the men disciples ran away and the women went to the cross with Jesus?

Useful words

Good Friday – the day that Jesus died on the cross; called 'Good' by Catholics as Jesus is seen as dying to forgive sins

A mural of the crucifixion at St Michael's Anglican church, Khayelitsha township, Cape Town, South Africa.

Section 1: Beliefs and teachings

The resurrection

Jesus' resurrection is when he miraculously rose from the dead three days after his crucifixion. Although there are some differences between the gospel accounts of Jesus' resurrection, as in the Passion story, they agree on the following events:

- Jesus' body was taken from the crucifixion site to a tomb by one of his followers (Joseph of Arimathea).
- Jesus' female followers visited the tomb on the Sunday following his crucifixion.
- The women found the stone that was covering the entrance to the tomb rolled away and the tomb empty.
- Jesus then saw and talked with his followers for 40 days after his resurrection.

The main differences between the gospels are:

- In the Gospels of Matthew, Mark and Luke the women are visiting the tomb to **anoint** Jesus' body, but in John's gospel, the body had already been anointed before being placed in the tomb.
- Matthew is the only Gospel to report that Pilate put guards on the door of the tomb and a large earthquake caused them to run away.
- There are differences about who told the women about the resurrection. Matthew says it was angels; Mark says it was a young man; Luke says it was two men in gleaming clothes; John says it was Jesus himself who met Mary Magdalene, who mistook him for a gardener before he revealed his true identity.
- There are differences about where Jesus met his disciples after the resurrection – Matthew only records Galilee, Luke only records Jerusalem, John and Mark record both Galilee and Jerusalem.

> **Useful words**
> **Anoint** – apply oil to the head or body as part of a religious rite

For the exam, you need to know Luke chapter 24, which records:

The resurrection – on the Sunday morning some women (including Mary Magdalene) went to the tomb to anoint the body. They found the stone rolled away and the tomb empty. When they came out, two men in gleaming clothes told them that Jesus had risen, as he had promised. They went back and told the disciples, who refused to believe them, but Peter went back to the tomb and saw it was true.

The road to Emmaus – two followers of Jesus (one called Cleopas) were walking to Emmaus, a village about 7 miles (11 km) from Jerusalem, when they were joined by a traveller and began to talk about what had happened in Jerusalem, including the crucifixion and the women's reports of the resurrection. The

The women at the empty tomb.

traveller explained to them that all these things had been foretold in the scriptures. He then joined them for a meal and when he broke bread for them, they realised the traveller was Jesus and he disappeared. They went back at once to Jerusalem to report to the Eleven, who told them that Jesus had appeared to Peter.

Appearance to the disciples in Jerusalem – as they were talking, Jesus appeared to them. They thought he was a ghost, but he showed them his hands and feet and allowed them to touch him and then asked for some food to eat. Then he explained the scriptures about the Messiah to them:

> He told them, 'This is what is written: The Messiah will suffer and rise from the dead on the third day, and repentance for the forgiveness of sins will be preached in his name to all nations, beginning at Jerusalem. You are witnesses of these things. I am going to send you what my Father has promised; but stay in the city until you have been clothed with power from on high.'
> (Luke 24:46–49)

The ascension

St Luke records that 40 days after his resurrection, Jesus told his remaining disciples to stay in Jerusalem, where they would receive the power of the Holy Spirit. Then he was taken up from them into a cloud and two men in white appeared and told them that Jesus had been taken into heaven (Acts 1:4–11). The narrative describes a cloud enveloping Jesus and the cloud can be a symbol of the presence and glory of God in the Bible. Jesus dematerialised, to use modern terms. He was taken into heaven, risen body intact.

Catholic teaching about these events and their redemptive efficacy

The Paschal mystery shows Catholics that the events of the Passion and resurrection were the work of God. They were part of a plan, what theologians call **salvation history**. The resurrection clearly demonstrates for Catholics that Jesus was who he said he was. As the Catechism puts it:

> The Resurrection above all constitutes the confirmation of all Christ's works and teachings. All truths, even those most inaccessible to human reason, find their justification if Christ by his Resurrection has given the definitive proof of his divine authority, which he had promised. (Catechism of the Catholic Church 651)

According to the Catholic Church, Christ, resurrected and ascended, has opened the way to heaven for humanity.

The Catholic Church teaches that the Paschal mystery – the death and resurrection of Jesus – guarantees our redemption because:

- Jesus freely offered himself for the salvation of humanity.
- Beforehand, during the Last Supper, Jesus both symbolised this offering and made it really present: 'This is my body which is given for you' (Luke 22:19).
- Christ came 'to give his life as a ransom for many' (Matthew 20:28) by his loving obedience to the Father.
- Christ's resurrection promises resurrection for all people.

Useful words

Salvation history – the plan and process of God's saving work on earth

Activities

1. What does the Catechism teach about the ascension and the way to heaven being open?
2. Why do you think atheists and Humanists do not believe in the resurrection of Jesus?

Section 1: Beliefs and teachings

Useful words

Ascension – the return of Christ to heaven

Only the One who 'came from the Father' can return to the Father: Christ Jesus. 'No one has ascended into heaven but he who descended from heaven, the Son of Man.' Left to its own natural powers humanity does not have access to the 'Father's house', to God's life and happiness. Only Christ can open to man such access that we, his members, might have confidence that we too shall go where he, our Head and our Source, has preceded us. (Catechism of the Catholic Church 661)

- 'By his **ascension** Jesus Christ, the Head of the Church, precedes believers into heaven so that believers may live in the hope of one day being with him forever' (Catechism of the Catholic Church 666).

The effects of the Paschal mystery are summed up in the Catechism as follows:

The Paschal mystery has two aspects: by his death, Christ liberates us from sin; by his Resurrection, he opens the way to a new life. (Catechism of the Catholic Church 654)

Activities

1. Look at the painting of the crucifixion on page 25. Why do you think the men disciples ran away and the women went to the cross with Jesus?
2. Explain the Church believes that the events of the Paschal mystery assures salvation.
3. What do you think about the Catechism's teaching on the ascension?

Practice questions

c. Explain two reasons why the Paschal mystery is important for Catholics. In your answer you must refer to a source of wisdom and authority.

d. 'The resurrection was the most important event in the life of Jesus.' Evaluate this statement considering arguments for and against. In your answer you should:
   - refer to Catholic points of view
   - refer to different Christian or non-religious points of view
   - reach a justified conclusion.

Summary

Catholic belief in the Paschal mystery refers to: the Last Supper when Jesus began the Eucharist, Jesus being betrayed by Judas, Jesus' arrest and trials by the Sanhedrin and then by Pontius Pilate and Herod, his crucifixion on Good Friday, burial by Joseph of Arimathea and resurrection from the dead on Easter Sunday. These events are important to Catholics because they guarantee humanity's salvation and entry to heaven.

Topic 1.1.7 The nature of salvation and grace

The nature of, and need for, salvation

Salvation means being saved from **sin**. Sin can be **original sin**, which is inherited from the actions of the first humans (symbolised as Adam and Eve), or personal sin, which is the consequence of a person's own actions. The Church teaches that everyone is born with original sin, which is washed away at baptism (which is why babies likely to die are baptised at birth).

Personal sins are actions that break God's law. Sin is also the state of being that comes about by committing a sinful action. Sin makes it difficult to have a relationship with God because sin separates a person from God, which is why Catholics seek repentance and forgiveness while on earth.

At the time of Jesus, the Jewish people sought to obey the law given to Moses in the Torah (the first five books of the Bible), which was a difficult task. They tried to honour God in this way, however imperfectly. However, the Catholic Church believes that Jesus came to earth in order for Christians to receive forgiveness, and a restored relationship with God, in a more direct way and personal way. 'Salvation' comes from the Latin word *salve*, to heal, Jesus healed a broken relationship between humanity and God.

The Church teaches that the death of Jesus on the cross:

- was a sacrifice for sin: while the Jews offered various animals to seek forgiveness, Jesus was the perfect offering and this can never be added to or repeated
- shows a victory of light over darkness, of life over death: God was in Christ and triumphed over death in the resurrection
- shows that God is involved in creation and in the suffering of the world, not being remote
- shows the love of God by giving himself for others.

An Evangelical placard in Belfast.

Thinking points

In this topic you need to:
- think about the significance of the life, death, resurrection and ascension of Jesus for Catholic beliefs about salvation and grace (including John 3:10–21 and Acts 4:12)
- consider the implications of these beliefs for Catholic practice today
- be able to evaluate the importance of salvation and grace for Catholics today.

Useful words

Salvation – the act of delivering from sin or saving from evil, of healing a broken relationship with God

Sin – an act that is against God's will

Original sin – the sin all humans are born with which is washed away at baptism, although its effects remain, such as a mortal nature and selfish will

Activities

1. Why do Catholics believe people need salvation from sin?
2. What does the Catholic Church teach about Christ's self-sacrifice?
3. Look at the placard in the photo. Do you think this would make people today look for salvation?

Section 1: Beliefs and teachings

Activities

1. What does the Catholic Church teach about Christ's self-sacrifice?
2. Look at the photo of the Mass. Why do Catholics need to go to Mass?

Catholics participating in the Mass.

This is how the death on the cross is summed up by the Catholic Church:

> The sacrifice of Christ is unique; it completes and surpasses all other sacrifices. First, it is a gift from God himself, for the Father handed his Son over to sinners in order to reconcile us with himself. At the same time it is the offering of the Son of God made man, who in freedom and love offered his life to the Father through the Holy Spirit in reparation for our disobedience. *(Catechism of the Catholic Church 614)*

Salvation from sin is important because:

- Without salvation, a person's sins will prevent them from having a relationship with God in this life and exclude them from God's presence after death.
- Salvation from sin was the purpose of the life, death and resurrection of Jesus. Jesus is the saviour of the world whose death on the cross brought forgiveness of sins and the assurance of eternal life.

Useful words

Grace – undeserved mercy as God's gift which gives the strength to be good and holy
Charisms – special gifts or callings

The nature of grace

Grace can mean differing things in today's society. It can mean being 'graceful', that is being gentle and dignified. It can mean what people say before meals. It means something more specific in the Bible and the language of the Church. It means mercy that is undeserved. Thus Christ is seen as having died for all even when many rejected him.

The Church teaches that grace is a participation in the life of God. By baptism, a Christian receives the grace of Christ. The Holy Spirit then breathes love and strength into them.

Grace also includes the gifts that the Spirit grants Christians to bring them into his work, helping them to collaborate in the salvation of others and in the growth of the Church. These gifts are:

- sacramental graces, which come from each of the different sacraments (see Topic 1.2.1, page 42), and special graces (**charisms**), such as the gift of miracles or words of wisdom
- the graces given to those exercising ministries in the Church such as priests, monks and nuns.

Topic 1.1.7 The nature of salvation and grace

A graceful dancer and an act of grace – this ballet about the prodigal son returning to his father (Luke 15) captures the two meanings of grace.

Biblical teachings on salvation and grace

You will be expected to know what these passages say about salvation and grace:

No one has ever gone into heaven except the one who came from heaven – the Son of Man. Just as Moses lifted up the snake in the wilderness, so the Son of Man must be lifted up, that everyone who believes may have eternal life in him. For God so loved the world that he gave his one and only Son, that whoever believes in him shall not perish but have eternal life. For God did not send his Son into the world to condemn the world, but to save the world through him. Whoever believes in him is not condemned, but whoever does not believe stands condemned already because they have not believed in the name of God's one and only Son. This is the verdict: Light has come into the world, but people loved darkness instead of light because their deeds were evil. Everyone who does evil hates the light, and will not come into the light for fear that their deeds will be exposed. But whoever lives by the truth comes into the light, so that it may be seen plainly that what they have done has been done in the sight of God. (John 3:13–20)

Then Peter, filled with the Holy Spirit, said to them: 'Rulers and elders of the people! If we are being called to account today for an act of kindness shown to a man who was lame and are being asked how he was healed, then know this, you and all the people of Israel: It is by the name of Jesus Christ of Nazareth, whom you crucified but whom God raised from the dead, that this man stands before you healed. Jesus is "the stone you builders rejected, which has become the cornerstone". Salvation is found in no one else, for there is no other name under heaven given to mankind by which we must be saved.' (Acts 4:8–12)

Section 1: Beliefs and teachings

Activities

1. Read the passage from John chapter 3 on page 31. What does it say about salvation?
2. Read the passage from Acts chapter 4 on page 31. What does it say about salvation?
3. Do you think people can be saved if they are not Catholic?

Useful words

Reconciliation – bringing together people who were opposed to each other

Catholics, and all Christians, believe that the death of Jesus brought salvation. However, some Catholics, and most Evangelical Protestants, would agree with the Bible passages above that anyone who does not confess faith in Jesus cannot possibly be saved.

The Catholic Church does not agree with such a view. No one knows what happens in other people's hearts and minds, so no one can say who will and who will not be saved.

Implications and significance for Catholic practice today

The Catholic Church teaches that grace and the salvation from sin brought by Jesus come to the world today through the Church (which Christians believe is Christ's body on earth). The Church teaches that grace and the salvation achieved by Christ are made present for Christians today by:

- receiving the sacraments of baptism and confirmation
- receiving the sacrament of **reconciliation**/confession
- receiving the sacrament of the Eucharist in the Mass
- leading a Christian life.

The overall significance of this is that believers can find a peace with God and a way back to him. Every religion seeks a path or a way to follow, and the Catholic Church has the way shown by Christ.

This means that the Catholic practice of encouraging Catholic families to have their children baptised, encouraging young adult Catholics to be confirmed, providing opportunities to receive the sacrament of reconciliation weekly, celebrating the Mass regularly and offering the weekly Mass on Sundays is important because it enables Catholics to have access to the grace and salvation necessary for entry to heaven. It is up to the individual Catholic to ensure that they back this up by living a good Christian life, which is not possible without the grace that comes from Christ through the sacraments.

Summary

People need salvation because without it they cannot enter heaven. Catholics believe that the death of Jesus brought salvation, which is given by the Church through the sacraments. These give Catholics the grace they need to live a Christian life.

Practice questions

c) Explain two reasons why salvation is important for Catholics. In your answer you must refer to a source of wisdom and authority.

d) 'Only those who have been saved from sin will get to heaven.' Evaluate this statement considering arguments for and against. In your answer you should:
- refer to Catholic points of view
- refer to different Christian or non-religious points of view
- reach a justified conclusion.

Topic 1.1.8 Eschatology

Catholic teachings about life after death

Catholic teachings about life after death

Catholics believe that this life is not all there is; they believe there will be life after death.

Judgement

The Church teaches in the Catechism that when people die, they are judged by God, 'Each man receives his eternal retribution in his immortal soul at the very moment of his death' (Catechism of the Catholic Church 1022).

After death:

- Christians who are perfectly purified will go to **heaven**: 'Those who die in God's grace and friendship and are perfectly purified will live for ever with Christ' (Catechism of the Catholic Church 1023).

- Christians who have died imperfect and impure, needing more forgiveness and healing (and possibly members of other religions and non-believers who have lived good lives) will go to **purgatory** to be purified of their sins.

- Very evil people who have totally rejected God's will will go to **hell**:

  To die in mortal sin without repenting and accepting God's merciful love means remaining separated from Him for ever by our own free choice. This state of definitive self-exclusion from God and the blessed is called hell. (Catechism of the Catholic Church 1033)

Resurrection

The Creed also says, 'I believe … in the **resurrection** of the body', so the Church also teaches that people receive glorified, new bodies in some way that Christ will return at the end of the world when the dead will be raised, God will judge everyone and make a new heaven and a new earth:

The holy Roman Church firmly believes and confesses that on the Day of Judgement all men will appear in their own bodies before Christ's tribunal in order to account for their own deeds. At the end of time the kingdom of God will come in its fullness. (Catechism of the Catholic Church 1059–1060)

> **Thinking points**
>
> In this topic you need to:
> - think about Catholic teachings about eschatology, including life after death, resurrection, judgement, heaven, hell and purgatory (including reference to John 11:17–27 and 2 Corinthians 5)
> - consider divergent beliefs about life after death (purgatory and the nature of resurrection)
> - be able to evaluate the importance of belief in life after death for Catholics today.

Useful words

Heaven – a place of infinite peace in the presence of God
Purgatory – a preparation for heaven, a place of purification and healing
Hell – a place of eternal separation from the love of God
Resurrection – a belief that the body will be raised again to life but in a new, spiritual, transformed way

Activity

Do you think there will be room in heaven for non-believers and members of other faiths?

Section 1: Beliefs and teachings

> **Activity**
>
> What is meant by the beatific vision? Why would this never be boring?

Icons of Christ rising again never show the moment of resurrection; that is a mystery. However, they depict Christ rising from the world of the dead, bringing Adam with him, representing the whole human race. There is an idea that Christ preaches in the realm of the dead, giving them a chance to hear the Gospel.

Heaven and hell

Catholics believe that heaven is perfection and eternal peace with God. It is described as the beatific vision, meaning the vision of God that is beautiful and blessed. It is not just carrying on but being immersed in life. Depictions of people on clouds with harps are simplistic and not what the Church means at all. 'The mystery of blessed communion with God (heaven) … is beyond all understanding and description. Scripture speaks of it in images: life, light, peace, wedding feast' (Catechism of the Catholic Church 1027). This hope is beyond imagination and will be a surprise:

> *What no eye has seen, nor ear heard, nor the human heart conceived, what God has prepared for those who love him.*
> *(1 Corinthians 2:9)*

Hell

The teaching of the Church affirms the existence of hell and its eternity ... The chief punishment of hell is eternal separation from God, in whom alone man can possess the life and happiness for which he was created. (Catechism of the Catholic Church 1035)

However, although it is an article of faith to believe that hell exists, it is not an article of faith to believe that anyone ever gets there. God wishes for everyone to enter heaven, but it is up to people's use of their free will to achieve this:

Those who, through no fault of their own, do not know the Gospel of Christ, or His Church, but who, nevertheless, seek God with a sincere heart, ... may achieve eternal salvation. (Catechism of the Catholic Church 847)

Purgatory

For Catholics, purgatory should not be understood as a lesser hell but as God's hospital, a place of healing and purification where people are prepared for heaven, which is why purgatory is often described as 'a waiting room for heaven'. Catholics believe that all who are in purgatory are saved, but not yet ready for heaven. This belief is summed up in the Catechism:

All who die in God's grace and friendship, but still imperfectly purified, are indeed assured of their eternal salvation; but after death they undergo purification, so as to achieve the holiness necessary to enter the joy of heaven. (Catechism of the Catholic Church 1030)

Activities

1. Look at the quotation from the Catholic Catechism about purgatory. What is the purpose of purgatory? Would you say it is a possible waiting room of hell or of heaven? Why?

2. Look at the painting of hell. Do you think a loving God would send people to a place like this forever? It can be said that people put themselves into that state and not God. Is this helpful?

An angel leading a soul into hell. Oil painting by a follower of Hieronymus Bosch.

Section 1: Beliefs and teachings

> **Activities**
>
> 1. What hope does the icon of Christ rising from the world of the dead give to people?
> 2. Read the passage from John 11. What does it say about a) life after death, b) the role of Jesus?
> 3. Read the passage from 2 Corinthians. What does it teach about life after death?

The Bible and life after death

All the Catholic beliefs in life after death are reflected in the Biblical witness. The Bible is full of teachings about life after death, judgement, heaven and hell, resurrection and the Last Day. However, you are only required to know about the teachings in John chapter 11 and 2 Corinthians chapter 5.

Jesus had a family of friends – Lazarus and his sisters Mary and Martha – who lived in the village of Bethany. Lazarus died and the sisters sent a message for Jesus to come.

> On his arrival, Jesus found that Lazarus had already been in the tomb for four days. Now Bethany was less than two miles from Jerusalem, and many Jews had come to Martha and Mary to comfort them in the loss of their brother. When Martha heard that Jesus was coming, she went out to meet him, but Mary stayed at home. 'Lord,' Martha said to Jesus, 'if you had been here, my brother would not have died. But I know that even now God will give you whatever you ask.' Jesus said to her, 'Your brother will rise again.' Martha answered, 'I know he will rise again in the resurrection at the last day.' Jesus said to her, 'I am the resurrection and the life. The one who believes in me will live, even though they die; and whoever lives by believing in me will never die. Do you believe this?' 'Yes, Lord,' she replied, 'I believe that you are the Messiah, the Son of God, who is to come into the world.' (John 11:17–27)

> For we know that if the earthly tent we live in is destroyed, we have a building from God, an eternal house in heaven, not built by human hands. Meanwhile we groan, longing to be clothed instead with our heavenly dwelling, because when we are clothed, we will not be found naked. For while we are in this tent, we groan and are burdened, because we do not wish to be unclothed but to be clothed instead with our heavenly dwelling, so that what is mortal may be swallowed up by life. Now the one who has fashioned us for this very purpose is God, who has given us the Spirit as a deposit, guaranteeing what is to come. Therefore we are always confident and know that as long as we are at home in the body we are away from the Lord. For we live by faith, not by sight. We are confident, I say, and would prefer to be away from the body and at home with the Lord. So we make it our goal to please him, whether we are at home in the body or away from it. For we must all appear before the judgement seat of Christ, so that each of us may receive what is due us for the things done while in the body, whether good or bad. (2 Corinthians 5:1–10)

Divergent Christian beliefs about life after death

All Christians believe that people are made up of a body and a soul (mind or personality). They believe that the soul is non-material and immortal and so will never die. However, Christians have different ideas about what will happen after death:

- Non-Catholic Christians do not believe in purgatory because they claim it is based on the teachings of the Church rather than the teachings of the Bible.

- Some Protestants (mainly Evangelicals) believe that the soul and body remain in the grave until the Last Day (which will follow the Second Coming of Jesus) when the dead will be raised and the living and the dead will be given resurrection bodies. Everyone will then be judged by God on the basis of what they have believed and how they have lived. Those who have been born again will go to heaven for eternity, everyone else will go to hell for eternity because they have rejected God's love in Christ. This is based on the teachings of St Paul in 1 Corinthians 15.

- Many Christians believe that when the body dies, the soul leaves the body to live with God in a spirit world where God can be experienced in a much more immediate way than on earth. They believe that the nature of this spiritual after-life is determined by what people believe and how they have lived. Good people (especially Christians) will go to heaven and bad people will go to hell.

- Some Christians do not believe in any form of hell. They believe that all should will have opportunities to learn from their mistakes on earth and so move up a variety of forms of heaven until they reach the presence of God.

> **Activity**
>
> Why do you think Christians have different ideas about life after death?

Why teachings about life after death are important for Catholics today

- Catholics believe that they will be judged by God after death. Therefore, belief in life after death gives Catholics an incentive to live a good Christian life following the teachings of the Bible and the Church, seeking to be faithful and loving to others.

- Living a good Catholic life means following scripture, tradition and the teaching authority of the Church. The teachings of Jesus taught that the two greatest commandments are to love God and to love your neighbour as yourself. So Catholics' beliefs about life after death are important as their lives will be affected as they try to love God by praying and by worshipping God as well as attending Mass every Sunday.

- Catholics believe that sin can prevent people from going to heaven. The Catholic Church teaches that those who die saved by grace but not yet ready for heaven will go to purgatory to be purified and made whole. Clearly, these beliefs mean that Catholics will try to avoid committing sins in their lives so that they will go to heaven.

- Christian beliefs about life after death give their lives meaning and purpose. They feel that for life to end at death does not make sense.

- Trying to love your neighbour as yourself is bound to affect a Catholic's life. In the Parable of the Sheep and the Goats (Matthew 25:31–46), Jesus said that only those who fed the hungry, clothed the naked, befriended strangers, and visited the sick and those in prison, would be allowed into heaven. This is a similar teaching to the Good Samaritan, where Jesus taught that loving your neighbour means helping anyone in need. These teachings are bound to affect Catholics' lives and explain why Catholic charities like the Catholic Agency For Overseas Development (CAFOD) are so involved in helping those in need.

Section 1: Beliefs and teachings

> **Practice questions**
>
> **c** Explain two reasons why belief in life after death is important for Catholics. In your answer you must refer to a source of wisdom and authority.
>
> **d** 'When you are dead, you're dead and that's the end of you.' Evaluate this statement considering arguments for and against. In your answer you should:
> - refer to Catholic points of view
> - refer to different Christian or non-religious points of view
> - reach a justified conclusion.

Summary

Catholics believe that when people die, they are judged by God: the perfectly purified go to heaven, those who have died with unforgiven sins go to purgatory to be purified of their sins and very evil people go to hell. On the Last Day, God will judge everyone and make a new heaven and a new earth where the resurrected souls from heaven and purgatory will live, but the souls from hell will return to hell. Other Christians do not believe in purgatory, some do not believe in resurrection, some do not believe in the Last Day. Belief in life after death is important for Catholics because they know they will be judged after death on how they have lived.

How to answer questions

a) State three religious traditions other than Christianity in Britain. [3]

Islam is a non-Christian religious tradition practised in Britain. Another would be Judaism and a third religious tradition is Hinduism.

A high mark answer because three non-Christian religious traditions are clearly stated.

b) Explain two reasons why belief in the incarnation is important to Catholics. [4]

The incarnation is important for Catholics because it shows them that God cared so much about the world that he sent his Son to show humans what God is like and to teach them how to live.

The incarnation is also important because through Jesus coming to earth, God began the process of salvation from sin, so making it possible for humans to have a full relationship with him and go to heaven after death.

A high mark answer because two correct reasons are given and each reason is developed.

c) Explain two Catholic teachings about the Trinity. In your answer you must refer to a source of wisdom and authority. [5]

Catholics believe that there is only one God who reveals himself to the world in three persons (the Holy Trinity). This is expressed in the Nicene Creed and in the Catechism of the Catholic Church which says, 'From the very beginning, the revealed truth of the Holy Trinity has been at the very root of the Church's living faith' (Catechism 249).

The Church explains the Trinity by speaking of God's substance when referring to his unity, and speaking of the three persons of God (Father, Son and Holy Spirit) when speaking of God at work in the world.

A high mark answer because two correct reasons are given and each reason is developed with a reference to the Nicene Creed and the Catechism, which are both sources of authority for Catholics.

d) 'Belief in hell is very important.' Evaluate this statement considering arguments for and against. In your response you should:
- refer to Catholic Christian points of view
- refer to different Christian points of view
- reach a justified conclusion. [12 marks + 3 spelling, punctuation and grammar (SPaG) marks]

Many Christians would agree with this because the Bible says there is a place called hell and Jesus used the idea of hell to persuade people to be good, as in the Parable of the Sheep and the Goats. They might also believe that the concept of justice requires a hell to ensure that not only are the good rewarded in heaven, but the evil are punished in hell. Some Protestants might believe hell is needed for those who reject God's offer of salvation.

Other Christians might think hell is not important because they believe in purgatory, where bad people can be purified of their sins. They might also believe that God is all-loving and all-forgiving and so would not condemn anyone to eternal hell. Others might feel there can be no hell because St Paul said that nothing can separate us from the love of God.

It seems to me that belief in hell is not that important for Catholics; belief in purgatory is much more important.

[Continued]

Section 1: Beliefs and teachings

A high mark answer because it gives three clear developed Christian reasons for thinking that hell is important. It then gives three reasons for Catholic Christians disagreeing and then reaches a fully justified conclusion.

Spelling, punctuation and grammar are correct and a wide range of specialist vocabulary (Parable of Sheep and Goats, justice, heaven, Protestant, salvation, purgatory, all-loving, all-forgiving) is used appropriately.

2 Practices

Area of study 1: Study of Catholic Christianity

Section 2: Practices

Topic 1.2.1 The sacramental nature of reality

Thinking points

In this topic you need to:
- think about Catholics' beliefs that the whole of creation manifests the presence of God
- consider the meaning and effects of each of the seven sacraments
- understand the practice and symbolism of each sacrament
- consider how sacraments communicate the **grace** of God
- understand divergent Christian attitudes to sacraments
- be able to evaluate the importance of the sacraments for Catholics, and explain Catholic teachings (including Catechism 1210–1211).

Useful words

Grace – undeserved blessing from God

How the whole of creation shows the presence of God

Catholics believe that God created the universe and everything in it, and so the whole of God's creation shows his presence. This belief is shown in the Bible:

- In the Psalms, for example:

    The heavens declare the glory of God; the skies proclaim the work of his hands. Day after day they pour forth speech; night after night they display knowledge. There is no speech or language where their voice is not heard. Their voice goes out into all the earth, their words to the ends of the world. (Psalm 19:1–4)

- Job shows that all living things reveal the presence of God:

    Ask the animals, and they will teach you, or the birds of the air, and they will tell you; or speak to the earth, and it will teach you, or let the fish of the sea inform you. Which of these does not know that the hand of the Lord has done this? In his hand is the life of every creature and the breath of all mankind. (Job 12:7–10)

- As the Catechism says:

    God transcends creation and is present to it. God is infinitely greater than all his works: 'You have set your glory above the heavens.' Indeed, God's 'greatness is unsearchable'. But because he is the free and sovereign Creator, the first cause of all that exists, God is present to his creatures' inmost being: 'In him we live and move and have our being.' In the words of St Augustine, God is 'higher than my highest and more inward than my innermost self'. (Catechism of the Catholic Church 300)

God is both within and beyond the universe, as St Paul said, 'In him we live and move and have our being' (Acts 17:28).

Topic 1.2.1 The sacramental nature of reality

What is a sacrament?

The Catechism of the Catholic Church defines the sacraments as

> *efficacious signs of grace, instituted by Christ and entrusted to the Church, by which divine life is 'dispensed' to us.* (Catechism 1131)

The Catechism goes on to say:

> *Christ instituted the sacraments of the new law. There are seven: Baptism, Confirmation ... the Eucharist, Penance, the Anointing of the Sick, Holy Orders and Matrimony. The seven sacraments touch all stages and all the important moments of Christian life. ...* (Catechism of the Catholic Church 1210)

These seven sacraments all work together to form an 'organic whole':

> *... the sacraments form an organic whole in which each particular sacrament has its own vital place. In this organic whole, the Eucharist occupies a unique place as the 'Sacrament of sacraments': 'all the other sacraments are ordered to it as to their end'.* (Catechism of the Catholic Church 1211)

For Catholics, the Eucharist has the fullest presence of Christ out of all the sacraments as it is the body and blood of Christ.

Sacraments are outward signs and symbols that that an inward gift of grace has been given by God. The Catholic Church celebrates seven sacraments:

- baptism
- Eucharist
- confirmation
- reconciliation (confession or **penance**)
- anointing of the sick
- marriage
- holy orders.

Originally, in Greek, sacraments were known as 'mysteries' (*mysterion*) but in Latin the term *sacrament* (meaning sacred action) was preferred. One term stressed the mystery of God's presence and the other the sacred rite, the ceremony and action.

> *The seven sacraments are the signs and instruments by which the Holy Spirit spreads the grace of Christ the head throughout the Church which is his Body. The Church, then, both contains and communicates the invisible grace she signifies.* (Catechism of the Catholic Church 774)

Useful words

Penance – an action showing contrition
Form – the words used in the sacrament
Matter – the symbolic actions performed in the sacrament

The sacrament of baptism

Baptism is a sacrament marking a person's entry to the Church. The central act of a ceremony of baptism is the pouring of water three times. Water is poured over the child's head as the priest recites the words, 'I baptise you in the name of the Father, and of the Son, and of the Holy Spirit. Amen.'

Other ceremonial signs are used such as making the sign of the cross on the forehead, anointing with two types of holy oil, dressing in a white garment and the gift of a lighted candle.

Sacraments have an essential **form** and **matter**. The form is the words used, the matter is the symbolic action or thing. So in Baptism the pouring of water is the matter and the form is the words 'I baptise you in the name of the Father and of the Son, and of the Holy Spirit.' The matter is the pouring of water. If water is not poured in the manner prescribed, or the words are not, or are incorrectly said, then the sacrament has not occurred. The sacramental effect is the giving of grace, the washing from sin and the presence of the Holy Spirit.

Activity

Look at Catechism 774 above. What do you think it means?

Section 2: Practices

Activities

1. Look at the photo. Why do you think water is used in baptism?
2. Do you agree that only those who are baptised will go to heaven?

The baptism of a baby.

The meaning and effects of the sacrament of baptism

- Baptism comes from a Greek word which means to dip, bathe or wash. In baptism, the old life is washed away and a new one is entered.

- At baptism a person, usually a child, becomes part of the Christian Church. The sacrament is done in public so that it is recognised by the whole Church community. The baptised person can be called a Christian and is joined in faith with other Christians.

- Baptism is the first of the sacraments of **initiation** (the others are confirmation and the Eucharist), marking the beginning of the sacramental life which is essential for Catholics.

- At baptism, parents and godparents promise to bring the child up according to the Church's teachings.

- In infant baptism, the original sin with which the child is born is washed away, leaving the baptised baby free of sin. Adult baptism frees people also from the sins they have already committed, so the sacrament is a sign of God's forgiveness and love.

- The anointing with oil (**chrism**), and the candle that is lit, show that in baptism the person has been claimed by Christ.

Baptism is important for Catholics because the Catechism teaches that it is the basis of the Christian life and, without it, a person cannot receive the other sacraments. It is through receiving the sacraments that a person can receive grace to live a Christian life. The Catechism teaches that baptism is necessary for salvation, and without salvation one cannot enter heaven. (However, people can have what is known as a 'baptism of desire'; in their hearts, if they seek God and follow their conscience, even if they do not understand the teachings of Christ and the Church. God is the only final judge of human hearts.)

The sacrament of the Eucharist

See Topic 1.2.2 (page 50).

Useful words

Initiation – a ritual action admitting someone into a group
Chrism – the oil used in baptism, confirmation and ordination

Topic 1.2.1 The sacramental nature of reality

The sacrament of confirmation

Meaning and effects

- The sacrament of confirmation is a sacrament of initiation after being baptised. The traditional order is: baptism, confirmation and Eucharist as practised in adult conversions. A different practice was introduced for children with First Holy Communion after baptism and confirmation later. This has not always been so and could change back again.
- The sacrament gives strength through the Holy Spirit, which is needed in order to live a Christian life.
- Confirmation gives people the chance to complete their baptism, which is shown by the baptismal vows being spoken at the confirmation.

The matter of the sacrament is seen in the signing with the holy chrism oil. The sacramental effect is the strengthening by the Holy Spirit.

A boy being confirmed by Bishop Telesphor Mkude in Bagamoyo, Tanzania.

How the sacrament of confirmation is celebrated

- The bishop holds his hands above the candidate and then lowers them to touch the top of their head. This laying on of hands symbolises the coming down of the Holy Spirit.
- The bishop makes the sign of the cross using chrism oil on the candidate's forehead, confirming the candidate using the words 'be sealed with the gift of the Holy Spirit'. The candidate replies 'Amen'.

> By the sacrament of Confirmation, [the baptised] are more perfectly bound to the Church and are enriched with a special strength of the Holy Spirit. Hence they are, as true witnesses of Christ, more strictly obliged to spread and defend the faith by word and deed. (Catechism of the Catholic Church 1285)

> The link between Baptism, Eucharist and Confirmation is made clear by the rules and regulations of the Catholic Church (Canon Law);
>
> The sacraments of Baptism, Confirmation and the blessed Eucharist so complement one another that all three are required for full Christian initiation. (Canon Law 842 §2)

Activities

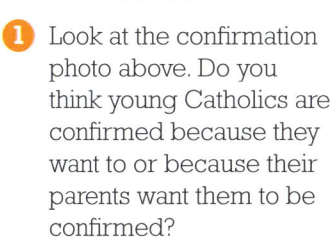

1. Look at the confirmation photo above. Do you think young Catholics are confirmed because they want to or because their parents want them to be confirmed?
2. Look at the quotations from the Catechism and Canon Law on this page. What do they tell us about confirmation?

Section 2: Practices

The sacrament of reconciliation

Meaning and effects

- The sacrament of reconciliation brings forgiveness of sins. It can be used for lesser sins, but is necessary for serious sins. Once these are forgiven, Catholics can receive the Eucharist.
- The sacrament of reconciliation allows someone to recognise that they have separated themselves from God and that they need God's forgiveness and his help not to commit sins again. This part of the sacrament is called **contrition**, the act of being sorry for the sin committed and determining not to commit it again.
- Receiving the sacrament of reconciliation at least once a year is one of the **Precepts of the Church**. Although people are encouraged to go more frequently as this is helpful to their spiritual life, helping them to be humble and reflect on their lives.

How the sacrament of reconciliation is celebrated

- The penitent (person making their confession) makes the sign of the cross and says words such as, 'Bless me Father, for I have sinned. It has been [length of time] since my last confession.'
- The penitent confesses their sins.
- The priest might give a few words of advice or encouragement and then gives the penitent a penance (prayers to say) and will often ask the penitent to pray for anyone they have confessed to hurting.
- The penitent says an act of contrition, a prayer of sorrow, such as 'Lord Jesus Christ, Son of God, have mercy on me, a sinner. Amen.'
- The priest says the words of **absolution**, blessing the person as he does so. '... and I absolve you from your sins in the name of the Father, and of the Son, and of the Holy Spirit. Amen.'

The form of this sacrament is seen in the words of absolution by the priest. The matter is the confession of sins. The effect is the forgiveness of these sins.

> *Anyone conscious of a grave sin must receive the sacrament of reconciliation before coming to communion.* (Catechism of the Catholic Church 1385)

The sacrament of anointing of the sick

Meaning and effects

- The sacrament of anointing of the sick is a strengthening sacrament. It is for anyone who is sick or deeply troubled, as well as those in danger of death.
- The sacrament gives grace, spiritual strength and healing to the person, and so is a very supportive sacrament.
- The sacrament allows the person's sins to be forgiven, if this is needed.

A Catholic priest blesses a girl as part of the sacrament of reconciliation in an open confession.

Useful words

Contrition – sorrow for the sin committed and deciding not to commit the sin again

Precepts of the Church – rules Catholics are expected to follow

Absolution – through the actions and words of a priest or minister pardon of sins is assured

Topic 1.2.1 The sacramental nature of reality

How the sacrament of anointing of the sick is celebrated

Because this sacrament is often given to people who are extremely ill, the format of the sacrament is frequently changed. However, the normal form is:

- The priest will lay his hand on the person as a symbol of bringing down the Holy Spirit and the gifts of the Holy Spirit, including strength.

- The matter of the sacrament is that the oil of the sick (previously blessed by the bishop in Holy Week) is marked in a sign of the cross on the person's forehead. The form is that the priest uses the words 'Through this holy anointing, may the Lord in his love and mercy help you with the grace of the Holy Spirit.' The priest repeats this on the hands, saying, 'May the Lord who frees you from sin save you and raise you up.' The sacramental effect is the giving of healing strength through the Holy Spirit.

A priest at the anointing of the sick.

> *The Anointing of the Sick 'is not a sacrament for those only who are at the point of death. Hence, as soon as anyone of the faithful begins to be in danger of death from sickness or old age, the fitting time for him to receive this sacrament has certainly already arrived.'*
> *(Catechism of the Catholic Church 1514)*

All Catholics should take part in the first five sacraments, but the next two are nevertheless very important:

> *Two other sacraments, holy orders and **Matrimony**, are directed towards the salvation of others; if they contribute as well to personal salvation, it is through service to others that they do so. They confer a particular mission in the Church and serve to build up the People of God. (Catechism of the Catholic Church 1534)*

Useful words

Matrimony – marriage

The sacrament of marriage

Meaning and effects

The Catholic Church teaches that God created man and woman for each other in the sacrament of marriage so that a couple can have a lifelong relationship of love and faithfulness for the procreation of children and the bringing up of a Christian family.

The sacrament of marriage is a sign of grace, instituted by Christ himself and, through the Church, imparting God's grace and strength to the couple. A secular, non-religious marriage involves only the bride and groom. For Catholics, sacramental marriage also involves God himself, like any sacrament that is celebrated.

How the sacrament of marriage is celebrated

- The exchange of vows committing the partners to lifetime marriage and restricting sex to each other is the key moment in the sacrament:

  I take you ... to be my wedded wife/husband,
  to have and to hold from this day forward,
  for richer, for poorer, in sickness and in health,
  to love and to cherish,
  till death do us part.

Activities

1. Do you think the sacraments of confession, reconciliation and anointing of the sick are important for Catholics?
2. Look at the photo above. Do you think a nun needs the sacrament of anointing?
3. Why does the sacrament of marriage makes divorce impossible for Catholic couples?

Section 2: Practices

> But 'the members do not all have the same function.' Certain members are called by God, in and through the Church, to a special service of the community. These servants are chosen and consecrated by the sacrament of holy orders, by which the Holy Spirit enables them to act in the person of Christ the head, for the service of all the members of the Church. The ordained minister is, as it were, an 'icon' of Christ the priest.
> (Catechism of the Catholic Church 1142)

Useful words
Nuptial blessing – a special blessing on the bride and groom
Consecrated – to be dedicated to a religious purpose
Ordination – making someone a priest, bishop or deacon by the sacrament of holy orders
Chalice – the goblet used for the wine in the Mass
Paten – small plate used to hold the Eucharistic bread

- The exchange of rings symbolising the unending nature of marriage and the **nuptial blessing** is a special blessing on the newly married couple.
- The form of the sacrament is the exchange of vows between the couple, before the Church (a priest or deacon and two witnesses). The matter is the couple themselves and their mutual consent. The effect is the joining together in sacramental union through the Holy Spirit.

The sacrament of holy orders

Meaning and effects

The sacrament of holy orders is given to those men who have received a special vocation from the Church and from God. In doing this, they are copying the work of the apostles when they gave up everything to follow Jesus and to serve people in the way that he did. When they take holy orders they show discipleship and they promise to serve. By taking holy orders, men show witness to other people that is visible to the entire world.

Through the sacrament, men are **consecrated** into the ordained ministry and become a deacon, priest or bishop. They are given the grace, strength and authority to serve and administer the sacraments as appropriate.

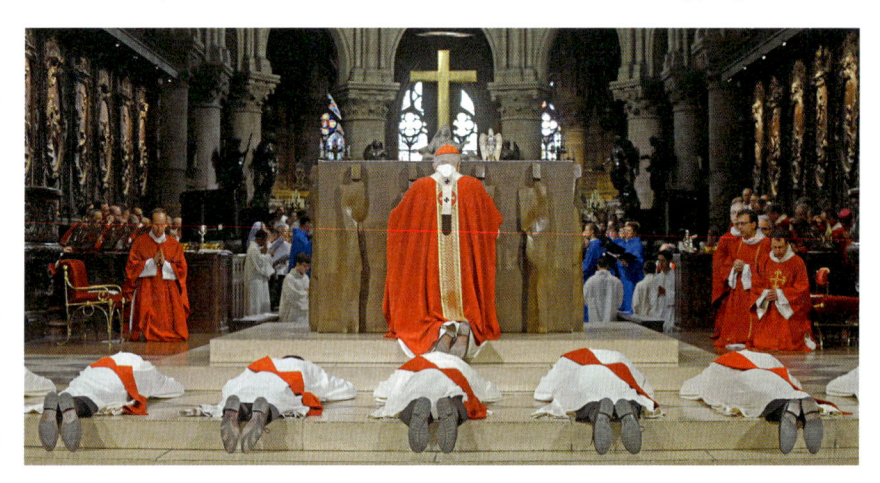

An ordination ceremony at the Notre Dame cathedral in Paris, France.

How the sacrament of holy orders is celebrated

A special Mass is held:

- The man for **ordination** promises to perform the duties of the office, either the priesthood (priests), the diaconate (deacons) or episcopacy (bishops), and to respect and obey his bishop.
- The candidate lies prostrate (full length) before the altar, while the congregation kneel and pray for the help of all the saints.
- The bishop silently lays his hands on the candidate (followed by all the priests present), before offering the consecratory prayer invoking the power of the Holy Spirit on those being ordained.
- The newly ordained priest is vested with the stole and chasuble of the Ministerial Priesthood and then the bishop anoints his hands with chrism before presenting him with the **chalice** and **paten** which he will use when presiding at the Eucharist.
- The gifts of bread and wine are brought forward by the people and given to the new priest.

Activities

1. Why do you think candidates for ordination prostrate themselves before the altar?
2. Why do you think there is a difference between matrimony and holy orders and the other sacraments?

- All the priests present **concelebrate** (they all join in the consecration prayers together) the Eucharist with the newly ordained priest.
- The matter of the sacrament is the laying on of hands and the anointing with chrism. The matter is the prayer of consecration. The sacramental effect is the grace of the ministry conferred.

Useful words

Concelebrate – when priests join together in the consecratory prayers of the Eucharist

How grace is communicated through the sacraments

'Grace' is an 'undeserved blessing', given out of God's free love. This comes through the presence of the Holy Spirit within the words and actions of each sacrament. To be a sacrament, the words and actions need to have been given by Christ. The sacraments have great significance for the life of Catholic Christians because:

- Through sacraments Catholics receive grace and blessing from God.
- Sacraments mark the journey of faith that Christians go through in life.
- Sacraments make Christians stronger in their faith.
- Sacraments bring Christians closer to God as a sacrament is an outward and visible sign of an inward, spiritual grace.

Divergent Christian understandings of the sacraments

Orthodox Christians also believe in and celebrate the seven sacraments, and their understanding of their meaning and significance is the same as in the Catholic Church.

However, Protestant Churches have every different views about the sacraments:

- Most Protestants only accept two sacraments – baptism and Holy Communion – as necessary for salvation because they believe these are the only sacraments sanctioned by Jesus in the Gospels and referred to in the rest of the New Testament.
- Some Protestants, such as Baptists and Pentecostals, believe that only adults should be baptised when they know and can agree to what is happening.
- Some Protestants, such as the Quakers and the Salvation Army, do not have any sacraments at all. They are not baptised and their worship, which for Quakers involves a lot of silent meditation, never includes the Eucharist.

Activities

1. Why do Protestants only accept two sacraments?
2. Why do you think some Protestants only baptise adults?

Practice questions

c Explain two reasons why the sacraments are important for Catholics. In your answer you must refer to a source of wisdom and authority.

d 'The sacraments make it easier to be a good Christian.' Evaluate this statement considering arguments for and against. In your answer you should:
- refer to Catholic points of view
- refer to different Catholic or non-Catholic Christian points of view
- reach a justified conclusion.

Summary

Catholics believe that the presence of God is visible in the whole of creation. The Catholic Church celebrates seven sacraments (outward signs and symbols that an inward gift of grace has been given by God): baptism, Eucharist, confirmation, reconciliation (confession or penance), the anointing of the sick, marriage and holy orders. The first five of these are compulsory for Catholics.

Section 2: Practices

Topic 1.2.2 Catholic liturgical worship

Thinking points

In this topic you need to:
- think about liturgical worship within Catholic Christianity, including the nature and significance of the Mass (including *Lumen Gentium*)
- consider the significance of liturgical worship for Catholics
- understand divergent Christian attitudes towards liturgical worship, including evangelical worship
- be able to evaluate the importance of liturgical worship for Christians.

Useful words

Host – sacramental unleavened bread
Lectionary – a list of Bible readings to be read at certain times of the year
Liturgical year – the year in the Church's calendar based on the special festivals from Advent to the Ordinary Sundays
Penitential Rite – the confession and absolution at the beginning of the Mass

Liturgical worship

Liturgical worship is public worship in church that uses a service book with set prayers and rituals so that everything follows the same format. The worshippers can follow the service and join in certain parts as they read the prayers and responses. The words have been in use for many years, which allows worshippers to think about them and continue to develop greater understanding. The set form also means that rituals have developed to help the worshippers to feel closer to God (for example, the elevation of the **host** in a Catholic Mass helps the worshippers to honour the presence of Christ coming into the unleavened bread).

The Bible readings for a year are set out in a **lectionary**, which follows the **liturgical year**. This begins at Advent, and follows through Christmas, Lent, Easter, the Feasts of the Lord to the Ordinary Sundays of the Year. The readings follow a three-year cycle so that congregations in liturgical churches hear most of Gospels read and also follow the main events of the Church's year.

The Mass

The Mass is a weekly celebration of the resurrection of Jesus. According to the Gospels, Jesus rose from the dead on a Sunday. This became known as the Lord's Day by the early Christians and was celebrated as a day of rest in the same way that the Sabbath was by the Jews.

It is the duty of all Catholics to attend Mass on Sundays and Holy Days, although Mass is often celebrated each day in most parishes and people can also go during the week. It is at the centre of Catholic life as it is when Catholics meet as a community to worship and learn the teachings of the Church. The Mass has a specific structure and wherever a Catholic attends Mass in the world it will be the same.

Structure of the Mass

The Introductory Rite

This is the first part of the Mass. It makes Catholics aware that they are sinners and need the forgiveness of God on a weekly basis. If they have committed a serious sin they are expected to go to confession before receiving Holy Communion.

- Greeting: the priest welcomes the congregation to the Mass.
- The **Penitential Rite**: this is when Catholics confess that they have sinned and ask for forgiveness and mercy of God. The rite includes the prayers 'I confess', the Kyrie (Lord Have Mercy) and the Gloria.

The Liturgy of the Word

This part of the Mass contains Bible readings which usually have a common theme, frequently linked to the liturgical year. For example, Easter readings will often be about receiving Jesus in Holy Communion.

Activity

Why do many Christians use liturgical worship?

- The First Reading: this is usually from the Old Testament and will be linked to the theme of the Mass or the time in the liturgical year.
- The Responsorial Psalm: this is the congregation's response to the reading and can be sung or said.
- The Second Reading: this is used on a Sunday or special holy days, and not usually on weekdays. This is often from the New Testament and will be linked to the theme of the Mass or the time in the liturgical year.
- The Gospel: this will be read by a deacon or a priest, and is a reading from one of the Gospels. This is one of two central high points in a Mass. The words of Christ are especially important and the people stand for this.
- The Creed: on Sundays and certain holy days. This a declaration by all present of their faith.

The Gospel reading and the **Liturgy** of the Eucharist are the two high points of the Mass because they are the moments when the worshippers come into direct contact, as it were, with Christ in his word and in the flesh.

The Liturgy of the Eucharist

This part of the Mass is all about the **Eucharist**. Eucharistic prayers are said calling on the Holy Spirit to change the bread and wine into the body and blood of Jesus. The priest then repeats the words used by Jesus during the Last Supper over the bread and the wine, 'This is my body … this is my blood …'. The form of the liturgy is:

- Presentation of the Gifts: this is the offertory (when the bread and wine are brought to the altar to be offered to God).
- Eucharistic Prayer: this is when the Last Supper is re-enacted and the bread and wine are changed into the body and blood of Christ, which is called by **transubstantiation**.
- Rite of Communion: this is when Catholics receive Communion. Hosts consecrated at Mass, but not given out during Communion, are stored (reserved) in the **tabernacle** for distribution to the sick or the housebound that day or during the week.

The Concluding Rite

This is the fourth and final part of the Mass:

- The congregation gives thanks for what it has received.
- Final Blessing: this concludes with the sign of the cross, 'in the name of the Father, and of the Son, and of the Holy Spirit'.
- Dismissal: this is the sending out of the congregation from the Mass into their community with words such as, 'Go forth, the Mass is ended.' Or 'Go in peace.'

The form of the sacrament of the Eucharist is the use of bread and wine, giving thanks over them, including calling down the Holy Spirit, and repeating the words of Jesus. The matter of the sacrament is the presence of Christ's risen body and blood.

Activities

1. Look at the illustration below. Why are both the vertical and horizontal dimensions important?
2. Why do you think the Eucharist is regarded as the most important sacrament?

Useful words

Liturgy – a set form of public worship
Eucharist – a sacrament commemorating the Last Supper
Transubstantiation – the belief that during the Mass the bread and wine become the body and blood of Jesus through the power of the Holy Spirit
Tabernacle – a safe place in which is kept the Blessed Sacrament

There is a horizontal, human level to the Mass, where people share with one another. There is a vertical direction, where people share with the presence of the risen Christ.

Section 2: Practices

The importance and significance of the Mass

The Mass is important and significant to Catholics because:

- During Mass, bread and wine are turned into the body and blood of Christ. This process is called transubstantiation. Catholics believe that Jesus is actually present with them during Mass.

- The Eucharist is a sacrament. It is a daily or weekly gift of grace that Catholics wish to receive, and by receiving this grace they are strengthened in their faith so that they can grow closer to God.

- The Mass is a celebration of the resurrection. It shows all Catholics that there is eternal life, so Catholics attend Mass to remember this and pray that one day they too will be able to receive eternal life.

- Catholics attend Mass to be in the real presence of Christ and to receive the body and blood of Christ. This is important as it joins them with Jesus, and so brings them closer to salvation.

- The Mass is a communal activity. During Mass, the congregation join to show their love of God. This is important as by doing this together they strengthen their faith and copy the community of apostles around Jesus at the Last Supper.

- It is important that Catholics attend Mass since it was commanded by Jesus when he said at the Last Supper, 'Do this in memory of me'. The Catechism says it is a sin to knowingly miss Sunday Mass and Mass on holy days of obligation.

> *The Eucharist is the source and summit of the Christian life. The other sacraments, and indeed all ecclesiastical ministries and works of the apostolate, are bound up with the Eucharist and are oriented toward it.* (Catechism of the Catholic Church 1324)

Lumen Gentium is one of the documents of the Second Vatican Council. This teaches the power and effect of sharing in the Eucharist at the Mass:

> *Really partaking of the body of the Lord in the breaking of the Eucharistic bread, we are taken up into communion with Him and with one another. 'Because the bread is one, we though many, are one body, all of us who partake of the one bread.' In this way all of us are made members of His Body.* (Lumen Gentium 1:7.53–55)

Activities

1. What do you think are the three most important reasons for going to Mass?
2. Look at Catechism 1324 above. What do you think it means?

Divergent Christian understanding of liturgical worship

Liturgical worship is the main form of worship in Catholic (service book The Missal), Orthodox (The Liturgy of John Chrysostom) and many Anglican Churches (service book Common Worship), but is only used for Holy Communion, baptism, marriage and funerals in Nonconformist Churches.

Most Protestant Churches have non-liturgical worship, which is worship in church without set prayers or rituals. The leader of the worship is free to choose the hymns, prayers and Bible readings, and the main focus of the service is the sermon, which can be on a theme of the leader's choice.

Music is often a major part of non-liturgical worship with hymns (accompanied by an organ in more traditional churches) or gospel songs/choruses (accompanied by guitars, keyboard or bands in more evangelical type churches). Prayers are extempore (without preparation) rather than following a set form, although they usually include thanksgiving, confession and intercession in the same way as liturgical services.

In evangelical type churches, there will often be more congregational participation, with members of the congregation offering prayers or expressing their approval of what the leader says by saying such things as 'Amen', 'Hallelujah', 'Praise the Lord'.

Practice questions

c Explain two reasons why there are different attitudes to liturgical worship among Christians. In your answer you must refer to a source of wisdom and authority.

d 'Sunday Mass is the most important celebration a Catholic can take part in.' Evaluate this statement considering arguments for and against. In your answer you should:
- refer to Catholic points of view
- refer to different Catholic points of view
- reach a justified conclusion.

Summary

Christians have two types of worship: liturgical, which is worship using set forms of worship with set prayers and Bible readings (the main worship in Catholic, Orthodox and most Anglican churches); and non-liturgical, which has no set forms and tends to focus on music and the sermon (the main form of worship in Protestant churches), and can be very lively and unstructured in evangelical churches. Mass is a form of liturgical worship that is important for Catholics. It uses set prayers and rituals so that everything follows the same format. It has its origins in the Last Supper and allows worshippers to be in the presence of Christ and to be close to God by receiving the body and blood of Christ.

Section 2: Practices

Topic 1.2.3 The Catholic funeral rite

Thinking points

In this topic you need to:
- think about the funeral rite as a liturgical celebration of the Church
- understand the practices associated with the funeral rite in the home, the church and the cemetery, including the ideas raised in 'Preparing for my funeral' by Vincent Nichols, Archbishop of Westminster
- consider the aims of the funeral rite, including communion with the deceased, the communion of the community and the proclamation of eternal life to the community
- be able to evaluate the importance of the funeral rite for Catholics.

Useful words

Vigil – a period of devotional staying awake on the eve of a religious festival/funeral

Activity

Do you think there is a need for a vigil service before the Funeral Mass?

The vigil in the home or the church

The funeral rite for Catholics will be the same all over the world, but various local customs surrounding the funeral itself will vary.

A **vigil** service can take place the night before the funeral and is held in the family home, although it can take place in the funeral home or in the church. The vigil service can take the form of a Service of the Word with readings from the Bible accompanied by reflection and prayers. Many families take the body to stay in the church overnight, sometimes with a rota of people keeping vigil.

The funeral rite in the church

The Church encourages funerals for Catholics to take the form of a Funeral Mass (Requiem Mass) for the repose of the souls of the dead. A Mass does not have to be celebrated, though.

The funeral liturgy remembers the deceased and expresses grief, but it is also an act of worship with hope in God and in the risen Christ.

The priest incenses the coffin and sprinkles it with holy water with final prayers and chants at the end of the rite including passages such as:

> May the angels lead you into paradise; may the martyrs receive you at your arrival and lead you to the holy city Jerusalem. May choirs of angels receive you and with Lazarus, once (a) poor (man), may you have eternal rest.

A priest waves incense over a coffin at a Catholic Funeral Mass.

Topic 1.2.3 The Catholic funeral rite

The funeral rite at the cemetery

The rite of **committal** is the final act of the community of faith in caring for the body of its deceased member. It should normally be celebrated beside the open grave or place of **interment**.

The tomb or burial plot is then blessed, if it has not been blessed previously. This is followed by a scripture reading about resurrection, prayers of farewell and commendation. The coffin is sprinkled with holy water and lowered into the ground with a prayer for the eternal rest of the soul of the departed, 'May his/her soul and the souls of all the faithful departed through the mercy of God rest in peace.' The priest then blesses the mourners.

A priest blesses the coffin before it is lowered into the ground.

The aims of the funeral rite

Communion with the deceased

The nature of the Funeral Mass allows there to be a link with the deceased. As the Catechism says:

> It is by the Eucharist thus celebrated that the community of the faithful, especially the family of the deceased, learn to live in communion with the one who 'has fallen asleep in the Lord,' by communicating in the Body of Christ of which he is a living member and, then, by praying for him and with him. (Catechism of the Catholic Church 1689)

The communion of the community

In committing the body to its resting place, the community expresses the hope that, with all those who have gone before them marked with the sign of faith, the deceased awaits resurrection and a reunion with God in heaven. The Catechism says of the rite of committal:

> A farewell to the deceased is his final 'commendation to God' by the Church ... By this final greeting 'we sing for his departure from this life and separation from us', but also because there is a communion and a reunion. For even dead, we are not at all separated from one another, because we all run the same course and we will find one another again in the same place. We shall never be separated, for we live for Christ, and now we are united with Christ as we go toward him ... we shall all be together in Christ. (Catechism of the Catholic Church 1690)

Useful words

Committal – the burial of a dead body
Interment – burial of a dead body

Activities

1. Do you think it is important that the Funeral Mass expresses hope as well as grief?
2. Look at the photo above. Why do you think the rite of committal is important?

Section 2: Practices

Activities

1. Why do you think the Archbishop of Westminster published a guide to Catholic funerals?
2. Do you think it's important to have a funeral for a dead person?

'Preparing for my funeral' by Vincent Nichols

Cardinal Vincent Nichols has issued a leaflet called 'Preparing for my funeral'. This sets out the types of liturgical prayer than can be involved and many practical concerns such as whether it should be a Mass, what the readings from the Bible should be, and whether it is followed by a burial or a cremation. He has done this because, 'it can be difficult for our next of kin to make detailed arrangements for our funeral at the same time as dealing with the grief and loss they will experience at our passing'. He also states: 'Our great hope is that we will be redeemed from death by Christ's great victory.'

According to the pamphlet, a Mass at a funeral is 'the highest form of prayer in which the Sacrifice of Christ himself is made present. In offering this Sacrifice, we commend to God the soul of the deceased in union with Christ himself.'

The proclamation of eternal life to the community and its significance for Catholics

Whether at home, in church or in the cemetery, the funeral rites all involve a proclamation of the Church's faith that the Paschal mystery assures the Catholic community of their eternal life, and can give hope to any non-Catholics, whatever their faith or lack of it:

> The Christian meaning of death is revealed in the light of the Paschal mystery of the death and resurrection of Christ in whom resides our only hope. The Christian who dies in Christ Jesus is 'away from the body and at home with the Lord'. (Catechism of the Catholic Church 1681)

Practice questions

c Explain two reasons why the communion with the community and the proclamation of eternal life are significant at Catholic funerals. In your answer you must refer to a source of wisdom and authority.

d 'Church funerals help Catholics come to terms with death.' Evaluate this statement considering arguments for and against. In your answer you should:
- refer to Catholic points of view
- refer to different Catholic or non-Catholic Christian points of view
- reach a justified conclusion.

Summary

The funeral rite begins with the vigil the night before the funeral. The funeral itself involves a church service, which should be a Mass, followed by the rite of committal and the internment in a cemetery. The rite involves communion with the deceased, communion with the community and the proclamation of eternal life.

Topic 1.2.4 Prayer

Prayer as the 'raising of hearts and minds to God'

Prayer can be defined as 'the raising of the heart and mind to God'. So the main purpose of prayer is attempting to experience a relationship with God. The Catechism describes prayer as 'the raising of one's heart and mind to God or the requesting of good things from God' (Catechism of the Catholic Church 2559). Prayer tries to put thoughts, feelings and requests before God and there are many ways of trying to do this.

The nature and significance of different types of prayer

Often prayer is **vocal prayer**, when words are used, either out loud or mentally, to express the prayer. However, prayer can also include **meditation** (thinking about religious matters) and **contemplation** (communion with God).

Prayer can have several subsidiary purposes:

- **Adoration**: praising or adoring God for what he is, for example, 'O God, how great and marvellous you are'.
- **Thanksgiving**: thanking God either for his general goodness or for some specific thing such as getting better from an illness.
- **Confession**: confessing sins to God, asking his forgiveness and determining to do better.
- **Supplication**: asking for God's help, either for oneself or for others (praying for God's help for others is known as intercession).

Thinking points

In this topic you need to:

- think about prayer as the 'raising of hearts and minds to God', in particular the nature and significance of different types of prayer:
  - the Lord's Prayer (Matthew 6:5–14)
  - set (formulaic) prayers
  - informal (extempore) prayer
- understand when different types of prayer might be used and why
- consider the importance for Catholics of having different types of worship
- be able to evaluate the importance of prayer for Catholics.

Useful words

Vocal prayer – prayer using words
Meditation – thinking about religious matters
Contemplation – communion with God
Adoration – praising or adoring God for what he is
Thanksgiving – prayers thanking God
Confession – prayers saying sorry for sins and asking God's forgiveness
Supplication – prayers asking for God's help

Activity

Look at the photo. Why do you think people pray?

Section 2: Practices

> **Activity**
>
> Why do you think the Lord's Prayer is important for Catholics?

Prayers can be expressed and different ways:

The Lord's Prayer

Most Catholics will use the Our Father (Lord's Prayer) a lot in their personal prayers with God as this is what Jesus asked them to do. This is the advice Jesus gave about prayer in the Sermon on the Mount:

> *And when you pray, do not be like the hypocrites, for they love to pray standing in the synagogues and on the street corners to be seen by others. Truly I tell you, they have received their reward in full. But when you pray, go into your room, close the door and pray to your Father, who is unseen. Then your Father, who sees what is done in secret, will reward you. And when you pray, do not keep on babbling like pagans, for they think they will be heard because of their many words. Do not be like them, for your Father knows what you need before you ask him. This, then, is how you should pray:*
>
> *This, then, is how you should pray:*
> *'Our Father, who art in heaven*
> *Hallowed be thy name*
> *Thy Kingdom come, thy will be done*
> *On earth as it is in heaven*
> *Give us this day our daily bread*
> *And forgive us our trespasses*
> *As we forgive those who trespass against us*
> *And lead us not into temptation*
> *But deliver us from evil.'* (Matthew 6:9–13)

The Lord's Prayer is a very brief prayer which expresses:

- Adoration: 'hallowed be your name, your kingdom come, your will be done on earth as it is in heaven'.

- Confession: 'forgive us our debts, as we also have forgiven our debtors'.

- Supplication: 'give us today our daily bread … And lead us not into temptation, but deliver us from the evil one'.

Set prayers

Liturgical worship is full of prayers expressing all four types of prayer. Many Christians come to know these prayers off by heart and use them as their own prayers, especially as their own private prayers. The ones most commonly used by Catholics are listed in the box on page 59.

Informal (extempore) prayers

Most Christians also use informal prayers as part of their devotions. They will express their innermost thoughts to God as a prayer, using their own words and their own language. Such prayers are known as **extempore** prayers. By making up their own prayers in their own words, they feel that they are in a personal relationship with God.

When Catholics pray

Obviously, Christians, Catholic or otherwise, pray when they attend public worship and informal worship in groups of Christians, but they also say private informal prayers:

> **Useful words**
>
> **Extempore** – spontaneous, personal prayers in a person's own words

Set prayers commonly used by Catholics

Glory Be
'Glory be to the Father, and to the Son, and to the Holy Spirit. Amen.'

The Hail Mary
Hail Mary, full of grace,
the Lord is with thee;
blessed art thou amongst women,
and blessed is the fruit of thy womb, Jesus.
Holy Mary, Mother of God,
pray for us sinners,
now and at the hour of our death. Amen.

Come Holy Spirit
Come Holy Spirit, fill the hearts of your faithful and kindle in them the fire of your love. Send forth your Spirit and they shall be created. And You shall renew the face of the earth. O, God, who by the light of the Holy Spirit, did instruct the hearts of the faithful, grant that by the same Holy Spirit we may be truly wise and ever enjoy His consolations, Through Christ Our Lord, Amen.

Hail Holy Queen
Hail, Holy Queen, Mother of mercy,
our life, our sweetness and our hope.
To thee do we cry, poor banished children of Eve:
to thee do we send up our sighs,
mourning and weeping in this valley of tears.
Turn then, most gracious Advocate,
thine eyes of mercy toward us,
and after this our exile,
show unto us the blessed fruit of thy womb, Jesus.
O clement, O loving, O sweet Virgin Mary! Amen.

Guardian Angel Prayer
Angel of God, my Guardian dear, to whom God's love commits me here, ever this day (or night) be at my side, to light and guard, to rule and guide. Amen.

Activities

1. Read the set prayers. Why do you think set prayers use such respectful language?
2. Why do some people find it easier and more appropriate to use their own words and make up their own prayers?
3. Why do you think some people have a set time for praying?

- At set times, for example when they wake up or before they go to bed.
- At any moment when the thought of God enters their mind, for example when they see a beautiful landscape they may pray prayers of adoration and thanksgiving or if they watch a scene of suffering on the television news, they may offer a prayer of supplication (intercession).
- Many Christians set aside a particular time each day for devotions when they offer informal prayers, read the Bible or think about religious things.

Why Catholics pray

- Prayer (especially *adoration* prayers) can help a person to get things into perspective. By stepping aside from the pressures of daily life and focusing on God, they can be brought to realise the reality of life.
- Prayers of *thanksgiving* help a person not to be selfish, to realise they depend on others and not to take things for granted.

Section 2: Practices

Activities

1. Do you think it is a good idea to have different forms of prayer and worship?
2. What do you think is the point of praying?
3. Look at the photo. Do you think it's a good idea to have a special place for prayer in the home?

An icon corner in the home of Orthodox Christians.

- Prayers of *confession* stop a person from bottling up feelings of guilt, help them to come to terms with what they have done and help them to learn from their mistakes so that their life improves.
- Prayers of *supplication* can help a person to feel they are doing something for those who suffer if only by praying, but can also inspire them to do something practical to help the less fortunate. Such prayers help people to face up to life better.
- *Contemplative* and *meditative* prayers can bring inner peace so that a person feels refreshed from within.

Why it is important to have a variety of types of prayer and worship

Worship is tremendously important for Catholics because Jesus told them that the greatest commandment is:

Love the Lord your God with all your heart, and with all your soul, and with all your mind, and with all your strength. (St Mark 12:30)

Catholics believe that to worship God fully, people must be able to worship in a variety of ways because people have different personalities with different feelings, aptitudes and interests. They therefore practise various types of worship, including:

- Worship in the home: people need to be able to worship in the home because this is the heart of people's lives and worshipping as a family brings the family together.
- Private worship: people need to be able to worship God in private so they can communicate with God one to one and express emotions they cannot express in front of others.
- Public worship: worshipping with others in church, especially at Mass, gives a sense of belonging to a whole community of believers and an opportunity to feel the strength of the faith and make friends with others in the faith.
- Prayer for different moods: sometimes people need to be serious or sorrowful, at other times joyful.

All Christians would agree with the above, although some Christians are more ready to use set, traditional prayers, while others prefer extempore prayer. Some would use actions such as cupped or raised hands, some prefer to kneel, others to stand or sit. Some Christians would use symbols such as lighted candles and some would be uneasy with this. Orthodox Christians have an icon corner in the home with several holy icons and lit candles. The family will gather there to pray.

Summary

Prayer is an attempt to experience a relationship with God, usually through words. For Catholics it is the raising of hearts and minds to God, and usually includes adoration, thanksgiving, confession and supplication. Jesus taught Christians to use the Lord's Prayer (Our Father). Catholics also use set prayers such as the Hail Mary and their own informal prayers.

Practice questions

c) Explain two reasons why prayer is important for Catholics. In your answer you must refer to a source of wisdom and authority.

d) 'Praying helps to make you a better person.' Evaluate this statement considering arguments for and against. In your answer you should:
- refer to Catholic points of view
- refer to different Catholic or non-Catholic Christian points of view
- reach a justified conclusion.

Topic 1.2.5 Forms of popular piety

Popular piety

Popular piety means the various forms of prayer and worship that Christians (especially Catholic Christians) use, which are inspired by people's culture rather than by the Church's liturgy.

> *The religious sense of the Christian people has always found expression in various forms of piety surrounding the Church's sacramental life, such as the veneration of relics, visits to sanctuaries, pilgrimages, processions, the stations of the cross, religious dances, the rosary, medals etc. These expressions of piety extend the liturgical life of the Church, but do not replace it.*
> (Catechism of the Catholic Church 1674–1675)

The main forms of Catholic popular piety are:

The Rosary

This is a form of prayer named after the string of beads (a **rosary**) used to count prayers. The Rosary is thought to look like a crown of roses surrounding a crucifix. The prayer is based on the Fifteen Mysteries of the Rosary, established by Pope Pius V in the sixteenth century, and an optional set of five, called the Luminous Mysteries, established by Pope John Paul II in 2002.

Joyful Mysteries

- The Annunciation.
- The Visitation.
- The Nativity.
- The Presentation of Jesus at the Temple.
- The Finding of Jesus in the Temple.

Luminous Mysteries

- The Baptism of Jesus in the Jordan.
- The Wedding at Cana.
- Jesus' Proclamation of the Kingdom of God.
- The Transfiguration.
- The Institution of the Eucharist.

Sorrowful Mysteries

- The Agony in the Garden.
- The Scourging at the Pillar.
- The Crowning with Thorns.
- The Carrying of the Cross.
- The Crucifixion and Death of our Lord.

Glorious Mysteries

- The Resurrection.
- The Ascension.
- The Descent of the Holy Spirit.
- The Assumption of Mary.
- The Coronation of the Virgin.

Thinking points

In this topic you need to:
- think about the nature and significance of the Rosary, Eucharistic adoration and the Stations of the Cross
- consider how each of these types of worship might be used and why
- be able to evaluate the importance to Catholics of having different types of worship.

Useful words

Popular piety – worship, respect and devotion shown to God and the saints

Rosary – the prayer beads used to help in saying the set series of prayers based on the rosary beads

Activities

1. Read the quotation from Catechism 1674–1675. What do you think it means?
2. Why do some Catholics call praying the Rosary a time of Bible study?

A set of rosary beads. Certain prayers are said on each bead.

Section 2: Practices

Luminous Mysteries

1. The Baptism of Jesus in the Jordan.
2. The Wedding at Cana.
3. Jesus' Proclamation of Kingdom of God.
4. The Transfiguration.
5. The Institution of the Eucharist.

All but two of these mysteries are based on the Gospels, and the Rosary is a type of Bible study, in a way. It was originally composed by St Dominic in the Middle Ages to help teach people the basics of Catholic faith and to give them a form of reciting the office that was more compatible with their secular lives. A full praying of the Rosary contains 150 Aves as a full recitation of the office over a liturgical year contains 150 psalms. The two Marian meditations – the Assumption and the Coronation – are extra to the Bible. The Luminous Mysteries were added more recently by Pope John Paul II.

The praying of the Rosary is started on the short strand, with the sign of the cross on the crucifix followed by reciting: the Apostles' Creed, the Lord's Prayer at the first large bead and three Hail Marys on the next three beads (for faith, hope and charity), the Glory Be to the Father on the next large bead. Then follow the **decades**, prayers arranged in sets of Ten Hail Marys. For each decade, one of the Mysteries is followed.

The importance and significance of the Rosary

Praying the Rosary is significant for Catholics because:

- It provides a structured, calm time of prayer and meditation.
- It gives an opportunity to remember the main events in the life of Jesus.
- It gives an opportunity to remember the life and work of the Virgin Mary.
- It brings many blessings (Mary made fifteen promises to St Dominic about the benefits of praying the Rosary), including receiving the Virgin Mary's special protection from evil and heresy, and great graces such as being delivered from purgatory swiftly.

Eucharistic adoration

Eucharistic adoration is adoration focused on the **Blessed Sacrament**. It may be performed both when the Eucharist is exposed for viewing and when it is not. Catholics can pray quietly before the Tabernacle where the hosts are reserved whenever the church is open.

In the 'Exposition of the Blessed Sacrament', the Eucharist is displayed in a **monstrance**, typically placed on an altar, at times with a light focused on it, or with candles flanking it. The exposition usually occurs during a special service of devotions to the Blessed Sacrament, or at a set time where specific people attend the exposition for a certain period of time. Official Catholic teachings consider the exposition and adoration of the Blessed Sacrament an important practice which 'stimulates the faithful to an awareness of the marvellous presence of Christ and is an invitation to spiritual communion with Him' ('Instruction on Eucharistic Worship', Sacred Congregation of Rites).

Many Catholics perform Eucharistic adoration for an uninterrupted hour known as the **Holy Hour**, when they keep watch with Christ for an hour. The inspiration for this is the story of the disciples in the Garden of Gethsemane the night before Christ's crucifixion, when he asked them to keep watch

---

Useful words

Decades – the ten Hail Marys said during the Rosary

Blessed Sacrament – the consecrated hosts used in the Mass

Monstrance – vessel used for the exhibition of the Blessed Sacrament

Holy Hour – an hour spent in Eucharistic adoration

A golden tabernacle in a Catholic church.

while he prayed, but returned to find them sleeping. Jesus asked Peter: 'Could you men not keep watch with me for one hour?' (St Matthew 26:40).

The importance and significance of Eucharistic adoration

Eucharistic adoration is important for Catholics because:

- Pope John Paul II showed its importance by spending many hours in silent Eucharistic adoration.
- Pope John Paul II said that eucharistic adoration provides contact with the 'very wellspring of grace'; that is, the worshipper gets in touch with the presence of Christ.
- Jesus himself is present in the blessed sacrament and so 'The Blessed Sacrament is the "Living Heart" of each of our churches and it is our very sweet duty to honor and adore the Blessed Host, which our eyes see, the Incarnate Word, whom they cannot see' (Pope Paul VI, *Credo of the People of God*).

Pope John Paul II said in 'Dominical Cenae' that an hour spent with Jesus in the Blessed Sacrament will repair for evils of the world and bring about peace on earth.

Stations of the Cross

The Stations of the Cross is a series of images depicting Jesus Christ on the day of his crucifixion. It also refers to the prayers that Catholics say when contemplating those images. Often, a series of fourteen images will be arranged in numbered order around a church **nave** or along a path, and worshippers travel from image to image, in order, stopping at each 'station' to say the selected prayers or simply to meditate and reflect on what happened.

A monstrance is placed on an altar, alongside the blessed sacrament. This forms part of the 'Exposition of the Blessed Sacrament'.

Useful words

Nave – the main part of a church building where the worshippers stand, sit or kneel

The Stations of the Cross

1. Jesus is condemned to death.
2. Jesus carries his cross.
3. Jesus falls the first time.
4. Jesus meets his mother.
5. Simon of Cyrene helps Jesus carry the cross.
6. Veronica wipes the face of Jesus.
7. Jesus falls the second time.
8. Jesus meets the women of Jerusalem.
9. Jesus falls the third time.
10. Jesus is stripped of his garments.
11. Crucifixion: Jesus is nailed to the cross.
12. Jesus dies on the cross.
13. Jesus is taken down from the cross (Deposition or Lamentation).
14. Jesus is laid in the tomb.

Some details are not exactly in the story of the Passion, such as the idea of Veronica wiping the face of Jesus or the number of times that Jesus fell. These are later interpretations and traditions.

Although not traditionally part of the Stations, the Resurrection of Jesus is sometimes included as a fifteenth station, to emphasise that Jesus did not stay dead in the tomb.

Activities

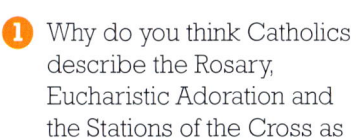

1. Why do you think Catholics describe the Rosary, Eucharistic Adoration and the Stations of the Cross as non-liturgical worship?
2. Look at the photos of the monstrance and the tabernacle. Do you think it is a good idea to spend an hour adoring the Blessed Sacrament?

The devotion may be conducted by individuals making their way from one station to another and saying the prayers or simply meditating on the station. Sometimes there is a person leading the stations and everyone follows him or her (it does not need to be a priest or deacon); they move from station to station while the worshippers make the responses.

The celebration of the Stations of the Cross is often carried out on the Fridays of Lent, especially Good Friday. When a church community celebrates the stations, they are usually accompanied by various songs and prayers such as the Stabat Mater or Adoramus Te, or a modern chant such as the Taizé chant, 'Jesus remember me when you come into your kingdom'.

The significance of the Stations of the Cross

The Stations of the Cross are important for Catholics because:

- They give Catholics a chance to identify with the sufferings of Jesus.
- They give Catholics a chance to pray through the journey of Jesus to the cross.
- They give Catholics a chance to give thanks for what Jesus did for them.
- They give Catholics a chance to remember the cost of the salvation which Jesus brings them.

The Catholic Church believes that popular piety is extremely important because, as the Catechism says:

> *In addition to the liturgy, Christian life is nourished by various forms of popular piety, rooted in different cultures. While carefully clarifying them in the light of faith, the Church fosters the forms of popular piety that express an evangelical instinct and a human wisdom that enrich Christian life. (Catechism of the Catholic Church 1679)*

In other words, there might be many forms of prayer and aids to worship, but the Church is happy to encourage any which are based upon the Catholic faith and enrich a person's understanding of the Gospel or their prayer life.

A collage of the Stations of the Cross from the Portuguese Church in Kolkata, India.

Divergent Christian views towards popular piety

Protestant Christians tend to have a very different view of popular piety from Catholics:

- They do not pray the rosary because of its connections with adoration of the Virgin Mary. Most Protestants believe that Mary had other children (see Mark 6:3) and so was not a perpetual virgin, and they do not believe in the assumption and immaculate conception because those beliefs are not in the Bible.
- Most Protestants do not practise Eucharistic adoration because they do not believe in transubstantiation. They believe the elements are simply symbols and so they do not reserve the hosts.
- Most Protestants do not follow the Stations of the Cross because some of them are not based on the Bible and also they think there is an element of idolatry, which is strictly condemned by Protestants (there are no statues in Protestant churches).

Activities

1. What do you think about the Protestant attitude to popular piety?
2. Look at the collage of the Stations of the Cross on page 64. Compare this to any others you can find out about online or in a local parish church. Which versions do you prefer and why?

Practice questions

c. Explain two reasons why the Rosary is important for Catholics.
d. 'You can gain more from contemplation and reflection than from liturgical worship.' Evaluate this statement considering arguments for and against. In your answer you should:
   - refer to Catholic points of view
   - refer to different Christian points of view
   - reach a justified conclusion.

Summary

Popular piety is prayer and worship based on people's culture rather than the liturgy of the Church. For Catholics this includes Eucharistic adoration, Stations of the Cross and the Rosary. These are important because they help Catholics to pray regularly, to feel the presence of Christ and to understand, and be grateful for, the cost involved in their salvation.

Section 2: Practices

Topic 1.2.6 Pilgrimage

Thinking points

In this topic you need to:
- think about the nature, history and purpose of pilgrimage
- understand why pilgrimage is important for Catholics today
- consider the significance of the places people go on pilgrimage, with specific reference to Jerusalem, Lourdes, Rome and Walsingham
- know what Catholic Catechism 2691–2696 has to say about pilgrimage
- think about divergent Christian attitudes to the importance of pilgrimage
- be able to evaluate the importance of pilgrimage.

Useful words

Relics – parts of a dead saint's body or belongings
Shrine – a place of worship holding the tomb or relic of a saint

Activity

Look at the photo of St Catherine's head. Do you think such relics should be on public display?

The nature, history and purpose of Catholic pilgrimage

Pilgrimage is a journey to a location of importance to a religion for spiritual reasons and not just out of interest as a tourist. When you think of it, life can be like a pilgrimage, for a believer, from birth to death, a journey from and to God.

People have gone on pilgrimages for many years. Many archaeologists think that the ancient monument of Stonehenge was a place of pilgrimage and the ancient Greeks went on pilgrimage to Mount Olympus, for example. All religious have their places of pilgrimage, such as the Muslim annual pilgrimage to Makkah (Mecca). Catholics and other Christians have been going on pilgrimage to the Holy Land (Israel and Palestine) since the Emperor Constantine's mother went there after she converted to Christianity. Other Catholic places of pilgrimage can involve the tombs of saints and places where the Virgin Mary is said to have appeared.

There were many centres of pilgrimage usually connected with the **relics** of a saint (the physical remains of a saint or the personal effects of the saint or holy person), preserved and displayed in a reliquary in a **shrine** at the pilgrimage site.

Pilgrims undertook these journeys to holy places because it was important for their faith. If they had committed sins, they believed that by going on a pilgrimage they could show God how sorry they were. Sometimes they were sent on such journeys by a priest as a penance for a bad sin. Sometimes they went to be healed of an illness. The popularity of these pilgrimages can be seen from Geoffrey Chaucer's *The Canterbury Tales* (1400) about a group of pilgrims journeying from London to the shrine of Thomas Becket at Canterbury Cathedral.

The head of St Catherine of Siena displayed in the Church of San Domenico in Siena. Other parts of her can be found in Venice and England.

Nowadays pilgrimage is very popular with Catholics; for example, almost 6 million Catholics went on pilgrimage to Lourdes in 2015. Lourdes, in the south of France, is a healing place of pilgrimage and the Virgin Mary is believed to have appeared there in the nineteenth century.

Why Catholics go on pilgrimage

- Some feel that life is a search for God and that going on a pilgrimage helps them in their search for God.
- Many pilgrims feel that they become closer to God on a pilgrimage.
- Making a pilgrimage takes planning, time and effort, and this process can help in determining what your priorities in life are.
- Pilgrimage adds discipline to a Christian's spiritual life – they have to get up and do something.
- Pilgrims go to places like Lourdes in the hope of being cured of an illness, and although few are cured, many claim that the pilgrimage gave them greater inner strength to cope with their illnesses and other problems of life.
- Places of pilgrimage have special connections with great figures or events in the Christian faith and so are full of holiness. Pilgrims hope that if they visit these places some of the holiness will rub off on them.

Places Catholics go on pilgrimage

You need to know why the four pilgrimage sites of Jerusalem, Rome, Lourdes and Walsingham are important for Catholic Christians today.

Jerusalem

A major centre of Christian pilgrimage is Jerusalem, where the crucial events in the final week of Jesus' life took place; the events that are still celebrated in Christianity today. Pilgrims visit:

- The **Cenacle**, thought to be the site of the Upper Room, which is important to pilgrims because it is where the Last Supper took place, and the Last Supper is when Jesus instituted the Eucharist.

Jewish tombs under the Church of the Holy Sepulchre.

Activities

1. Why do some Catholics say life is like a pilgrimage?
2. Look at the photo on page 66. Do you think relics like this should be on public display?
3. Explain why Catholic Christians go on pilgrimage to Jerusalem.

Useful words

Cenacle – the Upper Room in Jerusalem where the Last Supper took place

Section 2: Practices

> **Activity**
> Which do you think is the most important pilgrimage site in Rome?

Useful words

Via Dolorosa – 'the way of tears', the route Jesus took from Pilate's court to Golgotha
Basilicas – important church buildings and place of pilgrimage

- The Church of All Nations on the Mount of Olives, which is important to pilgrims because it is where Jesus prayed to his Father to take the cup from him and where Jesus was arrested.
- The Convent of the Sisters of Zion, which is important to pilgrims because it is built on top of the pavement where Jesus was tried before Pontius Pilate and from which Pilate offered to release Jesus.
- The **Via Dolorosa**, or way of suffering, which is important to pilgrims because it is the route Jesus took as he was made to carry his cross to Golgotha, the place of crucifixion (pilgrims usually walk along the Via praying at places where Jesus stopped and where Simon of Cyrene took over the cross).
- The Church of the Holy Sepulchre, which is perhaps the holiest place because it is believed to be the location of Golgotha, where Jesus was crucified (dying for the sins of the world), and Jesus' nearby tomb, where Jesus was buried and rose from the dead, so guaranteeing eternal life to Christians.

Rome

Rome is a major place of pilgrimage for Catholics because it contains Vatican City, the home of the Pope, special because St Peter was martyred and buried there. It also contains four papal **basilicas** (important church buildings), which are designated as pilgrim churches:

- St Peter's Basilica and the Basilica of St Paul Outside the Walls were designated as pilgrim churches by Pope Boniface VIII for the first Holy Year in 1300.
- Pope Clement VI added the Basilica of St John Lateran in 1350.
- Pope Gregory XI added Santa Maria Maggiore (St Mary Major) Basilica in 1375. This contains a statue of the Virgin Mary as the protector of the people of Rome.

These are the four major papal basilicas in Rome. Each contains a holy door, opened only during official Jubilee years, when special blessings are promised.

Pope Francis opens the Holy Door at St John Lateran in Rome for the Year of Mercy, December 2015.

Pope Francis visits the Basilica di Santa Maria Maggiore in Rome.

Topic 1.2.6 Pilgrimage

St Peter's Basilica is in Vatican City, the papal enclave within the city of Rome. Although it is neither the mother church of the Catholic Church nor the cathedral of the Diocese of Rome, St Peter's is regarded as one of the holiest Catholic shrines. Catholic tradition holds that the Basilica is the burial site of St Peter, the first Pope, whose tomb is directly below the high altar of the Basilica. For this reason, many popes are buried at St Peter's.

The Papal Archbasilica of St John Lateran is the cathedral church of Rome and is the episcopal seat of the Bishop of Rome (the Pope). As the cathedral church, St John Lateran is the most important of the basilicas and ranks above all other churches in the Catholic Church. It contains six papal tombs with pope Leo XIII (died 1903) being the last Pope to be buried there.

St John Lateran is near the Scala Sancta, or Holy Stairs. The Scala Sancta are white marble steps encased in wooden ones. According to Catholic tradition, they form the staircase which once led to the *praetorium* (headquarters) of Pontius Pilate in Jerusalem and which, therefore, were sanctified by the footsteps of Jesus Christ during his Passion.

The Papal Basilica of St Paul Outside the Walls was founded by the Roman Emperor Constantine I over the burial place of St Paul, where it was said that, after the Apostle's execution, his followers erected a memorial.

St Paul Outside the Walls in Rome.

Lourdes

Pilgrimage became very popular again in the nineteenth century among Catholics, especially after the experiences of St Bernadette of Lourdes.

In February 1858, fourteen-year-old Bernadette Soubirous saw a beautiful girl in a niche at a rocky outcrop near Lourdes. The apparition beckoned to her, but Bernadette did not move and the girl smiled at her before disappearing. Bernadette later described how she had seen a girl of about her own age and height, clothed in a brilliant and unearthly white robe, with a blue girdle round her waist and a white veil on her head. This was the beginning of eighteen apparitions during the spring and early summer of 1858. During one of these, Bernadette asked the girl her name and she said, 'I am the **Immaculate Conception**.' This title had only recently been given to Mary by the then Pope to make it clear that she was born holy, without the effect of original sin. During another appearance, the girl led Bernadette to a grotto where a miraculous spring appeared. Since these miraculous appearances of the Virgin Mary, Lourdes has become a great place of pilgrimage for Catholics and many healing miracles are alleged to have taken place there.

Today Lourdes hosts around 6 million visitors every year from all corners of the world. This constant stream of pilgrims and tourists transformed Lourdes into the second most important centre of tourism in France, second only to Paris, and the third most important site of international Catholic pilgrimage after Rome and the Holy Land.

The most important place for pilgrims to visit is the grotto where Bernadette saw visions of the Virgin Mary. Pilgrims today walk through the grotto touching the rock walls (which are now shiny smooth from millions of hands), look at the water spring that Bernadette dug, and pray in front of the niche where Mary appeared.

Useful words

Immaculate conception – the Catholic belief that Mary was protected from original sin from the moment of her conception so that Jesus was not born with original sin

Activity

Why do you think Lourdes is such an important place of pilgrimage for Catholics?

Section 2: Practices

The Virgin Mary told Bernadette to dig for and drink from the spring, and to wash in the water. This water is now piped to many taps near the grotto for people to drink and wash in. Many pilgrims fill bottles with this water to take home, or to take to their relatives who are staying in the Lourdes hospitals. There are also private baths, filled with this water, where volunteers dip pilgrims into the water.

There are two processions in Lourdes: the Eucharistic Procession every afternoon, where the Blessed Sacrament is processed around the grotto to the underground basilica; and the Rosary Procession in the evening, where thousands of pilgrims, holding candles, process from the grotto around the grounds of the Sanctuaries, and then to the front of the basilica.

While Lourdes is famous for miracles, and many of the sick who visit still hope for a miracle, the main purpose today is to give the sick strength and hope to bear their sufferings.

Walsingham

The Catholic Walsingham pilgrimage walk.

This village in Norfolk is known as 'the English Nazareth'. In 1061, the Lady of the Manor, Richeldis de Faverches, had a vision of the Virgin Mary and her home in Nazareth and Mary ordered her to build a copy of Mary's home. The house was eventually built and became a popular pilgrimage site when it became impossible for Christian pilgrims to get to Jerusalem because of Muslim conquests. In the shrine was a statue of Mary based on what Lady Richeldis saw in her vision and a phial which was supposed to contain milk from Mary's breasts. Many healings and visions were supposed to happen at the shrine.

The shrine was destroyed at the Reformation, but in the twentieth century an Anglican shrine was rebuilt and the Catholics reopened the old Slipper chapel as their shrine, one mile outside the village, on the site of an old chapel where medieval pilgrims used to remove their shoes before walking a mile barefoot to the shrine.

Modern pilgrims believe Walsingham is important because:

- they can feel close to the Virgin Mary (Our Lady of Walsingham) when praying there
- it is a place where other pilgrims claim their prayers have been answered
- it is a place where healings are claimed to have taken place
- it brings spiritual refreshment and brings Catholics and Anglicans closer together.

The Church's view on pilgrimage

The Catholic Church offers guidance on places of worship and includes places of pilgrimage among the 'most appropriate places for prayer'. The Catechism states that:

In prayer, the pilgrim Church is associated with that of the saints, whose intercession she asks. The different schools of Christian spirituality share in the living tradition of prayer and are precious guides for the spiritual life. The Christian family is the first place for education in prayer. Ordained ministers, the consecrated life, catechesis, prayer groups, and 'spiritual direction' ensure assistance within the Church in the practice of prayer.

The most appropriate places for prayer are personal or family oratories, monasteries, places of pilgrimage, and above all the church, which is the proper place for liturgical prayer for the parish community and the privileged place for Eucharistic adoration.
(Catechism of the Catholic Church 2692–2696)

Prayer is aided by special places, either in the home, or where there are family memories, or in places reserved for prayer such as a monastery or a church. Certain places have other associations, perhaps with saints or with the life of Jesus. These associations help people to pray better.

Divergent Christian attitudes to pilgrimage

Protestant Christians have always been critical of pilgrimages. Martin Luther said:

All pilgrimages should be stopped. There is no good in them: no commandment enjoins them, no obedience attaches to them. Rather do these pilgrimages give countless occasions to commit sin and to despise God's commandments. (To the Christian Nobility, 1520)

Protestants tend to feel that emphasising special 'holy places' is wrong because believers can encounter God anywhere since God is the same God everywhere. They are also opposed to any form of worshipping the Virgin Mary because they regard it as idolatry and because they believe that Mary had other children (Matthew 13:55–56) and that James the brother of Jesus was the first Bishop of Jerusalem (according to the early Church historian Eusebius), and so cannot be revered as the Virgin Mary. They also regard any veneration of saints as wrong because only God should be venerated; and they regard veneration of relics as idolatry.

So, Protestants will visit the holy places in Jerusalem and go to Iona and Taizé, but would not go to Walsingham or places like Lourdes.

Activities

1. What do you think are the benefits of going on a pilgrimage?
2. Why do you think Protestants do not go on pilgrimage to Lourdes?

Practice questions

c. Explain two reasons why pilgrimage is important for Catholics. In your answer you must refer to a source of wisdom and authority.

d. 'Pilgrimage to a holy place brings you closer to God.' Evaluate this statement considering arguments for and against. In your answer you should:
- refer to Catholic points of view
- refer to different Catholic or non-Catholic Christian points of view
- reach a justified conclusion.

Summary

Pilgrimage has always been important for Catholics, as they believe it brings them closer to God and involves going to holy places which might make them holy. Christians go to Jerusalem to feel close to Jesus in the places he spent his last days. They visit places like Rome as the heart of the Church, Lourdes in the hope of being cured and Walsingham to feel close to the Virgin Mary. Protestant Christians would only go to places connected with Jesus so they can avoid idolatry.

Section 2: Practices

Topic 1.2.7 Catholic social teaching

Thinking points

In this topic you need to:
- think about how Catholic social teachings show love of their neighbours, justice, peace and reconciliation (including *Laudato Si* and *Evangelii Gaudium* – the inclusion of the poor in society)
- consider how these teachings might be reflected in the lives of individual Catholics, including reference to Matthew 25:31–46
- understand the work of CAFOD, what it does and why
- be able to evaluate the importance to Catholics of the Church's social teaching.

Useful words

Cardinal virtues – the major virtues: justice, prudence, fortitude and temperance
Reconciliation – bringing together people who were opposed to one another

Activities

1. Do you think the love of God and love of neighbour are inseparable?
2. How do you think peace and reconciliation are connected to justice?

Catholic social teachings

Catholic social teaching is about loving God and your neighbours as inseparable parts of a whole, like two indivisible sides of a coin. It is based on what Jesus said when he was asked, 'Of all the commandments, which is the most important?'

> 'The most important one,' answered Jesus, 'is this: 'Hear, O Israel: The Lord our God, the Lord is one. Love the Lord your God with all your heart and with all your soul and with all your mind and with all your strength.' The second is this: 'Love your neighbour as yourself.' There is no commandment greater than these.' (St Mark 12:29–31)

Love of neighbour is at the heart of everything the Church teaches about living in society and is reflected in this statement from the Catechism:

> Love is itself the fulfilment of all our works. There is the goal; that is why we run: we run toward it, and once we reach it, in it we shall find rest. (Catechism of the Catholic Church 1829)

Justice

Justice is one of the four **cardinal virtues** of Christianity, along with *prudence* (being wise and careful), *fortitude* (determination and commitment) and *temperance* (moderation). These are explained in the Catechism of the Catholic Church 1805–1811. This teaching has its basis in the Bible, which says that God is just and will reward the righteous (another word for those who are just) and punish those who sin, if not in this life then in the life to come. The Bible says that God wants the world to be ruled justly and that this means people should be treated fairly and not cheated. Jesus said that the rich should share with the poor and there are many statements in the New Testament about how Christians should treat people fairly and equally.

> Anyone who does not do what is right is not a child of God; nor is anyone who does not love his brother. (1 John 3:10)

Peace and reconciliation

Peace and **reconciliation** are at the heart of the Christian Gospel. Jesus said, 'Blessed are the peacemakers, for they will be called sons of God' (Matthew 5:9). St Paul said, 'Let us therefore make every effort to do what leads to peace and to mutual edification' (Romans 14:19).

The Catechism says:

> Earthly peace is the image and fruit of the peace of Christ, the messianic 'Prince of Peace.' By the blood of his Cross, 'in his own person he killed the hostility,' he reconciled men with God and made his Church the sacrament of the unity of the human race and of its union with God. 'He is our peace.' He has declared: 'Blessed are the peacemakers.' (Catechism of the Catholic Church 2305)

Christianity is based on the concept of forgiveness and reconciliation. Christians should be committed to forgiveness and reconciliation because the power of forgiveness and love can lead to reconciliation and the ending of conflict. St Paul said that Christians should try to live in peace with everyone, and the only way to live in peace with everyone is to try to bring about reconciliation through forgiving those who wrong you.

Laudato Si

This is the second **encyclical** of Pope Francis (the current pope) and has the subtitle 'On Care For Our Common Home'.

The encyclical is concerned about environmental issues and world poverty. It highlights the problems of pollution, climate change, a lack of clean water, loss of biodiversity which has led to an overall decline in human life, and a breakdown of society. 'Never have we so hurt and mistreated our common home as we have in the last two hundred years.' The encyclical accepts the scientific consensus that climate change is a product of human activity, especially the use of fossil fuels. It claims that climate change is 'a global problem with grave implications: environmental, social, economic, political and for the distribution of goods. It represents one of the principal challenges facing humanity in our day.' Pope Francis urges discussion on how to solve the problems, and urges people to use alternatives to fossil fuels wherever possible.

The encyclical also highlights the issue of world poverty. It states that developed nations are morally obliged to assist developing nations in combating the climate-change crisis since poor nations are often ill-prepared to adapt to the effects of climate change and yet will bear the brunt of its result. Linking the issues of poverty and the environment, the Pope insists that the world must listen to 'both the cry of the earth and the cry of the poor'.

Similar teachings are found in Pope Francis's *Evangelii Gaudium* (*The Joy of the Gospel*), which was published in 2013. This explored various aspects of the Gospel message, and our need to communicate it. Peace and justice in the world are part of that message:

Useful words

Encyclical – a letter addressed by the Pope to all the bishops of the Church

Hundreds of people took part in a 'March for the Earth' in Rome on 8 November 2015 to show their support for Pope Francis's call for climate action.

> Just as the commandment 'Thou shalt not kill' sets a clear limit in order to safeguard the value of human life, today we also have to say 'thou shalt not' to an economy of exclusion and inequality. Such an economy kills. How can it be that it is not a news item when an elderly homeless person dies of exposure, but it is news when the stock market loses two points? This is a case of exclusion. Can we continue to stand by when food is thrown away while people are starving? This is a case of inequality. Today everything comes under the laws of competition and the survival of the fittest, where the powerful feed upon the powerless. As a consequence, masses of people find themselves excluded and marginalized: without work, without possibilities, without any means of escape ... With this in mind, I encourage financial experts and political leaders to ponder the words of one of the sages of antiquity: 'Not to share one's wealth with the poor is to steal from them and to take away their livelihood. It is not our own goods which we hold, but theirs.' (*Evangelii Gaudium*, Pope Francis, 24 November 2013)

Pope Francis appealed for the inclusion of the poor, quoting Jesus when he told his disciples, 'You yourselves give them something to eat!' (Mark 6:37) He quoted the Brazilian bishops:

> We wish to take up daily the joys and hopes, the difficulties and sorrows of the Brazilian people, especially those living in the barrios and the countryside – landless, homeless, lacking food and health care – to the detriment of their rights. Seeing their poverty, hearing their cries and knowing their sufferings, we are scandalized because we know that there is enough food for everyone and that hunger is the result of a poor distribution of goods and income. The problem is made worse by the generalized practice of wastefulness. (Evangelii Gaudium 191)

How these teachings might be reflected in the lives of Catholics

Christians believe that they are called to discipleship; they are called for a special purpose in the same way that the apostles were. This is often referred to as a **vocation**, a call to love God and love one's neighbour as Jesus commanded his disciples in the greatest commandment. Christian vocation cannot be restricted to church or Sundays. The call to be a Christian must involve everything a Christian does and so Catholic Christians must follow the Church's social teaching in their daily lives. This means that things like peace, justice and reconciliation need to be practised as far as possible with those around them.

This may well affect a Catholic's choice of career; they may choose a caring profession such as a doctor, nurse, carer, teacher or counsellor, or a role campaigning for equal opportunities. It is also likely to affect their daily lives as they become involved in charities that help the poor, making lifestyle choices that help the environment, standing up for the rights of the poor if they are attacked, and working for justice for the oppressed.

Many Catholics are led by the Church's social teachings to work for and/or support the work of SVP (Society of St Vincent de Paul) and CAFOD (Catholic Fund for Overseas Development).

The Parable of the Sheep and the Goats (Matthew 25:31–46)

> When the Son of Man comes in his glory ... All the nations will be gathered before him, and he will separate the people from one another as a shepherd separates the sheep from the goats. He will put the sheep on his right and the goats on his left. Then the King will say to those on his right, 'Come you who are blessed by my Father ... For I was hungry and you gave me something to eat, I was thirsty and you gave me something to drink, I was a stranger and you invited me in, I needed clothes and you clothed me, I was sick and you looked after me, I was in prison and you came to visit me.' ... Then he will say to those on his left ... 'I tell you the truth, whatever you did not do for one of the least of these, you did not do for me.' Then they will go away to eternal punishment, but the righteous to eternal life. (Adapted from Matthew 25:31–46)

In the Parable of the Sheep and the Goats, Jesus showed that it is the duty of Catholics to feed the hungry, clothe the naked, give drink to the thirsty, visit the sick and help those in prison. These teachings should affect the way a Catholic votes and participates in politics, especially in terms of the inclusion of the poor.

Useful words

Vocation – the calling a person has to live their life in a certain way

---

Activity

Read the Parable of the Sheep and the Goats. Can you think of any situations where it might make you change your mind about what to do?

Topic 1.2.7 Catholic social teaching

A CAFOD banner at a rally to encourage world leaders to take action to tackle global hunger.

The work of CAFOD: what they do and why

The major Catholic agency working for world development and supported by the Catholics of England and Wales is CAFOD. It was established by the Catholic Bishops of England and Wales in 1962. It is the English and Welsh arm of Caritas International (a worldwide network of Catholic relief and development organisations) supporting 1000 development projects in over 60 countries. It tries to end world poverty through:

1. *Development programmes*. CAFOD promotes long-term development so that **LEDC**s can become self-supporting and have the opportunities to become **MEDC**s. Some examples of CAFOD's development aid are:
   - The area around Hola in south-eastern Kenya is arid and poor. Its 12,000 people make a subsistence living as nomadic farmers moving around with their cattle. These people have no access to state health care. Since 1985 CAFOD has been helping the Hola Catholic Mission health programme. During this time three clinics have been opened and 40 health workers (chosen by the local community and working for no pay) have been trained to provide basic medical care and advice on hygiene, nutrition and child health.
   - In Brazil, the richest ten per cent of the 150 million people enjoy 53.2 per cent of the wealth in that nation, while the poorest ten per cent receive 0.6 per cent. This has led to about 6 million homeless children living on the streets. CAFOD is helping the parish of Piexnhos in Olinda (part of Hélder Câmara's old diocese) to run a scheme known as 'The Community Taking Responsibility for its Children'. Street educators give the children literacy classes and training in skills so that they can earn a living.

Useful words

LEDCs – less economically developed countries
MEDCs – more economically developed countries

Section 2: Practices

Activities

1. What does the SVP do in your parish?
2. How does your parish support CAFOD?

- In Bangladesh, floods in the district of Khulna often wipe out poor farmers' entire rice crops. CAFOD is helping the Organisation of Peasant Farmers, which sets up savings schemes to help them when crops fail and which is starting up different farming projects such as duck-rearing units.

2 *Disaster and emergency fund*. CAFOD has a disaster fund to deal with natural disasters and refugees, which often have to take priority over long-term aid. CAFOD has provided over £2 million to support Church partners in Syria providing food parcels, medical aid and relief supplies to refugees from the civil war. They also helped people to find safe places to stay.

3 *Raising awareness*. About five per cent of CAFOD's budget is spent on educating the people and churches of England and Wales about the need for development and the ways in which Catholics can help less developed countries. It publishes a newspaper called *Friday* and many educational materials. These give information not only about what CAFOD is doing, but also about world development.

4 *Speaking out on behalf of poor communities to bring social justice*. CAFOD was heavily involved in the Make Poverty History campaign of 2005, the biggest ever global mobilisation to end poverty. It is now involved in the Trade Justice Campaign to change the rules and practices of international trade to help developing countries work themselves out of poverty. CAFOD is also campaigning to cancel the debt owed by some of the world's poorest countries. Many developing countries spend twice as much on debt repayments to rich creditors as they do on health care and education. CAFOD also promotes Fairtrade products to bring better prices, decent working conditions, local sustainability and fair terms of trade for farmers and workers in the developing world.

Summary

The Catholic Church prescribes different principles (social teaching) on how worshippers should live their lives in order to carry out the work of God and so to enter heaven in the afterlife. This includes loving their neighbour, treating people fairly and equally (social justice), and bringing about peace and reconciliation. Catholics can do this individually or through organisations such as SVP or CAFOD.

Practice questions

c Explain two reasons why Catholics support the work of CAFOD. In your answer you must refer to a source of wisdom and authority.

d 'It is more important to save people's souls than feed their bodies.' Evaluate this statement considering arguments for and against. In your answer you should:
- refer to Catholic points of view
- refer to different Catholic or non-Catholic Christian points of view
- reach a justified conclusion.

Topic 1.2.8 Catholic mission and evangelisation

The history and significance of missionary and evangelical work for Catholics

A missionary is a person sent by a church into an area to bring people into the Christian Church. **Evangelisation** is proclaiming the message of Christianity with the aim of converting people to Christianity. Fundamentally, missionary work and evangelisation are one and the same thing.

Jesus' final words to his disciples were:

> *All authority in heaven and on earth has been given to me. Therefore go and make disciples of all nations, baptising them in the name of the Father and of the Son and of the Holy Spirit, and teaching them to obey everything I have commanded you.* **(Matthew 28:19)**

This is known by Christians as the **Great Commission** and they believe it is something they must do.

The history of missionary and evangelical work

The disciples of Jesus began this work immediately. The Acts of the Apostles in the New Testament records how St Peter organised conversions throughout Palestine, then St Philip converted an Ethiopian, leading to Christianity spreading into Africa (the Ethiopian Church is one of the oldest Christian Churches). It then records the great missionary journeys of St Paul, who founded Christian churches in Syria, Turkey and Greece before ending up in Rome, where there were already many Christians (tradition says that this Church was founded and led by St Peter, and Catholics believe that St Peter was the first Bishop of Rome, the title of the Pope).

Tradition says that St Thomas took Christianity to Iran and then to India, with other disciples going to different areas. There were Christian churches in Egypt, Iraq, North Africa and the European parts of the Roman Empire, including Britain, by 100CE. Armenia and Georgia were Christian countries by 300CE and there were Christians in China by 600CE. St Cyril and his brother Methodius converted Russia and the Slavs of Eastern Europe in the ninth century. Cyril invented the Cyrillic alphabet so that he could translate the Bible into Russian and the Slavonic languages.

When Europeans began to colonise America and Africa, Christian missionaries went with them, so that conversion to Christianity went hand in hand with being colonised by Europeans. These missionaries were very successful, although there can be a legacy of imperialism and ill-feeling in some parts of the world. South and Central America became Catholic through the work of Spanish and Portuguese Catholics. North America and much of Africa south of the Sahara became Protestant through the work of British missionaries, although French and Belgian African colonies became Catholic. Ironically, Europe, from where these missions were sent out, has now declined in faith and numbers attending church.

Thinking points

In this topic you need to:
- consider the history and significance of missionary and evangelical work
- understand the divergent ways this is put into practice by the Church and individual Catholics locally, nationally and globally
- think about how this work fulfils the commission of Jesus and teachings of the Church (including *Evangelii Gaudium*, Chapter 5)
- be able to evaluate the importance of mission and evangelisation for Catholics.

Useful words

Evangelisation – proposing or spreading the faith through teaching about the religion helping others

Great Commission – Jesus' last command to his disciples to go out and convert the world

Section 2: Practices

Columban Missionaries are Catholic missionaries who 'promote the message and values of the Gospel' in Asia and Latin America.

Activities

1. Why do you think Christians call Matthew 28:19 the Great Commission?
2. Look at the photo of the Columban missionary. Can you see any problems arising from what is going on in the photo?

Useful words

Alpha – a Christian course trying to convert non-churchgoers

Local missionary and evangelical work

Local churches are a focal point of Catholic identity and worship:

- they are where people go to show their devotion to God in the celebration of Mass
- they provide special services for Christians to celebrate Christian festivals
- they offer the sacraments to the people by providing baptism, communion, regular confessions, confirmation and marriage
- they provide discussion and prayer groups, as well as Bible readings and sermons in worship, to give people a chance to learn more about God and how they should behave as Christians
- they support the local Catholic Christian schools
- they provide social facilities such as youth clubs, uniformed organisations such as scouts, lunch clubs for the elderly, and parent and toddler groups, so bringing people into the Church.

National missionary and evangelical work

The Alpha course (now known simply as **Alpha**) is a programme that aims to introduce non-churchgoers to the basics of the Christian faith through a series of talks and discussions. It describes itself as 'an opportunity to explore the meaning of life'. Alpha courses are run in churches throughout the UK by all the major Christian denominations, including the Catholic Church, with the blessing of the bishops.

Topic 1.2.8 Catholic mission and evangelisation

An advertisement for the Alpha course.

Catholic parishes organise missions led by different groups or religious orders which will encourage local worshippers and visit schools. The CAFE (Catholic Faith and Evangelisation) team produce lively DVDs and teaching programmes on the faith.

Besides teaching about the faith and preaching, there is the good work and witness of groups such as SVP, as mentioned earlier. Love in action comes first, according to those involved, and talking about the Gospel second.

In 2010, Pope Benedict XVI created the 'Pontifical Council for the Promotion of New Evangelisation' to reinvigorate Christianity in Europe. Archbishop Fisichella was appointed the first President of the Council and established **Mission Metropolis** in Lent 2012 to revive faith in Christianity in Europe by concentrating on major cities such as Barcelona, Brussels, Dublin, Liverpool, Paris, Warsaw and Vienna. The plan comprised two parts. The mission was centred on each cathedral and involved:

- a regular reading of the Gospel
- the local bishop teaching young people, families and those converting to Catholicism
- the promotion of confession
- a charitable initiative.

Global missionary and evangelical work

The global missionary work of the Catholic Church is organised by the Society for the Propagation of the Faith, which is funded by offerings from Catholics on World Mission Sunday and throughout the year, combined with offerings to the Propagation of the Faith worldwide. The Society is in charge of the mission dioceses of the Catholic Church (about 1100 of them) and works with them to provide **catechetical programmes** (teaching schemes) and **seminaries** (where priests are trained), and to support the work of religious communities (monks and nuns), and the building of chapels, churches, orphanages and schools.

Modern Christian missions work to provide for material as well as spiritual needs. As Pope Francis said:

> *It is not enough to offer someone a sandwich unless it is accompanied by the possibility of learning how to stand on one's own two feet. Charity that leaves the poor person as he is, is not sufficient. True mercy, the mercy God gives to us and teaches us, demands justice, it demands that the poor find the way to be poor no longer. (2014 Lenten message from the Vatican)*

Useful words

Mission Metropolis – the Catholic mission to start the re-evangelisation of Europe from the cities

Catechetical programmes – religious instruction given in preparation for Christian baptism or confirmation

Seminaries – educational institutions which prepare pupils for ordination as clergy

Activity

Look at the Alpha poster above. Would this make you want to join the course? What questions would you ask if you did?

Significance of missionary and evangelical work for Catholics

The main reason Christians feel it is their duty to evangelise is the Great Commission of Jesus, but Christians also feel they should share their faith with others out of love for them. Christians believe that being a Christian helps people to share God's love, which gives them strength to cope with life and assures people a place in heaven, and therefore should be shared with those outside the faith.

Another reason why missionary and evangelical work is becoming more important for Christians is the decline in religion. In 1993, 1.28 million Catholics attended Mass in England and Wales, but by 2010 attendance at Mass had dropped to 0.88 million.

How missionary work and evangelism fulfil the Great Commission and the teaching of Jesus

Jesus' final words to his disciples (the Great Commission) were:

> *All authority in heaven and on earth has been given to me. Therefore go and make disciples of all nations, baptising them in the name of the Father and of the Son and of the Holy Spirit, and teaching them to obey everything I have commanded you.* (Matthew 28:19)

In *Evangelii Gaudium* (Chapter 5), Pope Francis appealed for Catholics to renew their personal faith and their faith in the joy of the Gospel. He spoke of 'Spirit filled Evangelisers' and 'Personal encounter with the saving love of Jesus.' This will produce an enthusiasm and attractiveness in society. He goes on to say that Catholics need to come alongside people in their needs:

> *Sometimes we are tempted to be the type of Christian who keeps the Lord's wounds at arms length. Yet Jesus wants to touch human misery, to touch the suffering flesh of others. He hopes that we will stop looking for those personal or communal niches which shelter us from the maelstrom of human misfortune and instead enter into the reality of people's lives and know the power of tenderness.* (Evangelii Gaudium 5:270)

Divergent approaches to missionary and evangelical work in the modern world

Some Catholics and other Christians take a different view on evangelisation because of living in a multi-faith society in the UK and in a multi-cultural world feeling the effects of globalisation. Such people tend to evangelise by living a good Christian life and loving their neighbours because they feel that:

- Trying to convert followers of other religions when living in a multi-faith society is a type of prejudice and discrimination. Treating people differently because of their religion and trying to convert other religions is discriminating against those who do not have the same faith as you.

- It is impossible to regard all other religions as wrong unless you have studied all of them and compared them to decide which one is true.

- It can lead to arguments and even violence within a multi-faith society when people are told their religion is wrong, or not the one most fully speaking of the way to God.
- It can be resented in LEDCs as a new form of colonisation as it appears that people from MEDCs are imposing their values and culture on an LEDC (see earlier comment about imperialism).

Conclusion

The problems caused by evangelisation are about **proselytism**, converting others. Evangelisation is about sharing and witnessing to the Gospel, which means *teaching* the faith without pressure or condemnation of others. It also means *living* the faith and helping others, showing the love of Christ. Evangelisation can be about much more than converting people, and will be handled in more culturally sensitive ways today. This does not mean that mission cannot happen, or that it cannot be seen to do great good.

The emphasis is on social care and compassion, with communities of committed Catholics praying and worshipping in peace as they work at this. They can provide health care, food aid, education and other services where there is a lack. The only children's hospital in the Palestinian territories, for example, is run by Catholic nuns, as a part of the charitable group, Caritas. Their example and the faith of such men and women can inspire others, whatever the context or difficulties. When Mother Teresa was once asked why her sisters cared for the sick and poor on the streets of Calcutta, she replied, 'They do it for Jesus.'

Useful words

Proselytism – converting others, often through aggressive or coercive techniques, which are frowned upon by Catholics today

Activity

What do you think about the Muslim and Hindu missionaries working in the UK?

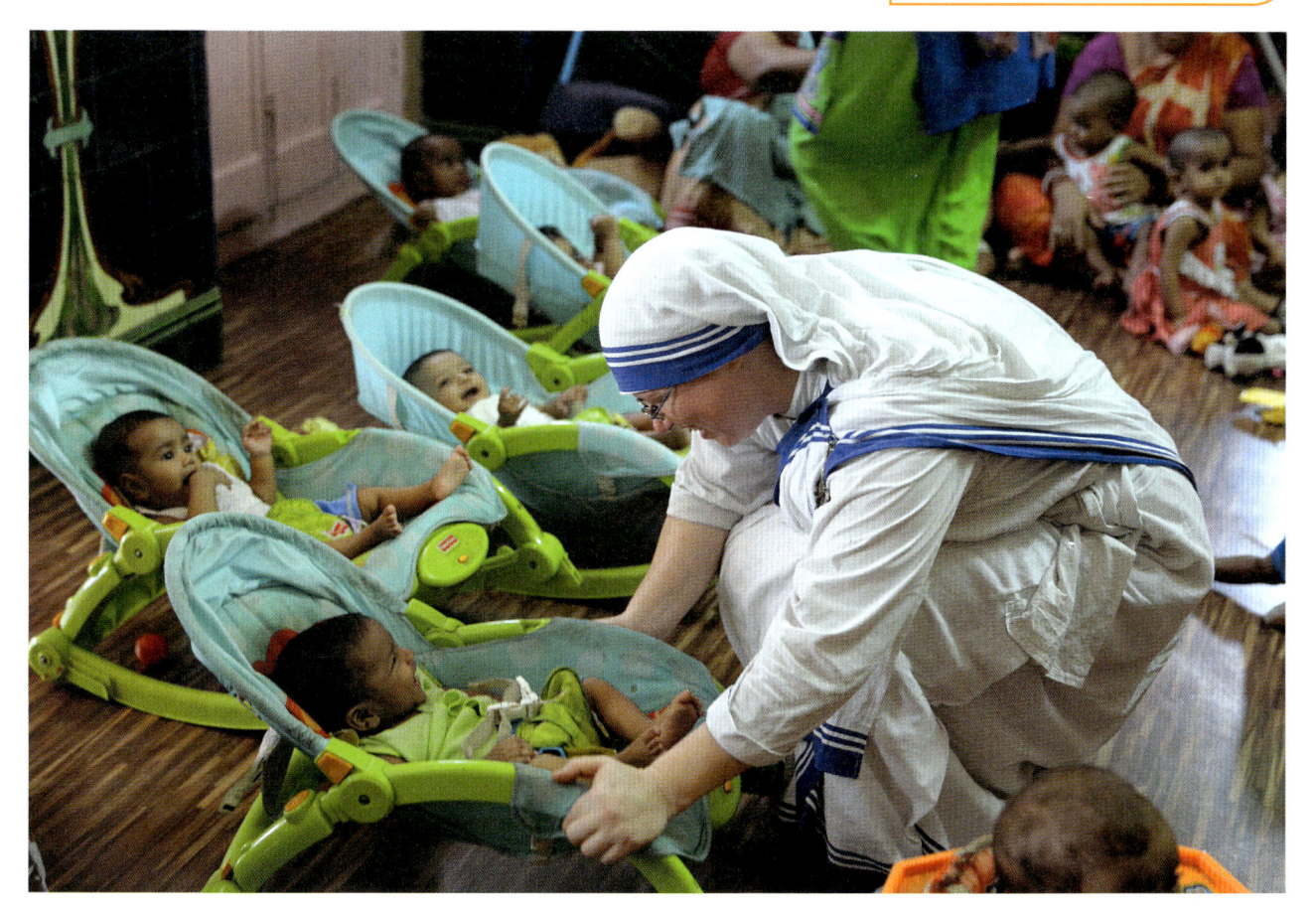

A nun caring for babies in India.

Section 2: Practices

Activities

1. How is the Caritas hospital an example of good Catholic service, witness and mission in Palestine today?
2. Do you think evangelisation has a place in a multi-faith, multi-cultural society?

Practice questions

c Explain two reasons why mission and evangelism are important for Catholics. In your answer you must refer to a source of wisdom and authority.

d 'There shouldn't be any missionaries in the modern world.' Evaluate this statement considering arguments for and against. In your answer you should:
- refer to Catholic points of view
- refer to different Catholic or non-Catholic Christian points of view
- reach a justified conclusion.

Summary

Catholics have a long history of mission, starting with the Great Commission that Jesus gave his disciples to preach the Gospel throughout the world. Thanks to the work of Catholic missionaries, there are now Catholic Christians throughout the world. The desire to expand the Church means that Catholics engage in missionary work locally, nationally and worldwide. However, the nature of the multi-faith and multi-cultural modern world has led to there being different approaches to missionary work.

How to answer questions

a) Outline three features of the sacrament of reconciliation. [3]

The penitent will talk to the priest about their sins, admitting their responsibility and resolving not to sin again. The priest will give the penitent their penance, which is something they have to do to show they are sorry. The penitent will then say a special prayer called the Act of Contrition which says how sorry they are.

A high mark answer because three features of the sacrament of reconciliation are clearly outlined.

b) Describe two differences between worship in a Catholic church and worship in the main religious tradition of Britain. [4]

The main religious tradition of Britain is Protestant. One main difference is that the main worship in a Catholic church is the Mass whereas the main worship in Protestant churches is non-liturgical with charismatic hymns and prayers. Another difference is the understanding of the Eucharist, in that Catholics believe in transubstantiation but Protestants believe the elements do not change and are purely symbolic.

A high mark answer because two correct differences are clearly described.

c) Explain two reasons why Catholics work for peace. In your answer you must refer to a source of wisdom and authority. [5]

Catholics work for peace because peace is the heart of the Christian Gospel. Jesus said, 'Blessed are the peacemakers, for they will be called sons of God' (Matthew 5:9). St Paul said, 'Let us therefore make every effort to do what leads to peace and to mutual edification' (Romans 14:19).

The Catechism says: 'Earthly peace is the image and fruit of the peace of Christ, the messianic "Prince of Peace". By the blood of his Cross, "in his own person he killed the hostility", he reconciled men with God and made his Church the sacrament of the unity of the human race and of its union with God. "He is our peace"' (Catechism of the Catholic Church 2305).

A high mark answer because two correct reasons are given and each reason is developed with a reference to the Bible's teaching and the Catechism, which are both sources of authority for Catholics.

d) 'Daily prayer is an essential element of life.' [12 marks + 3 spelling, punctuation and grammar (SPaG) marks]

Most Catholics would agree with this because daily prayer can help a person to get things into perspective. By stepping aside from the pressures of daily life and focusing on God, they can be brought to realise the reality of life. Daily prayers of thanksgiving help a person not to be selfish, to realise that they depend on others, and not to take things for granted. Daily prayers of supplication and intercession can help a person to feel that, by praying, they are doing something for those who suffer, and it can inspire them to do something practical to help the less fortunate.

However, some Catholics may feel that the pressures and demands of modern living make daily prayer too much of a burden and they just pray at Sunday Mass. Others might feel God prefers them to pray when they want to rather than praying out of duty or habit. Of course, atheists and Humanists would feel no need to pray to a god they don't believe exists!

[Continued]

Section 2: Practices

It seems to me that if you believe in God, you should want to pray every day to keep your relationship with God going. But, obviously, those who do not believe in God are not going to find any form of prayer an essential feature of life.

A high mark answer because it gives three clear developed Catholic reasons for thinking that daily prayer is an essential feature of life. It then gives three reasons for both Christians and non-Christians disagreeing before reaching a fully justified conclusion.

Spelling, punctuation and grammar are correct and a wide range of specialist vocabulary (perspective, thanksgiving, supplication, intercession, Sunday Mass, atheists, Humanists) is used appropriately.

3 Sources of wisdom and authority

Area of study 1: Study of Catholic Christianity

Section 3: Sources of wisdom and authority

Topic 1.3.1 The Bible

Thinking points

In this topic you need to:
- think about the structure, origins and development of the Bible as the revealed Word of God
- consider the Bible's different literary forms, such as the Old Testament (law, history, prophets and writings) and the New Testament (Gospels, letters)
- understand divergent Christian understandings about which books should be within the Bible, with reference to the Council of Trent.

Useful words

Biblia – the Greek word that 'Bible' is derived from, meaning 'the books'

The Bible as a source of wisdom

Catholics have various sources of wisdom and authority. The Bible and the Holy Scriptures are read out during Mass and can be read personally. Catholics believe that these words have an extra quality, a spiritual dimension that guides and brings peace to the reader or listener.

Then there is the Tradition of the Church, going back to the teaching of the first apostles who followed Jesus. The role of the Pope and the bishops is to guard this knowledge and to teach it. Sometimes they sit together and delve into the tradition and into the scriptures to decide what is right and wrong in modern society, with its many new ideas and challenges.

The development and structure of the Bible as the revealed Word of God

Origins

The word 'Bible' comes from the Greek word **Biblia**, meaning books. The Bible is not one book but a collection of books all in one cover. It is a library of books, and at the time of Jesus these would have been usually written on scrolls that were rolled up and kept on shelves or even in clay jars to protect them. The Bible used by Catholics has 73 different books within it, 46 in the Old Testament and 27 in the New Testament. These were written down over a long period of time. The books in the Old Testament took about 1000 years to put together. The books in the New Testament, by contrast, were all written within about 70 years.

The Bible did not 'fall from heaven' as one complete book. Although Catholics believe it was inspired by God, many ordinary people wrote the different books in different times and places.

The Bible is like a library of books or ancient scrolls.

Structure of the Bible

There are two distinct parts to the Bible. The Old Testament contains the history and calling of the Jewish people. The New Testament is based on Christ and the first apostles. Christians see the New Testament as being prepared for in the Old, and as its fulfilment when the Messiah had come.

> *The New Testament lies hidden in the Old and the Old Testament is unveiled in the New.* (St Augustine of Hippo)

The word 'Testament' is a translation of a Hebrew word **Berith**, which perhaps would be better translated as **covenant**. In the ancient world, a covenant was a binding, sacred promise, often sealed in the blood of sacrificed animals, between people. The Jews were the only ancient people to believe that God had made a covenant with humanity. This came about when the Hebrew slaves were freed from Egypt by Moses and the people were given the **Torah**, the law, to follow in thanksgiving and service.

The New Testament for Christians is the binding, sacred agreement sealed by the blood of Christ on the cross, showing that all can be forgiven and draw close to God as Father.

Although Jews and Christians disagree about Jesus being the **Messiah**, Christians today recognise and are grateful for all that Judaism has given to their religion. As the documents of the Second Vatican Council state:

> *... the Church cannot forget that she received the revelation of the Old Testament by way of that people with whom God in his inexpressible mercy established the ancient covenant.* (Nostra Aetate 4)

Useful words

Berith – the Hebrew for covenant
Covenant – a binding, sacred agreement
Torah – the five books of law which are the first five books of the Old Testament
Messiah – the Hebrew word for Christ, meaning God's Anointed King, the coming deliverer

Israelites crossing the Red Sea as shown in a fifteenth-century manuscript.

Section 3: Sources of wisdom and authority

A section of the Dead Sea Scrolls.

> **Activity**
>
> Do you think the Old Testament is still important for Christians?

The origins, structure and different literary forms of the Bible

The Old Testament (the Hebrew Bible)

The books making up the Old Testament are as follows:

- the Torah (law): the first five books
- the Prophets: for example, Books of Prophets such as Isaiah, Jeremiah and Ezekiel, but also history books such as Joshua, Judges, 1 & 2 Samuel
- the Writings: for example, Psalms, Proverbs, Song of Songs, Daniel (the history books are placed mainly in the Prophets in the Jewish understanding of the Old Testament).

The Bible contains many different type of writing: there are law books, history books, prophet books, poetry books and wise sayings. Some of the oldest copies of Old Testament books were found in caves by the Dead Sea in 1947 and these are known as the **Dead Sea Scrolls**.

Old Testament laws

The first five books of the Old Testament are known as 'the Books of Moses' or 'the Torah'. They contain all the laws and rules of Judaism (there are 613 commandments). These laws are summed up in the Decalogue (Ten Commandments) which were inscribed on stone tablets and kept in the Ark of the Covenant. Orthodox Jews follow all 613 laws, but Christians believe they do not need to follow the food and ceremonial laws because the sacrifices required by the Torah have been replaced by Christ's offering of himself on the cross.

> **Useful words**
>
> **Dead Sea Scrolls** – copies of Old Testament books discovered in the Holy Land in about 1947

Topic 1.3.1 The Bible

Christian monks say or sing the Old Testament Psalms daily in their times of common prayer.

Old Testament history

The historical parts of the Old Testament are mainly in the Deuteronomic history, the books of Joshua, Judges, 1 & 2 Samuel, and 1 & 2 Kings. This is named after the teachings of the Book of Deuteronomy, which has a clear message of a call to obedience. If people follow the laws, they are blessed; if not, they will fail and face disaster. Thus, when kings followed other gods, disaster often struck. Besides the historical books, there are also some historical narratives about the Patriarchs, the ancestors of the Jews, in Genesis, and the travels of the Hebrews with Moses in the other books of the Torah. Later, the books of 1 & 2 Chronicles were added, retelling much of the Israelite history from the viewpoint of being in exile in Persia, as well as Ezra and Nehemiah, about the returning exiles.

Old Testament prophets

The Prophets are collections of oracles that often begin 'Thus says the Lord', although messages can also come in the forms of symbolic visions such as Jeremiah seeing a budding tree, or Ezekiel's heavenly chariot or Daniel's vision of the son of man coming on the clouds. Biblical **prophecy** was not just about *foretelling* the future, but mainly and usually about *forthtelling*. This means that the prophets believed they had a message from God for the people, about what God was like and how they should behave. These words can still ring true today and be contemporary lessons.

Old Testament writings

The Writings contain the Psalms (hymns of praise, petition and lament); wisdom literature (collections of wise sayings such as the Proverbs) and also highly symbolic works with many codes, dreams and visions, known as **apocalyptic** writings, such as the Book of Daniel.

The New Testament: Gospels

The New Testament is based on the life and teaching of Jesus Christ and the first apostles. It was put together relatively quickly within the first century CE, unlike the Old Testament which spans more than 1000 years of composition.

Useful words

Prophecy – speaking the Word of God, either for the future or for the present

Apocalyptic – a style of writing that used symbols and codes to teach spiritual truths and to try to foretell the future

Activity

Why do you think Jesus so often quoted from the Old Testament in his teachings?

Section 3: Sources of wisdom and authority

Activities

1. Read Daniel 7:9–14 and Revelation 21:1–8. These are examples of apocalyptic literature in both testaments. What type of symbols are used, and what ideas are being communicated?
2. How might these apocalyptic passages make sense for Catholics reading today?

Useful words

Gospel – literally 'Good News', telling the life and teachings of Jesus

Synoptic – the Gospels of Matthew, Mark and Luke that have similar styles

Canon – a rule or list of approved books

The New Testament has 27 different books:

- four **Gospels**: Matthew, Mark, Luke and John
- the Acts of the Apostles
- 21 Epistles or letters
- one apocalyptic, prophetic book.

Gospels are a particular type of writing, being a proclamation. They contain history but are preaching books to announce who Jesus was and what he taught. 'Gospel' derives from a Greek word *evangelion*, which means good news. The Gospels announce the good news about Jesus.

Mark's is thought to be the earliest Gospel, based on the testimony of St Peter, probably composed during the persecution in Rome in 65CE. Matthew and Luke use parts of Mark, adding their own material. The first three Gospels are known as the **Synoptic** Gospels as they see things along the same lines. John has a very different style. The narrative is divided into seven signs of Jesus and his speeches are long and not the short, simple sayings in the other Gospels.

The New Testament: the letters

The letters are said to be from Paul, Peter, Jude, James and John. One is unnamed: Hebrews. These were written to encourage and instruct early groups of Christians in certain places, and they were copied and passed around the Roman Empire from church group to church group. They were written on the move and are not careful, detailed explanations of doctrine or textbooks. There are debates about the identity of the John writing his three letters. Was it the same as the apostle John and/or the writer of the Gospel? Scholars have debated how many of the letters are actually from Paul, or whether some are from his later disciples, using his name as they follow his teaching, develop it and pass it on. Everyone accepts that Paul wrote Romans, 1 & 2 Corinthians and Galatians. Others think that he wrote many more, if not all of them.

Most of the early churches had a similar list of books to be included, although a few were disputed, until it was finally decided by the Council of Carthage in 397CE. This final list is known as the **canon** of the New Testament books, from a word meaning rule. All had accepted the four Gospels and the ten letters of St Paul. Some disputed the other books or added others. Most ancient lists of what should have been in the New Testament were very similar and we see a clear pattern established by the second century CE.

Divergent Christian understandings about which books should be in the Bible

In the early days of the Church there was no agreement as to which books were to make up the Bible. The Hebrew Old Testament (the Tenakh for the Jews) with 39 books was supposedly agreed upon at a Jewish council called the Council of Jamnia at the end of the first century, but the Christian Churches (which did not speak Hebrew) used the Greek translation of the Old Testament known as the Septuagint with 47 books. The Churches did not finally agree on which books were to be in the New Testament until the Council of Carthage in 397CE, when the 27 books of the New Testament were agreed. This was the Bible accepted by both Catholics and Orthodox, and was the Bible translated into Latin by St Jerome for the Catholic

Topic 1.3.1 The Bible

The **Rylands fragment** of part of John's Gospel.

Church (the Vulgate). These books were confirmed as the Catholic Bible at the Council of Trent in 1546.

At the Reformation, the Protestant scholars, who made translations into European languages, determined that the Hebrew Old Testament agreed at Jamnia was more reliable than the Greek and so the Protestant Bible is the Hebrew Old Testament plus the New Testament agreed at the Council of Carthage. This means that Protestant Bibles only have 39 books in their Old Testament whereas Catholic and Orthodox Bibles have 47 books. Protestant Bibles have the books left out from the Catholic and Orthodox Bibles as a separate book they call the Apocrypha.

Useful words

Rylands fragment – the earliest definite fragment of a Gospel, the Gospel of John

Practice questions

c Explain two reasons why the Bible is important for Catholics. In your answer you must refer to a source of wisdom and authority.

d 'If the Bible came from God, all Christians would use the same Bible.' Evaluate this statement considering arguments for and against. In your answer you should:
- refer to Catholic points of view
- refer to different Catholic or non-Catholic Christian points of view
- reach a justified conclusion.

Summary

Christians believe the Bible to be the Word of God. It is divided into the Old and New Testaments. The Old Testament is also the Jewish Bible and contains law, history, prophets and writings. The New Testament was written by Christians and contains the Gospels, letters by the apostles, a book about the origins of the Church (Acts) and Revelation. There was some dispute about what should be in the Bible, and although Catholics and Orthodox have the same Bibles, Protestant Bibles have fewer Old Testament books.

Section 3: Sources of wisdom and authority

Topic 1.3.2 Interpretation of the Bible

Thinking points

In this topic you need to:
- think about Catholic interpretation of the Bible and understanding of inspiration
- consider divergent interpretations of the authority of the Bible within Christianity, including different understandings about the literal Word of God and the revealed Word of God as a source of guidance and teaching (2 Timothy 3:16, Catechism 105–108)
- be able to evaluate the implications of these ideas for Catholics today.

Catholic interpretation of the Bible and the meaning of inspiration

Catholics believe that the Bible was inspired by God. The catechism explains this in these words:

God is the author of Sacred Scripture. 'The divinely revealed realities, which are contained and presented in the text of Sacred Scripture, have been written down under the inspiration of the Holy Spirit.' 'For Holy Mother Church, relying on the faith of the apostolic age, accepts as sacred and canonical the books of the Old and the New Testaments, whole and entire, with all their parts, on the grounds that, written under the inspiration of the Holy Spirit, they have God as their author, and have been handed on as such to the Church herself.' God inspired the human authors of the sacred books. 'To compose the sacred books, God chose certain men who, all the while he employed them in this task, made full use of their own faculties and powers so that, though he acted in them and by them, it was as true authors that they consigned to writing whatever he wanted written, and no more.' The inspired books teach the truth. 'Since therefore all that the inspired authors or sacred writers affirm should be regarded as affirmed by the Holy Spirit, we must acknowledge that the books of Scripture firmly, faithfully, and without error teach that truth which God, for the sake of our salvation, wished to see confided to the Sacred Scriptures.' Still, the Christian faith is not a 'religion of the book'. Christianity is the religion of the 'Word' of God, 'not a written and mute word, but incarnate and living'. If the Scriptures are not to remain a dead letter, Christ, the eternal Word of the living God, must, through the Holy Spirit, 'open (our) minds to understand the Scriptures'.
(Catechism of the Catholic Church 105–108)

'Saint Matthew and the Angel', a painting of 1534.

Catholics believe the Bible has authority because:

- The Bible is inspired by the Holy Spirit which means it comes from God and is therefore holy and considered authoritative (giving the truth and to be accepted and followed) by Catholics.
- It reveals God. God speaks through both the Old Testament and New Testament showing his character and commands, so it should be followed.
- It contains God's laws on how to behave, such as the Ten Commandments. These rules are there to help people live as God intends so it has authority by showing them how God wants them to live.
- It contains the teachings of Jesus on how to live the Christian life. They believe Jesus is the second person of the Holy Trinity so what he taught has authority, which means that the Bible that records his teaching also has authority.
- The Bible can bring people into a closer relationship with God by learning about what God wants and how God cares for them.

Christians see the Bible as being inspired, but what does that mean? There are two extremes on offer, that of the liberal and that of the fundamentalist.

Divergent interpretations of the authority of the Bible

Christians interpret the authority of the Bible in different ways:

- The **fundamentalist** sees everything in the Bible as literally the Word of God. Every word is absolutely true, including anything said about history or science. Thus, the fundamentalist will believe in a six-day creation, a literal Adam and Eve and a worldwide flood.
- The **liberal** sees much of the Bible as human words, but there are teachings and ideas that are striking and spiritual, angles on truth. It is like saying that any great writer or composer is inspired. They have original, good, helpful ideas and say something about God. Many things will be questioned: miracle stories, events, whether Jesus actually said this or that and also morals. These will sometimes be seen as of their day and not always relevant now.

The Bible as a source of guidance and teaching

The Bible is not like a novel or a straightforward textbook. It is a collection of many different books and styles of writing, put together over 1000 years. Some sections seem hard, dated and unclear. Some parts are striking and stand out, giving clear ideas and inspiring people. People reading the Bible need guidance and in the Catholic Church small sections of the text are selected day by day for the Mass. Usually, there is a passage from the Old Testament and from the New Testament, a Psalm and a Gospel passage. People study and pray with the Bible. Believers feel that the words of scripture sometimes seem to come alive and speak to their hearts, to their situation, and go right to the point. At other times, reading the Bible might be spiritually refreshing but there is no particular guidance or encouragement.

Activities

1. Look at the painting of St Matthew on page 92. What is it saying about how Matthew wrote his Gospel?
2. Do you think it matters if the Bible is not scientifically correct?
3. Do you think it is a good idea to use the Bible for guidance when you have to make a moral decision?

Useful words

Fundamentalist – one who believes the Bible is the literal word of God

Liberal – one who believes the Bible was written by humans inspired by God and so may need reinterpreting in light of the modern world

Section 3: Sources of wisdom and authority

Activities

1. What do you think about *Lectio Divina*?
2. Can you think of any Bible stories or passages that have inspired you?

Useful words

Lectio Divina – sacred or divine reading; a way of praying and studying a passage from the Bible

Lectio Divina: using the Bible today

Lectio Divina, meaning Sacred, Holy or Divine Reading, is a method of reading the Bible carefully and prayerfully that many Catholics are encouraged to follow today. This was worked out in monasteries in the past, but is used widely by many ordinary Catholic laypeople. It follows a series of steps:

- *lectio* – reading
- *meditatio* – meditation
- *oratio* – praying
- *contemplatio* – contemplation.

A person sits in a quiet place, enters a state of calm, says a prayer and then opens the Bible at a particular passage. They read what it says. Then they read through it again and see what strikes them. A word, an idea, a phrase might stand out. Then they pray, thinking about what spoke to them. Finally, they sit quietly, letting the message sink in.

The Psalms have a saying:

> *Your word is a lamp to my feet and a light to my path.*
> *(Psalm 119:105)*

Catholics can seek help and guidance from the scriptures as well as just finding peace of mind from reading them. If the Bible is like a sacrament, they believe, then God's presence will come through the words.

The implications of interpretation of the Bible for Catholics today

The above passage in the New Testament is an important one for Christians. It states clearly that it is 'inspired by God' and offers insight into both interpreting the Bible and using it in everyday life. Christians accept the Bible as inspired and use it widely, but there are different approaches to this idea of inspiration. There are debates about the interpretation of some passages of the Bible among Christians in general, and Catholics have extra help with this. Whereas Protestant Christians use the Bible alone to work out what they believe, Catholics have tradition. This is the oral teaching coming down from the apostles, for they did not write everything down in the documents of the New Testament. There are also the wise teachings and reflections of holy men and women down the ages, and all this is guided by the present teaching authority of the Catholic Church with the Pope and the bishops.

Summary

There are alternative interpretations for the authority of the Bible and the extent that it can be seen as the 'literal' Word of God. Catholics believe that the words of God are not literally those of God but that the Bible contains wider truths that must be interpreted with the help of the Catholic Church.

Practice questions

c Explain two reasons why Catholics regard the Bible as a source of guidance and teaching. In your answer you must refer to a source of wisdom and authority.

d 'You don't need any help to understand the Bible.' Evaluate this statement considering arguments for and against. In your answer you should:
- refer to Catholic points of view
- refer to different Catholic or non-Catholic Christian points of view
- reach a justified conclusion.

Topic 1.3.3 Scripture, tradition and the magisterium

The meaning, function and importance of the magisterium (both conciliar and pontifical)

The living teaching office of the Church is known as the **magisterium**, from the Latin word *magister*, for 'teacher'. It is exercised by the Pope with the bishops. There are different levels:

- The ordinary magisterium is where all the bishops teach what has always been taught.
- The **conciliar** magisterium, where the Pope calls a General Council, assembling his bishops to discuss certain issues, as happened, for example, in the Second Vatican Council in the 1960s, and many centuries ago at Nicaea in 325CE to debate how Christ was fully God and fully human at the same time.
- The **pontifical** magisterium uses **papal infallibility**. At certain times, when a matter is not decided by all the bishops, the Pope can make a statement that settles the issue. To do this he has to consult many people and opinions and spend much time in prayer. He has this role as the successor of St Peter. The infallibility of the Pope does not mean that he never gets anything wrong, or that anything he says is infallible. It is careful, limited and tested by reference to the tradition. The last time (and only the second time) that papal infallibility was used was in 1950 by Pope Pius XII. He had listened for some time to options around the world from his bishops about the idea of Mary being assumed body and soul into heaven. This had been a longstanding idea in the Church, east and west, but it had never been proclaimed as an official doctrine. The doctrine of the assumption was then defined and proclaimed but the Pope was careful to leave questions open that neither he nor anyone else could answer. He did not decide the question of whether Mary had died and then been taken, or simply been taken before she died. The Pope does not claim extraordinary revelation and knowledge. He is a keeper of the faith, and not its inventor.

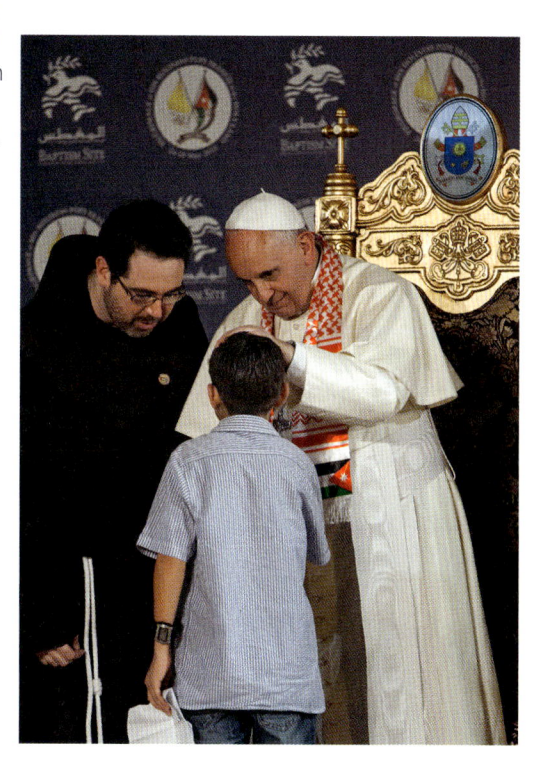

Thinking points

In this topic you need to:
- think about the meaning, function and importance of the magisterium of the Church (both conciliar and pontifical), with reference to Catechism 100
- consider the magisterium as a living teaching office of the Church and authentic interpreter of the affirmations of scripture and tradition
- understand why scripture and tradition are important for Catholics today.

Useful words

Magisterium – the teaching office of the Church, from the Latin word *magister*, for 'teacher'

Conciliar – the Church meeting and working as a Council of Bishops with the Pope

Pontifical – relating to the office of the Pope as the Supreme Pontiff, the Head of the Church on earth

Papal infallibility – when the Pope speaks authoritatively on a disputed matter of doctrine

Pope Francis blesses a Syrian refugee during his visit to the Catholic church at the Baptism Site of Jesus in Jordan.

Section 3: Sources of wisdom and authority

Within the Catholic faith, the Pope and the magisterium are servants of the faith that is handed down, as the following Catechism makes clear:

> Yet this Magisterium is not superior to the Word of God, but is its servant. It teaches only what has been handed on to it ... All that it proposes for belief as being divinely revealed is drawn from this single deposit of faith.

> It is clear therefore, that in the supremely wise arrangement of God, sacred Tradition, sacred Scripture and the Magisterium of the Church are so connected and associated that one of them cannot stand without the others. (Catechism of the Catholic Church 86, 95)

> The task of interpreting the Word of God authentically has been entrusted solely to the Magisterium of the Church, that is, to the Pope and to the bishops in communion with him. (Catechism of the Catholic Church 100)

The above Catechism of the Catholic Church makes it clear that the magisterium of the Church (that is, the Pope and his bishops) shares the task of interpreting the 'Word of God', that is to say, the scriptures.

Scripture and tradition

The Protestant view of authority in the Church is that it is based on the Bible alone (*sola scriptura* in Latin). The Catholic view, however, sees the Bible as a part of God's revelation in Christ, albeit a very important one. Remember that the Bible did not just 'fall out of the sky' but was composed over many years by many people. When the New Testament was written, within the first century CE, not everything taught by the apostles was written down. Much was taken for granted for the early churches would have had their own training (catechesis) as they were set up. Much of this would have been oral, covering beliefs about God, Jesus and the Holy Spirit, or about ways of worshipping. Some things may have been written down, such as lists of sayings of Jesus (before the Gospels were written) and maybe lists of passages from the Old Testament that Jesus was believed to have fulfilled.

The oral tradition from the apostles was handed down from generation to generation and the Church itself decided which books should be included as scripture in the New Testament. The Church formed the Bible, and not the Bible the Church. As one of the documents of the Catholic Church states:

> God graciously arranged that the things he had once revealed for the salvation of all peoples should remain in their entirety, throughout the ages, and be transmitted to all generations ... It was done by those apostles and other men associated with the apostles who, under the inspiration of the same Holy Spirit, committed the message of salvation to writing. In order that the full and living Gospel might always be preserved in the Church the apostles left bishops as their successors. They gave them 'their own position of teaching authority' (Council of Trent). This sacred Tradition, then, and the sacred Scripture of both Testaments, are like a mirror, in which the Church, during its pilgrim journey here on earth, contemplates God, from whom she receives everything, until such time as she is brought to see him face to face as he really is. (Dei Verbum *II:7*)

Pope Pius XII declared the **assumption of Mary** to be official teaching. He did so on the papal throne, *cathedra* in Latin. When the Pope speaks *ex cathedra* from his throne in this way, he is invoking infallibility.

Useful words

Sola scriptura – 'Scripture alone'; the Protestant idea that the Bible alone is the source of authority in the Church
Assumption of Mary – the belief that Mary was assumed body and soul into heaven
Ex cathedra – 'from the chair'; from the throne of St Peter

Tradition, scripture and magisterium: the three legs of a stool. Each is needed by the others.

Topic 1.3.3 Scripture, tradition and the magisterium

Tradition, or the **Apostolic Tradition**, is not the same as cultural traditions. It is the teaching of the apostles. There might be many customs that could change, such as the style of dress that priests have, or even the white cassock that the Pope wears. They are human ideas. They did not come from the apostles.

> *Sacred Tradition and sacred Scripture, then, are bound closely together, and communicate one with the other. For both of them, flowing from the same divine well-spring, come together in some fashion to form one thing, and move towards the same goal.*
> (Dei Verbum II:9)

> *Sacred Tradition and sacred Scripture make up a single deposit of the Word of God, which is entrusted to the Church.*
> (Dei Verbum II:10)

The Catholic Church sees God's revelation as coming to people through the Bible and tradition.

Catholics do not differentiate between the written Word of God and the Apostolic Tradition or teaching. They form one revelation of God in Christ, covering different angles. So, when a Protestant Christian asks where Catholics find something in the Bible, it might not be in the Bible, but it is in the tradition. Usually, though, Catholics will point out that seed thoughts, the basis of the idea, can be seen in the Bible and teachings about it grew and developed from that basis, like oak trees from tiny acorns.

Apostolic Succession

Linked with the idea of Apostolic tradition is the idea of **Apostolic Succession**. This states two things. First, the teaching from the apostles is passed down to their successors, the bishops. Second, a bishop must have been ordained by a recognised bishop in that succession. In a way, the hands laid on a candidate to be a bishop are an extension of those of the first apostles in an unbroken line. Yet, it is not just the ordained character that is passed on, but the faith. This allows there to be a living teaching office within the Church, and not just old scriptures and writings.

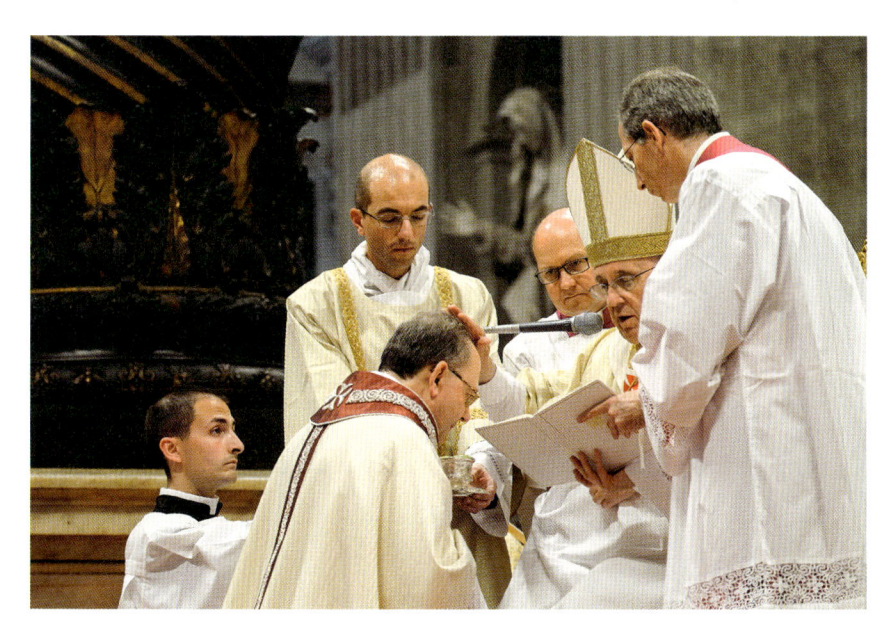

Useful words

Apostolic Tradition – the teaching passed down orally from the apostles

Apostolic Succession – the line of bishops going back to the apostles

Pope Francis ordains a new bishop.

Section 3: Sources of wisdom and authority

Activities

1. What is meant by the Apostolic Tradition, Apostolic Succession and the magisterium?
2. Why is papal infallibility important for the Catholic Church?
3. Catholics believe that many ideas in the tradition can be found as seed thoughts in the Bible itself. Explain how the immaculate conception of Mary can be found in the Bible in this way.

The magisterium as the living teaching office of the Church and authentic interpreter of the affirmations of scripture and tradition

The Pope and the bishops guide the Catholic Church today. One way in which we see the Church's magisterium helping with the interpretation of scripture is with doctrines that are special to Catholics but are contested by Protestants. Protestants will challenge Catholics with the question 'Where is it in the Bible?'

Take one example, the immaculate conception of Mary. This states that Mary was conceived without original sin, kept pure and ready to carry Christ within her. The Bible does not say this exactly, but she is described by the Angel Gabriel as 'full of grace' in Luke 1:28, which is also stated in the 'Hail Mary' prayer, 'Hail Mary, full of grace, the Lord is with thee.' This can be seen as one doctrine developed from an idea in the Bible. Yet, nothing in the tradition must contradict anything in the Bible, even if it can develop things within it.

Why the magisterium is important for Catholics today

The purpose of the magisterium is to guide people today on how to understand scripture and to evaluate modern debates and issues in the light of the faith.

Below is an example of one important issue that has caused debate and controversy within the Catholic Church: women priests.

Women priests

Having women as priests has been a hotly debated topic in the Catholic Church as other denominations are ordaining female ministers. Pope John Paul II issued a statement in the 1980s that this was not possible from all that had been handed down from the apostles, although no one questioned that women were not equal in dignity or skill with men. Jesus had not called any women to be his apostles; women had never been ordained as priests in the past; it was taught that a priest had to be male as his was a sacramental office, representing Christ at the altar, and Christ was male.

The then Pope said that he had no way and no authority to change what he saw as being handed down from the apostles. Later popes such as Francis have affirmed this teaching, saying, 'The Church has spoken', but he recognises the need to promote other forms of women's ministry and the role of women as a voice in the Church.

It is interesting to compare this debate with that of whether priests should be allowed to marry. There were married priests in the early Church. It is recognised that the Pope could allow priests to marry as it is only a useful convention and not actual tradition, or it is described as a matter of discipline and not doctrine (which is why some former Anglican clergy who are married have been ordained as Catholic priests and allowed to continue their ministry as exceptions to the normal rule).

Anglican women priests.

Practice questions

c Explain two reasons why the magisterium is important for Catholics. In your answer you must refer to a source of wisdom and authority.

d 'The magisterium is the only authority Christians need.' Evaluate this statement considering arguments for and against. In your answer you should:
- refer to Catholic points of view
- refer to different Catholic or non-Catholic Christian points of view
- reach a justified conclusion.

Summary

The magisterium (the teaching office of the Catholic faith) has different administrative levels, with the Pope at its head. The function of this office is to interpret scripture and to hand down belief about the Catholic faith to future generations (the Apostolic Tradition).

Section 3: Sources of wisdom and authority

Topic 1.3.4 The Second Vatican Council

Thinking points

In this topic you need to:
- think about the nature, history, and different understandings of the importance of the Second Vatican Council
- understand the nature and significance of four of its key documents for the Church and for Catholic living: *Dei Verbum*, *Lumen Gentium*, *Sacrosanctum Concilium* and *Gaudium et Spes*.

Useful words

Council – a meeting of the Pope and the bishops
Aggiornamento – the Italian for bringing something up to date

The Second Vatican Council (also known as Vatican II) was opened in October 1962 and closed in November 1965. The **Council** was called by Pope John XXIII and closed by Pope Paul VI (Pope John had died in 1963); 2908 men were invited to attend, including all the bishops and superiors of religious communities. There were also a small number of ecumenical observers, the first time ever at a Catholic Council, rising to 100 by the end of the Council. Theological experts were also involved, known as *periti*, who included Father Joseph Ratzinger, later to become Pope Benedict XVI. The Council met during the autumn over four years, although smaller groups met for study and debate throughout the year. The Councils of the Church are usually named after the place where they assemble, such as Nicaea, Ephesus or in this case the Vatican. The earliest Council was in Jerusalem, held by the apostles (see Acts 15).

Pope John XXIII was elected Pope in 1958 at the age of 76 and he was expected to be a 'safe pair of hands', a 'caretaker'. He caught everyone by surprise. The previous Pope, Pius XII, had been in office since 1939 and many Catholics were expecting changes in the Church and the way some things were done. Pope John called the Council, saying that he wanted a 'New Pentecost' to dawn in the Church, with the Holy Spirit renewing and shaking the people. He desired to throw the windows of the Church open to the wind of the Holy Spirit. He sought **aggiornamento**, a bringing up to date of the Church. He did not wish to change teaching or doctrine, but the way things were expressed. The Second Vatican Council was therefore a pastoral Council, rather than a dogmatic one, in comparison with earlier Councils, such as the First Vatican Council in the nineteenth century that affirmed the infallibility of the Pope or much earlier ones that debated the nature of the incarnation and the Holy Trinity.

Catholic bishops assemble for the Second Vatican Council.

Pope John had a humble, affectionate style and when he greeted the crowds outside St Peter's in Rome at the start of the Council, he told them:

> *Dear children, returning home you will find your children. Give your children a hug and say, 'This is a hug from the Pope'.*

There was an air of excitement and expectancy. One delegate, Patrick O'Donoghue, commented later:

> *The world flocked to Rome – through the media – during the Council, knowing that something wonderful was happening. Christ was speaking His words of hope and healing with authority to the peoples of our times.*

Among the various documents to come from the Council were four key ones on the nature of the Church: *Lumen Gentium* ('Light of Humanity'), on the Church in the modern world, *Gaudium et Spes* ('Joy and Hope'), on worship and the Mass *Sacrosanctum Concilium* ('Sacred Council'), and on the Word of God (*Dei Verbum*).

Activities

1. Why was Vatican II called?
2. Do you think the Church needs a Vatican III?

Divergent understandings of the importance of the Council

- Many Catholics saw the Second Vatican Council as a great relief and encouragement as the Church listened to the people and opened up to the modern world.

- Some thought the reforms of Vatican II went too far. For example, Archbishop Marcel Lefebvre led a breakaway group of priests who rejected the reforms of Vatican II by forming the Society of St Pius X (SSPX) which celebrates the Tridentine Mass (the Latin Eucharistic liturgy used by the Catholic Church from 1570 to 1964). They have entered negotiations with Rome to come back into the Catholic Church under Pope Francis but they have to accept the teachings of Vatican II.

- Some thought that the changes did not go far enough and that there should be married priests, changes in Church teachings about contraception, shared communion with non-Catholic Christians and allowing divorced and remarried people to take communion.

In the 1970s and 1980s, some thought that the changes from Vatican II would go much further, that there would be married priests before too long, as well as changes in Church teachings about contraception, sharing communion between Christians and also allowing the divorced and remarried to take communion. These changes did not happen and were never expected to.

The nature and significance of the four key documents for the Church and Catholic living

Four key documents were produced by Vatican II:

Dei Verbum

The title *Dei Verbum* means 'Word of God'. This document deals with divine revelation in the Bible and also in the tradition handed down from the apostles. The document begins:

> *It pleased God, in his goodness and wisdom, to reveal himself and to make known the mystery of his will ... His will was that men should have access to the Father, through Christ, the Word made flesh, in the Holy Spirit, and thus become sharers in the divine nature ...* (Dei Verbum *I:2)*

Section 3: Sources of wisdom and authority

Tradition and scripture were two expressions of the Word of God, as coming from one 'spring of life', or source. They were not in competition and were gifts to ensure that God's revelation would always be known:

> *God graciously arranged that the things he had once revealed for the salvation of all peoples should remain in their entirety, throughout the ages, and be transmitted to all generations.* (Dei Verbum II:7)

The magisterium is also a gift of God, the living teaching office of the Pope and the bishops to guide the Church:

> *It is clear, therefore, that, in the supremely wise arrangement of God, sacred Tradition, sacred Scripture and the Magisterium of the Church are so connected and associated that one of them cannot stand without the others.* (Dei Verbum II:10)

The Bible is to be read and understood intelligently, although recognising the culture of the writers and the many types of literary form within it, such as poetry, symbol, myth and history:

> *... Look for that meaning which the sacred writer, in a determined situation and given the circumstances of his time and culture, intended to express and did in fact express, through the medium of a contemporary literary form.* (Dei Verbum III:12)

Scripture and tradition can guide, teach and inspire Catholics today, and having the Bible in the language of the people in the Mass helps people to understand how to apply these teachings to their own lives.

Lumen Gentium

The title came from the opening words meaning 'the light of humanity'. Christ was declared as the light of humanity. The Church was united as the **pilgrim people** of God on a journey together towards the Second Coming of Christ and the kingdom of God. The role of the baptised was emphasised, recognising the priesthood of all believers (**common priesthood**). Each Christian was called to serve Christ, to work for peace and to speak his word to others. The ordained priesthood was taken from this more general priesthood and called to special tasks within the Church such as hearing confessions and consecrating the bread and wine at the Eucharist:

Useful words

Pilgrim people – the idea that Christians are pilgrims whose life is a pilgrimage to heaven

Common priesthood – all the baptised who follow Christ and serve him

> *Though they differ essentially and not only in degree, the common priesthood of all the faithful and the ministerial ... priesthood are none the less ordered one to another; each in its own proper way shares in the one priesthood of Christ.* (Lumen Gentium II:10)

In the past, the Church had often been seen as a pyramid, with the Pope at the top descending to the people at the base. Now the Church was more like a circle as people joined together, but with the Pope and the bishops leading and holding things together in unity.

The Church had been seen as being like a fortress, keeping the outside world and its ways at bay. Now the doors were 'open' and the Church was linked to all people, regardless of their beliefs. For Catholics, when God became a human being, God touched all of humanity in Christ, an example which they follow in this 'opening up' to the world, seeking to move closer to God and to constantly learn and serve one other.

Two different models of how the Church is organised, from the top down or trying to involve as many as possible, but with a clear leadership.

Topic 1.3.4 The Second Vatican Council

Sacrosanctum Concilium

The title simply means 'the sacred council' and this was the earliest document to be produced by the Council. The subject was liturgy and worship, the Mass in particular. A new rite of the Mass was to be produced, simplifying the old Mass with its many rituals, symbols and exclusive use of Latin. Latin was still to be encouraged for parts of the Mass, but sections of it could now be in the **vernacular**, the language of the local people, and thus many different translations of the Mass would be needed.

There was to be more active lay participation in reading parts of the Bible, and in leading the bidding prayers. The people should be informed and taught what was happening during the Mass:

> *Christ's faithful, when present at this mystery of faith, should not be there as strangers or silent spectators. On the contrary, through a good understanding of the rites and prayers they should take part in the sacred action, conscious of what they are doing, with devotion and full collaboration.* (Sacrosanctum Concilium II:48)

More responses were said by the people, and not just the clergy and servers at the altar.

The document made clear that Christ is present in the Mass not only in the consecrated bread and wine, but also in the Word of God that is read out, in the person of the priest, and in the assembled people. The Mass, including all the people in the celebration, is:

> *the summit toward which the activity of the Church is directed; it is also the fount from which all her power flows.* (Sacrosanctum Concilium I:10)

This is because it celebrates the presence of the resurrected Christ.

The changes of Vatican II led to Latin Mass disappearing and priests facing the congregation during Mass.

Useful words

Vernacular – the language of the people

A priest elevating the host during Mass.

Gaudium et Spes

The title means 'Joy and hope' and this document addressed the world and not just the Church. The dignity of each person is affirmed through this document, as well as their human rights. There was a desire for justice and a need for dialogue with others, including Humanists and atheists. The world was changing rapidly, with social upheaval, new ideas and advances in science and technology, for example the first man in space was a recent event in 1961 and the world was having to cope with the proliferation of nuclear weapons.

> *The human mind is in a certain sense broadening its mastery over time – over the past through insights of history, over the future by foresight and planning. Advances in biology, psychology, and the social sciences not only lead man to greater self-awareness, but provide him with the technical means of moulding the lives of whole peoples as well ... The accelerated pace of history is such that one can scarcely keep abreast of it.* (Gaudium et Spes 5)

The document expressed concern over morals and values in the midst of all this change and advocated following Christ who 'died and was raised for the sake of all' as the way to achieve human dignity. It explained to people that the incarnation of Christ was the key to life and human fulfilment and that through this event, God touched the whole of humanity. The document claimed that peace and justice are necessary for all, whatever their belief, and encouraged dialogue with atheists and secular groups for social action and change.

Section 3: Sources of wisdom and authority

> **Activity**
>
> Do you think it is better for a leader to make decisions or for a group of people to make decisions?

In Vatican II, Catholics were encouraged to pray with other Christians and to seek to work for greater unity.

Useful words

Separated brethren – non-Catholic Christians

Other Christians

Among many other areas discussed at the Council there was a warm and friendly opening up to Christians of other traditions. Protestants and others were now known as '**separated brethren**' who all share a common baptism into Christ that gives them a real but imperfect unity. Catholics were encouraged, for the first time, to pray with other Christians and to seek to work for greater unity, however, communion was not to be shared without a greater unity in the faith and the fullness of the Church resided in the Catholic Church, in communion with the Pope as the successor of St Peter.

Practice questions

c Explain two reasons why the Second Vatican Council was important for Catholics. In your answer you must refer to a source of wisdom and authority.

d 'The most important decision of Vatican II was to allow the Mass to be in English instead of Latin.' Evaluate this statement considering arguments for and against. In your answer you should:
- refer to Catholic points of view
- refer to different Catholic or non-Catholic Christian points of view
- reach a justified conclusion.

Summary

The Second Vatican Council constituted a 'bringing up to date' of the Church and was assembled by Pope John XXIII. There are four key documents associated with this Council: the *Dei Verbum*, *Lumen Gentium*, *Sacrosanctum Concilium* and *Gaudium et Spes*.

Topic 1.3.5 The Church as the Body of Christ and the People of God

The nature and significance of the Church as the Body of Christ and as the People of God

The Body of Christ

Catholics are used to speaking of the consecrated host as the Body of Christ but the term is also used for the Church community itself, an idea which has its foundation in the New Testament, in particular this extract from the Epistle to the Romans.

> *For as in one body we have many members, and not all the members have the same function, so we, who are many, are one body in Christ, and individually we are members of one another. We have gifts that differ according to the grace given to us ... (Romans 12:4–6)*

The many people that make up the Church community are said to be part of Christ's Body. This idea of the Church as a unified body is one which has continued throughout the Church's history.

Like all good symbols, the symbol of the Body works at different levels:

- The people are the Body.
- The consecrated bread of the Eucharist is the Body.
- The people are the Body as the assembly of the faithful because they are baptised into Christ.

The 'entry point' to become part of this 'Body of Christ' is the sacrament of baptism, which not only washes away sin but gives the gift of the Holy Spirit and brings a person's soul into relationship with Christ. According to the Bible, baptism is open to all races and ages, to every social status:

> *For in the one Spirit we were all baptised into one body – Jews or Greeks, slaves or free – and we were all made to drink of one Spirit. (1 Corinthians 12:13)*

Thinking points

In this topic you need to:
- understand the idea of the Church as both the Body of Christ and the People of God at one and the same time
- think about the nature and significance of the Church as the Body of Christ and the People of God, including Romans 12:4–6 and 1 Corinthians 12
- consider why the Church as the Body of Christ and the People of God is important for Catholics today
- understand divergent Christian attitudes towards these ideas.

Catholics taking communion together as one 'Body'.

Section 3: Sources of wisdom and authority

Activities

1. Look at the photo on the page 105. Do you think the Eucharist unites Christians?
2. Look at the photo below. Do you think nuns are more important in the Church than ordinary members?

Useful words

People – in the Bible, more than a collection of human beings; a special set, tribe, nation who were called and blessed by God for service, and who belonged to God

The People of God

The Church as the **People** of God derives from baptism. People from different backgrounds are made members of the Church. God loves all people but not all believe or seek a relationship with the Creator. The Old Testament has the covenant with Moses and the calling of the Jews to worship the one God and to be witnesses to the pagans. The new covenant in Christ is seen as a call to all people to join together. Where people were strangers and far away from God's teaching and covenants, they are now brought close:

> But now in Christ Jesus you who were once far off have been brought near by the blood of Christ. For he is our peace; in his flesh he has made both groups into one and has broken down the dividing wall ... (Ephesians 2:13–14)

The desire for God is thought to be planted in each human being:

> The desire for God is written in the human heart, because man is created by God and for God; and God never ceases to draw man to himself. (Catechism of the Catholic Church I:27)

The Church teaches God's love for all people, whatever their religion (or lack of it). However, the Church offers baptism to bring them into a knowledge of Christ and all his blessings he is believed to have revealed to humanity, and thereby they belong to one Body, one People of faith.

Why the Church as the Body of Christ and the People of God is important for Catholics today

This belief is important for Catholics because:

- The teaching that the Church is the Body of Christ means that Christ did not leave the earth at his ascension; his body remained on the earth in the Church.
- It means that the Church is carrying on the work of Christ in the world.
- It means that Christians form one body and so are united with each other as well as with Christ.
- It is how the Church is described in the New Testament.
- At baptism, Christians are baptised into the body of Christ.
- At Mass, by sharing the bread at communion, Christians share in the Body of Christ.
- The Church teaches that Christians continue the work of Jesus and so are the Body of Christ on earth.
- Describing the Church as the Body of Christ shows how Christians can perform different tasks and yet be a unity.

As Catechism 805 says: 'The Church is the Body of Christ. Through the Spirit and his action in the sacraments, above all the Eucharist, Christ, who once was dead and is now risen, establishes the community of believers as his own Body.'

Topic 1.3.5 The Church as the Body of Christ and the People of God

In 1 Corinthians 12, St Paul gives an analysis of the Church as the Body of Christ. He begins by explaining how Christians receive different gifts from the Spirit (service, wisdom, knowledge, healing and so on), but the gifts come from the one Spirit so that none are superior: 'All these are the work of one and the same Spirit, and he distributes them to each one, just as he determines' (1 Corinthians 12:11). Just as the parts of the human body are interdependent (the hand cannot say to the foot that it doesn't need it), so in the Body of Christ all are interdependent and none are superior – 'so that there should be no division in the body, but that its parts should have equal concern for each other' because 'you are the body of Christ, and each one of you is a part of it' (1 Corinthians 12:24,27).

Divergent Christian understandings of these ideas

Although all Christians believe that the Church is the Body of Christ and the People of God, there are different ideas about its structure, leadership and authority.

- Catholic Christians accept the authority of the Pope and believe that the Pope is the Head of the Church. They believe it is the role of the Pope to rule and guide the Church and to pass on the true teachings of Christ.
- Orthodox Christians believe that they follow the right beliefs and teachings of the Church (the meaning of Orthodox). They reject the authority of the Pope and believe authority comes from councils of bishops or patriarchs acting together.
- The Protestant Churches believe that the Bible is the sole authority. They believe that the Pope has no authority to decide on beliefs; that the Bible is the sole authority for Christians; that salvation comes from faith rather than the sacraments; that all Christians are equal and all are priests; that Churches should be ruled democratically.

The Ecumenical Movement believes that the teachings of St Paul mean Christians should unite as the Body of Christ and Protestants and Orthodox Christians have come together in the World Council of Churches. The Catholic Church in England and Wales is working as a member of Churches Together to show the unity of Christians in action.

A girl, Proscovia, cooking on an open fire in front of her tiny house in Uganda.

Practice questions

c) Explain two reasons why Catholics believe the Church is the Body of Christ. In your answer you must refer to a source of wisdom and authority.

d) 'The Church is too divided to be called the Body of Christ.' Evaluate this statement considering arguments for and against. In your answer you should:
- refer to Catholic points of view
- refer to different Catholic or non-Catholic Christian points of view
- reach a justified conclusion.

Summary

Catholics believe that the Church is the Body of Christ on earth because the Church carries on the work of Jesus on earth, and is one even though it has lots of different parts. This is based on the teaching of St Paul and has been important in trying to bring Christian Churches together.

Section 3: Sources of wisdom and authority

Topic 1.3.6 The four marks of the Church

Thinking points

In this topic you need to:
- think about the nature of the Church as one, holy, catholic and **apostolic**
- consider the four marks and the Nicene Creed and the First Council of Constantinople
- explain how the marks may be understood in different ways within Christianity
- evaluate why the four marks are important for Catholics today.

Useful words

Apostolic – based on the teaching of the twelve apostles
Sister Churches – the Eastern Orthodox Churches which have most of the Apostolic Tradition and Succession, although separate from the Pope
Ecumenical – working together for unity, from the word for 'the whole world'

The meaning of the four marks of the Church

In Christian teaching the Church is frequently described as the one, holy, catholic and apostolic Church. This is stated in the Nicene Creed and so is part of the belief of all Christians. It indicates the four marks of the Christian Church: unity, holiness, universality and apostolicity.

The Church is one

This description of the Church means that even though there may be differences in practice between Catholics and Protestants, Orthodox and Catholic, Christians form one Church united in belief. Churches Together allows Christians in England and Wales to work as one group.

Catholics believe that the Church is one because:

- God is a unity, so his Church must be one.
- The Church is based on one Lord, Jesus Christ.
- The Church has one baptism for the forgiveness of sins.
- The Church is inspired by one Spirit.
- The Church has one faith as agreed in the Apostles' and Nicene Creeds.

The Second Vatican Council declared that other Christians are 'separated brethren', sharing a common baptism into Christ. The Council spoke of 'ecclesial communities' and not 'other Churches' as it was felt that Protestant groups had neglected important aspects of the Church and the gifts given to the Church. An exception was made for the Eastern Orthodox Churches, which were classed as **Sister Churches** as they had preserved so much of the faith.

Catholics are now encouraged to pray with other Christians at times and to work ecumenically. The word '**ecumenical**' comes from the Greek word for the whole world.

The nature of the Church as holy

Catholics believe that the Church is holy because:

- God made it, therefore it belongs to God, and so his Church is holy.
- Christ gave his life to make his Church holy. His Church is devoted to God.
- The Church is the source of the sacraments which bring God's grace to humanity. Therefore it is empowered by God and so is holy.
- The Church has been given the true faith and is guided by the Holy Spirit. Therefore it is spiritually excellent.

Catholics believe that what Christ gave to the apostles to hand on was pure, good and holy. Nothing can change that intrinsically. However, human beings are not all saints and their failings can obscure the light

Topic 1.3.6 **The four marks of the Church**

A Catholic saint: Mother Teresa.

that tries to shine from the Church in each generation. When someone does let that light shine, they make an impact. Think of Mother Teresa tending to the sick and the dying who had been abandoned on the streets of Kolkata, or Maximilian Kolbe, a Franciscan friar, who was sent by the Nazis to Auschwitz concentration camp. He volunteered to die in place of a man who was a husband and father.

The nature of the Church as catholic

Catholic means universal and the Christian Church includes people who believe from all over the world. Not only are the Christians all over the world, but the Christian message is for everyone whatever their race, gender or colour.

Catholics believe that the Church is catholic because:

- Whereas the Jewish religion was for one race, Christianity is for the whole world.
- There are Christians all over the world.

The Christian message can be understood and believed by anyone wherever they are in the world.

Jesus told his disciples:

> *Go therefore and make disciples of all nations, baptising them in the name of the Father, and of the Son and of the Holy Spirit.*
> *(Matthew 28:19)*

There is one liturgy, one Mass, for the people but regional variations can be used in style, music and singing, and decoration. In some countries, such as Britain, people stand when the Gospel is read, as a mark of respect. In other countries, they are already standing and they sit down deliberately. Standing in those countries suggests they are ready for action, to challenge people and even to fight. Sitting down means peace and listening.

There are also Eastern Churches who rejoined the Pope in Rome and they retain their distinctive dress and **Eastern Rite** of the Mass, which they call the liturgy.

Useful words

Catholic – means 'whole world' or 'universal'

Eastern Rite – eastern customs and liturgy followed by Catholics who were once Orthodox

Eastern Rite Catholics at worship.

The nature of the Church as apostolic

The Church is apostolic

This means that the Church is based on the teaching and tradition of the apostles. The first apostles were disciples of Jesus specially chosen by him to proclaim his message to the whole world. The twelve apostles, led by St Peter, founded the Christian Church for Jesus.

Catholics believe that the Church is apostolic because:

- It was founded by the apostles.
- It teaches what the apostles taught.
- The bishops are the successors of the apostles who maintain and proclaim the message of Jesus.
- The authority of St Peter has been passed down by the Apostolic Succession to the current Pope.

An apostolic Church involves not only the Apostolic Tradition, but also the Apostolic Succession. The Succession means that the overseers or bishops that the first apostles ordained then ordained others in turn, so that today's Catholic bishops trace their orders right back to St Peter and the original apostles.

Activities

1. Make a list of things Catholics and Protestants agree about.
2. Make a list of things Catholics and Protestants disagree about.
3. Make a list of things Catholics and Orthodox agree about.
4. Make a list of things Catholics and Orthodox disagree about.

How the four marks may be understood in different ways by Christians today

For many Protestants, the oneness of the Church is seen as something spiritual, based on baptism and a belief in Christ, rather than something requiring agreement across various doctrines. Orthodox Christians, while they also see the oneness of the Church as based in the faith as well as Christ, differ in their approach to doctrine, viewing agreement on things like the Creeds as an essential aspect of 'oneness'. Protestants would therefore allow any believer to receive communion, but Orthodox and Catholics would not. All would agree that the Church is essentially holy.

The term 'catholic' means 'universal' in the Creed, and all agree that Christians are part of a movement that is across all races and nations. For Catholic and Orthodox Christians it means that they are based on the teaching of the apostles and the bishops that have come from them, too.

The apostolic nature is differently understood. For Protestants, this is about being based on the scriptures that came from the apostles; for Catholic and Orthodox Christians it is about their teaching, the scriptures and the line of bishops that have come from the first apostles.

Why the four marks of the Church are important for Catholics today

The four marks of the Church – one, holy, Catholic and apostolic – are important for Catholics because the marks remind Catholics that:

- The Church is not a human creation but a divine gift formed and guided by Christ.
- Jesus did not form many different groups but one faith and the Catholic Church has preserved that unity in faith.
- The Church is worldwide and does not belong to any one nation or cultural style.
- The Church traces itself back to the apostles through the line of bishops and the faith that has been passed down.
- The Church is holy, it comes from God and so Catholics cannot remake it and make it say what they want it to. Catholics are guided and formed by the Church, not the other way round.

Catholics joining together to say the Creed in Mass.

Practice questions

c Explain why the Apostolic Succession is important for Catholics. In your answer you must refer to a source of wisdom and authority.

d 'The Church is too divided to be called One and Holy.' Evaluate this statement considering arguments for and against. In your answer you should:
- refer to Catholic points of view
- refer to different Catholic or non-Catholic Christian points of view
- reach a justified conclusion.

Summary

Catholics believe that the Church is one because all Christians are united in their belief in the Apostles' Creed and the Nicene Creed and so in their beliefs about God and Jesus. They believe that the Church is holy because it comes from God and God is at work in his Church. They believe that the Church is catholic (universal) because anyone can join the Church whatever their race and there are Christians all over the world. They believe that the Church is apostolic because the Church was founded by the apostles of Jesus, and the Church today teaches the same message about Jesus as the apostles did.

Section 3: Sources of wisdom and authority

Topic 1.3.7 Mary as a model of the Church

Thinking points

In this topic you need to:
- understand the role of the Virgin Mary for Catholics
- consider how Mary joined with Christ in the work of salvation
- think about the significance of Mary as a model of the Church and of discipleship
- consider Mary as a model of faith and charity (including Luke 1:26–39 and Catechism of the Catholic Church 963–975)
- evaluate the implications of this teaching for Catholics.

Useful words

Shrine – a building or container for holy things, a holy place
Ark – a container; the Ark of the Covenant contained the Ten Commandments and was seen as being especially blessed
Theotokos – Greek for 'God bearer'

The importance and significance of Mary as a model of the Church

Mary is a model of the Church as she is the mother of Christ, the one who gave him to the world. Early Christian devotion described her as a **shrine**, as the **Ark** of the Covenant that had contained the Ten Commandments and a special presence of God. Mary became known as the Madonna, the **Theotokos**, the God bearer. The Church, for Catholics, is to show the presence of Christ to the world just as Mary did:

> The Virgin Mary … is acknowledged and honoured as being truly the Mother of God and of the redeemer … She is 'clearly the mother of the members of Christ' … since she has by her charity joined in bringing about the birth of believers in the Church, who are members of its head.' 'Mary, Mother of Christ, Mother of the Church'. (Catechism of the Catholic Church 963)

Mary is a model of the Church as one in whom Christ dwelt and was then shown to the world. The Church is also like a mother to believers as they find new life through baptism from the Church.

Mary, the young Jewish woman from Nazareth, is also seen as the faithful Israelite, the fulfilment of 2000 thousand years of faith, expectation and longing.

Activity

Look at the icon of Mary. Do Catholics pray to Mary or do they ask for her prayers. What is the difference?

This icon or image of Mary is called the Orans, meaning the One who Prays, raising her arms. She is shown, symbolically, carrying Christ within her and offering him to the world.

Topic 1.3.7 Mary as a model of the Church

These images come together in an apocalyptic passage in the Book of Revelation:

> *A great portent appeared in heaven: a woman clothed with the sun, with the moon under her feet, and on her head a crown of twelve stars. She was pregnant and in birth pangs ...* (Revelation 12:1–2)

Here we see symbolism at work superbly. The woman is Mary, is the Church and is Israel: three things at once. The twelve stars can represent the apostles *and* the twelve tribes of Israel. This passage has a sense that the woman is in glory, that Mary was taken up into heaven. The doctrine of the **assumption** of Mary, body and soul into heaven, is a very early tradition and a dogma of the Catholic Church, although nothing is mentioned about it directly in the New Testament, apart from this possible hint.

> *Finally, the Immaculate Virgin, preserved free from all stain of original sin, when the course of her earthly life was finished, was taken up body and soul into heavenly glory, and exalted by the Lord as Queen over all things.* (Catechism of the Catholic Church 966)

The assumption of Mary into heaven.

The importance of Mary as a model of discipleship

Catholics believe that the Virgin Mary shows Christians how to be a model disciple:

- Mary obeyed God's plan for her: she did not question what was to happen to her, rather she accepted that it was God's will.
- Mary was conceived without sin (**Immaculate Conception**) and remained a pure virgin throughout her life. By following her example, Catholics can also try to live pure lives.
- Mary showed complete devotion to Jesus. She loved her son and was with him right to the end, even sharing in his sufferings on the cross. This is how Christians should love Christ.
- Even when she did not always understand what was happening (for example, Mary did not understand Simeon's prophecy at the circumcision of Jesus and could not understand why Jesus stayed behind in the Jerusalem Temple when he was twelve), Mary trusted God and was supportive and faithful to Jesus.
- Mary was always a help and support to her son, for example, at the wedding feast in Cana (John 2:5) she told the people to ask Jesus and to 'do whatever he tells you'.
- Mary was without sin from the moment of her conception (Immaculate Conception) and continued to be sinless throughout her life.

The importance of Mary as a model of faith and charity

Mary is an example of faith because:

- She believed the message of the Angel Gabriel at the **Annunciation** even though she had no proof that it would happen.
- She believed that Jesus was God's Son before he performed any miracles simply because of what Gabriel had said.
- She trusted that God would make sure death was not the end for her son.

Useful words

Assumption – the belief that the Virgin Mary was taken into heaven body and soul

Immaculate conception – the belief that the Virgin Mary was conceived without original sin and was always full of grace

Annunciation – the greeting of the Archangel Gabriel to the Virgin Mary when he announced that she was to have a son who would be the Christ

Activities

1. Look at the painting of the Annunciation on the page 114. What does it teach about the Virgin Mary?
2. Look at the painting of the Virgin Mary on this page. What is meant by the assumption of the Virgin Mary?
3. In what ways can the Virgin Mary be seen as a model of the Church?

The annunciation of the angel to Mary.

Mary is an example of charity because:

- She gave up her own life and career to bear God's son when she could have refused.
- She was always ready to help people.
- She continues to pray for those who need her help.

The implications of teachings about Mary for Catholic life today

The teachings about Mary are important for Catholic life today because:

- As the Mother of all the baptised since she is the Mother of Christ, her prayers are asked for as candles are lit, the 'Hail Mary' and the Rosary is recited, and her shrines are visited such as at Lourdes and Walsingham.
- As the Theotokos, the God bearer, she encourages Catholics today to be 'God bearers' in a lesser sense, being open to the Holy Spirit.
- As an example of faith in the way she responded to the Angel's message, she encourages Catholics to be firm in their faith.
- In the way she gave herself to God's will, she is a reminder of the value of women in the Church in so many ways and the blessedness of all mothers who give the gift of life.

By her complete adherence to the Father's will, to his Son's redemptive work, and to every prompting of the Holy Spirit, the Virgin Mary is the Church's model of faith and charity. Thus she is a 'pre-eminent and ... wholly unique member of the Church'; indeed, she is the exemplary realisation of the Church. Her role in relation to the Church and to all humanity goes still further. 'In a wholly singular way she cooperated by her obedience, faith, hope, and burning charity in the Saviour's work of restoring supernatural life to souls. For this reason she is a mother to us in the order of grace'.
(Catechism of the Catholic Church 967–968)

Activity

Read the passage from Catechism 967–968 and try to put it into your own words.

Summary

Mary is an important figure for Catholics. She is seen as the model of discipleship through her important role in the birth, life and resurrection of Christ so helping him to bring about the salvation of humanity. She is also seen as a model of faith and charity because she gave up everything to bear God's son.

Practice questions

c) Explain two reasons why the Virgin Mary is regarded as a model of discipleship. In your answer you must refer to a source of wisdom and authority.

d) 'The Virgin Mary has too much importance for Catholics.' Evaluate this statement considering arguments for and against. In your answer you should:
- refer to Catholic points of view
- refer to different Catholic or non-Catholic Christian points of view
- reach a justified conclusion.

Topic 1.3.8 Sources of personal and ethical decision-making

The example and teaching of Jesus as the authoritative source of moral teaching

Catholics look for guidance with moral choices as they go through life. Jesus, the Bible, the tradition and the Church can provide this.

Jesus was the perfect human being according to Catholics, as he was God made man. He is the example of a holy life and of what God is like in human terms. Jesus' moral teaching can be summed up in two sayings. The first is the **golden rule**:

> *In everything do to others as you would have them do to you; for this is the law and the prophets.* (Matthew 7:12)

The second is in Mark 12:28–34, where Jesus is asked what the greatest of the commandments might be. Jesus took two of the Laws from the **Torah** and joined them together:

> *The first is 'Hear, O Israel: the Lord your God, the Lord is one; you shall love the Lord your God with all your heart, and with all your soul, and with all your mind, and with all your strength'. The second is this, 'You shall love your neighbour as yourself.' There is no other commandment greater than these.*

Thus, love of God and of neighbour are both vital and are like two sides of the same, inseparable coin.

> *The entire Law of the Gospel is contained in the 'new commandment' of Jesus, to love one another as he has loved us.*
> (Catechism of the Catholic Church 1970, following John 15:15)

The greatest commandment was like the two sides of a coin. You cannot have one without the other.

Jesus as the fulfilment of the Law

The Torah, the Law of Moses, in the Old Testament is a collection of hundreds of different laws concerning ritual and ethics. The ritual laws can be written down alongside ethical ones, such as Leviticus 19:14–15, which has the command to love your neighbour as oneself, and be equal and fair to the poor. However, many rules concerning offerings and the cult are mixed in with these. The ritual laws, concerning what can be offered in sacrifice and what should be done in the Temple, are seen by the Church as no longer relevant as Christ has come. The ethical laws still stand, true forever, based on **natural law**. The ritual laws are no longer relevant as Christ has come. They were seen as pointing the way and preparing for him, to teach people about sin, sacrifice and forgiveness.

Thinking points

In this topic you need to:
- think about sources of personal and ethical decision-making for Catholics
- think about the example and teaching of Jesus as the authoritative source for moral teaching
- think about Jesus as the fulfilment of the law, including Matthew 5:17–24
- think about different understandings of the place and authority of natural law
- think about virtue and the primacy of conscience
- be able to explain and evaluate the importance of different sources of authority for Christians today.

Useful words

Golden rule – do to others what you would wish them do to you
Torah – the Law of Moses
Natural law – the inbuilt moral order to the universe

> Do not think that I have come to abolish the Law or the Prophets; I have not come to abolish them but to fulfil them. For truly I tell you, until heaven and earth disappear, not the smallest letter, not the least stroke of a pen, will by any means disappear from the Law until everything is accomplished. Therefore anyone who sets aside one of the least of these commands and teaches others accordingly will be called least in the kingdom of heaven, but whoever practises and teaches these commands will be called great in the kingdom of heaven. For I tell you that unless your righteousness surpasses that of the Pharisees and the teachers of the law, you will certainly not enter the kingdom of heaven.
> (Matthew 5:17–20)

Jesus did not deny the old laws, but claimed to have fulfilled them and done away with any need for some of them. As Messiah, the Christ, he saw himself as wielding that authority and the Church sees that he fulfilled the ritual laws about offerings in his own person on the cross. Christ had made the most perfect offering to the father that could ever be made; that is recalled by Catholics in the Mass each time it is celebrated.

The new law is summed up in the Sermon on the Mount (Matthew 5–7), especially the nine Beatitudes (Matthew 5:3–11), which turn secular values upside down, exalting the poor, the weak and merciful. Jesus often goes to the heart of the matter, looking at attitudes and the desires that start to form wrong actions. A lustful look could lead to adultery, and Jesus refused the lax attitude to divorce shown by some contemporary Jewish rabbis. Looking again at Matthew 5:17 we are reminded that Jesus did not reject the old laws but fulfilled them. The ritual sacrifices were no longer needed as he had come.

Natural law

> The natural law is nothing other than the light of understanding placed in us by God; through it we know what we must do and what we must avoid. God has given this light or law at the creation.
> (St Augustine)

Jesus giving the Sermon on the Mount.

Topic 1.3.8 Sources of personal and ethical decision-making

Different societies, cultures and ages have different moral rules about what is right and wrong. The Catholic Church believes that beneath all of these differences there is an absolute moral law which is the same in all times and all places and applies to all people. This is what is meant by 'natural law'. These universal laws can be discovered by anybody by the right use of reason – that is, by thinking clearly about what leads to the good of all human beings. The theory of natural law is based on the teaching of Aquinas. It claims that there are some things which are always wrong because of how the universe has been established. Natural law has nothing to do with the laws of nature.

The Catechism recognises, as well, that the sinfulness of humanity and society can obscure and confuse the promptings of the natural law. Someone could think it would be all right to be kind to their own class or race but not to others:

> *The precepts of natural law are not perceived by everyone clearly and immediately. In the present situation sinful man needs grace and revelation so moral and religious truths may be known by everyone …* (Catechism of the Catholic Church 1960)

> *The natural law expresses the original moral sense which enables man to discern by reason the good and the evil, the truth and the lie.* (Catechism of the Catholic Church 1954)

Different understandings of the place and authority of natural law

Some Protestant Christians reject the idea that human beings can work out for themselves what is right and wrong and believe that all morality comes from God. They believe that the sinfulness of human beings means that they cannot use their own reason to arrive at the truth because sin has damaged their ability to reason clearly. Therefore, Christian morality comes from what God has revealed in the Bible and how this is interpreted by Church leaders.

The Catholic response would be that sin has affected the will (the ability to choose what is right) but not the intellect (the ability to know what is right) – in fact, the story of the Fall makes clear that what makes human beings different from the animals is their knowledge of right and wrong. It is because human beings know what is right but don't do it that makes an action wrong in the first place.

Virtue and the primacy of conscience

> *Deep within his **conscience** man discovers a law which he has not laid upon himself but which he must obey. Its voice, ever calling to him to love and to do what is good and to avoid evil, sounds in his heart at the right moment … For man has in his heart a law inscribed by God.* (Catechism of the Catholic Church 1776)

The Catholic Church believes that God has placed the moral law within every person and 'In all he says and does, man is obliged to follow faithfully what he knows to be just and right. And this demand man finds in his heart is the natural law' (Catechism of the Catholic Church 1778). This is part of what the scripture calls being created in 'the image of God' (Genesis 1:27).

When conscience is followed and the commandments of the Church are upheld, good habits form and these are known as the virtues. A virtue is an ingrained good habit.

> **Activity**
> What do you think is the most important commandment?

> **Useful words**
> **Conscience** – a reasoned approach to what is right and wrong using our innate moral faculty

Section 3: Sources of wisdom and authority

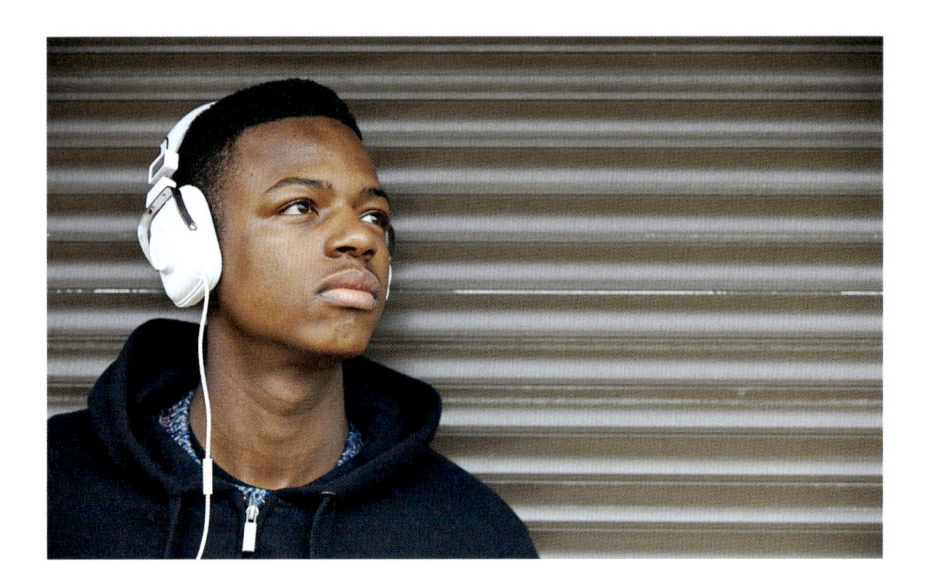

Sometimes take off the headphones and switch off the mobile and just be still.

It is important for every person to be sufficiently present to himself in order to hear and follow the voice of his conscience. (Catechism of the Catholic Church 1779)

Modern life can be full of distractions, with multimedia, social media and instant messaging, and it is not always easy to be still, alone and quiet. This stillness is also called **interiority**.

Useful words

Interiority – taking space and time for quiet, self-reflection

There can be many and varied influences in the media and among friends and family. There are fashions for behaviour as well as music and clothes. There are attitudes which are pushed at us, maybe because others are doing the same thing, or some people want to sell a product. It can be difficult to stand against the crowd and think for yourself. Resisting peer pressure is not easy, and peer pressure comes not only from your own age group, but also from society. What values do we see played out before us on television in dramas and soap operas? What values are present in film and music, and in the lifestyle of celebrities?

Informing conscience

Conscience is a judgement of reason whereby the human person recognises the moral quality of a concrete act ... (Catechism of the Catholic Church 1778)

We need to inform our consciences as a conscience works on a rational foundation, weighing up situations and arguments. Catholics are encouraged to understand what the Church teaches about a topic, and not to rely on misunderstandings. The scriptures need to be consulted and as many facts about the matter should be gathered. If people do not understand various facts and moral arguments, then they cannot always be held responsible for some of their actions. There are difficult issues in modern society too, with fast-paced changes in technology and medicine that pose new challenges. The Catechism of the Catholic Church 1789 admits this but states, clearly, that certain principles must always be followed:

Activity

What does it mean to have an informed conscience? Give an example from modern issues.

- First principle: Never do evil that good may come.
- Second principle: Follow the golden rule: 'Whatever you wish that men would do to you, do so to them' (Mark 7:12).
- Third principle: Have charity towards your neighbour and respect their right of conscience even when you disagree with them.

Different implications of these sources of authority for Christians today

Let us take four examples that make use of the three principles outlined above, based on the teaching of Christ and the Catechism of the Catholic Church:

- *Abortion*: terminating a pregnancy might seem the caring thing to do in some circumstances, but what about the life of the unborn? ('Never do evil that good may come'). Other Christians might disagree, seeing the well-being of the mother as more important.

- *Stealing*: a person might have a clever plan to cover their tracks and try to get away with it, but would you want someone to do that to you? (Follow the golden rule.) Still, there might be life-and-death situations where theft would be allowable, some would say, such as if you are starving.

- *Respect*: a friend might be unable to eat a meal you have given them as a guest. Perhaps they are vegetarian or their religion prohibits them from eating certain foods (respect their conscience). This would be widely agreed on by all Christians.

- *Homosexuality*: gay partners who are in love and are committed to each other would be counselled to follow chastity and abstain from sex by the Catholic Church and other Christians, but some Catholics and Protestants would disagree, seeing the love of the partners as most important.

> **Activity**
>
> Look at the photo on page 118. Do you think practising interiority is a good idea?

Practice questions

c) Explain two reasons why natural law is important for Catholics. In your answer you must refer to a source of wisdom and authority.

d) 'You only need the two great commandments of Jesus to make moral decisions.' Evaluate this statement considering arguments for and against. In your answer you should:
- refer to Catholic points of view
- refer to different Catholic or non-Catholic Christian points of view
- reach a justified conclusion.

Summary

Catholics look to Jesus as the authoritative source for moral teaching. Many Catholics refer to Matthew 5:17 (the fulfilment of the law) for guidance, and the Bible also contains important passages on natural law and the importance of virtue and conscience in providing moral guidance.

Section 3: Sources of wisdom and authority

How to answer questions

a) Outline three features of the New Testament. [3]

The New Testament contains the four Gospels of Matthew, Mark, Luke and John. These record the life and teachings of Jesus Christ. The New Testament also contains letters from the apostles such as St Paul and St Peter giving advice to Christians.

A high mark answer because three features of the New Testament are clearly outlined.

b) Explain two reasons why the Church is called apostolic. [4]

The Church is called apostolic because it is based on the teaching and tradition of the apostles. The first apostles were disciples of Jesus specially chosen by him to proclaim his message to the whole world, and the twelve apostles, led by St Peter, founded the Christian Church for Jesus. Another reason is because the bishops are the successors of the apostles who maintain and proclaim the message of Jesus. As the Catechism says, 'Christ governs her through Peter and the other apostles, who are present in their successors, the Pope and the college of bishops'.

A high mark answer because two correct reasons are identified and developed.

c) Explain two reasons why a Catholic might obey their conscience when making a moral decision. In your answer you must refer to a source of wisdom and authority. [5]

Catholics might obey their conscience because the Church teaches that conscience is the voice of God. As Catechism 1795 says, 'Conscience is man's most secret core and his sanctuary. There he is alone with God whose voice echoes in his depths.' Catholics follow their conscience because it is a God-given faculty that helps them to do good and avoid evil. The voice of conscience tells us what to do and what not to do.

A high mark answer because two correct reasons are given and each reason is developed with a reference to the teaching of the Catechism, which is a major source of authority for Catholics.

d) 'Christians must only obey the Bible.' [12 marks + 3 spelling, punctuation and grammar (SPaG) marks]

Some Christians would believe that the Bible is the only authority because they believe that it is inspired by the Holy Spirit which means it comes from God. They also believe that it should be obeyed because it contains God's laws on how to behave, such as the Ten Commandments, which help people to live as God intended. They also believe that the Bible should be obeyed because it contains the teachings of Jesus on how to live the Christian life. They believe that Jesus is the second person of the Holy Trinity so what he taught has authority.

However, Catholics would disagree because they believe that the Bible needs interpreting by the Pope and the college of bishops under his leadership (the magisterium) for the life of Christian people in the twenty-first century. The magisterium can address issues that did not exist in the time of the Bible, for example same-sex partnerships. This is important as Catholics cannot look in the Bible to find answers to these issues. The magisterium is the supreme authority for Catholics, telling them what to believe. If the magisterium states something to be true then it is true.

So it seems that Catholic Christians need to obey more than the Bible given the supreme authority of the magisterium. Therefore, it is not true that Christians must only obey the Bible.

A high mark answer because it gives three clear developed Christian reasons for thinking that only the Bible should be obeyed. It then gives three correct Catholic reasons for disagreeing before reaching a fully justified conclusion.

Spelling, punctuation and grammar are correct and a wide range of specialist vocabulary (Holy Spirit, Ten Commandments, second person, Holy Trinity, Pope, magisterium, college of bishops) is used appropriately.

4 Forms of expression and ways of life

Area of study 1: Study of Catholic Christianity

Section 4: Forms of expression and ways of life

Topic 1.4.1 The architecture, design and decoration of Catholic churches

Thinking points

In this topic you need to:
- think about the common and divergent forms of architecture, design and decoration of Catholic churches
- consider how they reflect belief, are used in and contribute to worship, including reference to Catechism of the Catholic Church 1179–1181.

The common and divergent architecture of Catholic churches

Exteriors of Catholic churches can vary in style greatly. Some will have bell towers, some will not. Many will look very plain, some more ornate, such as the exterior of Notre Dame Cathedral in Paris, France, with its carvings and images of saints. This was a product of the **Gothic** style of building with pointed arches and ribbed vaults that flourished in the later Middle Ages. The later **Baroque** style of the seventeenth century was more opulent and expressive, showing off wealth with ornamentation, magnificent statues and paintings.

Modern styles are plainer and simpler, but can be imaginative too, such as the elaborate Sagrada Familia in Barcelona, Spain.

Useful words

Gothic – style of medieval church building with pointed arches

Baroque – elaborate style of church building and decoration from the seventeenth century onwards

Exterior details of Notre Dame Cathedral in Paris, France.

Activity

Look up examples online of Gothic and Baroque church buildings. Make a display of different types and write a description of them.

La Sagrada Familia in Barcelona, Spain, designed by Antoni Gaudi. Construction started in 1882 and completion is estimated in 2028.

Topic 1.4.1 The architecture, design and decoration of Catholic churches

The design of Catholic churches

All the senses are engaged in Catholic worship: sight, smell, touch, taste and hearing. There are colourful symbols to look at and the perfume of incense; communion wafers are taken in the hand and eaten, and prayers and readings are listened to.

People will stand, sit or kneel, make the sign of the cross over themselves at various points or dip their fingers in holy water. Catholic worship reminds us that we have bodies and are not just minds.

All of this rich tapestry of images and actions reminds the worshipper that Catholics believe in the incarnation, that God became a human being in Jesus of Nazareth. God speaks and moves within and through his creation, within and through natural things. The material world is thus seen as blessed by God's presence and is not to be treated as inferior or of little concern.

All Catholic churches have features in common, although the building can be ancient or modern, plain or highly ornate. In a few cases, the main area will be circular so that people can sit and face each other. The building will have the following features:

- An entrance area, a porch or **narthex**: this will be used to display posters and messages, booklets and rotas, and for greeting people before or after Mass.
- A gathering area or **nave**: this will have seating, either rows of fixed pews or seats that can be moved.
- A special area for the priests and servers at the altar, or **sanctuary**: the sanctuary will contain the altar, a **lectern** (or ambo) and usually the **tabernacle** (although this could be in a side chapel).
- At least one side chapel with a small, separate altar, the **Lady Chapel**. The Virgin Mary, often called 'Our Lady' by Catholics, always has a place of honour in a Catholic church as the Mother of God (**Madonna**), but her images and devotions are never in the sanctuary itself as this is set aside for honouring Christ. The Virgin Mary is honoured and her prayers are asked for, but she is not worshipped. She is human and not divine.

The decoration of Catholic churches

Catholicism has a rich assortment of symbols, visual aids, rituals and rites that aid worship and express the belief of the people. In a Catholic church, during Mass or at other times, there will be colourful vestments and cloths, candles, sweet-scented incense, sacred vessels, bread and wine, holy pictures and statues, crosses, crucifixes and holy water. Passages will be read from the Bible, and at the reading of the Gospel there will be a special focus and ceremonial actions. This may also be enhanced by sacred music, whether traditional or modern, hymns or unaccompanied voices using a style called plainchant.

All of this expresses belief in God as Father, Son and Holy Spirit, belief that mankind is created in God's image, and belief in Jesus as the 'Word made flesh'.

There will be statues, paintings, **icons** (painted holy images on wood), banners and stained-glass windows. There will usually be a statue of the Sacred Heart of Jesus and of the Virgin Mary as well as other saints. The Sacred Heart is a heart with a flame above it and thorns surrounding it, symbolising the eternal fire of God's love in Christ.

Activity
Do you think Catholic churches need a Lady Chapel?

Useful words

Narthex – the porch area at the entrance of a church building

Nave – the main worship and seating area

Sanctuary – the sacred space where the altar is and where Mass is celebrated

Lectern – raised stand where the Bible is read from

Tabernacle – where the Blessed sacrament is kept in Catholic churches

Lady Chapel – a side chapel in a Catholic church reserved for devotion to the Blessed Virgin Mary

Madonna – 'Mother of God', referring to how Mary carried God in Jesus in her womb. God as Spirit ultimately does not have or need a mother, but the incarnation of God in Christ did

Icon – painted image of Christ or the saints on wood

Section 4: Forms of expression and ways of life

Interior of the Lady Chapel at Westminster Cathedral in London.

Divergent forms of architecture, design and decoration

- In much older churches, especially in the Middle Ages, there were screens that partly separated the sanctuary area from the nave. There was a cross on top of these and they were known as **rood screens**. Few survive today and in most Catholic churches the sanctuary is perfectly visible from the nave. (In Eastern Orthodox churches and Eastern Catholic churches, a screen still exists and is covered with beautifully painted icons of Christ, Mary, the angels and the saints. Doors are opened and closed to the sanctuary area at different times during worship. This screen is known as the **iconostasis**.)

- Different architectural styles are used for Catholic churches, depending upon the architects and the age in which they were built. For example, Westminster Cathedral (the largest Catholic cathedral in England) is Neo-Byzantine in style and built with bricks, and reflects the late Victorian/Edwardian era when it was built, whereas Liverpool Metropolitan Cathedral has a 'modern style' and is built with concrete and aluminium, reflecting the fact that it was built in the 1960s.

- The decoration of Catholic churches also reflects the era when they were built. For example, the decoration in Westminster reflects Victorian style and the decoration in Liverpool reflects the 1960s' style.

However, Catholic churches always have the common features of the sanctuary with altar and tabernacle, the nave, and usually a Lady Chapel.

Useful words

Rood screen – a medieval, Western version of the Eastern iconostasis separating the sanctuary from the nave
Iconostasis – the screen separating the sanctuary from the nave in Eastern churches, which is decorated with icons
Holy of Holies – the Holy Place in the ancient Jerusalem Temple

How the architecture, design and decoration of Catholic churches reflect belief

The layout of Catholic churches and their architecture are highly symbolic. The separation of the sanctuary area, used only by the clergy and servers, is a reminder that God is holy, and this echoes the ancient Jewish notion of the **Holy of Holies** in the Jerusalem Temple which only certain priests could enter. The priests and ministers come down from the sanctuary to the nave, to the people, representing God's movement to humanity, and especially his coming in Jesus as God made man.

Activity

Give examples of how the five senses of sight, touch, taste, hearing and smell might be engaged in Catholic worship.

Topic 1.4.1 The architecture, design and decoration of Catholic churches

A golden iconostasis in Kykkos Monastery, Cyprus.

For Catholics, 'the Church' is the people of God, baptised and having the gift of the Holy Spirit. The special building consecrated, blessed and set aside for worship us 'a church'. The buildings are special and teach aspects of the faith in their own way through their architecture and symbolism. This idea is summed up in the Catechism:

> *For the Body of the risen Christ is the spiritual temple from which the source of living water springs forth: incorporated into Christ by the Holy Spirit, 'we are the temple of the living God'. When the exercise of religious liberty is not thwarted, Christians construct buildings for divine worship. (Catechism of the Catholic Church 1179–1180)*

The 'spiritual temple' and a 'source of living water' refer to the People of God who build a church for worship wherever the authorities allow it (religious liberty). The church building is in one sense only a meeting place for the people, who are the church as the assembly of the faithful. However, it is also a **consecrated** building, set apart and blessed for worship. When a bishop consecrates church buildings, there is an elaborate ceremony and rich symbolism with holy oil and crosses marked along the walls.

As the building is set apart and blessed, the consecrated hosts (the **Blessed Sacrament**) are kept in there in the tabernacle; Catholics believe that these are the body of Christ.

The term 'nave' comes from the Latin for ship, and suggests the keel of a ship, a sense that worshippers are in Christ's boat, being steered by him and on a journey to heaven. This is the area where the congregation sit.

Useful words

Consecrated – blessed and set apart for sacred use
Blessed Sacrament – consecrated hosts kept in the tabernacle

125

Section 4: Forms of expression and ways of life

Activities

1. How are the five senses involved in Catholic worship?
2. How is the sanctuary like the Holy of Holies in the Jewish Temple?
3. How do the features of a Catholic church reflect Catholic beliefs?

How the architecture, design and decoration of Catholic churches are used in, and contribute to, worship

For Catholics, churches should be places of assembly, worship, prayer and ceremony. They should be both 'in good taste' and a 'worthy' place for these functions. In keeping with this, church buildings for Catholics are usually sacred places, decorated with symbols and designed to be worshipped in. The symbols point to the mystery of Christ and his offering on the cross, represented on the altar.

These ideas are expressed fully in the following Catechism:

> *A church is a 'house of prayer' in which the Eucharist is celebrated and reserved, where the faithful assemble, and where is worshipped the presence of the Son of God our Saviour, offered for us on the altar for the help and consolation of the faithful – this house ought to be in good taste and a worthy place for prayer and sacred ceremonial. In this 'house of God' the truth and harmony of the signs that make it up should show Christ to be present and active in this place.* (Catechism of the Catholic Church 1181)

The layout of a church building reminds worshippers that there is the otherness of God but that God also comes among them. The people assemble in the nave area, and only the clergy and servers venture into the sanctuary and around the altar. Great reverence is shown for this area, both bowing to the altar and genuflecting (going down on one knee) to the Blessed Sacrament in the tabernacle. The priest and ministers bring the Body and Blood of Christ in the consecrated bread and wine down into the nave area for the people to receive. God is other, God comes among his people. The building as a consecrated place containing the reserved sacrament, the Blessed Sacrament in the tabernacle, has a holy quality of awe, quiet and prayerfulness for Catholics who enter it.

Practice questions

c Explain two ways in which the architecture of a Catholic church reflects Catholic beliefs.

d 'The design of Catholic churches helps people to worship God properly.' Evaluate this statement considering arguments for and against. In your answer you should:
- refer to Catholic points of view
- refer to different Catholic or non-Catholic Christian points of view
- reach a justified conclusion.

Summary

Catholic churches were built with worship in mind, and their architecture, design and decoration, from the opulent design and decoration to elements of the layout such as the nave, sanctuary and side chapel (Lady Chapel), all reflect the different functions of Catholic worship.

Topic 1.4.2 The different internal features of a Catholic church

Entering the building

Catholics feel that entering the church building is to enter a sacred place. It is a place of prayer and of spiritual presence as the **Blessed Sacrament** is kept there.

Catholic Catechism speaks of this as being like crossing a threshold, like going through a door into a special place, a place of prayer and blessing. As Catechism 1186 puts it:

> *To enter into the house of God, we must cross a threshold, which symbolises passing from the world wounded by sin to the world of new Life to which all men are called. The visible church is a symbol of the Father's house toward which the People of God is journeying and where the Father 'will wipe every tear from their eyes'. Also for this reason, the Church is the house of all God's children, open and welcoming. (Catechism of the Catholic Church 1186)*

The meaning and significance of the lectern

The lectern (or **ambo**) is the raised stand or platform where the Bible is read from. An important part of worship in a Catholic church is the reading of the Bible, both Old and New Testament scriptures.

> *The dignity of the Word of God requires that in the church there is a suitable place from which it may be proclaimed. (Catechism of the Catholic Church 1184)*

A Mass will usually have an Old Testament reading, a **Psalm** of praise, and always a Gospel reading. On Sundays and holy days there will be an extra reading from the New Testament. At the end of the first (and second) reading, the reader concludes with, 'The Word of the Lord' and the people reply, 'Thanks be to God.'

The Bible for Catholics is the Word of God as well as the words of many men and women in ancient times. The Old Testament looks forward to the coming of Christ, but speaks of the same God who has the same love and mercy for his people. The Church honours the writings of the Hebrew Bible and Catholics are expected to be thankful for all that Judaism has given them in the past. Jesus was a Jew, the twelve disciples were Jews, and Peter as the first Pope was a Jew.

The Gospel

The most important parts of the Bible for Catholics are the Gospels as these are believed to contain the words and deeds of Jesus. The Gospel can only be read by an ordained deacon or a priest, or a bishop. The ordained ministers each represent Christ to the people and they proclaim his words and deeds. The reading of the Gospel is treated as special by having **acolytes** holding candles beside the lectern. The Book of the Gospels may also be perfumed with incense. A special chant of 'Alleluia, Alleluia,

Thinking points

In this topic you need to:
- think about the different internal features found inside a Catholic church, with reference to Catechism 1182–1186
- consider the meaning and significance of the lectern, altar, crucifix and tabernacle
- evaluate how these features express the importance of redemption and facilitate Catholic worship.

A Bible reading from the lectern.

Useful words

Blessed Sacrament – the consecrated bread and wine
Ambo – a raised platform where people read or speak from
Psalm – a prayer of praise, petition or lament in the Old Testament
Acolyte – a server who carries a candle

Section 4: Forms of expression and ways of life

Activities

1. Look at the photo on page 127. How do you know she is not reading the Gospel?
2. Why do you think the altar is at the centre of the church?

Useful words

Eucharistic prayer – the prayer of thanksgiving and consecration over the bread and wine

Altar – the place where the bread and wine are consecrated; it is a place of sacrifice and a table of sharing

Alleluia' (meaning 'Praise God') precedes the reading of the Gospel of the day with a sentence summing up its message, such as:

Alleluia, Alleluia! Your words are spirit, Lord, and they are life: you have the message of eternal life.
Alleluia!

The Gospels are also placed on the lectern as they are raised up and special.

The meaning and significance of the altar

Catechism reminds Catholics of how special the altar is. It is about the cross, where the **Eucharistic prayer** is offered and the Lord's sacrifice is present each time:

The altar of the New Covenant is the Lord's Cross. From which the sacraments of the Paschal mystery flow. On the altar, which is the centre of the church, the sacrifice of the Cross is made present under sacramental signs. The altar is also the table of the Lord, to which the People of God are invited. (Catechism of the Catholic Church 1182)

The **altar** is made of stone that has been consecrated by a bishop. There is a relic of a saint under the central part of it. This is both an altar of sacrifice and a table of sharing. The sacrifice is the offering of all prayers and praises made by worshippers and also that of Christ on the cross. Christ is not re-sacrificed. That happened once and for all in history, but for Catholics his offering is brought into the present, right among the people. His redemption still affects people today:

... the sacrifice of Christ offered once for all on the cross remains ever present. (Catechism of the Catholic Church 1364)

A priest saying the Eucharistic prayer.

Topic 1.4.2 The different internal features of a Catholic church

In the Catholic Mass, bread and wine are taken, prayed over and consecrated. The Holy Spirit is called down on them and the words of Jesus are repeated over them – 'This is my body … This is my blood …' – so that a change is believed to take place. They become the Body and Blood of Christ at their deepest level of reality. On the surface they are still bread and wine, and yet, in an unseen way, Christ is present. They retain the form of natural things, but they have the inner substance of Christ's Body and Blood. This is the doctrine of **transubstantiation** which says that the exterior form of bread and wine remains (the accidents) but the inner reality changes (the substance). (See Topic 1.2.3, page 54.)

In the Mass, for Catholics, it is as though the worship of heaven and earth is joined together briefly. The people praise on earth, offering up Christ who stands in heaven with the saints and the angels praising and praying for the people.

The meaning and significance of the crucifix

Catholic churches will always have a crucifix. This is a cross with an image of Christ on it. It might be a carving or a painting. The crucifix reminds the worshippers that Jesus died for them. To an outsider, it can seem to be a cruel and sadistic image of torture. For the Christian it speaks of love, as well as the unjust suffering of innocent people. It is a sign that God entered his creation as Jesus and became one of them, sharing the suffering and darkness in life.

Some non-Catholic Christians fear that Catholics are fixated with the death of Jesus and they complain; 'Jesus is not on the cross any more!' This is to misunderstand the purpose of depictions of the crucifixion. They are reminders of his death and nothing more.

The meaning and significance of the tabernacle

The Catechism reminds Catholics why the tabernacle is special, as a focus and in helping people to adore the presence of Christ:

> *The dignity, placing and security of the Eucharistic tabernacle should foster adoration before the Lord really present in the Blessed Sacrament of the altar.* (Catechism of the Catholic Church 1183)

The tabernacle is a container for consecrated hosts. The hosts are the pieces of bread that were taken and transformed. 'Host' comes from the Latin for victim, reminding people of Christ's sacrifice. Hosts are kept there both to take out to the sick, so that they can receive Holy Communion at home, and also for adoration. Catholics believe that there is a holy and special presence in a church building that keeps the hosts in the tabernacle. The word tabernacle is an old word meaning 'tent' or dwelling.

Catholics like to sit and pray before the tabernacle, sensing that God is with them. There is a service of prayer and blessing called adoration where a host is taken out of the tabernacle and put in a decorative container on the altar for all to see. This is called a **monstrance**, from the Latin for 'to show'. This will often be exposed for a Holy Hour when people pray in silence, say the Rosary, and finally sing or say prayers as a priest or a deacon who makes the sign of the cross over the people, blessing with the monstrance that contains a consecrated host, the Body of Christ. The layout of the sanctuary and the placing of the tabernacle remind the worshipper that this is a holy place.

Activity

Imagine that a non-Catholic Christian visits a Mass, watching what happens at the altar, and also notices the use of the tabernacle. She complains to her Catholic friend: 'Catholics are trying to re-sacrifice Christ and they are worshipping the bread and the wine!' How would you answer this charge?

Useful words

Transubstantiation – the belief that the bread and wine change into the Body and Blood of Christ in an unseen way

Monstrance – a receptacle in which the host is displayed

The San Damiano Cross, a twelfth-century crucifix.

Section 4: Forms of expression and ways of life

> **Activity**
>
> Why is the Tabernacle so important for Catholics?

A woman praying in Basilica dos Martires Catholic Church, Lisbon, Portugal.

How the internal features of a Catholic church express the importance of redemption

The focus on the altar and the cross at the centre of the sanctuary area, the focal point of the church building, remind the worshipper that the Catholic faith is about redemption. God was in Christ, reconciling the world to himself. The reserved sacrament in the tabernacle reminds the worshipper of the sacrifice of Christ and also of the resurrection. Images of saints remind people that they worship a living God who sent Christ to redeem and forgive. The saints are great examples of that redemption in individuals. A place where private confessions are heard, either in a confessional or in a corner of the church, reminds people that God still forgives through Christ. The crucifix reminds people of the death of Christ, and the lectern is where the Bible is read aloud.

The Catechism reminds Catholics that Christian life begins at baptism:

> *The gathering of the People of God begins with Baptism; a church must have a place for the celebration of Baptism (baptistery) and for fostering remembrance of the baptismal promises (holy water font).* (Catechism of the Catholic Church 1185)

There is also a need for a place to offer forgiveness in the sacrament of confession (or penance), and the Catechism concludes this section with the idea that a church building is a place of prayer:

> *A church must also be a space that invites us to the recollection and silent prayer that extend and internalise the great prayer of the Eucharist.* (Catechism of the Catholic Church 1185)

Topic 1.4.2 The different internal features of a Catholic church

How the internal features of a Catholic church facilitate Catholic worship

The building is designed to be prayed in and is not a meeting hall. Catholics pray before the tabernacle, or before an image of Christ, the Virgin Mary or a saint. They light candles and say a prayer. They walk around, praying at the Stations of the Cross.

The lectern and the altar are especially important and are a focus for worship in a Catholic church during the Mass. The scriptures are read from the lectern, so the Word of God is proclaimed from there for Catholics. The homily teaches about the Gospel and readings of the day, and is usually delivered from the lectern.

The altar is the place of offering. Here, gifts of bread and wine are brought and thanksgiving prayers are offered as the Holy Spirit is called on the gifts to transform them in to the sacramental Body and Blood of Christ which are given out in Holy Communion. The altar is given special reverence as the place of this offering and is approached with care. The altar stands at the front of any Catholic church as the central feature and focal point.

A priest in a confessional listening to a confession.

Activities

1. What might the candles in the Gospel procession suggest?
2. Do you think the internal features of a Catholic church help you to worship God?

Practice questions

c. Choose two internal features of a Catholic church and explain why they are significant.

d. 'The tabernacle is the most important feature of a Catholic church.' Evaluate this statement considering arguments for and against. In your answer you should:
   - refer to Catholic points of view
   - refer to different Catholic or non-Catholic Christian points of view
   - reach a justified conclusion.

Summary

There are various internal features of Catholic churches that are symbolic and which facilitate worship especially the lectern, the altar, the crucifix and the tabernacle.

Section 4: Forms of expression and ways of life

Topic 1.4.3 The meaning and significance of sacred objects within Catholicism

Thinking points

In this topic you need to:
- think about the meaning and significance of certain sacred objects within Catholicism, including sacred vessels, sarcophagi and hunger cloths
- consider how these objects are used to express Catholic beliefs, including the belief that 'All the signs in the liturgical celebrations are related to Christ …' (Catechism 1161)
- evaluate the different ways these objects may be used in church and other settings.

Useful words

Paten – a silver or gold plate that has the priest's host
Ciborium – the silver or gold container for the hosts
Chalice – a silver or gold cup for the wine to be consecrated at the Mass
Stoup – a container on the wall to hold holy water

Activities

1. Look at the photo of the chalice and paten. Why are these important for Catholics?
2. Look at the photo of the water stoup. Why is holy water important for Catholics?

The meaning and significance of sacred vessels

All the signs in the liturgical celebrations are related to Christ …
(Catechism of the Catholic Church 1161)

Catholics have sacred objects expressing their belief that God cares about and expresses himself through the material world. These are used in prayer and worship and are always treated with respect because of this.

The vessels used for the bread and the wine are the most central sacred objects in use as it is believed that these hold the Body and Blood of Christ in sacramental form.

- The **paten** is a silver or gold plate which the priest's host (bread) is placed on. The priest's host is larger as it can be held up for the people to see, and broken up to share out at the altar.
- The **ciborium** is a silver or gold container that holds the people's hosts (bread).
- The **chalice** is a silver or gold cup to hold the wine and the water.

These are handled with care and washed and wiped clean after each Mass.

Holy water is ordinary water that has been blessed in the name of the Trinity. It is kept by the entrance in a **stoup** on the wall, and also is carried in silver or gold buckets so it can be sprinkled over people and objects. A smaller, hand-held sprinkler can also be used. Holy water is a reminder of baptism and the washing clean from sin through the cross of Christ. It is also a reminder of the promise of eternal life for Catholics because that gift is promised in baptism.

Christian Holy Communion; holding a gold chalice with wine and the host on a paten.

A stoup in a village church in Teotitlan del Valle, Oaxaca, Mexico.

Topic 1.4.3 The meaning and significance of sacred objects within Catholicism

Cloths and vestments

Cloths on the lectern and altar frontals are also used throughout the year, having certain colours for certain seasons. The priest's vestments (colourful robes) for the Mass will also reflect this colour scheme:

- White and gold are used for special celebrations such as Christmas and Easter, and on saints' days for saints who were not martyrs.
- Green is used for 'ordinary time', when there are no special celebrations.
- Red is used for events involving martyrs, recalling their shed blood, and also for Good Friday, and for the Day of Pentecost to symbolise the fire of the Holy Spirit.
- Purple is used for penitence or sorrow, during Advent or Lent.

For the Mass, a priest will wear a long white garment known as an **alb**, then a colourful **stole** like a scarf, and a **chasuble** over this. These reflect the old Roman style of dress centuries ago, but they became sacred and decorated with Christian symbols for use in church. Catholics feel that using these old-style ceremonial vestments keeps us linked with the early Church, where everything began.

The meaning and significance of sarcophagi

A **sarcophagus** is a stone container for bones. Some ancient churches and monasteries had sarcophagi within them containing the bones of significant people. They were often decorated with various symbols and scenes from the person's life (as in knights) or biblical scenes. Such objects are only found in older churches and monasteries.

The meaning and significance of hunger cloths

Traditionally, hunger cloths were widely used during Lent to depict scenes from the life of Christ and were hung over the rood screen in front of the altar. This was similar to covering holy images and statues with purple cloths during Lent, which is still often done today. They showed scenes from the Gospels reminding people of Christ's suffering and love for them. They have fallen into disuse in parts of the Catholic Church but are still made in some areas of the world.

A Christian–Roman sarcophagus lid from the fourth century CE showing the Virgin Mary with the baby Jesus in the manger.

Useful words

Alb – a long white garment worn by a priest during the Mass
Stole – a colourful scarf worn by the priest beneath the chasuble
Chasuble – a colourful garment worn by a priest over the alb and stole
Sarcophagus – a stone container for bones (plural: sarcophagi)

Hunger cloths

Contemporary hunger cloths tend to be themed towards justice and peace for people in the world, and are produced by charities such as CAFOD. This is part of a prayer suggested by CAFOD to bless a hunger cloth:

Leader: We bless this cloth and dedicate it to God's glory
In the name of the Father who cares for us
In the name of the Son who inspires us
In the name of the Spirit who walks with us

All: May it be a symbol
Both of our unity and our diversity
A reminder that to do God's work there are many ways
That in God's house there are many rooms
And a sign
Of welcome at God's banquet
Where a table is set for all peoples to share.
Amen.

Activities

1. Why do you think modern Catholic churches do not have sarcophagi?
2. Make a pie chart showing the liturgical colours of the Church's year and explain what they represent. Why do you think white and gold represent resurrection and incarnation?

Section 4: Forms of expression and ways of life

The ways sacred objects are used to express belief

The precious metals used for the communion vessels show that something special and sacred is going on. The colours used for the liturgical seasons reflect parts of the Christian story:

- the resurrection and the incarnation use white or gold to show something holy, special, glorious or joyful
- red is used for the martyrs, symbolising their shed blood
- purple is for sorrow, for penitence such as in Advent and Lent
- green is for creation and is used when there are no special festivals, as 'ordinary time'
- the special vestments for the priests show that they are performing a sacred role and are celebrating the mysteries of the Mass.

The divergent ways sacred objects may be used in the church and other settings

The chalice and paten are used to consecrate and distribute Holy Communion. Holy images, crosses and crucifixes will be used in private devotions and prayer, either in the church or at home. Holy water is used to bless oneself, and can be sprinkled at home too. **Votive candles** are lit to symbolise prayers being offered, as a candle is lit and placed on a stand. Hunger cloths, when used, remind Catholics of Christ's offering. Sarcophagi, although not actually used in worship as such, unless they contain the bones of saints, are respectful carvings where the bones of the dead are kept in old churches. If a saint lies within, prayers will be said beside the sarcophagus and candles lit.

Tapestries of the life of the Virgin Mary are brought out every December in the nave of Notre Dame Cathedral, Strasbourg, France.

Useful words

Votive candles – candles that are lit as a prayer is offered

Activities

1. What sort of things do Catholics light votive candles for?
2. Do you think priests should dress up in different, colourful ways during Mass or just wear ordinary clothes?

Summary

Sacred objects such as sacred vessels, sarcophagi and hunger cloths play an important role in Catholic worship, both in churches and in other settings. The choice of decoration, whether that be colour (with hunger cloths) or materials (sacred vessels), is highly symbolic.

Practice questions

c. Choose two sacred objects and explain how they are used to express Catholic beliefs.
d. 'Sacred objects help Catholics to understand their faith.' Evaluate this statement considering arguments for and against. In your answer you should:
   - refer to Catholic points of view
   - refer to different Catholic or non-Catholic Christian points of view
   - reach a justified conclusion.

Topic 1.4.4 The meaning and significance of paintings, frescos and drawings within Catholicism

Paintings, fresco, and drawings: meaning and significance

Catholicism uses images in many ways. It is a very visual faith. Paintings, frescos and drawings are visual aids that help people to remember aspects of their faith.

The Catechism explains that sacred art is more than skilful and beautiful. It must also be spiritual and have meaning. Its aim should be to help believers understand more about God and draw them into deeper worship of God:

> *Sacred art is true and beautiful when its form corresponds to its particular vocation: evoking and glorifying, in faith and adoration, the transcendent mystery of God.* (Catechism of the Catholic Church 2502)

Icon of Christ, St Catherine's Monastery, Sinai

The oldest holy images are paintings on wood known as icons, from the Greek for image.

The oldest known icon of Christ, from St Catherine's Monastery in Sinai, dates from the sixth, century CE. The two different facial expressions on either side may emphasise Christ's two natures as fully God and fully human.

Apart from this stylistic detail, it uses a very realistic portrait style, and early icons followed the Greek and Roman custom of realistic representation. Such portraits were painted for funerals and monuments.

Images of Christ like this one were made to honour him and to help the people to worship, recognising that Jesus was God made human. They were not just decorations, but precious images that were blessed and helped people to be close to God through them. For Catholics, God has entered creation and these images help worshippers to remember that.

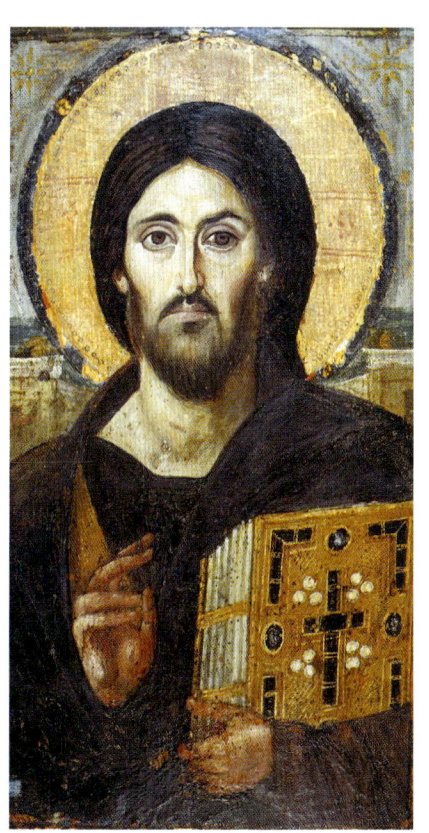

Thinking points

In this topic you need to:
- think about the meaning and significance of paintings, frescos and drawings within Catholicism, and be able to talk about these with reference to two specific pieces and Catechism 2502–2503
- consider the divergent ways paintings, frescos and drawings are used to express belief by the artist and those who observe the art
- consider the divergent ways paintings, frescos and drawings may be used in church and other settings.

The oldest known icon of Christ.

Section 4: Forms of expression and ways of life

> **Activity**
>
> Explain why artists put halos around saints' heads.

Later icons became more stylised with many symbolic features. In the West, realistic representation was more common and remains so today. Traditional icons are sometimes used in Catholic churches, but many other types of image are as well. In such icons, people can see holiness and the presence of God, symbolised by the light shining from their faces. Such holy images are sometimes referred to as 'windows into heaven' for they help people to draw close to God, to something invisible through something visible. These visual aids can move a person to pray and to worship. They are far more than decorations. People pray before them, using them as a focus to help their devotions.

Fresco by Giotto of St Francis of Assisi

A **fresco** is a method of painting on freshly laid plaster so that the colours fuse with the wall. This was a common form of church decoration in the West in the past. The works of Giotto from the thirteenth and fourteenth centuries CE in Italy show the early influence of the movement known as the Renaissance, where realistic representation was used in painting. Giotto painted a number of scenes from the life of St Francis of Assisi in the Basilica of St Francis in Assisi in Italy. St Francis was the son of a rich merchant in the twelfth and early thirteenth centuries. He gave away all his possessions and became a wandering **friar** with a group of brothers, the Franciscans. He was known for his great holiness and humility.

The Sermon to the Birds by Giotto (1266–1377).

The Giotto fresco shows St Francis preaching to the birds. St Francis would sometimes stop and do novel and surprising things to make a point. He had a great love for nature and animals, seeing birdsong as praising 'the Creator'. There are various stories of him calming and taming wild animals such as a wolf, and in the illustration the birds are calm and listening, coming close to him. This is part of a longer tradition of holy men and women having the calming presence of God within them, found in the Bible in the story of Daniel in the lions' den. St Francis also has a golden **halo** (only faintly shown because of the age of the fresco), which is often used in Christian artwork to show sanctity, the holy quality of his life and God's presence within him.

> **Useful words**
>
> **Fresco** – a painting rendered on fresh plaster
> **Friar** – a wandering preacher who had taken vows of poverty
> **Halo** – the golden circle around Christ's or a saint's head to show that they are holy

The artist shows St Francis with one hand lowered, open in welcome. The other hand is raised in blessing, with three fingers reflecting the Trinity.

St Francis did not care what other people thought (notice the nervous person watching him) and only cared about the praise of God and the love of God's creation above all else.

Looking at this fresco tells us that being a saint is refreshing but not easy. Saints stand out, upset social conventions and surprise people, and have to be ready for rejection and mockery in the name of Christ. It also reminds us of the key Christian belief in the incarnation: God became a human being. Hence, all creation is important and is blessed.

Topic 1.4.4 The meaning and significance of paintings, frescos and drawings within Catholicism

The Catechism reminds Catholics that sacred art used in churches should either back up or give greater insight into the truths of the Catholic faith:

For this reason bishops, personally or through delegates, should see to the promotion of sacred art, old and new, in all its forms, and with the same religious care, remove from the liturgy and from places of worship everything which is not in conformity with the truth of faith and the authentic beauty of sacred art. (Catechism of the Catholic Church 2503)

The divergent ways Catholic art is used to express belief by the artists and those who observe the art

For Catholics, holy images of Christ, the saints and the angels who are alive in the glory of heaven, praying for the world, are very important:

They truly signify Christ, who is glorified in them. They make manifest the 'cloud of witnesses' who continue to participate in the salvation of the world and to whom we are united, above all in sacramental celebrations. (Catechism of the Catholic Church 1161)

The Council of Nicaea in 325CE stated:

venerable and holy images of our Lord and God and Saviour, Jesus Christ, our inviolate Lady, the holy Mother of God, and the venerated angels, all the saints and the just, whether painted or made of mosaic, or any other suitable material, are to be exhibited in the holy churches of God, on sacred vessels and vestments, walls and panels, in houses and on streets.

Some people are uneasy with the use of imagery in Catholic churches. They fear this will cause idolatry, that people will worship the images rather than God, and goes against the warnings in the Ten Commandments such as:

You shall not make yourself a carved image or any likeness of anything in heaven above or on earth beneath or in the waters under the earth. (Exodus 20:4)

St John of Damascus defended the use of holy images in churches when he wrote *On Defence of Holy Images* in the eighth century CE:

I am emboldened to depict the invisible God, not as invisible, but as he became visible for our sake, by participation in flesh and blood. I do not depict the invisible divinity, but I depict God made visible in the flesh.

When you see the Bodiless become man for your sake, then you may depict the figure of a human form; when the Invisible becomes visible in the flesh, then you may depict the likeness of something seen.

So, as God became incarnate (taking human form) in Christ, then believers can make images of that human form. What people cannot and must not try to do is to make pictures of God as a transcendent spirit, beyond human forms. The author of the Ten Commandments was banning any pictures of God in spiritual form. St John of Damascus taught that followers should not worship holy images, but show them respect and honour for they depict holy things – Christ and the saints. Such images were allowed of physical people.

Activities

1. 'You should not have images in churches.' Why would someone say this, and what arguments would Catholics make to argue against it?
2. Study the fresco of St Francis preaching to the birds by Giotto on page 136. What three points can be made by this painting about Christian belief and discipleship?

Section 4: Forms of expression and ways of life

Catholics believe that holy images show human beings glorified, full of the Holy Spirit and shining with interior light:

Through their icons, it is man 'in the image of God', finally transfigured 'into his likeness', who is revealed to our faith.
(Catechism of the Catholic Church 1161)

The divergent ways paintings, frescos and drawings may be used in church and other settings

Sacred images and paintings are used not only for decoration but as an aid to worship. The images themselves are not worshipped, but what they represent. Catholicism is a very visual faith as the belief in the incarnation is so central, as is the belief that objects can provide a vehicle for the spirit.

Individual believers will typically have prayer cards with holy images and, at home, pictures or statues.

There are some images, however, that are extra special as they are believed to be miraculous in origin – not made by human hands.

Useful words
Shroud – burial cloth

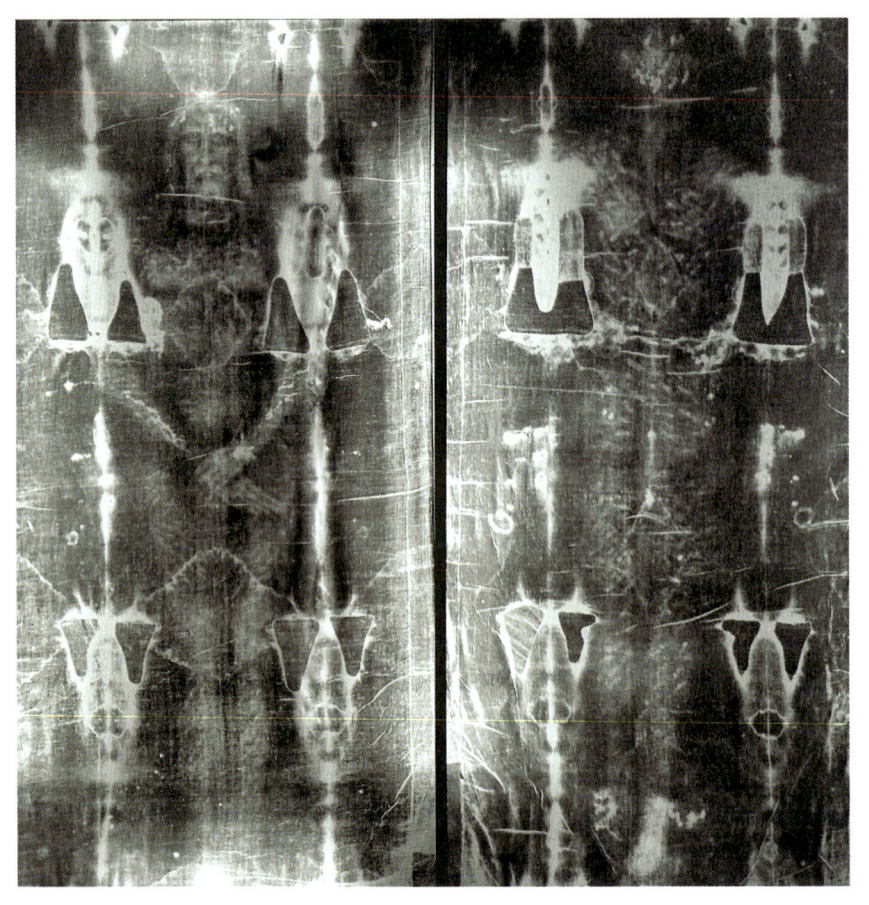

One example is the Shroud of Turin. This is a long burial sheet with the imprint of a crucified man on the front and the back. It is now kept in Turin Cathedral in Italy. It is believed by many to be the actual burial **shroud** of Jesus. The wounds are accurate from what is known of Roman crucifixion, including wounds that only Jesus would have had, such as marks from the crown of thorns and a wound to his side. There is no paint on the shroud and the image is on the surface of the fibres, as though scorched.

The Shroud's first documented appearance was in France in the fourteenth century, where it was owned by a descendant of a Crusader. It may have come from Constantinople, where many relics were kept, and from Edessa in Turkey before this. Edessa claimed to have a holy face of Christ, 'made without human hands' – a miraculous image. Pollen samples taken from the cloth indicate that it could only have come from Turkey and the Holy Land. All of this suggests that it could well be the burial cloth of Jesus. However, radiocarbon dating in the 1980s suggested the fabric was from the Middle Ages. The debate is still open as the samples used had been handled frequently and were corrupted.

Shroud of Turin.

Topic 1.4.4 The meaning and significance of paintings, frescos and drawings within Catholicism

Our Lady of Guadalupe (the Virgin Mary) is another example. This dates from 1531, when a local farmer, Juan Diego, was walking up the Tepayac Hill in Mexico. He saw what he described as a beautiful lady, in a ball of light, as bright as the sun. She asked that a church be built there in her honour. She revealed that she was the Virgin Mary and called herself 'Coatallope', meaning 'treader on snakes' in the local dialect. It is likely that Guadalupe is the Spanish mistranslation of this word. At first, the bishop did not believe him, but Juan returned and found roses growing on the hill which he was instructed to take back to the bishop. When he unfurled his tunic, known as a **tilma**, made of cactus fibres, the image of the Virgin Mary was revealed. He claimed to know nothing of this. Within six years, 6 million Aztecs were converted to Catholicism, largely as a direct result of this image, in a rapid spread of faith that contributed to many people turning from pagan sacrifice far faster than the Spanish authorities had ever dared to hope.

In 1977, infrared photography was used on the image and it revealed no pigment and no lines drawn as an outline. The image seems to be just on the surface and has not penetrated the fibres. Tilmas do not normally last long as they decay. This one is intact after centuries. Some also claim that microscopic analysis shows images of people in the eye of the Virgin Mary, as though these were snapshots of the first people to see the image.

Our Lady of Guadalupe.

Useful words

Tilma – simple tunic made of cactus fibres worn by ancient Mexicans

Activities

1. What do you think about the Shroud of Turin?
2. Why do you think the image of Our Lady of Guadalupe converted so many people?

Practice questions

c. Choose a specific painting and explain two ways in which it is used to express belief by the artist.
d. 'Paintings help Catholics to understand their relationship with God.' Evaluate this statement considering arguments for and against. In your answer you should:
   - refer to Catholic points of view
   - refer to different Catholic or non-religious points of view
   - reach a justified conclusion.

Summary

Paintings, frescos and drawings have important symbolic importance within Catholicism, and are often used to express wider beliefs in terms of their individual elements, for example the use of a halo to symbolise blessedness, or in their wider theme, such as the incarnation.

Section 4: Forms of expression and ways of life

Topic 1.4.5 The meaning and significance of sculptures and statues

Thinking points

In this topic you need to:
- think about the meaning and significance of sculpture and statues, and the way they are used to express belief by the artist and those who observe the art
- consider the way these are used to express belief
- evaluate how sculptures and statues may be used in church and other settings.

Sculptures and statues: meaning and significance

Sacred statues

The Catechism explains that human art expresses humans' relationship with God and that creativity is a reflection of God's gifts and power given to human beings:

> Created 'in the image of God', man also expresses the truth of his relationship with God the Creator by the beauty of his artistic works. Indeed, art is a distinctively human form of expression … To the extent that it is inspired by truth and love of beings, art bears a certain likeness to God's activity in what he has created. (Catechism of the Catholic Church 2501)

While two-dimensional paintings were widely used in the Eastern churches, statues began to be made in the West towards the end of the first millennium CE. Any Catholic church will have a number of these. There will usually be one of the **Sacred Heart** of Jesus and one of the Blessed Virgin Mary, as well as other saints.

The Sacred Heart is based on the visions of St Margaret Mary Alacoque in seventeenth-century France. The visions were a new form of a much older devotion to the wound in Jesus' side. She saw the heart of Jesus exposed, surrounded by the crown of thorns and with a fire burning within it. The thorns are believed by Catholics to refer to the Passion of Christ and the fire to refer to his eternal love. Her visions were recognised as authentic by the Church and the image of the Sacred Heart became a popular devotion.

Useful words

Sacred Heart – an image where the heart of Jesus is surrounded by thorns with a flame burning on top of it

A statue of Our Lady of Walsingham, Little Walsingham, Norfolk.

The Sacred Heart of Jesus, Castaño del Robledo, province of Huelva, Spain.

Topic 1.4.5 The meaning and significance of sculptures and statues

Some statues of the Blessed Virgin Mary are based on visions of the Virgin Mary appearing (**apparitions**), such as Our Lady of Walsingham and Our Lady of Lourdes. The Walsingham vision dates from 1061 in Norfolk, and Lourdes from the nineteenth century in France.

Our Lady of Walsingham appears in the dress of an Anglo-Saxon queen and the budding lily she holds represents the ancestry of Jesus as the Messiah. Mary points to Christ, a detail that is often present in images of the Blessed Virgin. She is a witness to her son, who is more important than her.

In Lourdes, the Virgin Mary appeared to an ordinary girl, Bernadette. The Virgin Mary, Our Lady of Lourdes, asked for pilgrims to come to the spring of water that had been uncovered at her feet to be healed. Both shrines have recounted many stories and claims of answered prayer and healings, with plaques placed along the walls giving thanks for these.

Statues are respected and honoured for what they represent, just like icons and other paintings. They are not worshipped but they will be blessed in the name of the Trinity and can become a focus for prayer.

The seal of Walsingham Priory.

Sacred sculptures

Many statues are simple works and lay no claim to be great art. However, the Catholic world has a number of impressive sculptures. Michelangelo's *Pieta* was made in 1498–9 and rests in the **Basilica** of St Peter in Rome. *Pieta*, from an Italian word meaning sorrow or lamentation, shows the dead Christ held in Mary's arms. Michelangelo's sculpture is a pyramid shape getting wider as it reaches the rock of Golgotha that Mary sits on. It is a loving and moving scene of a mother cradling her dead son as he is taken down from the cross. Christ's face is serene and resigned, rather than wracked with pain. He is shown as the saviour who gives himself up willingly. Mary is young, too young to be the mother of the child she holds. This might be a sign of her holiness and the fact that there is an irony in all-Christian devotion involving her; she is her son's daughter as much as he is her son. Christ was her creator and redeemer.

> **Useful words**
>
> **Apparitions** – visions of the Virgin Mary, an angel or a saint
> *Pieta* – lamentation, a scene of Mary holding the dead Christ
> **Basilica** – an important church building
> **Keys of the kingdom** – the authority Catholics believe that St Peter (and then the popes) received from Christ

A large bronze sculpture of St Peter stands in St Peter's Basilica in Rome. This is attributed to the sculptor Anolfo di Combio, who lived in the thirteenth and early fourteenth centuries. St Peter's Basilica is built on the site of an earlier basilica dedicated to the saint from the time of the Emperor Constantine, built in the fourth century CE. This was erected over what is believed to be the burial site of St Peter, the disciple of Jesus. Bones believed to be those of the saint have been found in a chamber marked with Christian inscriptions beneath the high altar.

The bronze sculpture shows St Peter holding his hand up in blessing while the other hand clutches the **keys of the kingdom** of heaven. Jesus told St Peter that he would have such keys:

Statue of St Peter in the Vatican.

Pieta – the statue of Mary holding the body of Jesus by Michelangelo.

141

Section 4: Forms of expression and ways of life

Activities

1. Study the statues of Our Lady of Walsingham and the *Pieta*. What do they signify about Christ and his mother?
2. Study the statues of Our Lady of Walsingham and the *Pieta*. Each has a different way of suggesting that Christ is more important than the Blessed Virgin Mary in these. Explain how this works.
3. Why are bronze statues of St Peter often found in Catholic churches?
4. Do you think Christmas cribs help Catholics understand and celebrate Christmas?

I will give you the keys of the kingdom of Heaven: whatever you bind on earth will be bound in heaven; whatever you loose on earth will be loosed in heaven. (Matthew 16:19)

The popes believe that they are the successors of St Peter who look after the Church on earth. Pilgrims often touch the foot of St Peter and kiss it in devotion and respect.

The divergent ways sculptures and statues are used to express belief by the artist and those who observe the art

Sculptures and statues are expressions of the Catholic faith. These include faith in the incarnation of God in Christ, of the blessing given to the Virgin Mary and the grace of the Holy Spirit in the saints. Visual images are also useful in spreading and teaching the faith, such as St Augustine of Canterbury carrying a crucifix before him when he landed among the Saxons in Kent in the early seventh century CE, or when St Francis of Assisi set up the first Christmas crib to educate the illiterate villagers about the Christmas story.

How sculptures and statues may be used in church and other settings

Scenes from the life of Christ may be reproduced for reflection and quiet prayer. Human beings need visual aids and symbols to help them with this, as transcendent, spiritual, abstract things are difficult to think about on their own. Holy images, sculpted or painted, are used primarily for personal prayer and to teach and remind the faithful of certain important doctrines and also of important saints. They can be used for evangelisation and missionary work, but this is a secondary function.

Practice questions

c. Choose a specific sculpture or statue and explain two ways in which it is used to express belief by those who view the art.

d. 'Statues and sculptures help Catholics to understand their faith better.' Evaluate this statement considering arguments for and against. In your answer you should:
- refer to Catholic points of view
- refer to different Catholic or non-religious points of view
- reach a justified conclusion.

Summary

In a similar way to paintings, sculpture and statues provide an important expression of belief for Catholics. They are also useful in spreading and teaching the faith, for example about the saints, and as a tool for personal prayer.

Topic 1.4.6 The purpose and use of symbolism and imagery in religious art

Religious art: the purpose and use of symbolism and imagery

The cross

The cross can be a simple sign, a reminder that Jesus died on the cross. It can also speak of divine love and forgiveness. It moves beyond a mere sign to work as a symbol. It appears regularly in religious art. Believers make the sign of the cross as they start to pray, the priest makes it over them as he blesses them, and a cross will be present clearly in every Catholic church.

The crucifix

The crucifix is a representation of Jesus on the cross which appears regularly in religious art. It is a visual aid reminding people of the Passion of Christ, symbolic of his death for the sins of the world. This is at the front of a church, over the altar, as a focus of devotion and a reminder of Christ's sacrifice. Individuals might have one on a wall at home or wear one around their neck, as a reminder of Christ's sacrifice.

The fish

A fish is used to symbolise Christianity as fish frequently featured in the Gospels because some of the first disciples were fishermen. Jesus often took fish and blessed them, sharing them out. He told his disciples that he would make them 'fishers of men' (Mark 1:18). The Greek word for fish, *Ichthus*, was a secret code for the early Christians as the word is formed from the first letters of 'Jesus Christ, Son of God, Saviour' in Greek, *'Iesus Christos, Theos Uios Soter'*. Here, a secret sign works also as a symbol, pointing to deeper truths of Christ as saviour.

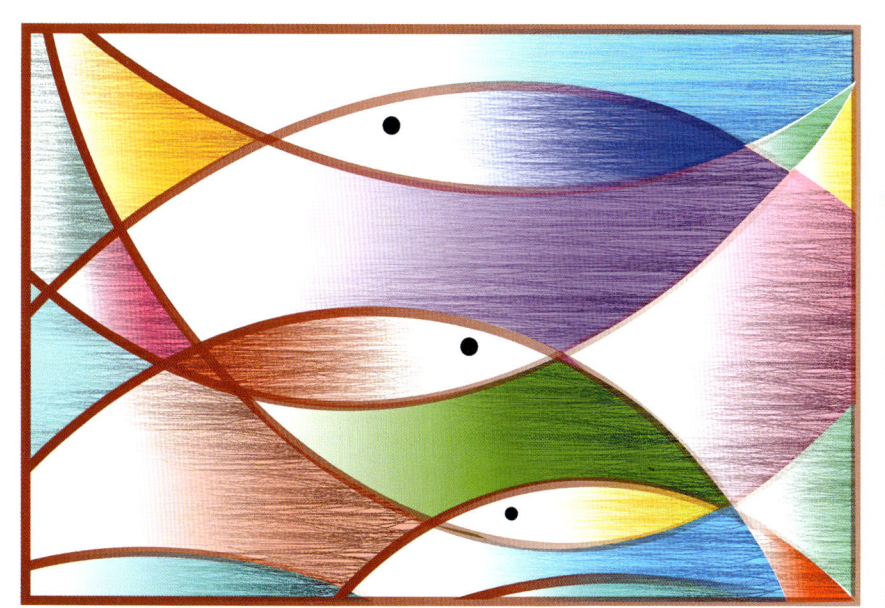

> **Thinking points**
>
> In this topic you need to:
> - think about the purpose and use of symbolism and imagery in religious art
> - consider the symbols of the cross, crucifix, fish, Chi Rho, eagle, **alpha and omega**, and the symbols of the four evangelists
> - evaluate the way the symbolism is used to express belief, and be able to explain and evaluate the use of symbolism in religious art
> - consider how these symbols may be used in church and other settings.

> **Useful words**
>
> **Alpha and omega** – the first and the last, the start and end of the Greek alphabet
> *Ichthus* – Greek for fish; an early Christian symbol

A modern, digital painting of symbolic fishes in a pattern background.

> **Activity**
>
> Explain the difference between a sign and a symbol, giving an example of each.

Section 4: Forms of expression and ways of life

> **Useful words**
> **Chi-Rho** – a sign made up of the first two letters for Christ in Greek
> **Evangelist** – a Gospel writer

The Chi Rho, symbolising the victory of the resurrection.

A painting of a dove in St Etienne du Mont Church, Paris, France.

An eagle lectern at St Mary Redcliffe Church, Bristol.

The Chi Rho

The **Chi-Rho** symbol is sometimes found in churches. This is an example of a sign that can only suggest one thing. It is a design made from the first two letters of Christ in Greek. It would have been formed as a secret sign in the days when Christians were persecuted in ancient Rome. Constantine, who later became emperor, claimed he had a vision of a Chi Rho as he advanced on Rome in the early fourth century CE. He was told, 'In this sign, conquer.' This symbol is not used in worship and devotion today but only in religious decoration in churches.

The dove

The dove is often used in religious art to symbolise the Holy Spirit, following on from the story of Noah, when a dove returns bearing an olive branch to show that the floods have stopped. At Jesus' baptism, the spirit comes down on him like a dove.

> *The Spirit comes down and remains in the purified hearts of the baptised. (Catechism of the Catholic Church 701)*

The eagle

Eagles are symbols in the scripture of the power and speed of God's message. A passage in Isaiah states:

> *… but those who wait for the Lord shall renew their strength, they shall mount up with wings like eagles, they shall run and not be weary, they shall walk and not faint. (Isaiah 40:31)*

Sometimes churches have had carvings or brass sculptures of an eagle on the lectern, although this is not common in modern buildings.

Alpha and omega

Jesus is said to be the 'Alpha and the Omega'. These are the first and the last letters of the Greek alphabet. Jesus is symbolically depicted as the first and the last:

> *Do not be afraid; it is I, the First and the Last; I am the Living One. I was dead and look – I am alive for ever and ever … (Revelation 1:18)*

The alpha and the omega may appear on church vestments and hangings, but are always on the Paschal or Easter candle, which is lit on Holy Saturday in the evening. The Vigil Mass is the first Mass of the resurrection.

The four evangelists

The four **evangelists** are sometimes symbolised in religious art as winged creatures, carrying the Gospel to the four corners of the earth: Matthew as a winged man, Mark as a winged lion, Luke as a winged ox and John as an eagle. The wings suggest that they are messengers, spreading their word across the globe. There is also a suggestion of being godly, called by heaven for the task, in a similar way to the angels:

- Winged man: Matthew's Gospel presents the birth stories and family tree of Jesus, stressing the incarnation and Jesus as a human being – a man. The wings on him, and all the others, suggest that he is a messenger spreading the Gospel.

- Winged lion: Mark's Gospel shows a courageous, miracle-working figure of Jesus who rises again to heaven, strong and victorious.

Topic 1.4.6 The purpose and use of symbolism and imagery in religious art

- Winged ox: Luke's Gospel stresses the sacrifice of Jesus, and oxen were often offered as sacrifices in the ancient world.
- The eagle: John's Gospel speaks more of the heavenly aspect of Jesus as the Word of God made man. The eagle soars high, suggesting divinity.

How religious symbolism is used to express belief

The mural of the resurrection by Piero della Francesca, a fifteenth-century artist, shows the mystery of the risen Christ. For believers this is a mystery beyond words and human comprehension, and hence the need to use symbolism.

Symbols point beyond themselves, suggesting ideas and feelings. A symbol is different from a sign; a sign has one meaning, while a symbol can mean different things all at the same time. Symbols, therefore, represent more than the thing they depict, suggesting a number of ideas and feelings. Both signs and symbols are used in Catholic worship. They communicate core beliefs, such as the cross pointing to Jesus dying to save the world, or the Easter candle suggesting the light and life of resurrection. The fish and the Chi Rho are signs that suggest Christ. The alpha and the omega symbolise the beginning and the end, the eternal nature of God and Christ. The winged creatures symbolise aspects of the different Gospels and how they present Christ.

Activities

1. Can you think of any symbols not referred to here which are used in Catholic churches?
2. What sort of symbol would you give yourself?
3. Look at the fresco of the resurrection. What symbols are used in this fresco?

'The Resurrection of Christ', a fresco from about 1462, by Piero della Francesca.

Section 4: Forms of expression and ways of life

The divergent ways religious symbolism may be used in church and other settings

Human beings use pictures and symbols to express ideas and feelings. We keep photos and paintings of people special to us, loved ones, family members. These are extra special if we are separated for a length of time, and especially if they have died. They are precious mementos and reminders. People might take them out, sit before them, touch them and kiss them. The pictures themselves are not the person and it is not the pictures themselves that are being loved; it is what they represent.

Symbols convey mystery and the Catholic faith celebrates the holy mysteries, meeting God through sacraments and material things. Fire, water, oil, bread and wine convey the divine, symbolising holiness, life, the Body and the Blood of Christ. Light speaks of God's mystery and presence in flickering candles. Even human hands can convey blessing.

The laying on of hands suggests the power and presence of the Holy Spirit coming on people or on the bread and wine at the consecration. This practice was taken from Jesus himself, who often laid a hand on people to heal them, and from the practice of the apostles when blessing, healing and ordaining. Touch is so important for human beings, to feel loved, wanted, included. For Catholics, God has touched the world, as it were, in Christ, rather than being separate from it.

A priest conducts a healing Mass at a Catholic Church in New York, USA.

Practice questions

c Choose a Christian symbol and explain two reasons why it is important for Catholics. In your answer you must refer to a source of wisdom and authority.

d 'Catholic symbols only have meaning for Catholics.' Evaluate this statement considering arguments for and against. In your answer you should:
- refer to Catholic points of view
- refer to different Catholic or non-Catholic Christian points of view
- reach a justified conclusion.

Summary

There are a number of important symbols in the Catholic faith that worshippers will see often in religious artwork and adorning churches and shrines. The key ones are the cross, crucifix, fish, Chi Rho, dove, eagle, alpha and omega, and symbols of the four evangelists.

Topic 1.4.7 The meaning and significance of drama: mystery plays and passion plays

The meaning and significance of mystery plays

The Catechism teaches that God has gradually revealed himself to the world through his actions. This has clear parallels with drama, which is about revealing mysteries and inspiring its audience.

In prayer, the faithful God's initiative of love always comes first; our step is always a response. As God gradually reveals himself and reveals man to himself, prayer appears as a ... call, a ... drama. Through words and actions, this drama engages the heart. It unfolds throughout the whole history of salvation. (Catechism of the Catholic Church 2567)

In fact, the story of Christ is so 'dramatic' that it has inspired a whole type of play, that of the medieval **mystery play**.

The Bible is full of action and these inspired the medieval mystery plays. The big story of the Bible as a whole, starting with the creation, the fall of the devil, the flood and so on, and ending with the Gospels and the death and resurrection of Christ, was staged by local groups of players. These were known as mystery plays, telling the mystery of human redemption. They would be performed at festivals on the street, and especially at Easter. These were mainly popular in the Middle Ages among Catholics who could not read and write, and who relied on visual interpretations to find out about the Bible stories and the great mysteries of their faith.

Groups of traders would compete for the noisiest, most colourful play and one of the most popular to perform was the **Harrowing of Hell**, where the resurrected Christ frees people from the devils in hell, and pots and pans and instruments would bang and hoot.

A medieval mystery play in a Frankish town in the thirteenth century.

> **Thinking points**
>
> In this topic you need to:
> - think about the meaning and significance of drama, including mystery and passion plays
> - consider the way in which drama is used to express belief, and how drama may be used in the church and other settings.

> **Useful words**
>
> **Mystery play** – a medieval play about the great stories of the Bible
>
> **Harrowing of Hell** – a medieval play about the risen Christ freeing people from hell

> **Activity**
>
> Why do you think mystery plays were so popular in the Middle Ages?

Section 4: Forms of expression and ways of life

This mystery play told people about Christ's resurrection and gave hope not only of life after death, but of forgiveness after people died if people responded to God's love.

The meaning and significance of passion plays

A **passion play** tells the story of Jesus' journey to the cross, his '**passion**'. Early passion plays grew out of the Easter liturgy in churches and these went out into the streets and market places with local people taking the roles.

Passion plays are still popular in different parts of the world, such as in Latin America and the Philippines. In Europe they are more seldom performed, but there are good examples. In 1634 in Oberammergau in Germany a vow was made that a passion play would be held every ten years if the village was spared from the bubonic plague. The vow was kept and this has been followed at the start of each decade. It was also performed in 1934 and 1984, the 300th and the 350th anniversaries. Nearly half the villagers took part in 2010, about 2000 people.

In England, an annual play of the entire life of Christ takes place on the estate at Wintershall in Surrey. After the enactment of the feeding of the 5000 from the Gospels there is an interval as people stop for lunch. In Brighton there is Soul by the Sea, a passion play performed on Easter

'The Harrowing of Hell', about 1190.

Useful words

Passion plays – plays retelling the story of the passion and resurrection
Passion – the journey of Jesus to the cross

During the Good Friday Mass at St Timothy's Catholic Church, California, USA, parishioners participate in the Solemn Veneration of the Cross.

Topic 1.4.7 The meaning and significance of drama: mystery plays and passion plays

Oberammergau Passion Play, Germany.

Activity
Do you think passion plays are a good way of explaining the mysteries of salvation to people?

Sunday which moves venue, on the beach or in the town. A large number of Coptic Christians from Egypt and Sudan live in the town (the Coptic Christians are part of the Eastern Churches) and many help. One year Mary was played by a Coptic woman and she sang a traditional Good Friday lament when Christ was taken down from the cross, with a haunting and moving effect.

The passion plays all retell the story of Christ's journey to the cross and are an act of devotion for both performers and viewers. They convey the message of salvation and forgiveness.

The way drama is used to express belief

The Mass has dramatic features; colourful vestments, sacred gestures, objects and symbols. At Easter these multiply with a re-enactment of the passion and the Easter story. Just as human beings need visual aids and symbols, so too we move and express ourselves in our actions. Catholic worship involves standing, kneeling, raised hands, the sign of the cross, processions and walking up to receive communion. Special acted-out plays telling part of the Bible story or the Gospel story are an extension of this, proclaiming their message through drama.

The divergent ways drama may be used in church and other settings

Each Mass is a drama in a way, and the retelling and memorial of Christ's sacrifice and Last Supper in the Eucharistic prayer are like something worshippers see on the stage in front of them. This multiplies in the Easter liturgy. The Gospel of the Passion is broken down into many voices for the different characters. At the **veneration of the cross**, a cross is displayed and people file up to kiss it. Feet are washed on Holy Thursday. At most Masses bells are rung. All of these actions and physical symbols remind people of their belief in the incarnation of God in Christ.

At the Easter Vigil on Holy Saturday, the Paschal candle is lit from the new fire of Easter. This represents the light of the resurrected Christ and it is brought into the darkened church. It has symbols of Christ, a cross and the alpha and the omega on it.

Useful words
Veneration of the cross – kissing and honouring a cross on Good Friday

Section 4: Forms of expression and ways of life

First communion: a priest lighting the Paschal candle in St Bernard's Church, Sussex.

All of these things are dramatic actions, but drama sketches as such would now be rarely used in the church itself. They would take place outside, on the street or at a separate venue. While the faith can be expressed through plays, it is wrong to see drama as just being about this. Rituals, symbolic actions and costume are used at the altar.

Activity

Why do you think the Mass is sometimes referred to as 'the drama of the Mass'?

Practice questions

c Explain two ways in which drama expresses Catholic beliefs. In your answer you must refer to a source of wisdom and authority.

d 'Mystery plays are just a mystery to most people.' Evaluate this statement considering arguments for and against. In your answer you should:
- refer to Catholic points of view
- refer to different Catholic or non-Catholic Christian points of view
- reach a justified conclusion.

Summary

As with art, drama can also be used to symbolise Catholic belief, as well as to spread the word of Christ. Key formats are the mystery and passion plays, while the Mass can also be seen as a dramatic re-enactment of the story of Christ and the salvation of mankind.

Topic 1.4.8 The nature and use of traditional and contemporary styles of music in worship

The nature and use of traditional and contemporary styles of music in worship

Hymns

Hymns are a collection of verses that tell a story. They present beliefs, sentiments and experiences. Early Christian hymns had few verses, capturing a central belief such as:

> Sleeper, awake!
> Rise from the dead,
> And Christ will shine his light upon you. *(Ephesians 5:14)*

Medieval hymns were longer, such as those praising Christ's presence in the Mass as in Tantum Ergo, or the Stabat Mater, composed to accompany the Stations of the Cross.

Victorian hymns flourished, such as John Newton's 'Amazing Grace'. Modern hymns are still composed, such as those by Catholic composer Bernadette Farrell with numbers such as 'Christ Be Our Light'.

Plainchant

The early Christians developed a tradition of unaccompanied singing and chanting from the worship in Jewish synagogues throughout the Roman Empire. Chants were sung in parish Masses and in monasteries in both the East and West. In the West, the style known as **plainchant** developed. The use of the human voice reflects Catholic belief and awe in God, and emphasises the redemption of human beings.

Thinking points

In this topic you need to:
- think about the nature and use of traditional and contemporary styles of music in worship, with reference to Catechism 2641, including hymns, plainchant, Psalms and worship songs
- consider the way different music is used to express belief
- evaluate the divergent ways music may be used in church (including the Mass) and other settings.

Useful words

Plainchant – a style of unaccompanied singing for monastic offices or the Mass

Nuns singing during the World Mission Week in Rio de Janeiro, Brazil.

Part of Missa De Angelis.

Section 4: Forms of expression and ways of life

Psalms

The Psalms are songs of praise and lament in the Old Testament, many of which were probably composed by King David. Eastern cultures would sing in joy and also sorrow, expressing the feelings of the community together. King David was a harpist, and the Psalms were probably composed not only for voices but also for instruments. Judaism used musical instruments in the worship of the ancient Temple in Jerusalem, before it was destroyed in 70CE. For example, Psalm 150 mentions trumpets, harps, lyres, tambourines, strings, pipes, cymbals and dancing. The use of instruments became more common in the West, but they were hardly used in the early Church. The ancient Ethiopian Orthodox Church, one of the Eastern Churches, uses stringed instruments and the **sistrum**, a hand-held collection of small cymbals. Clergy have prayer staffs to beat rhythm. There can also be drums and wooden flutes. The Ethiopian Church has always drawn a great deal of influence from the worship of the old Jerusalem Temple.

The Western, Catholic Church tended to use the human voice only, or mainly, until recent years when a variety of instruments have also been sued. Although this can be seen as 'modern', what has been said about the Old Testament, and groups such as the Ethiopian Christians, reminds us that using various instruments in worship is also very ancient.

The early Church used the Psalms in their worship, and monasteries still gather daily at different times to sing through them.

Useful words
Sistrum – Ethiopian musical instrument with small cymbals
Worship song – a short, modern song with one or two verses

Sistrum rattles used during the Ethiopian Orthodox Timkat Epiphany festival, Lalibela, Ethiopia.

Worship songs

A **worship song** is a modern religious song shorter than a hymn. It will have only one or two verses. It will put a Bible verse to music or tell a simple message about the love of God or forgiveness in Christ. The use of pipe organs in churches spread in the West in the medieval period, with woodwind and strings also often found in parishes. In recent years, a range of musical instruments have been used during Mass, including percussion, string and wind instruments such as guitars, flutes, tambourines and hand drums. Masses using modern folk-style music flourished in the latter part of the twentieth century, using a collection of Protestant modern worship

Activities

1. Why do you think many Catholic churches still use plainchant?
2. Listen to examples of Eastern and Western chant, plainchant, Ethiopian church music with instruments, modern praise songs and adoration songs. Search online, on YouTube, iTunes or on CDs. In English songs, look for material that reflects the song of creation and also the song of redemption. Write out some examples.

Topic 1.4.8 The nature and use of traditional and contemporary styles of music in worship

songs or those of the **ecumenical** community of Taizé in France with its short chants, some in Latin. Taizé has Catholics and Protestants living together.

Modern worship songs can be lively praise songs, sometimes with dance moves or actions; or gentle, calm adoration songs which try to lead into times of profound stillness. These can be repeated like simple mantras or chants to calm the mind and to focus on key beliefs of the Gospel, such as:

The Lord is my light, my light and salvation.
In him I trust, in him I trust.
Or;
'O Christe, Domine Jesu' ('O Lord Jesus Christ').

Useful words

Ecumenical – different types of Christians meeting together

Taizé Community: Church of the Reconciliation Saturday evening prayers.

Youth 2000 is a Catholic youth movement that sings worship songs. These include upbeat praise songs and gentle, meditative songs accompanying traditional Catholic devotions such as the Rosary or adoration of the Blessed Sacrament.

Putting hymns and songs into the Mass is a relatively modern custom since the liturgy of the Mass is designed to be complete in itself either said or with parts of the prayers and responses sung.

The way different music is used to express belief

There are two basic songs that are sung in the Bible: the song of creation and the song of redemption. The Old Testament has many Psalms that praise the glory of the Creator and echo the song of the angels in heaven:

Holy, holy is Yahweh Sabaoth.
His glory fills the whole earth. (Isaiah 6:1)

Then there is the new song of the Lamb of God, the Saviour:

Worthy is the Lamb that that was sacrificed
to receive power, riches, wisdom,
strength, honour, glory and blessing. (Revelation 5:12)

The songs of the Church echo both these themes, whether in plainchant for human voices alone, or using wind and string instruments, or organs and keyboards. Some music is designed to be background music and listened to by the congregation, and some to be joined in with as communal singing. Every song, whatever style it has, will express a belief about God, Christ, the Church or the sacraments.

Activities

1. What are the song of creation and the song of redemption?
2. Do you think modern music helps to make worship more relevant?

Section 4: Forms of expression and ways of life

Activity

Why might someone feel it is inappropriate to have modern songs and instruments in the Mass? Maybe they feel that only things like plainchant or the organ should be used. How might you answer them?

Divergent ways in which music may be used in church (including the Mass) and other settings

The Catholic Church believes that music and song is an appropriate response to the wonder of God's love seen in the coming of Christ. This idea is summed up in Catechism 2641, which talks about the early Christians composing hymns and canticles (songs) about the work of Christ and praises of God (doxology) for the wonderful salvation brought about by Christ.

In the newness of the Spirit, they also composed hymns and canticles in the light of the unheard-of event that God accomplished in his Son: his Incarnation, his death, which conquered death, his Resurrection, and Ascension to the right hand of the Father. Doxology, the praise of God, arises from this 'marvellous work' of the whole economy of salvation. (Catechism of the Catholic Church 2641)

Useful words

Doxology – the praise of God in words, music or song

God's saving work causes praise to rise in human beings, and songs and music to be played. **Doxology** is the praise of God, and it is birthed in awe and gratitude. The liturgy of the Mass was always designed to have sung parts, and important points are often sung today, such as the Gloria, the Psalm, the Gospel acclamation and parts of the Eucharistic prayer, particularly where the people join in the acclamations and the final 'Amen'. Hymns and songs were later additions and are not part of the liturgy. Plainchant and simple, gentle worship songs and chants like those from Taizé are calming and express the sense of adoration. This sort of quiet, often repetitive music is used for more meditative worship. Some worshippers find it helpful to play such chants as they sit down quietly to pray and meditate at home.

More rousing, loud music, particularly with the organ, or cymbals and trumpets, expresses celebration and joy, such as the rousing Easter hymn 'Thine be the Glory Risen, Conquering Son'. Music will open the Mass as the priest and servers enter, and a simple chant is often sung at the Gospel reading, such as 'Alleluia, Alleluia'. A hymn or worship song can be sung as the bread and the wine are brought to the altar. Parts of the Eucharistic prayer might be chanted and a quiet piece sung after communion. A more lively, rousing piece might end the Mass. Music will express thanksgiving and praise.

Summary

Hymns, plainchant, psalms and worship songs are all types of music familiar to Catholics, and play an important part in both traditional and contemporary worship. Music is used in Church as part of the Mass, and can also have an important role to play as a form of prayer.

Practice questions

c Explain two ways in which music is used to express belief. In your answer you must refer to a source of wisdom and authority.

d 'All music used in Catholic churches should be modern and lively.' Evaluate this statement considering arguments for and against. In your answer you should:
- refer to Catholic points of view
- refer to different Catholic or non-Catholic Christian points of view
- reach a justified conclusion.

How to answer questions

a) Outline three features found in a Catholic church. [3]

Three features would be an altar to celebrate the Mass, a tabernacle to contain and preserve the consecrated hosts, and a font to contain the water for baptism.

A high mark answer because three features found in a Catholic church are clearly outlined.

b) Explain two ways hunger cloths are used by Catholics. [4]

Hunger cloths are used to help children understand the Bible better as they provide simple images of Bible stories. Another way of using hunger cloths is to remind Catholics of Jesus' suffering in the desert as some contain images of self-denial to mark the season of Lent.

A high mark answer because two correct ways of using hunger cloths are clearly explained.

c) Explain two ways music can make worship more relevant to the life of a Catholic. In your answer you must refer to a source of wisdom and authority. [5]

Music can lift the soul and therefore help Catholics to express the joy and love of God necessary for true worship of God, as explained in the Catechism of the Catholic Church 2641(1). Another reason is that children enjoy music and so appropriate age-related music will help them to understand some of the Church's teachings, enabling them to worship from a young age, and Jesus said, ' let the little children come to me' (Matthew 19:14).

A high mark answer because two correct reasons are given and each reason is developed with a reference to the Bible's teaching and the Catechism, which are both sources of authority for Catholics.

d) 'Paintings help a Catholic understand their relationship with God.' Evaluate this statement considering arguments for and against. In your response you should:
- refer to Catholic Christian points of view
- refer to different Christian points of view
- reach a justified conclusion. [12 marks + 3 spelling, punctuation and grammar (SPaG) marks]

Many Catholics would agree with this statement because most Catholic churches have Stations of the Cross which show the final hours of Jesus' life in graphic form, helping Catholics to be grateful for the sacrifice he made to atone for sins. Paintings in churches portray Bible stories such as the baptism of Jesus which help Catholics to understand God the Holy Trinity. The Catechism of the Catholic Church teaches that art which reflects the glory of God draws the worshipper to adoration and prayer.

Some Catholics might disagree because most religious paintings show God as male, which could put off some Catholic women who could find that paintings undermine their relationship with God. Some Christians believe that any image of God lessens his greatness, which could weaken a Christian's sense of awe before God. Many paintings in churches are medieval, portraying a different age, and this might confuse a Catholic's faith rather than enhance it.

From this consideration it seems to me that words might help and some are needed here. Religious paintings might help some Catholics to understand their relationship with God, but they might not help other Catholics.

[Continued]

Section 4: Forms of expression and ways of life

A high mark answer because it gives three clear developed reasons for thinking that paintings help Catholics to understand their relationship with God. It then gives three reasons for disagreeing before reaching a fully justified conclusion.

Spelling, punctuation and grammar are correct and a wide range of specialist vocabulary (Stations of the Cross, sacrifice, atone, sins, Holy Trinity, adoration, sense of awe, medieval) is used appropriately.

1a Beliefs and teachings

Area of study 2: Study of second religion, either Islam or Judaism

Section 1a: Beliefs and teachings

Area of study 2: Introduction (Islam)

For those of you studying the area based on Islam, it is important that you should understand some of the different groups within Islam. This will allow you to understand their beliefs and attitudes.

Islam should be one religion, but within 30 years of Muhammad's death, Islam split into two groups:

- Sunnis: Muslims who follow only the example of Muhammad.
- Shi'as: Muslims who follow the example of Ali, Muhammad's son-in-law, as well as Muhammad.

About 80–85 per cent of Muslims are Sunni, the rest are Shi'a. The first division arose because when Muhammad died, many Muslims believed that the leader should be Ali as he was Muhammad's first convert, closest relative and father of Muhammad's grandchildren. However, the majority of Muslims elected three of Muhammad's best companions as caliphs before eventually Ali was elected as the fourth caliph. After Ali's death, there was more conflict as some Muslims wanted Ali's sons, Hasan and Husayn (who were Muhammad's grandsons), to be caliph, but Hasan was poisoned and Husayn and his followers were massacred at Karbala. Those who followed Ali became Shi'as and those who followed the Umayyad caliphs became Sunnis.

Most Sunni Muslims are not aware of any differences within Sunni Islam and think all Sunnis have the same beliefs of following the Five Pillars and the holy law of Islam known as the Shari'ah. However, there are different groups in Sunni Islam:

- The Salafis (often connected with a Saudi Arabian group which began in the eighteenth century, the Wahhabis) teach that Islam should be based solely on Qur'an and hadith, Muhammad must not be worshipped and festivals connected with him should not be celebrated. They also teach that Muslims should not celebrate birthdays, listen to music, dance, or have their photos taken or displayed (a form of idolatry). They should not worship at the graves of saints or follow special holy men. The Taleban, al-Qaeda and Isis are developments from these groups.

- The most numerous Sunni group among British Muslims is the Barelvi, who originated in northern India as a reaction against Wahhabism. They revere the Prophet Muhammad, celebrate his birthday, do not ban music and dancing, and have close connections with Sufism.

Sufism is the name given to the Islamic mystical movement which tries to unite individual believers with Allah. Some Muslims regard the Sufis as very important because they encourage Muslims to look at their relationship with Allah and emphasise the value of religious experience. Others regard Sufis as non-Muslim because they seem to think that finding Allah is more important than following the Shari'ah and the Five Pillars.

Pilgrims mourning the death of Husayn at the Karbala Mosque.

The Shi'as have split into many different groups. Most Shi'as believe in the Twelve Imams as successors of Ali and that the twelfth Imam did not die, but went into hiding in a mosque in Baghdad and will return before the end of the world. Iran is a Twelver Shi'a country. Ismaili Shi'as believe that the seventh Imam should have been Isma'il and that his descendants are the true Imams. There are many offshoots of the Ismailis such as the Nizari Khojas, whose leader, the Aga Khan, is regarded as the Imam of the age, and the Druze, some of whom believe in reincarnation. Other Muslims have Christian names and some believe there is no need to follow the Five Pillars. Shi'as have their own Shari'ah based on the hadith of Ali as well as the Qur'an and the hadith of Muhammad.

Section 1a: Beliefs and teachings

Topic 2.1a.1 The six beliefs of Islam

Thinking points

In this topic you need to:
- think about the nature, history and purpose of the six beliefs and their importance for Muslims
- be able to explain and evaluate how the beliefs are understood and expressed in Muslim communities.

The six beliefs of Islam

Sunni Muslims believe that there are six principal beliefs, commonly referred to as articles of faith, that a Muslim must believe to be accepted as a Muslim. These six beliefs are:

- belief in Allah
- belief in His angels
- belief in His holy books
- belief in His messengers
- belief in the Last Day
- belief in life after death.

The first five beliefs are based on Qur'anic verses such as:

Whoever disbelieveth in God and His angels and His scriptures and His messengers and the Last Day, he verily wandered far stray. (4:136)

It is righteousness to believe in God and the Last Day and the Angels and the Book and the Messengers. (2:177)

The men of faith. Each one believeth in God and His angels, His books and His apostles. (2:285)

Hadith Sayings of Muhammad, Social Guidance and *Forgiveness*.

Topic 2.1a.1 The six beliefs of Islam

However, the full six beliefs are based on a **hadith** of the Prophet Muhammad recorded by Sahih Muslim:

A man came up to Muhammad and said; 'Prophet of Allah tell me what is Iman (faith)?' Upon this the Holy Prophet replied, 'You must believe in Allah, his angels, his holy books, his Messengers, in the Last Day and life after death.' (Kitab al-iman 1:4)

Hadith are second in authority to the Qur'an for Sunni Muslims because Sunni Muslims believe:

- Muhammad was the final prophet so his words must be important.
- The best person to interpret the Qur'an must be Muhammad.
- If the Qur'an is not clear, a Muslim must follow hadith.
- Hadith are one of the bases of the **Shari'ah**.

History

There has always been some disagreement among Muslims about the sixth belief. Some believe that it simply refers to life after death, others believe that it refers to 'destiny', meaning Allah's control of the future of humans and their fate in the afterlife, an idea known as predestination (*al-Qadr*, see Topic 2.1a.7, page 183). Perhaps this is why Sunni Muslims now describe the six beliefs using these three categories:

- *Tawhid* (the oneness of Allah) – belief in Allah
- *Risalah* (the messengers of Allah) – belief in angels, holy books and messengers
- *Akirah* (the last things) – belief in the Last Day and life after death.

Importance

The six beliefs are very important for Sunni Muslims because:

- Believing in *Tawhid* shows that Muslims believe God is the only one, and if God is the only one, He must be the creator of everything, and so He must be all-powerful and in control of everything. It also means that God must be present everywhere in the universe He has created and so people can be in contact with God anywhere.
- Believing in *Tawhid* also shows that the God Muslims worship is the same God worshipped by Jews and Christians.
- Believing in angels shows that God can communicate with humans using His special beings.
- Believing in the prophets of God shows that Islam is both the first religion (it began with the Prophet Adam) and the last religion (the final prophet is Muhammad).
- Believing in the holy books of God demonstrates that God has sent books to show humans what to believe and how to live. This belief also shows that the holy books given to Jews and Christians were distorted, and so are no longer God's true word. Most importantly, it shows that the Qur'an is God's final word to humanity, which shows humanity what to believe and how to live.
- Believing in *Akirah* is important for Muslims because believing that all people will be judged by Allah on the Last Day is bound to have a major effect on how Muslims live their lives. Muslims believe they will be judged on the basis of how they have lived their lives and will be sent to heaven or hell as a result of that judgement.

Useful words

Hadith – sayings of the Prophet Muhammad
Iman – faith
Shari'ah – the holy law of Islam which covers all aspects of life
Tawhid – belief in Allah's unity
Risalah – belief in Allah's angels, prophets and holy books
Akirah – belief in the Last Day and life after death

Hadith are things that Muhammad is recorded as having said. There are several collections of hadith, but the ones which most Sunni Muslims accept as genuine are the Hadith of Bukhari and the Hadith of Sahih Muslim. These are regarded as genuine because they have a line of guarantors going back to a companion of the Prophet who heard Muhammad say them.

Activities

1. Why do you think hadith are important for Muslims?
2. What are the six beliefs based on?

Section 1a: Beliefs and teachings

Useful words

Piety – religious devotion

Activity

How are the six beliefs understood by Muslim communities today?

The understanding of the six beliefs in Muslim communities today

Most Sunni Muslim communities believe that the six beliefs mean that all people are created equal in the sight of Allah. No one is superior to another except because of their **piety** and righteousness. The beliefs also mean that Muslims are required to respect the dignity of mankind, regardless of religion, race, nationality or place of birth. People should not be judged on factors over which they had no choice such as gender, colour, ethnicity or disability.

The six beliefs mean that in Sunni Islam there are no priests, priesthood or holy men with special authority. The only intermediaries between God and humans are angels, and the only humans given special authority by God were the prophets. However, since belief in *Risalah* means that there can be no prophets after Muhammad, no humans can have God's special authority.

From the six beliefs, Muslims believe that people are born free of any sin and bear no responsibility for the faults and sins of other people. It is only after they reach the age of puberty and knowingly commit sins that people will be held responsible for their actions in this life. Salvation in Islam comes through believing the six beliefs and living in the way set out by Islam.

Shi'a Muslims have expressed the six beliefs as five roots. The five roots are covered in the next section.

Practice questions

c Explain two reasons why the six beliefs are important for Muslims. In your answer you must refer to a source of wisdom and authority.

d 'You can't be a Muslim if you don't believe in the six beliefs.' Evaluate this statement considering arguments for and against. In your answer you should:
- refer to Muslim points of view
- refer to different Muslim points of view
- reach a justified conclusion.

Summary

The six beliefs are the basis of Islam and are summarised by Sunni Muslims as:
- *Tawhid* – belief in only one God
- *Rislah* – belief in God's angels, messengers and holy books
- *Akirah* – belief in the Last Day and life after death.

Topic 2.1a.2 The five roots in Shi'a Islam

The five roots in Shi'a Islam

Shi'a Muslims have five roots of faith (known as **Usul ad-din**), which are the basis of Shi'a faith. The roots are:

- Belief in the oneness of Allah (*Tawhid*) and all Allah's characteristics that come from his oneness:

  Say, 'He is God, the One and Only, God the Eternal, the Absolute; He begetteth not nor is He begotten; and there is none like unto Him.' (Surah 112)

- Belief in Allah's justice (**Adalat**). Allah is described in the Qur'an as 'the All-just'. Justice means fairness and the maintenance of what is right. Muslims believe that Allah created the world in a just way. Shi'a Muslims believe the universe works according to laws established by Allah and the way it operates is fair and just.

- Belief in Allah's prophets from Adam to Muhammad (**Nubuwwah**).

- Belief in the successors of Muhammad (**imamah**) and belief that chosen descendants of the Prophet Muhammad were given special powers by Allah. The Imam is the one who determines what the Qur'an means and who determines what the law should be – the problem is to know what the Imam says! There is a Shi'a hadith which says,

  whosoever knows not the Imam of his age dies the death of a heathen.

  Some Shi'as believe that specially chosen descendants of the prophet are in touch with the **Hidden Imam** and pass on his messages; others believe that specially chosen leaders called **mujtahids** or **ayatollahs** interpret his messages.

- Belief in the Day of Judgement, with judgement being based on believing the five roots and following the Shi'a Shari'ah (which is based on hadith from Imam Ali as well the Prophet Muhammad).

History, purpose and importance

The five roots developed in order to sum up what one must believe to be a Shi'a Muslim. They are based on the Qur'an and the teachings of the Twelve Imams, especially when it became necessary to differentiate Shi'a beliefs from those of the Sunnis. At one point, some Shi'a scholars taught that only belief in the Oneness of Allah, the prophets of Allah and the Day of Judgement were essential beliefs for being a Muslim, and belief in the Imams and Allah's justice were what differentiated Shi'as from Sunnis. However, nowadays Shi'as regard belief in all five roots as essential.

The five roots are important because:

- They are the basis of Shi'a Islam; it is from the roots that the religion grows.
- They are the five principles of faith and show a person what they must believe to be a Muslim.

Thinking points

In this topic you need to:
- think about the nature, history and purpose of the five roots in Shi'a Islam, and their importance for different Shi'a communities today
- be able to explain and evaluate the importance of the five roots.

Useful words

Usul ad-din – the five roots of Shi'a Islam
Adalat – God's attribute of justice
Nubuwwah – prophets of God
Imamah – belief in the successors of the Prophet Muhammad. For Shi'as, Imam is a successor, but 'imam' with a small 'i' is a prayer leader for Sunnis
Hidden Imam – the twelfth Imam who disappeared and is believed to be in contact with the ayatollahs
Mujtahid – a Shi'a scholar with sufficient training and knowledge to interpret the Shari'ah
Ayatollah – the highest ranking religious leader in Twelver Shi'ism

Activities

1. What are the five roots based on?
2. What are the main differences and similarities between the six beliefs and the five roots?

Section 1a: Beliefs and teachings

Qom is one of the holiest cities in Iran and has the largest theology school in Iran.

Useful words

Sects – group with different religious beliefs from those of a larger group to which they belong
Ismaili – Shi'as who believe that the seventh Imam, Isma'il, was the final Imam
Imamate – the office of the Imam
Fatimid – an Ismaili caliphate that ruled North Africa from 909CE to 1171CE
Caliph – leader of the Islamic community
Ahmadiyya – a Muslim sect founded in Pakistan by Yirza Ahmad

- They come from the teachings of the Qur'an and the Twelve Imams, which means they are of utmost important to Shi'a Muslims.
- Shi'a Muslims believe that unless they understand and believe the five roots, they will not be able to perform the acts of worship necessary to live the Muslim life.
- They are the beliefs that Muslims must hold if their practices are to be correct and to ensure that they go to heaven.

Importance in different Shi'a communities

There are many different **sects** within Shi'a Islam (although the vast majority of Shi'as are Twelvers who believe in the Twelve Imams and all five roots) and their origins have led to the five roots having different levels of importance, in particular the fourth root about the successor of Muhammad.

The **Ismaili** Shi'as (Seveners) believe that the seventh imam, Isma'il, was the final Imam. The Nizari Khoja branch of Ismailis believe that the **Imamate** continued from Isma'il to the present day, that there is no Hidden Imam and that their current leader, the Aga Khan, is the Imam. The Druze (found mainly in Syria, Lebanon and Israel) believe in reincarnation as part of the afterlife and accept a **Fatimid caliph**, al-Hakim, as the final Imam.

The **Ahmadiyya**, who developed from Ismailis in Pakistan 150 years ago, accept the Sunni six beliefs rather than the Shi'a five roots, although they believe that their founder, Mirza Ahmad, received a special message.

Sunnis and the five roots

Sunnis accept four of the five roots since they are contained in the six beliefs. Root 1 is *Tawhid*, and Sunnis believe that the second root, God's justice, is part of God's oneness. Root 3 (belief in the prophets from Adam to Muhammad) is *Risalah* and Root 5 (belief in the Day of Judgement) is *Akirah*. However, Sunnis cannot accept Root 4 (belief in the successors of Muhammad) since they believe that Muhammad was the last of the prophets and there can be no messengers after him. Root 4 is the basis of conflicts between Shi'as and Sunnis.

Activity

Why are there different understandings of the five roots among Shi'a Muslims?

Summary

The five roots are the basic beliefs of Shi'a Muslims. They are belief in God's oneness, God's justice, God's messengers from Adam to Muhammad, the Last Judgement and Muhammad's successors. Sunni Muslims do not accept the root about Muhammad's successors and some Shi'a groups do not accept that there were twelve successors.

Practice questions

c Explain two reasons why the five roots are important for Shi'a Muslims. In your answer you must refer to a source of wisdom and authority.

d 'It doesn't matter what you believe as long as you worship God and live a good life.' Evaluate this statement considering arguments for and against. In your answer you should:
- refer to Muslim points of view
- refer to different Muslim points of view
- reach a justified conclusion.

Topic 2.1a.3 The nature of Allah

Allah

Muslims always refer to God as **Allah** because this is the word used for God in the Qur'an and is the word the Prophet Muhammad used for God.

Allah is the Arabic for God, but, unlike the English word God, Allah has no plural form. It is impossible to say Allahs in Arabic, so referring to God as Allah is confirming the absolutely fundamental Muslim belief about God: that Allah is the one and only God.

Muslim beliefs about the characteristics of God are found in the book he has given to the world, the Qur'an. Muslims believe that the Qur'an has total authority because they believe that the Qur'an:

- contains God's actual words to humanity
- was revealed to Muhammad in such a way that it can never be distorted
- is God's final word: there will never be another book from God
- tells humans all they need to know about God, religion and how to live their lives.

Muslims believe that God's nature is shown in the 99 names of God which can be found in the Qur'an. These names are the titles given to God within the Qur'an itself and include such titles as:

- the Creator
- the Tremendous
- the Bestower
- the All-knowing
- the Ever-providing
- the All-seeing
- the Judge.

Many Muslims like to remind themselves of God's nature by having a rosary of 33 beads (which they pass through their fingers three times) or 99 beads to remind themselves of what God is like and how great He is.

> *This is the Book, in it is guidance sure without doubt to those who fear Allah. (Sura 2:2)*

A *shahadah* inside the Taynal Mosque, Tripoli, Lebanon.

Thinking points

In this topic you need to:
- think about how the characteristics of Allah are revealed in the Qur'an: *Tawhid*, immanence, transcendence, omnipotence, beneficence and mercy, fairness and justice, *Adalat* in Shi'a Islam
- be able to explain and evaluate the importance of these characteristics for Muslims.

Useful words

Allah – the Arabic for God

Activity

Why do you think the Qur'an has total authority for Muslims?

Section 1a: Beliefs and teachings

The Qur'an

The main characteristics of God revealed in the Qur'an are considered below.

Oneness (*Tawhid*)

Tawhid is belief in Allah's oneness. This is the absolute basis of Islam, as the first part of the Muslim creed (**shahadah**, the first pillar) states, 'I bear witness that there is no god, but God'.

Allah's oneness means that he has no partners, no helpers and especially no equals. Muslims feel that the Christian belief in God as a Trinity, and especially the belief in Jesus as the Son of God, is an insult to Allah's oneness.

Belief in Allah's oneness means that Allah must be the creator of everything since he is the only God. It also means that Allah must be all-powerful and in control of everything and that Allah must be present in the universe He has created.

> *And verily, We have sent among every nation a Messenger proclaiming: 'Worship Allah Alone, and avoid all false deities'.*
> *(Surah 16:36)*

Omnipotence

Two of the **ninety-nine names** of Allah are: 'the Absolute' and 'the All-powerful' and it is a fundamental belief that Allah has complete power. He has created the universe and so must have complete power over it.

This belief in Allah's **omnipotence** can be seen in the name of the religion. Islam means submission to God's will and Muslims are those who have submitted their wills to God's will because God is so great.

Allah's omnipotence also implies his **omniscience**, as another of his names is 'the All-knowing'. The first **surah** of the Qur'an says that Allah is 'the Master of the Day of Judgement' and for Allah to be in charge of the Day of Judgement, he must know everything about what humans do in order to have the power and authority to judge them.

Beneficence and mercy

Every surah except Surah 9 begins with the **bismillah**:

> *In the name of Allah, Most Gracious, Most Merciful,*

showing that a major characteristic of Allah is his beneficence. This means not only that Allah is good, but that he is kind and loving to his creation. Islam teaches that when God created humans, he did not leave them alone to get on with their lives as best they could, he sent prophets with his word to show humans how to live their lives in the best way so that they would go to heaven.

The Qur'an also teaches that Allah's mercy is such that if people are not perfect and fail in their attempts to live the perfect Muslim life, he will forgive them. He is 'the All-forgiving', which is why Muslims believe that trying to be a good Muslim by doing things like fasting in Ramadan (the pillar of **sawm**, see page 200) and going on pilgrimage to Makkah (the pillar of **hajj**, see page 199) can ensure that a Muslim's sins are forgiven by Allah.

Useful words

Shahadah – the Muslim creed and first pillar
Ninety-nine names – the titles or characteristics given to Allah in the Qur'an
Omnipotence – unlimited power
Omniscience – God's characteristic of being all-knowing
Surah – a chapter of the Qur'an (there are 114 surahs)
Bismillah – the words at the beginning of each surah, 'in the name of Allah, the Merciful, the Compassionate'
Sawm – fasting, the fourth pillar
Hajj – pilgrimage, the fifth pillar

Activities

1. Look at the illustration on page 165. Why do you think many Muslims prefer to translate this as, 'There is no deity except Allah'?
2. How do the words Islam and Muslim show Muslims' belief in God's omnipotence?

Justice (*Adalat*)

Allah is described in the Qur'an as 'the All-just'. Justice means fairness and the maintenance of what is right. Muslims believe that Allah created the world in a just way. They believe that the universe works according to laws established by Allah and the way it operates is fair and just. The composition of the earth provides food and liquid for humans which enables them to survive and prosper. Allah has designed everything to work well together and provide a fair life for people.

Muslims believe that Allah's justice is also shown in the way he has provided his holy law, the **Shari'ah**, to make sure that humans deal fairly and justly with each other. They believe that if everyone followed the Shari'ah, the world would have a just society.

Allah's justice is also shown in the way he deals with humans. At the end of the world all humans will be brought before the court of Allah to be judged by him and he will judge everyone justly. The good will be rewarded and the evil punished, which is the basis of justice.

> *In Allah's creation there is no extremism, immoderation or contradiction; the earth is most rightly and justly spaced apart from the sun. If the earth were closer to the sun, it would be a blazing furnace; if it were farther, it would be an ice grave. Distances between the sun and the earth, and between all of the heavenly objects are most rightly and justly designed. ('Understanding God's Attributes', Dr Muhammad Ratib An-Nabulsi, www.onislam.net)*

Transcendence

Transcendence refers to the aspect of God's nature and power which is totally beyond the material and so beyond human experience. This attribute can be seen in some of the 99 names of God to be found in the Qur'an. 'The Greatest', 'the Highest', 'the Glorious', 'the Supreme One', 'the Magnificent' all show how far beyond any human description God is.

Immanence

Although Islam believes that Allah is transcendent, is also teaches that Allah has the attribute of immanence, he is close to humans and can be contacted by humans:

> *We are nearer to man than his jugular vein. (Surah 50:16)*

This is Allah's attribute of immanence; Allah is within the universe he has created:

> *Whithersoever ye turn, there is the presence of God. (Surah 2:115)*

> *When My servants ask thee concerning Me, I am indeed close to them: I listen to the prayer of every suppliant when he calleth on Me. (Surah 2:186)*

Transcendence and immanence are a great mystery in Islam, and indeed in most religions. God is both far beyond humans and yet also closer to them than their own jugular veins.

Activity
Which characteristic of Allah is most important for Muslims and why do you think so?

Useful words
Shari'ah – the holy law of Islam

Thy Lord is self-sufficient, full of Mercy: if it were God's will, God could destroy you, and in your place appoint whom God will as your successors, even as God raised you up from the posterity of other people. (Surah 6:133)

God! There is no god but He – the Loving, the Self-Subsisting, Eternal. No slumber can seize Him nor sleep. His are all things in the heavens and on earth. (Surah 2:255)

God Most Gracious is firmly established on the throne of authority. To Him belongs what is in the heavens and on earth and all between them. (Surah 20:5)

The most beloved of speech according to Allah is when the servant says, 'Subhanallahi wa bihamdihi' [How Transcendent is Allah and we praise him!]. (Muslim)

Section 1a: Beliefs and teachings

Why the characteristics of Allah are important for Muslims

Tawhid

Belief in *Tawhid* is important for Muslims because it means that:

- There is only one God who created everything that exists.
- If one God created everything, then Muslims must try to preserve the oneness of the world he has created.
- If the universe was made by and belongs to one God, then the Muslim community must itself be a unity (this is called the **ummah**).
- There can only be one law for Muslims, Allah's law, which is known as the Shari'ah.
- Muslims must only worship Allah; the worst sin a Muslim can commit is the sin of **shirk**, which is to associate others with Allah. This is why there can be no images or statues in the mosque and why Muslims decorate with calligraphy rather than representational art.

Omnipotence

Belief in Allah's omnipotence is important for Muslims because:

- It means that Muslims believe Allah is in control of everything that happens.
- It means that Allah has a plan for the world and the power to make sure that that plan actually happens.
- Part of that plan is that God will bring the world to an end on the Last Day and God's omnipotence means that he has the power to do this:

> *Blessed be He in whose hands is dominion, and He over all things hath power. (Surah 67:1)*

Benevolence

Belief in Allah's benevolence is important for Muslims because:

- If God is compassionate and merciful to sinners, Muslims should be merciful and forgiving to those who cause them offence.
- On the Day of Judgement, Muslims will be able to request Allah's mercy for their sins, but how can Muslims ask for Allah's forgiveness if they themselves are not prepared to forgive?

Justice

Belief in Allah's justice is important for Muslims because:

- The Qur'an teaches that God is a just God who will reward the good and punish the bad on the Last Day; therefore Muslims need to work for justice, so they are not sent to hell on the Last Day.
- Islamic teaching on the Last Day is concerned with the need for the good to be rewarded and the evil punished, which is the basis of justice.
- The fact that Allah is just means that Muslims must behave justly to other people and ensure that the world is governed in a fair way by following the Shari'ah.

Useful words

Ummah – the Muslim community
Shirk – the sin of associating other things with God; it is the worst sin

Activities

1. Do you think it is possible for God to be both transcendent and immanent?
2. Do you think it is possible for humans to say what God is like?

- Allah's justice means that Muslims must work to make sure that all people have equal rights before the law and that Muslims should work for a fairer sharing of the earth's resources through the pillar of *zakah* (see page 205) and groups such as Muslim Aid and Islamic Relief.

Transcendence

Belief in transcendence is important for Muslims because:

- It shows that Allah is worthy of humanity's worship and praise since he is greater than anything.
- It shows that Allah is in control because nothing is as great as Allah.
- It shows that Allah is not restricted in any way – by time, space or matter. He is **self-subsistent** and eternal and so can be contacted by humans wherever they are and whenever they ask.

Immanence

Belief in Allah's immanence is important for Muslims because:

- It means that Allah is within the universe he has created and so science and learning can comprehend Allah.
- It means that, despite his greatness, Allah can be contacted by humans.
- It means that Allah is present for all the religious activities of a Muslim, especially such things as **salah** and *sawm*.

Conclusion

For Muslim theologians, all the characteristics of Allah can be summed up by *Tawhid*. Everything comes from Allah's oneness to express their faith in the oneness of Allah.

Useful words

Self-subsistent – without dependence on or support from anything else
Salah – ritual prayer, the second pillar

Practice questions

c Explain two reasons why God's justice is important for Muslims. In your answer you must refer to a source of wisdom and authority.

d 'No one knows what God is like.' Evaluate this statement considering arguments for and against. In your answer you should:
- refer to Muslim points of view
- reach a justified conclusion.

Summary

Muslims call God Allah because this is the word used in the Qur'an. The Qur'an says that the main characteristics of God are:

- oneness
- omnipotence (all-powerful)
- beneficence (love and compassion) and mercy
- justice (*adalat*)
- transcendence
- immanence.

God's oneness is the basis of Islam and is the first part of the Muslim creed.

Section 1a: Beliefs and teachings

Topic 2.1a.4 *Risalah* (prophets)

Thinking points

In this topic you need to:
- think about the nature and history of prophethood, especially the Qur'an's teachings about the prophets: Adam, Ibrahim, Isma'il, Musa, Dawud, Isa and Muhammad
- be able to explain what these beliefs teach Muslims, and evaluate their importance for Muslims.

Useful words

Khalifahs – Allah's stewards or vicegerents
Vicegerent – a person appointed to look after things on behalf of a ruler

The nature of the prophets

Muslims believe that Allah created humans to look after the earth for him (Allah's **khalifahs** or **vicegerents**) and humans need prophets to know how to do this. Muslims do not believe that Islam began with Muhammad; rather, it began with the creation of humans and so it is the original religion begun by Allah and his first prophet, Adam.

Islam teaches that the prophets were all ordinary human beings; what made them different was that they were chosen to receive Allah's messages. Muslims believe it is wrong to treat prophets in the same way Christians treat Jesus, because they are not divine. All the prophets except Isa were married and had children.

However, most Muslims believe that the prophets were sinless after they had been called by Allah to be his messenger. This is why they believe that prophets should be blessed whenever their name is mentioned: 'Peace be upon him' (p.b.u.h. or in Arabic *alayhi al-salām*, a.s.), although many Muslims use s.a.w. or s.a.a.w. ('May Allah honour him and grant him peace'; *ṣallā llāhu 'alay-hi wa-sallam* in Arabic) when they mention Muhammad.

According to the Qur'an, each prophet was given Allah's word for their generation, so each prophet brought Islam in its perfect form. However, humans either ignored, distorted or forgot Allah's word so that Allah had to keep sending a new prophet until, Muslims believe, Muhammad was given the Qur'an in a form that could never be distorted.

Activities

1. Which prophets were married?
2. Why did Allah have to keep sending new prophets?

Arabic calligraphy for the name of Muhammad and peace be upon him.

Topic 2.1a.4 *Risalah* (prophets)

The main prophets of Islam are:

Adam

According to the Qur'an, the first prophet of Islam was the first man, Adam. He was created by Allah to be Allah's vicegerent to look after the earth for Allah in the way Allah wanted. At first, Adam and his wife **Hawwa** (Eve), though she is not named in the Qur'an, lived in the Garden, and were told by Allah not to eat the fruit of a certain tree. However, Iblis tempted them by telling them that Allah did not want them to eat because he did not want them to become like the angels. Adam and Hawwa succumbed and ate the fruit and so had to leave the Garden.

Allah placed Adam and his wife on earth to live. They realised they had been wrong to follow Iblis' advice and asked Allah for forgiveness. Allah forgave them and gave Adam his guidance, and in Islam those who receive Allah's guidance are his prophets. The hadith record that as a sign of his thanks for Allah's forgiveness and guidance, Adam built a House for Allah in **Makkah** (Mecca) called the **Ka'aba**.

> **Useful words**
>
> **Hawwa** – the first woman, Adam's wife (Eve)
> **Makkah** – the city in Arabia where Muhammad was born
> **Ka'aba** – the shrine in Makkah which Muslims face to say prayers and which is the centre of *hajj*
> **Ishaq** – Ibrahim's son Isaac, the father of the Jewish people

Ibrahim (Abraham)

Muslims regard Ibrahim as the greatest of the prophets before Isa. He was born into a polytheistic (worshipping many gods) family, which shows that the message of the previous prophets had been ignored or forgotten. However, Ibrahim rejected polytheism. He argued with his father and his father's people about the wrongness of false gods. He broke down the idols they worshipped to show that they had no power. When the people tried to burn Ibrahim, Allah saved him from the fire. So he condemned idolatry and showed the people the truth of Islam.

> *Abraham was not a Jew nor yet a Christian, but he was true in faith and bowed his will to God's, which is Islam.* (Surah 3:67)

The Qur'an records that Ibrahim and his wife had no children into their old age, but then Allah granted them the gift of two sons, Isma'il and **Ishaq**. Muslims believe that Ishaq was the prophet for the Jews and Isma'il the prophet for the Arabs.

The Qur'an records that Ibrahim had a vision from Allah where he sacrificed his son. His son urged him to obey Allah's command in the vision, but as Ibrahim was about to sacrifice his son, Allah called out and stopped the sacrifice and rewarded them for being obedient to his will and doing right. Ibrahim and Isma'il are also recorded in the Qur'an as restoring the Ka'aba after it had been destroyed in Noah's flood. They established the Ka'aba as a place of assembly and pilgrimage for Muslims.

Ibrahim was given the holy book of Sahifah (The Scrolls of Ibrahim), the first of the holy books mentioned in the Qur'an. The Qur'an teaches that Ibrahim was specially chosen by Allah to deliver 'A message for the nations' (Surah 6:90), and that all the prophets between Ibrahim and Muhammad (Moses, David, Solomon, John the Baptist and Jesus) were descendants of Ibrahim. Muslims regard Ibrahim as a role model for how to live the Muslim life.

> *Abraham was indeed a model devoutly obedient to God, true in faith, and he joined not gods with God.* (Surah 16:120)

> *Say ye: 'We believe in Allah and the revelation given to us, and to Abraham, Ismail, Isaac, Jacob and the Tribes, and that given to Moses and Jesus, and that given to all prophets from their Lord: We make no difference between one and another of them: And we bow to Allah in Islam.'* (Surah 2:136)

Activity

Look at the quotation from Surah 2:136 above. What does it tell us about Muslim beliefs?

Section 1a: Beliefs and teachings

The holy Ka'aba. Muslims believe the blocks are the ones used by Ibrahim and Isma'il.

Isma'il (Ishmael)

As discussed above, Isma'il was the eldest son of Ibrahim (in Muslim tradition his mother was Ibrahim's second wife Hagar) who helped his father in the rebuilding of the Ka'aba and establishing it as a place of pilgrimage. He was also the one who encouraged Ibrahim to sacrifice him to show his obedience to Allah. Isma'il is regarded as the prophet to the Arabs and is believed by Muslims to be the ancestor of Muhammad.

Isma'il: he was strictly true to what he promised, and he was an apostle and a prophet. (Surah 19:54)

Musa (Moses)

Musa has more mentions in the Qur'an than any other prophet. The Qur'an records how Musa was born a Jew but brought up by Pharaoh's wife. He killed an Egyptian and fled to Midian, where God called him to go back to Egypt and lead the Jews out of slavery in Egypt and into God's promised land. Musa was chosen to receive the holy book of Tawrat (Torah), but the people rejected or distorted his message.

Also mention in the Book (the story of) Moses: for he was specially chosen, and he was a messenger (and) a prophet. And we called him from the right side of Mount (Sinai), and made him draw near to Us, for mystic (converse). And, out of Our Mercy, We gave him his brother Aaron, (also) a prophet. (Surah 19:51–53)

Dawud (David)

The Qur'an teaches that Dawud, the great king of Israel, was chosen as a prophet and was given the holy book of Zabur (Psalms) because of the distortion of the Tawrat. The Zabur was not written down until long after Dawud's death, so it was never written down properly. However, part of the Zabur is recorded in the Qur'an (this is the only quotation from the Bible in the Qur'an):

Activity

Look at the photo above. Why do you think the Ka'aba is important to Muslims?

Before this we wrote in the Psalms, after the message given to Moses: 'My servants the righteous shall inherit the earth.' (Surah 21:105 and Psalm 37:29)

Isa (Jesus)

Isa and his mother Maryam are major figures in the Qur'an. Surah 19 is called Maryam and is all about her and Isa. This surah records that Isa had a virgin birth. His mother never had sex and was 'the most virtuous of women' who conceived Isa by the power of Allah. The Qur'an records many miracles of Isa such as healing lepers, making the dumb speak and the lame walk, raising the dead and making clay birds fly. According to the Qur'an, the Jewish authorities wanted to have Isa executed and attempted to crucify him, but Allah prevented this from happening:

> They said in boast, 'We killed Christ Jesus, the son of Mary, the Apostle of God'; but they killed him not nor crucified him, but so it was made to appear to them. (Surah 4:157)

Muslims believe that Allah took Isa to heaven from the cross so that Isa never died.

Isa was given the holy book Injil (Gospel). However, the Qur'an makes it plain that he was only a prophet, an ordinary man, not the son of God:

> Christ the son of Mary was no more than an Apostle: many were the apostles that passed away before him. His mother was a woman of truth. They both had to eat their daily bread. (Surah 5:78)

Muhammad

There are many references in the Qur'an to the Messenger of Allah, the Apostle of Allah and Allah's prophet, which are clearly references to Muhammad. These references show that:

- Muhammad was called by Allah to bring his final message to humanity.
- His message must be followed and those who follow his message will be rewarded, but those who reject it will be punished.
- His life was a perfect example for people to follow.
- The message of the prophets was distorted or forgotten so Allah sent Muhammad with a message that could not be distorted and a holy book (the Qur'an) which could never be distorted.

However, there are only four references to Muhammad's name in the Qur'an plus one that refers to Ahmad which is assumed to refer to Muhammad:

> Muhammad is no more than an Apostle: many were the Apostles that passed away before him. (Surah 3:144)
>
> Muhammad is not the father of any of your men, but he is the Apostle of God, and the Seal of the prophets. (Surah 33:40)
>
> Those who believe and work deeds of righteousness, and believe in the revelation sent down to Muhammad – for it is the truth from their Lord – He will remove from them their ills. (Surah 47:2)
>
> Muhammad is the Apostle of God; and those who are with him are strong against Unbelievers, but compassionate amongst each other. (Surah 48:29)
>
> Jesus the son of Mary said, 'O Children of Israel! I am the apostle of God sent to you confirming the Law which came before me, and giving glad tidings of an Apostle to come after me, whose name shall be Ahmad.' (Surah 61:6)

Activities

1. Why might Christians disagree with what the Qur'an says about Isa?
2. Why do you think Muhammad is so important to Muslims?

Section 1a: Beliefs and teachings

So Muhammad is:

- The final prophet; there will never be another prophet.
- The final example of how humans should live.
- The seal of the prophets; he acts like the seal people used to prove origin and to show that the message hadn't been tampered with. As the seal, Muhammad is the final prophet with Allah's final message for humanity.

What the prophets teach Muslims

- Islam is the original religion. Allah taught Islam to his first prophet, Adam, and then taught the same religion to all the prophets through to the final prophet, Muhammad.
- Every prophet was called by Allah and given Allah's true message to give to the people of earth and so Muslims should follow the teachings of the prophets.
- Prophets were just ordinary human beings who were chosen by Allah to be his messengers. They were not angels, they were not divine. Even Isa was only human even though he had a virgin birth. This teaches Muslims that they should have nothing to do with religions which claim any sort of divine status for their leaders and that Muslims should beware of treating their prophets as if they were semi-divine.
- Because prophets were given their message from Allah in the form of a holy book, Muslims should follow the teachings of the holy book given by God to his final prophet, Muhammad – the Qur'an.
- People before Muhammad were able to ignore, forget or even distort Allah's message, so Muslims should treat the Qur'an respectfully and make sure they do not distort it. They must also read it regularly so that there is no chance of them ignoring or forgetting its message.
- Muhammad received Allah's message in a way that could not be distorted or forgotten, so his message is the final message from Allah, which means that Islam is both the first religion (God sent it to Adam) and the last religion (Muhammad was the final prophet).
- All the prophets lived lives whose example could be followed, but Muhammad's has to be the most important one. Muhammad was the final prophet, there will be no more prophets of God and so Muhammad's life provides a perfect example for Muslims. Good Muslims should follow the **Sunnah** of the Prophet Muhammad because his is the last example people have of how to live their lives.

Useful words

Sunnah – the example and way of life of the Prophet Muhammad

Summary

Muslims believe that God sent prophets with his message telling humans how to look after the world. Prophets were ordinary human beings who brought God's message in a perfect form, but the messages of Adam, Ibrahim, Ism'ail, Musa, Dawud and Isa were altered or forgotten so that God had to send his final message to Muhammad in a form that could never be altered or forgotten. This means there can be no more prophets after Muhammad.

Practice questions

c Explain two beliefs which the prophets teach Muslims.

d 'Prophets show how much God loves humanity.' Evaluate this statement considering arguments for and against. In your answer you should:
- refer to Muslim points of view
- reach a justified conclusion.

Topic 2.1a.5 Muslim holy books

The nature, history and purpose of Muslim holy books

Muslims believe that God sent prophets (*rasul*) with his message and the most important of these were given the message in the form of God's holy book.

There is some dispute about the exact nature of the holy books (*kutub*):

- Most Muslims believe that God made one holy book, the Qur'an, which is his eternal word, and each holy book given to a prophet was simply a copy of that 'heavenly original'. Unfortunately, over time these holy books became distorted by humans. Sometimes God sent a prophet to correct the distortions, but on four occasions he sent a new copy of the holy book until finally he sent the Qur'an to Muhammad in a form that could never be distorted.

- Some Muslim scholars believe that the earlier holy books were not the Qur'an as they only contained certain parts of the Qur'an. They contained God's message appropriate to the needs of the prophet's time. They believe that only Muhammad was given God's full eternal word in the undistortable Qur'an.

The purpose of holy books was so that Muslims would know what to believe and how to live. Muslims believe that God created humans to look after the world for him in the way he wanted – they were to be God's *khalifahs* or vicegerents. However, in order to do this, they needed to know what God's way of living was.

The history of holy books begins with Adam. God gave the Qur'an to his first Prophet, Adam, so that he could tell people what to believe and how to live. Unfortunately, according to Islam, humans subsequently distorted God's words and so God had to send other messengers.

Muslims believe that God sent his word three times to prophets of Judaism:

- Prophet Ibrahim (Abraham) was given the message in a book known as **Sahifa Ibrahim** (the Scrolls of Abraham).

    But We have already given the family of Abraham the Book and Wisdom, and conferred upon them a great kingdom. (Qur'an 4:54).

    However, this book became so distorted that all copies were lost.

- Prophet Musa (Moses) was given the message in the holy book known as **Tawrat** (Torah). Although Musa's message became distorted, some parts remained in the Torah of the Old Testament, which is why many elements of Judaism (including the food laws) are still very similar to Islam.

    It was We who revealed the to Moses: therein was guidance and light. By its standards have been judged the Jews by the prophets who bowed (as in Islam) to God's will by the Rabbis and the Doctors of Law: for to them was entrusted the protection of God's Book. (Surah 5:47)

Thinking points

In this topic you need to:
- think about the nature, history and purpose of Muslim holy books: the Qur'an, Tawrat (Torah), Zabur (Psalms), Injil (Gospel) and Sahifah (Scrolls)
- be able to explain why the holy books are important in Muslim life.

We have been commanded to believe in previously revealed Books only in the sense of admitting that, before the Qur'an, God also sent down books through His Prophets, that they were all from the same God, the God who sent the Qur'an, and the sending of the Qur'an ... confirms, restates and completes those divine instructions. ('Towards Understanding Islam', Abul Ala Mawdudi, Islamic Foundation, 1980)

Useful words

Kutub – holy books (singular *kitab*)
Sahifa Ibrahim – the holy book given to Ibrahim (Abraham)
Tawrat – the holy book given to Musa (Moses)

Activity

Look at the quotation above and put it into your own words.

Section 1a: Beliefs and teachings

Useful words

Zabur – the holy book given to Dawud (David)
Injil – the Gospel given to Isa (Jesus)
Apostles – Prophets or messengers: the titles given to those who brought God's message

And in their footsteps We sent Jesus the son of Mary, confirming the Law that had come before him: We sent him the Gospel: therein was guidance and light, and confirmation of the Law that had come before him: a guidance and an admonition to those who fear Allah. (Surah 5:46)

Activities

1. Which is the only other Muslim holy book actually quoted in the Qur'an?
2. Look at the picture of holy books below. Why is it difficult to find them in their original form?
3. What are the differences between the Injil of Islam and the Gospels in the Christian New Testament?

- Prophet Dawud (David) was given the message in the **Zabur** (Psalms), some of which, Muslims believe, have survived undistorted in the Psalms of the Old Testament. The Qur'an has a direct quotation from the Psalms of the Old Testament in Surah 21:105,

Before this We wrote in the Psalms, after the message given to Moses, 'My servants the righteous shall inherit the earth',

which quotes Psalm 37:29:

We have sent thee inspiration as We sent it to Noah and the Messengers after him ... And to David We gave the Psalms. (Surah 4:163)

Injil

The final prophet before Muhammad was Isa (Jesus), who was given the holy book the **Injil** (Gospel). However, Muslims believe the holy book Injil was not the same as the New Testament or the four Gospels, it was the book given to Isa by God which he then preached to the Jewish people:

Muslims believe that the Gospels in the New Testament are human records of what people remembered of the true Gospel preached by Isa.

The main distortions of the Injil contained in the New Testament are that:

- Isa was the Son of God when he was really the prophet of God.
- Isa died on the cross when Muslims believe he was taken to heaven.
- Christians removed those parts of the Injil which foretold the coming of Muhammad.

*Christ Jesus the son of Mary was no more than an Apostle of God, and His Word, which He bestoweth on Mary, and a Spirit proceeding from Him: so believe in God and His **apostles**. Say not 'Trinity': desist: it will be better for you: for God is One God. Glory be to Him far exalted is He above having a son. (Surah 4:171)*

A selection of Islamic holy books.

Topic 2.1a.5 Muslim holy books

The Qur'an

Muslims believe that God decided that his word needed revealing in a new way because:

- He had sent it five times and each time it had been distorted.
- People had ignored or disobeyed what God's word said.
- People no longer knew what the Qur'an was.

This meant that the Qur'an needed to be sent to a prophet who could not read and write and so would recite God's words. The prophet's only message would be the Qur'an in a form such that the Qur'an could be preserved in a book that could never be distorted.

Muslims believe that Muhammad was the ideal person to receive the revelation because he was highly intelligent; he could not read or write but he had an excellent memory and he had a perfect moral and religious character. This meant that God could give Muhammad his message as a dictation which Muhammad could learn by heart and recite to the people. So Muhammad recited the words God gave him:

Proclaim (recite) in the name of thy Lord and Cherisher who created.
(Surah 96:1)

Muhammad ensured that his followers memorised the revelations, although later he had secretaries who wrote down the revelations on whatever came to hand (bits of leather, pottery or paper). Muhammad checked that each written revelation was accurate, then put them into a chest kept by his wife Hafsa. In 631CE Muhammad sorted the revelations into 114 surahs based on their being revealed at the same time or being on a common theme.

History

When Muhammad died, his friend and first convert, **Abu Bak'r**, decided that it was essential for there to be an authorised version of the revelations. As Muhammad had used secretaries to write down the revelations and to help him in sorting out the revelations, Abu Bak'r decided to use the chief secretary, **Zayd ibn Thabit**, to make the authorised version.

The third Caliph, **Uthman** (644–56CE), ordered all the surviving secretaries of Muhammad to meet together to make an official version of the Qur'an based on Abu Bak'r's authorised version. When this was done, all other written versions were destroyed. Uthman organised the Qur'an by length of surah so that Surah 2 is the longest and Surah 114 the shortest. Surah 1 is a call to prayer used by Muslims in the five times a day prayer of *salah*.

Every surah apart from Surah 9 begins with the *bismillah*:

'In the name of God, the Merciful, the Compassionate', showing that what follows is the Word of God.

Muslims believe that the way the Qur'an was revealed to Muhammad and then compiled by the caliphs guarantees that the Arabic Qur'an, as used by Muslims today, is the exact words of God revealed to Muhammad. They believe that the Arabic Qur'an is 'An earthly copy of a heavenly original' because:

- All Arabic Qur'ans today have the same surahs, words and letters.
- All old copies of the Qur'an have the same surahs, words and letters.

Activity

Why might non-Muslims have some doubts about whether the Qur'an came directly from God?

Since Uthman's time, all Qur'ans in existence have had:

- 114 Surahs
- 77,639 Arabic words.

Useful words

Abu Bak'r – Muhammad's friend and first Caliph, who ordered the first collection of the Qur'an

Zayd ibn Thabit – Muhammad's chief secretary, who organised Uthman's Qur'an

Uthman – the third caliph, who ordered the final official copy of the Qur'an

Section 1a: Beliefs and teachings

Divergent Muslim views about the importance of the holy books

Muslim beliefs about the holy books revealed before Muhammad received the Qur'an are very significant because they show that God has always made sure people knew what to believe and how to live. They also show that these books are no longer important because they have been distorted and so are no longer God's word. This means that the Jewish Tenakh and the Christian Bible are not holy books for the majority of Muslims.

Other Muslims believe that since the Qur'an refers to these books as holy books, parts of them must still show what God revealed. So they believe that they are still holy and if what they say fits in with what the Qur'an says then their teachings should be followed by Muslims.

The importance of the Qur'an for Muslims today

The belief that the Qur'an used today is the exact Qur'an revealed to Muhammad, an earthly copy of a heavenly original, the very words of God himself, is hugely significant because it means that:

- Everything in the Qur'an must be true because God said it.
- Muslims must believe everything in the Qur'an because all of it is God's words.
- Muslims must follow everything that the Qur'an says if they want to do what God wants them to do.
- Nothing in the Qur'an can be altered because it is the eternal Word of God. There can be no greater authority, for Muslims, than the Qur'an.

The Qur'an tells Muslims what to believe:

- Belief in God as a unity who is omnipotent, omniscient and omnipresent is a fundamental teaching of the Qur'an.
- Belief in God's angels is clearly shown as Jibril revealed the Qur'an to Muhammad.
- Belief in God's messengers and holy books because they are a major theme of the Qur'an.
- Belief in the Last Day and life after death, which are referred to throughout the Qur'an.

The Qur'an sets out how Muslims should live, through:

- regular ritual prayer (*salah*), and assembling for worship on Friday
- fasting during the month of Ramadan (*sawm*) and celebrating the end of fasting with the festival of Id-ul-Fitr
- paying a religious tax to help orphans (*zakah*)
- going on pilgrimage to Makkah, to join in the pilgrimage around the world with the sacrificial festival of Id-ul-Adha
- not eating pork, not drinking alcohol or gambling, and not being involved in interest.

Activities

1. Look at the lists of what the Qur'an tells Muslims to believe and do. Which of these would Christians agree with?
2. Do you think non-Muslims would find it hard not to eat pork, drink alcohol or gamble?

Topic 2.1a.5 Muslim holy books

A copy of the Qur'an on a special stand in Dubai.

The importance of the Qur'an is shown in Muslims' daily lives. Muslims for whom Arabic is not their native language learn to read Arabic (even if they don't understand it) so they can read the Qur'an in Arabic, the language in which the Qur'an was revealed. They show they believe the Qur'an is holy by never touching it without first washing their hands (clean hands), always keeping it above all other books, never holding the Qur'an below their waist, and never eating, drinking or talking while reading it.

They also obey what the Qur'an says. A Muslim who performs the pillars does so because it is commanded in the Qur'an. A Muslim who follows the Shari'ah (Islamic law) does so out of respect for the Qur'an.

Summary

Muslims believe that God sent messengers (prophets) with holy books (*kutub*) which contained God's message on how people should live and what they should believe. God sent the Salifah to Ibrahim, the Tawrat to Musa, the Zabur to Dawud and the Injil to Isa. However, people altered these and God had to send his final word, the Qur'an, in a form that can never be changed. So the Qur'an is the most important book a Muslim can have as it contains God's words on how to live and what to believe.

Practice questions

c Explain two reasons why there are Muslim holy books other than the Qur'an. In your answer you must refer to a source of wisdom and authority.

d 'The Qur'an is God's final word to humanity and so should be obeyed.' Evaluate this statement considering arguments for and against. In your answer you should:
- refer to Muslim points of view,
- refer to different Muslim points of view
- reach a justified conclusion.

Section 1a: Beliefs and teachings

Topic 2.1a.6 *Malaikah* (angels)

Thinking points

In this topic you need to:
- think about the nature and importance of angels for Muslims and what the Qur'an teaches about Jibril, Mika'il and Izra'il
- be able to explain what these beliefs teach Muslims.

Useful words

Malaikah – angels
Shaytan – the devil

Activities

1. Why do you think Muslims believe God cannot communicate directly with humans?
2. What are the differences between angels and humans?

The nature of angels

Muslims believe that the unity and greatness of Allah mean that he is far too holy to communicate directly with humans.

The Qur'an teaches that Allah created the angels (*malaikah*) as immortal beings without free will. According to the Qur'an, angels are male and have wings. As they have no free will, they obey all of Allah's commands and so never commit sins. Because they are sinless, angels can have direct contact with Allah and pass his messages to humans; therefore Angels are the ones who can act as go-betweens between humans and Allah.

The Qur'an teaches that when he created Adam, Allah ordered the angels to bow down to him because Adam had been able to name Allah's creations while the angels (with no free will) had not. Muslims believe that Iblis (*Shaytan*) was an angel who refused to bow down to Adam and so was sent out of heaven and set up his own kingdom of hell. The Qur'an says that Iblis begged Allah to postpone his punishment for disobedience until the Last Day and this is why Iblis is able to tempt humans to go against Allah (Surah 7:11–18).

Muslims believe that Shaytan set up the kingdom of hell after being sent out of heaven by Allah.

Topic 2.1a.6 *Malaikah* (angels)

Muslims believe that angels have many functions:

- They praise Allah in heaven.
- They are the guardians of the gates of hell.
- They record the good and bad deeds of humans (humans are often thought to have a recording angel on each shoulder, one writing down good deeds, the other bad deeds) to present to Allah on the Last Day as the basis for his judgement.

> Allah created angels from intellect without sensuality, the beasts from sensuality without intellect, and mankind from both intellect and sensuality. So when a person's intellect overcomes his sensuality, he is better than the angels; but when his sensuality overcomes his intellect, he is worse than the beasts. (Hadith recorded by Bukhari)

Jibril (Gabriel)

Jibril is the chief of the angels whose main role, according to the Qur'an, is to deliver Allah's message to the prophets so that they could pass it on to humanity.

Muslims also believe that Jibril told the prophet Ibrahim about the birth of his sons, Ishaq (Isaac) and Isma'il (Ishmael). He also told the prophet Zechariah about the birth of **Yahya** (John the Baptist), and **Maryam** (Mary) about the birth of Isa (Jesus). According to the Qur'an, it was Jibril who told Maryam she would have a child even though she was still a virgin.

Jibril's most important role, however, was to reveal the Qur'an to Muhammad. In 610CE during the month of Ramadan, while Muhammad was meditating in a cave near Makkah, God sent the angel Jibril with the first revelation of the Qur'an.

Jibril continued to give Muhammad revelations for the next twenty years until the Qur'an was complete.

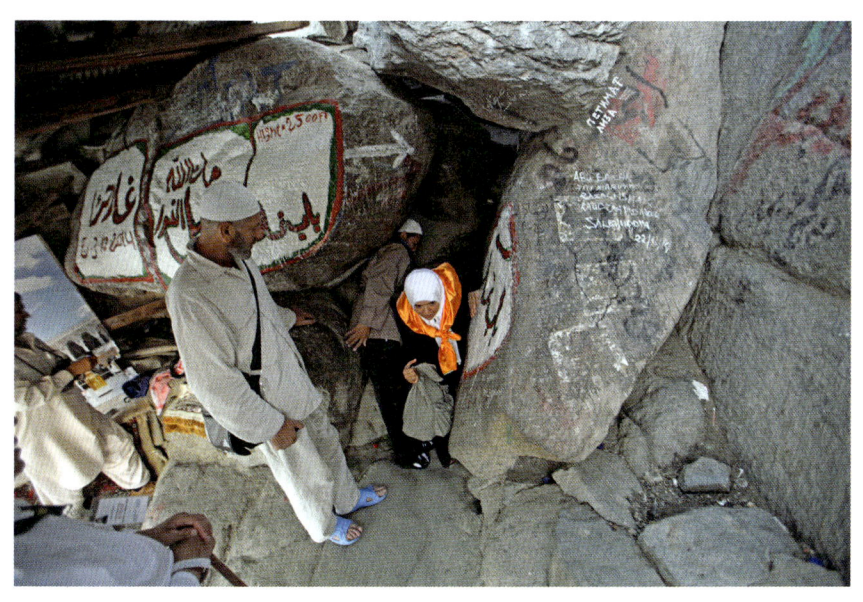

Muslim pilgrims at the entrance of Cave Hira, where the Angel Jibril appeared with the first revelation of the Qur'an.

Activities

1. Rewrite the hadith recorded by Bukhari in your own words.
2. Look at the photo of Cave Hira. Discuss what you think happened when Muhammad received his first revelation.

> Say: 'Whoever is an enemy to Gabriel – for he brings down the revelation to they heart by God's will, a confirmation of what went before and guidance and glad tidings for those who believe.' (Surah 2:97)

Useful words

Jibril – the archangel Gabriel
Yahya – John the Baptist
Maryam – the Virgin Mary

There is a whole Surah – Surah 19 – about the role of Jibril in telling Zechariah about the birth of Yahya (John the Baptist), telling Maryam about the birth of Isa (Jesus) and helping Maryam after the birth (which happened in the desert) by causing a small stream to flow to give her water and providing dates from the palm tree she was leaning against.

Section 1a: Beliefs and teachings

Useful words

Mika'il – the angel Michael
Izra'il – the angel of death

Mika'il (Michael)

Mika'il is the second most important angel. Mika'il is believed to be the guardian of heaven, protecting it from evil and the Devil. He also ensures that humans are nourished by sending rain to the earth. There is only one reference to Mika'il in the Qur'an, which states:

> *Whoever is an enemy of God or his angels or his apostles or Jibril or Mika'il, verily God is an enemy of the unbelievers. (Surah 2:98)*

Izra'il

Izra'il is the angel of death. The Qur'an says that the angel of death (his name is not mentioned) takes the soul of people at death and returns it to Allah:

> *The Angel of Death put in charge of you, will take your souls: then shall ye be brought back to your Lord. (Surah 32:11)*

However, Izra'il only acts at Allah's command because it is Allah alone who decides when a person will die:

> *Nor can a soul die except by God's leave. (Surah 3:145)*

There are hadith which record that the prophets met Izra'il during their lives and that Izra'il watches over the dying.

Why angels are important for Muslims

Angels are important for Muslims because:

- Angels communicated the Qur'an to Muhammad so without them Muslims would not have God's instructions on how to live and what to believe.
- Angels called the prophets to serve God and proclaim God's message; without angels, Muhammad would not have been the perfect example for Muslims.
- Angels ensure that on the Day of Judgement God will have all the facts when judging people on their lives.
- Angels make sure that heaven is safe from evil.

Summary

Muslims believe that angels:
- communicate God's messages to humans as God is so holy
- record people's good and bad deeds for God to use on the Day of Judgement
- guard the gates of hell.

Jibril communicates God's messages to the prophets, Mika'il is the guardian of heaven and Izra'il is the angel of death.

Practice questions

c Explain two of the roles of angels in Islam. In your answer you must refer to a source of wisdom and authority.

d 'Without angels there would be no Islam.' Evaluate this statement considering arguments for and against. In your answer you should:
- refer to Muslim points of view
- reach a justified conclusion.

Topic 2.1a.7 *Al-Qadr* (fate)

What Muslims believe about *al-Qadr*

Al-Qadr means power or fate or **predestination**, and is taken to mean that everything in the universe is following a divine plan. This belief comes from such Qur'anic verses as:

> The command of God is a **decree** determined (Surah 33:38)

and

> In all things the master-planning is God's. (Surah 13:42)

It also comes from numerous references in the Qur'an to the way in which things happened in the lives of the prophets that they did not understand at the time, but which they later came to see were a part of Allah's plan for them. As **Yusuf** (Joseph) says at the end of Surah 12 (a whole surah about the life of Yusuf):

> This is the fulfilment of my vision of old! God hath made it come true! He was indeed good to me when He took me out of prison and brought you out of the desert, even after Satan had sown enmity between me and my brothers. Verily my Lord understandeth best the mysteries of all He planneth to do. (Surah 12:100)

From such verses, Muslims believe that Allah has a plan for the universe that he created, that he has the power to make that plan happen (Allah is omnipotent) and that he knows what will happen (he is omniscient) so that in the end everything will work out as Allah willed and as Allah wanted. This is why many Muslims will say '*insh Allah*', meaning 'if Allah wills', after statements such as 'See you next week' – things will only happen if Allah wants them to. However, belief in *al-Qadr* is not without its problems.

Al-Qadr and the Day of Judgement

The Muslim teachings on *Akirah* are that people will be brought before Allah at the end of the world for the final judgement. Allah will judge everyone on the basis of their beliefs and actions and reward or punish them accordingly. But surely people can only be punished for something they did of their own free will? People can only be punished for actions for which they are responsible and which they could have done differently if they had so chosen. On this understanding, belief in *al-Qadr* and Allah's final judgement seem to be mutually contradictory.

This has led to two different Muslim explanations:

- Many Shi'a Muslims follow the explanation of the eighth-century Muslim theologians called **Mu'tazilites** who suggested that Allah created humans with free will and made them his vicegerents responsible for the world. So it is up to humans what happens and individual humans are responsible if misusing their free will results in them disobeying God. Therefore, they can be judged by God on the Last Day because they are responsible for their actions.

Thinking points

In this topic you need to:
- think about the nature and importance of predestination for Muslims
- consider how *al-Qadr* and human freedom relate to the Day of Judgement
- consider different understandings of predestination in Sunni and Shi'a Islam
- be able to explain and evaluate the implications of belief in *al-Qadr* for Muslims today.

Useful words

Predestination – the belief that everything that happens has already been decided
Decree – an official order from a high authority
Yusuf – the prophet Joseph (coat of many colours)
Insh Allah – if God wills
Mu'tazilites – eighth-century Muslim theologians regarded as non-Muslim by most Sunni Muslims today

Activities

1. Why do Muslims believe in *al-Qadr*?
2. How does belief in *al-Qadr* make it difficult to explain why there is evil and suffering in the world?

Section 1a: Beliefs and teachings

Useful words

Foreknowledge – knowing what is going to happen long before it does

The Prophet said, 'Allah says, "The vow, does not bring about for the son of Adam anything I have not decreed for him, but his vow may coincide with what has been decided for him, and by this way I cause a miser to spend of his wealth. So he gives Me (spends in charity) for the fulfilment of what has been decreed for him what he would not give Me before but for his vow."' (Sahih Bukhari 78:685)

- Sunni Muslims tend to follow the explanation of another eighth-century theologian, al'Ashari, who claimed that Allah knows what people will do before they do it, since he has the attribute of **foreknowledge**. Allah knows what people will do, but they do it of their own free will. This idea was explained more recently by a Sunni scholar:

By believing in al-Qadr we testify that Allah is the Absolute Controller of the affairs of His universe. It is He who decides what is good and what is bad ... We are unable to understand and interpret many of Allah's actions. It is meaningless to argue that human beings act without freedom and that we are forced to act in the way we do. We decide for ourselves what we will do, and what we will not, and we are responsible for our own actions. This freedom of action does not conflict with the foreknowledge of Allah.

The implications of belief in *al-Qadr* for Muslims today

Belief in *al-Qadr* means that Allah has a master plan for the universe, and, since Allah is omnipotent, that means that nothing happens without Allah's permission. This means that:

- Although they may face present sufferings, Muslims do not need to worry about their long-term future because God is in control, so all will be well.
- Any sufferings Muslims undergo must be accepted because what they suffer must be part of God's plan and so will have an eventual good outcome.
- Muslims cannot sit back and let God take responsibility for things because Muslims have free will and so although God's plans will happen, Muslims have to make their own choices and be responsible for their own actions and destiny.

Muslims need to work out what God wants them to do (for most Muslims this simply means observing the Five Pillars and living according to the Shari'ah) so they can be sure their choices are what God wants to happen.

Activities

1. Why does belief in *al-Qadr* make it difficult to accept Muslim beliefs about the Day of Judgement?
2. Do you think it is possible to believe in *al-Qadr* and that humans are free to choose what they want to do?

Summary

Al-Qadr is the belief that God has a plan for the world and so everything that happens is part of this. The Qur'an says that nothing happens unless God wants it to happen. Sunni Muslims believe that people choose what to do but they only choose what God wants. Shi'as believe that people have free will which somehow fits with God's plans.

Practice questions

c) Explain two reasons why Muslims believe in *al-Qadr*. In your answer you must refer to a source of wisdom and authority.

d) 'Nothing happens unless God wants it to.' Evaluate this statement considering arguments for and against. In your answer you should:
   - refer to Muslim points of view
   - refer to different Muslim points of view
   - reach a justified conclusion.

Topic 2.1a.8 *Akirah* (Muslim beliefs about life after death)

Muslim beliefs about life after death

Muslims believe that when people die their body stays in the grave until the Last Day.

The Qur'an teaches that this world will be brought to an end by God on a day of his choosing (the Last Day). Before that, Isa (Jesus) will return, the angel **Israfil** will sound the trumpet and the dead will be raised. Everyone will stand before God on the plain of Arafat (near Makkah) to be judged by God and sent to either heaven or hell:

> *They say, 'What when we are reduced to bones and dust should we really be raised up to be a new creation?' Say, 'Nay be ye stones or iron, or created matter which in your minds is hardest to be raised up, yet shall ye be raised up'. (Surah 17:49–51)*

> *That Day shall all men be sorted out. Then those who have believed and worked righteous deeds shall be made happy in a mead of delight. And those who have rejected faith and falsely denied Our signs and the meeting of the Hereafter, such shall be brought to punishment. (Surah 30:14–16)*

Most Muslims believe that the final judgement on the Last Day will be based on a mixture of faith and action. There are many Qur'anic references to those doing evil deeds as well as those rejecting faith being sent to hell; consequently, the most common belief is that only good Muslims will pass the test of the final judgement.

However, many Muslim think that the verse:

> *Whoever does evil will be requited accordingly, nor will he find, besides God, any protector or helper (Surah 4:123)*

means that in the end God will **intercede** for Muslims who have tried their best to be good Muslims, but have committed sins. After all, one of the major teachings of the Qur'an is that God is 'the Merciful' and 'the Compassionate'. There is another Muslim belief, based on the hadith, that the Prophet Muhammad will intercede for his followers who have sinned and that God will accept his intercession.

Muslims prepare for the Last Day when they confess their sins at Arafat.

Thinking points

In this topic you need to:
- think about Muslim beliefs about life after death: judgement, paradise, and hell, and how they are shown in the Qur'an
- think about the similarities and differences between Christian and Muslim beliefs
- be able to explain and evaluate why life after death is important for Muslims and how it might affect their lives.

Useful words

Israfil – the angel who begins the Last Day by blowing his trumpet

Intercede – to use your influence to persuade someone in authority to forgive another person

Activities

1. Read either Surah 17 or Surah 52 and write down any teachings about life after death that are not mentioned in the passages on this page.
2. Look at the photo of Arafat. Muslims believe they will have to read the book of their life in front of everyone there. Why might this be a frightening idea?

Section 1a: Beliefs and teachings

Useful words

Al'Jannah – heaven
Jahannam – hell
Barzakh – the period between death and the Last Day

Activities

1. Write out two different Muslim views about hell.
2. Look at the photo of the Muslim cemetery below. What is the big difference between this and a Christian cemetery? Why do you think this is?

One day He will gather them together: it will be as if they had tarried but an hour of a day: they will recognise each other. (Surah 10:45)

A relative prays in a Muslim cemetery in Algeria.

Muslim beliefs about paradise

All Muslims believe that heaven is paradise. The Qur'an describes heaven as **al'Jannah** (the Garden):

> Gardens of perpetual bliss: they shall enter there, as well as the righteous among their fathers, their spouses, and their offspring. Angels shall enter from every gate (with the salutation): 'Peace be with you, that you persevered in patience! Now how excellent is the final home!' *(Surah 13:23–24)*

The Qur'an also describes heaven as a place of delights:

> They will not hear therein ill speech or commission of sin. But only the saying of: 'Peace! Peace!' *(Surah 56:25–26)*

> Allah hath promised to Believers, men and women, gardens under which rivers flow, to dwell therein, and beautiful mansions in gardens of everlasting bliss. But the greatest bliss is the good pleasure of Allah. That is the supreme felicity. *(Surah 9:72)*

Muslim beliefs about hell

Hell is **Jahannam** and is portrayed in the Qur'an as a place of fire and torture. However, there are different Muslim attitudes about the nature of hell because of different statements in the Qur'an about hell. The general view is that people will stay in hell forever, but some Muslims believe that bad Muslims will only stay in hell for a short time to be punished for their sins. They believe this because Surah 15 says that there are seven classes of hell and Surah 6 says that people only stay in hell for as long as God wills. Some Muslims even believe that these verses mean that good followers of other religions will only stay in hell for a short time.

Between death and the Last Day

There are also differences about what happens between death and the Last Day. The belief that after death souls stay in the grave until the Last Day is challenged by the Qur'anic teaching that those who die when on *hajj* or fighting in a holy war will go straight to heaven after death. Some Muslims use these verses to claim that the afterlife is spiritual and that people's souls are judged immediately after death and then go to a spiritual heaven or hell.

Muslims also have different beliefs about what happens in the period between people dying and their body being raised on the Last Day (this period is known as **Barzakh**). Some Muslim traditions say that after death, souls are visited by the angel of death and questioned about their faith. If they answer with true Muslim belief, they are shown their place in heaven, and look at it until they are raised on the Last Day. If they answer wrongly, they are beaten with clubs until the Last Day.

Other Muslim traditions say that after the death of the body, the soul hovers over the grave until the Last Day. Other Muslim traditions claim that the soul simply sleeps until the Last Day so that *Barzakh* will just seem like a moment between death and the Last Day, as stated in the Qur'an quotation in the margin.

Topic 2.1a.8 *Akirah* (Muslim beliefs about life after death)

Of course, all these traditions explain why Muslims are so careful with the body after death, why they insist on burial and not cremation, and why they are doubtful about autopsies and transplants.

Why life after death is important for Muslims

- The Qur'an teaches that there is life after death. Muslims believe that the Qur'an is the Word of God which contains everything God wants humans to know, therefore they must believe whatever the Qur'an says.
- Muhammad taught that there is life after death. Muslims believe that Muhammad is the last prophet God will ever send and the perfect example for Muslims. Therefore, they must believe whatever he taught.
- Islam has six fundamental beliefs (Allah, his angels, his holy books, his messengers, the Last Day and life after death) which all Muslims are expected to believe. Since Muhammad said that all Muslims must believe these, Muslims must believe in life after death.
- Muslims believe that this life is a test from God. The idea of a test involves the need for a judgement, and rewards for those who pass. Judgement and reward can only happen if there is life after death, therefore Muslims believe in life after death because it makes sense of this life being a test.
- Many Muslims believe in life after death because it gives their lives meaning and purpose. A life after death, in which people will be judged on how they lived this life, with the good rewarded and the evil punished, makes sense of this life. If the purpose of life is to live your life in such a way that you spend eternity in heaven, then that gives life meaning.

How Muslim beliefs about life after death affect the lives of Muslims

- Islam teaches that on the Last Day, all humans will be gathered before God on a vast plain and judged by God. The judgement will be made on the nature of people's lives. Those who have lived good Muslim lives will pass the judgement and go to paradise; everyone else will fail and go to hell. This affects Muslims' lives because they must try to live good Muslim lives if they are to go to paradise and avoid hell.
- Living a good Muslim life means observing the Five Pillars of Islam. So belief in life after death means that Muslims will pray five times a day, they will fast during Ramadan, they will pay their *zakah* and they will go on *hajj* at least once. So their beliefs about life after death will have a big effect on their lives.
- Living a good Muslim life also means following the holy law of Islam, the Shari'ah. This will affect Muslims' lives because they will have to eat *halal* food, observe Muslim dress laws, not drink alcohol, not gamble and not be involved in lending at or receiving interest.
- Muslims believe that resurrection means that nothing should be removed from the body after death. This means that funerals take place within 48 hours and the body is simply embalmed and buried. This affects Muslims' lives because they try to avoid post-mortems and autopsies and many Muslims have concerns about transplant surgery.

Section 1a: Beliefs and teachings

- Muslim beliefs about life after death give their lives meaning and purpose. Living your life with a purpose and believing that this life has meaning both affect the way you live. It may be why in surveys Muslims suffer less from depression and are less likely to die by suicide than atheists and agnostics.

Muslim and Christian beliefs about life after death

Similarities:

- Both believe this life is not all there is and that there will be life after death.
- Both believe there will be some form of judgement after death based on how people have lived on earth.
- Both believe in heaven as a place of paradise with God.
- Both believe that good people will go to heaven.
- Both believe that life after death is important because it makes sense of this life because it makes sure that the good are rewarded.

Similarities between Catholics and Conservative Protestants and Muslims:

- Both believe that the dead will be raised on the Last Day.
- Both believe that the Last Day will bring the world as we know it to an end.
- Both believe that people will be judged on what they have believed as well as how they have behaved.
- Both believe in hell as well as heaven and that bad people and people with the wrong beliefs will go to hell.

Differences:

- Christians do not believe the dead need to be buried quickly.
- Christians believe bodies can be cremated.
- Some Christians believe in immortality of the soul not resurrection of the body.
- Some Christians do not believe in the Last Day and believe judgement will take place as soon as people die.
- Catholic Christians believe that people not ready for heaven will go to purgatory to be cleansed of their sins before the Last Day.
- Some Christians do not believe in hell and believe that eventually everyone will go to heaven.

Summary

Muslims have different beliefs about what happens after people die; this period is known as *Barzakh*. Muslims all agree that on the Last Day the dead will be raised and judged by God. Good Muslims will go to paradise and evil people will go to hell, but there are some different ideas among Muslims about what happens to bad Muslims and good non-Muslims.

Practice questions

c Explain two different Muslim views about the final judgement. In your answer you must refer to a source of wisdom and authority.

d 'When you're dead, you're dead and that's the end of you.' Evaluate this statement considering arguments for and against. In your answer you should:
- refer to Muslim points of view
- refer to different Muslim points of view
- reach a justified conclusion.

How to answer questions

a) **Describe two similarities between Muslim beliefs about life after death and the beliefs of the main religious tradition of Britain. [3]**

Christianity is the main religious tradition of Britain. One similarity is that both Christians and Muslims believe this life is not all there is and that there will be life after death. Another similarity is that both Christians and Muslims believe there will be some form of judgement after death based on how people have lived on earth.

A high mark answer because Christianity is identified as the main religious tradition of Britain and two similarities are clearly described.

b) **Explain two reasons why the five roots of Usul ad-din are important for Shi'a Muslims. [4]**

The five roots are important for Shi'a Muslims because they come from the teachings of the Qur'an and the twelve imams, which means they have total authority.

Shi'a Muslims also believe that unless they understand and believe the five roots, they will not be able to perform the acts of worship necessary to live the Muslim life.

A high mark answer because two correct reasons are given and each reason is developed.

c) **Explain two reasons why belief in *Akirah* is important for Muslims. In your answer you must refer to a source of wisdom and authority. [5]**

The Qur'an teaches that there is life after death. Muslims believe that the Qur'an is the Word of God which contains everything God wants humans to know, therefore they must believe whatever the Qur'an says.

Muhammad taught that there is life after death. Muslims believe that Muhammad is the last prophet God will ever send and the perfect example for Muslims. Therefore, they must believe whatever he taught.

A high mark answer because two correct reasons are given and each reason is developed with a reference to the authority of the Qur'an and Muhammad.

d) **'Allah's omnipotence is His most important characteristic.' Evaluate this statement considering arguments for and against. In your response you should:**
- refer to Muslim points of view
- refer to different Muslim points of view
- reach a justified conclusion. [12 marks + 3 spelling, punctuation and grammar (SPaG) marks]

Some Muslims might believe this because two of the 99 names of Allah are: 'The Absolute' and 'the All-powerful' and it is a fundamental belief of Islam that Allah has complete power. He has created the universe and so must have complete power over the universe he has created. Islam means submission to God's will and a Muslim is one who has submitted their will to God's will because God is so great. That phrase is repeated many times during salah prayers: 'Allahu akbar' – 'God is great'.

[Continued]

Section 1a: Beliefs and teachings

However, most Muslims would think that God's most important characteristic is his oneness. The shahadah begins, 'I bear witness that there is no god, but God.' Belief in God's oneness means that God must be the Creator of everything and he must be the all-powerful who is in control of everything.

It seems to me that for Islam omnipotence is not the most important characteristic of God, his oneness is because this is the basic belief of Islam and all God's other characteristics come from his oneness.

A high mark answer because it gives three clear developed reasons for thinking that omnipotence must be God's greatest characteristic. It then gives three reasons for disagreeing and then reaches a fully justified conclusion.

The answer would reach full marks for SPaG as spelling, punctuation and grammar are correct and a wide range of specialist vocabulary (99 names, the Absolute, *salah*, *Allahu akbar*, *shahadah*) is used appropriately.

SPaG

A high mark answer because the answer spells, punctuates and uses the rules of grammar with consistent accuracy and effective control of meaning. A wide range of specialist terms is used adeptly and with precision.

2a Practices

Area of study 2: Study of second religion, either Islam or Judaism

Section 2a: Practices

Topic 2.2a.1 The Ten Obligatory Acts

Thinking points

In this topic you need to:
- think about the nature, history and purpose of the Ten Obligatory Acts and why the acts are important for Shi'a Muslims
- be able to evaluate the importance of the Ten Obligatory Acts for Shi'a Muslims today.

Useful words

Shahadah – the confession and witness of faith, the first pillar
Salah – ritual prayers to be said five times a day, the second pillar
Zakah – charity tax, the third pillar
Sawm – fasting, the fourth pillar
Ramadan – ninth month of the Islamic year; the month of fasting
Hajj – pilgrimage to Makkah, the fifth pillar
Khums – an additional charity tax for Shi'a Muslims

What are the Ten Obligatory Acts?

Sunni Muslims often refer to their faith as 'the House of Islam', by which they mean their home. A house needs foundations, and for the House of Islam this is the Qur'an. This is the word of Allah and so is the foundation of Muslim faith and worship. In the Middle East, houses are supported on pillars, and Sunni Muslims believe that the House of Islam is supported on five pillars:

1 *Shahadah* – declaration of faith.
2 *Salah* – ritual prayer.
3 *Zakah* – compulsory giving to the poor.
4 *Sawm* – fasting during **Ramadan**.
5 *Hajj* – annual pilgrimage to Makkah.

For Sunni Muslims, performing the Five Pillars is the practical expression of being a Muslim, and observing all five shows that a Muslim is a good Muslim.

Shi'a Islam teaches that there are Ten Obligatory Acts that Muslims must perform to show that they are good Shi'a Muslims who truly believe the Five Pillars. These acts are as follows:

1 *Salah* – the ritual prayer performed at set times, five times a day (covered in Topic 2.2a.3, page 196). Shi'as have some slightly different practices, such as using a tablet of wood or holy soil rather than a prayer mat, as they were mentioned in a Shi'a hadith. Some Shi'as combine the second and third prayers, and the fourth and fifth prayers.
2 *Sawm* – fasting during the month of Ramadan (covered in Topic 2.2a.4, page 200).
3 *Zakah* – the obligatory charity tax (covered in Topic 2.2a.5, page 205).
4 *Hajj* – the annual pilgrimage to Makkah (covered in Topic 2.2a.6, page 209).
5 *Khums* – this is a special type of *zakah* where a fifth of certain types of income must go to charity. This is a special Shi'a act (covered in Topic 2.2a.5, page 205).
6 *Jihad* – the struggle to be a good Muslim (covered in Topic 2.2a.7, page 214).
7 *Amr-bil-ma'ruf* (always doing that which is good). Shi'a Muslims are obliged always to seek out that which is good. For example, a Shi'a should never walk past someone in trouble, they should help them.
8 *Nahi anil munkar* (always avoiding that which is evil). Although a Shi'a should always seek out that which is good, they should keep well away from that which is evil and tell off anyone doing, or about to do, evil.
9 *Tawalla* (loving the relatives of the Prophet). This is closely connected with the Shi'a belief in the Imams: if the Prophet nominated his descendants to be Imams, then his relatives must also be special. Those who can trace their ancestry back to Muhammad receive special treatment from Shi'a Muslims.
10 *Tabarra* – hating those who hate Allah and his chosen ones.

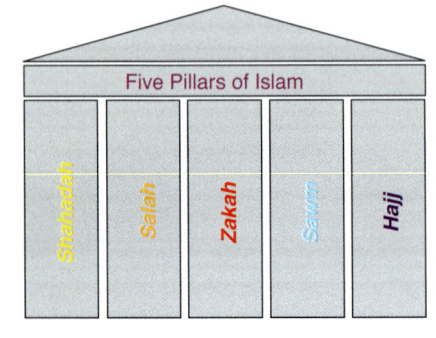

The Five Pillars of Islam in graphic form.

Topic 2.2a.1 The Ten Obligatory Acts

History

The Ten Obligatory Acts were developed by the Twelve Imams of Shi'a Islam (all of whom were descendants of the Prophet Muhammad). They perhaps developed at a point before Sunni Muslims had accepted the *shahadah* as the first pillar, which is why it is not one of the Ten Obligatory Acts but is regarded by Shi'as as essential for becoming a Muslim (see Topic 2.2a.2, page 194).

The acts were presumably developed to differentiate Shi'a Muslims from the Sunnis. The last six acts are not in the Five Pillars, but Sunnis would also agree that doing that which is good and avoiding evil are essential features of being a Muslim, and there was much debate in Sunni Islam as to whether *jihad* should be included as the sixth pillar. Sunnis have their own addition to *zakah* known as *sadaqah*, which is a voluntary tax to the poor that could be compared to the Shi'a obligatory act of *khums*.

Importance

Shi'a Muslims believe that fulfilling the Ten Obligatory Acts is important because:

- The Acts were established by Muhammad, Ali and the Imams.
- Allah will punish those who do not fulfil the acts.
- By observing the four practical pillars, a Muslim is following the example of the Prophet Muhammad, and following his example is the way to lead a good Muslim life.
- By fulfilling the acts a Shi'a Muslim feels confident that on the Day of Judgement, Allah will allow him or her into heaven.
- The obligatory acts are a major way of differentiating Shi'a from Sunni Muslims.

Advertisement for a *hajj* tour in a mosque in the UK.

The believers, men and women, are protectors of one another: they enjoin what is just, and forbid what is evil: they observe regular prayers, practise regular charity, and obey God and His Apostle. (Surah 9:71)

Practice questions

c Explain two reasons why the Ten Obligatory Acts are important for Shi'a Muslims. In your answer you must refer to a source of wisdom and authority.

d 'The Ten Obligatory Acts should be performed by all Muslims.' Evaluate this statement considering arguments for and against. In your answer you should:
- refer to Muslim points of view
- refer to different Muslim points of view
- reach a justified conclusion.

Activities

1. Which pillar is not in the Ten Obligatory Acts?
2. Which of the Ten Obligatory Acts are not pillars?
3. Look at the quotation from Surah 9:71. Which of the Obligatory Acts does it say Muslims should observe?
4. Who established the Ten Obligatory Acts?
5. Which of the Ten Obligatory Acts would cause problems for Sunni Muslims?
6. Look at the advertisement for the *hajj*. How might this unite the Sunni and Shi'a communities?

Summary

The Ten Obligatory Acts are: the four practical pillars (*salah*, *sawm*, *zakah* and *hajj*) plus *khums*, *jihad*, doing good, avoiding evil, following the relatives of the prophet and hating those who hate Allah and his chosen ones. They are only obligatory for Shi'a Muslims because the last two refer to the Shi'a Imams who are rejected by Sunni Muslims.

Section 2a: Practices

Topic 2.2a.2 *Shahadah*

Thinking points

In this topic you need to:
- think about the nature of *shahadah* as one of the Five Pillars, why reciting *shahadah* is important for Muslims and its place in Muslim practice today
- be able to explain and evaluate the significance of the *shahadah* for Sunni and Shi'a Muslims today.

Useful words

Minaret – the tower beside the mosque from which the call to prayer is announced
Muezzin – the prayer caller who announces the call to prayer five times a day
Ibadah – worship
Iman – faith

There is no god but He: that is the witness of God, His angels and those endued with knowledge standing firm on justice. There is no god but He, the Exalted in Power, the Wise. (Surah 3:18)

Activities

1. When is the *shahadah* said?
2. Look at the photo. Why is the *shahadah* often called the Muslim creed?
3. What is the difference between the *shahadah* and the other four pillars?

What the *shahadah* is

The *shahadah* in Arabic is

La Ilaha Illallah, Muhammadur Rasulullah,

which means,

There is no god but God. Muhammad is the prophet of God.

Shahadah means 'to observe, witness, testify', and the word sometimes comes at the beginning so that it becomes a statement of belief: 'I bear witness that there is no god but God and that Muhammad is the prophet of God'.

The *shahadah* is often called the Muslim creed because it contains all that Muslims must believe to call themselves Muslims.

The words of the *shahadah* are repeated many times a day by Muslims in the prayer ritual of *salah*. They are announced five times a day from the **minaret** of the mosque as the **muezzin** calls Muslims to prayer. They are the first words a baby hears, as his or her father should whisper them into the baby's ears. They should be the last words a Muslim utters if they know they are dying.

The *shahadah* text above a doorway in the Topkapi Palace, Istanbul, Turkey.

The *shahadah* as one of the Five Pillars

Some scholars believe that, although it is now the first pillar, *shahadah* was the last of the pillars and was not generally accepted as a pillar until about 50 years after the death of Muhammad. The four active pillars are prescribed in the Qur'an but the first pillar simply sums up the teachings of the Qur'an. The active pillars are ways of **ibadah** (worship), but you cannot worship without the faith (**iman**) on which the worship is based. Hence, *shahadah* is the first and the most important pillar, as if one does not believe that, he is not a Muslim, but if one does not believe one of the others he may still be a Muslim.

The *shahadah* has two simple beliefs: the unity of God and the prophethood of Muhammad. From these two beliefs come all the other beliefs. If you believe in God's unity then you believe in the oneness of creation and humanity, the **vicegerency** of humans, angels, prophets and holy books. If you believe that Muhammad is the prophet of God, then you accept the Qur'an as the Word of God and the *sunnah* of Muhammad as the path to follow in your life.

The importance of *shahadah* for Muslims today

The *shahadah* is important because:

- There are no ceremonies such as baptism or Bar Mitzvah to make you a Muslim; this is where the *shahadah* is of crucial importance because if someone converts, all they have to do is recite the *shahadah* in front of Muslim witnesses and then they are a Muslim.
- The *shahadah* shows that Muslims reject **polytheism** – there is no god but God.
- The *shahadah* shows that Islam rejects Christian beliefs about Jesus being the Son of God – Muhammad is nothing more than a prophet.
- The *shahadah* sums up the beliefs of Islam.
- Good Muslims recite it at least five times a day.

The *shahadah* in Shi'a Islam

In just the same way as Sunni Muslims, the Shi'a teach that reciting the *shahadah* in Arabic is all that is required for a person to become a Muslim. However, there are two important differences between Shi'as and Sunnis about the *shahadah*:

- Shi'as agree with the Sunnis that the oneness of God and divine guidance through his messenger Muhammad are essential to Islam. However, the Shi'as believe that for the spiritual and moral guidance of the community, God instructed Muhammad to designate Ali as the leader of the community, and so most Shi'as also add 'Ali is the vicegerent of God' at the end of the *shahadah* to show their belief that Ali is the leader of the believers along with God and Muhammad.
- *Shahadah* is not one of the Ten Obligatory Acts for Shi'as, whereas it is the first pillar for Sunnis.

This is the central pillar even though it is the only 'non-action' pillar. Iman [faith] provides the central pillar that sustains the whole structure. (Kurshid Ahmad, Islam – Its Meaning and Message, Islamic Foundation)

Useful words

Vicegerency – looking after something on behalf of someone else
Polytheism – worshipping many gods

Activities

1. Explain why is the *shahadah* important for Muslims today.
2. Are there any differences between Sunnis and Shi'as about the *shahadah*?

Practice questions

c) Explain two reasons why the *shahadah* is important for Muslims today. In your answer you must refer to a source of wisdom and authority

d) 'The *shahadah* is the most important of the Five Pillars.' Evaluate this statement considering arguments for and against. In your answer you should:
- refer to Muslim points of view
- refer to different Muslim points of view
- reach a justified conclusion.

Summary

The *shahadah* is the first pillar and says that Allah is the only God and Muhammad is his prophet. It is important because is sums up Muslim beliefs and is all that people have to say to be a Muslim. It is not an Obligatory Act for Shi'as but it is a pillar for Sunnis.

Section 2a: Practices

Topic 2.2a.3 *Salah*

Thinking points

In this topic you need to:
- think about the nature, history, significance and purpose of *salah* for Sunni and Shi'a Muslims
- consider how *salah* is performed (ablution, times, directions, movements and recitations) in the home and mosque
- think about *jummah* prayer and consider similarities and differences between Christian and Muslim worship
- be able to explain and evaluate the importance of *salah* for Muslims.

When ye prepare for prayer, wash your faces and your hands to the elbows, rub your head and your feet up to the ankles. If ye are in a state of impurity, bathe your whole body. (Surah 5:7)

Useful words

Prostrated – to put oneself flat on the ground so as to be lying face downwards, especially in respect of submission
Fajr – dawn prayer
Zuhr – midday prayers
As'r – afternoon prayer
Maghrib – sunset prayers
Isha – night prayer
Muezzin – the prayer caller
Adhan – the call to prayer
Minaret – the tower from which the prayer call comes
Wudu – the ritual washing before prayers

The history of *salah*

Salah is the five times a day ritual prayer of Islam. *Salah* as it is known today began with Muhammad (although Muslims would argue that *salah* began with Adam as it was part of the message given by God to the prophets).

According to the Muslim biographies, Muhammad began a system of morning and evening prayers during which Muslims faced Jerusalem and **prostrated** themselves as a sign of their submission to God. A hadith collected by al-Bukhari says that al-Bara' bin 'Azib narrated:

Allah's Messenger offered his prayers facing Bayt Al-Maqdis [Jerusalem] for sixteen or seventeen months.

When Muhammad set up the Muslim community in Madinah in 622CE, the direction of prayer was changed from Jerusalem to Makkah and an afternoon prayer was added.

By 628CE the ritual prayer of *salah* was established at five times a day, with Muhammad indicating how to perform the ritual on the basis of revelations as recorded in the Qur'an:

Set up regular prayers; for such prayers are enjoined on believers at stated times. (Surah 4:103)

Establish regular prayers at the sun's decline till the darkness of the night, and the morning prayer and reading: for the prayer and reading in the morning carry their testimony. And pray in the small watches of the morning an additional prayer. (Surah 17:78)

Turn thy face in the direction of the Sacred Mosque; that is indeed the truth. (Surah 2:149)

How *salah* is performed

- *Salah* should take place five times a day:
  - *Fajr* – between dawn and sunrise
  - *Zuhr* – after midday until afternoon
  - *As'r* – between late afternoon and sunset
  - *Maghrib* – between sunset and the end of daylight, and
  - *Isha* – between sunset and dawn.
- The time for prayer is announced by the **muezzin** making the **adhan** (call to prayer) from the **minaret** of the mosque.
- Muslims must prepare for *salah* by removing their shoes and then performing **wudu** (washing hands, arms to the elbow, face, nostrils, ears and head, and washing the feet three times). *Salah* is a sacred moment when a Muslim makes direct contact with God and so must be as pure as possible.
- Muslims must then find a clean place.

- To pray, Muslims must then face the direction of Makkah (*qibla*).
- A set prayer ritual must be carried out: repeat the call to prayer, make a prayer of intention, stand with hands to ears and recite Surah 1, kneel on the floor and touch the forehead to the ground as a sign of submission to God, raise the top half of the body and give God the glory, prostrate again, then stand up and say '*Allahu akbar*' (God is great). This ritual is called a **raka** and each prayer time has a set number of *rakat*.
- During each *salah* the prayer must repeat the *shahadah*, and request God's blessing on the people around them and Muhammad and all the prophets.
- *Salah* ends by saying 'the peace and mercy of Allah be upon you' over each shoulder.
- *Salah* must be said in Arabic, with all the people praying performing the same actions and facing the same direction.

Salah in the home

Many Muslims say their prayers at home as a family, with the whole family joining in. They often have a special room which they keep ritually clean and never enter when wearing shoes. They will perform their *wudu* in the bathroom and have prayer mats which are kept facing Makkah (the direction of the Ka'aba can be found using a *qibla* compass).

Many Muslims think that family *salah* is a good way of binding the family and even use the Christian saying 'the family that prays together stays together'. It is also often easier for women and girls to pray at home.

Salah in the mosque

Although *salah* can be said anywhere, it is thought preferable for it to be performed in the mosque because of this verse in the Qur'an:

> bow down your heads with those who bow down in worship.
> (Surah 2:43)

It is from the mosque that the muezzin makes the call to prayer:

> God is great. I bear witness that there is no god but God and that Muhammad is the prophet of God. Rush to prayer. Rush to success. God is great. There is no god but God.

Each mosque also has a prayer board with six clocks showing the times of the five daily prayers and **jummah** prayers on Friday. The prayer times vary from week to week (except near the equator) as they are based on the times of sunrise and sunset.

All mosques have communal *wudu* facilities and a prayer hall which can never be entered by anyone wearing shoes. The carpet in the hall will have lines directed to the prayer wall where the **mihrab** (*qibla* alcove) indicates the direction of the Ka'aba.

The worshippers stand in lines behind the **imam** (prayer leader), who leads them through the ritual.

Most mosques have a special area for women to perform *salah* (usually a gallery) as men and women must be separated. There is a tradition in the Indian subcontinent (India, Pakistan and Bangladesh) for women to pray at home.

Useful words

Qibla – direction of the Ka'aba in Makkah
Raka – the set actions in the prayer ritual (plural *rakat*)
Jummah – Friday midday prayers
Mihrab – alcove in mosques showing the direction of Makkah
Imam – prayer leader

Activities

1. What must happen before a Muslim performs *salah*?
2. Does the Qur'an tell Muslims all they need to know about *salah*?
3. Look at the photo of *salah* below. What can be learned from this about the nature and meaning of *salah*?
4. Why do you think many women prefer to pray at home?

Muslim sisters praying in their home.

Section 2a: Practices

Jummah prayer

O ye who believe! When the call is proclaimed to prayer on Friday, hasten earnestly to the remembrance of God, and leave off business: that is best for you if ye but knew! And when the Prayer is finished, then ye may disperse through the land and seek the bounty of God. (Surah 62:10)

This verse is the basis of the custom of Muslims attending mosque for *Zuhr* prayers on a Friday (many Muslim countries have a Friday to Saturday weekend). These prayers are now called *jummah* prayers and should be attended by at least 40 adult males, and so they are performed in mosques designated **jami mosques** where it can be expected there will be 40 adult males.

The imam leads the first two *rakat* and then preaches a sermon (**khutba**), often giving advice on how to live a good Muslim life (usually related to the country they are in), after which he leads the worshippers in the final *rakat*.

Muslims living in a non-Muslim country would only need an hour or so off from work on Friday to attend *jummah* prayers.

Why *salah* is important to Muslims today

- It puts them in direct contact with God five times a day.
- It reminds them every day that they have submitted themselves to God.
- It unites them with their fellow Muslims as they stand in lines performing the same actions and saying the same words.
- It is a discipline which forces Muslims to take their religion seriously.
- It reminds Muslims of the fundamentals of Islam: submission and peace.
- It is a way of having their sins forgiven, as a hadith says: 'the five prayers remove sins as water removes dirt'.
- It is commanded by the Qur'an in such verses as:

    But celebrate the praises of the Lord, and be of those who prostrate themselves in adoration. (Surah 15:98)

    Establish regular prayer, for prayer restrains from shameful and unjust deeds; and remembrance of God is the greatest thing in life. (Surah 29:45)

Shi'as and *salah*

Salah has the same importance for Shi'as as for Sunnis and *salah* is one of the Ten Obligatory Acts. The differences in practice have been covered in Topic 2.2a.1, page 192.

A mosque clock in Manchester showing the time of prayers.

Useful words
Jami mosques – mosques appointed for Friday prayers
Khutba – sermon

Activities
1. Why do you think *jummah* prayers are important?
2. Look at the prayer board above. Why do you think Muslims need to consult a board like this every week?

Christian and Muslim worship

Salah is Muslim worship and *du'a* is Muslim personal prayer. There are no differences between *du'a* and Christian personal prayer.

Differences:

- Muslims must perform *wudu* before worship, but Christians do not, although some Christians sprinkle themselves with holy water as they enter the church.
- Muslims must face Makkah for *salah* whereas Christians can worship facing any direction (although most Catholic, Orthodox and Anglican churches face the east).
- Muslims worship in Arabic, whereas Christians worship in their native language.
- Men and women worship separately in Islam, whereas the sexes worship together in Christianity.
- The Muslim special day for worship is Friday, whereas the Christian special day is Sunday.
- Muslims should perform *salah* five times a day at set times, whereas Christians are only required to go to church on Sunday, but are expected to pray every morning and evening.
- Muslims perform a set ritual to perform *salah*, but only Christian liturgical worship has set rituals; Pentecostals and other Protestants have no set rituals.
- Christian worship usually has musical accompaniment and often has hymns, Muslim worship does not.
- Christian worship often has visual stimuli (crosses, stained-glass windows, statues of Mary and the saints) Muslim worship does not.

Similarities:

- Weekly worship includes a sermon in both faiths.
- Worship involves the whole congregation saying a prayer together (even non-liturgical Christian worship includes saying the Lord's Prayer).
- Both worships involve praying for the needs of others.

Practice questions

c Explain two reasons why *jummah* prayers are important for Muslims. In your answer you must refer to a source of wisdom and authority.

d '*Salah* is the most important of the Five Pillars.' Evaluate this statement considering arguments for and against. In your answer you should:
- refer to Muslim points of view
- refer to different Muslim points of view
- reach a justified conclusion.

Summary

Salah should take place five times a day and can be performed wherever a Muslim is as long as they can find a clean place, face the direction of the Ka'aba and wash themselves according to the rules of *wudu*. There is a set ritual and the prayers must be said in Arabic. There is a special *salah* on Friday midday (*jummah* prayers) which must be said in the mosque. *Salah* is important because it gives direct contact with God five times a day.

Section 2a: Practices

Topic 2.2a.4 *Sawm*

Thinking points

In this topic you need to:
- think about the nature, history and purpose of *sawm*; and the nature and importance of *sawm* during Ramadan (Surah 2:183–185)
- consider the nature and significance of the Night of Power and why it is important for Muslims
- be able to explain and evaluate the importance of *sawm* and Ramadan for Muslims.

The nature of *sawm*

Sawm is the fourth pillar and means fasting. The Qur'an makes plain that Muslims must practise fasting. Muslims can fast voluntarily at any time (except the *ids*, when fasting is banned), but the month of Ramadan soon became a compulsory month of fasting,

The obligation to fast begins on the first day of Ramadan (the ninth month of the Islamic year), which occurs when the new moon is seen and lasts until the sighting of the next new moon.

Sawm means no food, drink, smoking, lying, gossiping, swearing, getting angry or sex from dawn to dusk. Families have two special meals a day, the **iftar** to break the fast at night and the **suhur** just before dawn to give strength to face the day's fast.

All Muslims above the age of puberty should fast, although there are special exemptions for those on journeys (often taken to cover doing exams), the elderly, the sick, breastfeeding mothers and menstruating women. However, the fast days should either be made up later or be compensated for by feeding a poor person.

Useful words

Iftar – the meal breaking the fast at night
Suhur – the meal just before fasting starts at dawn

> *O ye who believe! Fasting is prescribed to you as it was prescribed to those before you that ye may learn self-restraint for a fixed number of days; but if any of you is ill or on a journey, the prescribed number of days should be made up from days later. For those who can do it with hardship is a ransom, the feeding of one that is indigent. But he that will give more, of his own free will, it is better for him. And it is better for you that ye fast, if ye only knew. Ramadan is the month in which was sent down the Qur'an as a guide to mankind, also clear signs for guidance and judgement. So everyone of you who is present at his home in that month should spend it in fasting. But if anyone is ill or on a journey, the prescribed days should be made up by days later. God intends every facility for you. He does not want to put you to difficulties. He wants you to complete the prescribed period, and to glorify Him in that He has guided you; and perchance ye shall be grateful. (Surah 2:183–185)*

As part of the Ramadan fast, extra prayers are said and one thirtieth of the Qur'an is read each day so that at the end of Ramadan the whole Qur'an has been read. All Muslims try to attend mosque on the 27th of Ramadan (*Laylat al-Qad'r* – the Night of Power) to celebrate the night when Muhammad received the first revelation of the Qur'an.

Activities

1. What must Muslims do during Ramadan?
2. Why is *Laylat al-Qad'r* important for Muslims?

There are often social gatherings at *iftar* when traditional foods are consumed. This ASDA supermarket is making these foods easily available to its Muslim clients.

The history of *sawm*

Muslims believe that fasting has always been part of Islam:

Fasting is prescribed to you as it was prescribed to those before you. (Surah 2:183)

This can be seen in the religions of Judaism and Christianity, which both have fasting (for example, Yom Kippur for Jews and Lent for Christians) as part of the message they were given which was distorted, but not forgotten.

Ramadan had been a traditional holy month in Arabia. It was a truce month (no fighting was allowed) and holy men fasted. It fell at a fixed time of the year and by making the Muslim calendar a lunar one, Muhammad made sure that Ramadan was no longer connected with Makkan polytheism and a particular season of the year. Ramadan moves back eleven days each year so that over a period of 32 years it moves through all the seasons (which causes major problems in northern latitudes when Ramadan falls in May, June and July).

The biographies record that Muhammad observed his first Ramadan in 625CE after the instruction in Surah 2 had been revealed to him.

Why *sawm* during Ramadan is important for Muslims

Sawm is important because:

- Keeping the fast is fulfilling the fourth pillar of Islam.
- The Qur'an is the greatest gift God has for humanity and keeping the fast in Ramadan is a way of thanking God for the Qur'an.
- Fasting brings Muslims closer to God so they can concentrate on God rather than the ordinary things of life.
- Fasting promotes the self-control which any Muslim needs to practise their faith properly.
- Many Muslims see Ramadan as an annual training programme to recharge their spiritual batteries so they can carry out their duties to God for the rest of the year.

Fasting in the Arctic Circle

The Islam Society of Northern Finland claims there are two schools of thought about the problem. Egyptian lawyers say that if the fast lasts more than 18 hours, then Muslims can follow the Makkan time or the nearest Muslim country time. Saudi Arabian lawyers say that whether the hours of fasting are long or short, Muslims have to follow the local time. The Society recommends that Muslims in northern Finland observe either Makkah's fasting hours or Turkish time because Turkey is the nearest Muslim country to Finland.

Activities

1. Why can Ramadan be a problem for Muslims living in the Arctic Circle?
2. What do you think about the advice given to such Muslims above?

Section 2a: Practices

'The night of al-Qadr is better than a thousand months'

Dusk at the Sultan Omar Ali Saifuddin Mosque in Brunei.

- Fasting in Ramadan unites and strengthens the Muslim community.
- Ramadan brings Muslim families together and strengthens their bonds.

Useful words

Laylat al-Qadr – the Night of Power (destiny)
Destiny – what has been set out to happen
Sirah – a biography of the prophet Muhammad
Jibril – the angel Gabriel

Laylat al-Qadr

Laylat al-Qadr can be translated as either the 'Night of Power and Excellence' or the 'Night of **Destiny**'. It was the night when Muhammad received the first revelation of the Qur'an.

The biographies of Muhammad (known as *Sirah*) tell us that in the year before 610CE, Muhammad had become very dissatisfied with the polytheistic religion of Makkah and had begun to go to the nearby Mount Nur to fast, pray and meditate in Cave Hira. Muhammad decided to spend the whole month of Ramadan in contemplation. Towards the end of the month he was visited by the angel **Jibril**, who told him to 'recite', and Muhammad frightenedly replied that he had nothing to recite. This happened twice and then the angel said:

> *Proclaim in the name of thy Lord and Cherisher, who created, created man out of a clot of congealed blood. Proclaim! And thy Lord is Most Bountiful, He who taught the use of the pen, taught man that which he knew not.* (Surah 96:1–5)

This was the first revelation Muhammad received and the rest of the Qur'an came over the next 23 years. There is no indication in the Qur'an as to which date in Ramadan the revelation occurred, although it is generally agreed that the revelation occurred in the last ten days of the month.

Activity

Look at the photo of *al-Qadr* above. What do you think it means and do you think it is true?

As a result, those who can afford to, devote their time in **remembrance of Allah** (often retired people) and stay in the mosque for the final ten days of Ramadan. They fast during the day and occupy themselves with the remembrance of Allah, performing voluntary prayers and studying the Qur'an day and night. However, most Sunni Muslims celebrate the night on the 27th of Ramadan and attend mosque for special prayers and read the Qur'an.

Useful words

Remembrance of Allah – thinking about God in a meditative way

Muslim beliefs about the Night of Power

- Praying on that night is the best prayer (better than 1000 months of prayers).
- Praying in the mosque on the Night of Power can bring forgiveness of all a person's sins.
- There is a tradition that reciting Surahs 29 and 30 during the 23rd night of Ramadan will ensure admission into paradise.
- Praying on the Night of Power brings religious insight ('Therein come down the angels and the Spirit by Allah's permission').
- Meditating and retreating to the mosque for the last ten days of Ramadan can bring a special closeness to and relationship with Allah.

Many Muslims believe that *Laylat al-Qadr* is the night when Allah determines everyone's destiny (one meaning of *Qadr*) for the coming year:

> *During Lailatul-Qadr, the angels, the spirit, and the trusted scribes all descend to the lower heavens and write down whatever Allah decrees that year, and if Allah wishes to advance something or postpone it or add thereto, He orders the angel to erase it and replace it with whatever He decrees.* (Imam Abu Abdullah al-Sadiq)

According to this view, destiny includes life and death, sustenance, abundance of crops or famine, and everything good or bad. A Shi'a hadith claims that, 'Allah the Glorified and Exalted determines in this night each and every event to occur during the next year to any and all of His creation.'

Why the Night of Power is important for Muslims today

- It remembers and celebrates the revelation of the Qur'an, the final and unalterable Word of God.
- It remembers and celebrates the calling of Muhammad to be the last and final messenger of God to the world.
- Some Muslims believe this was the day Muhammad made his night journey to heaven (*al Mi'raj*) when God gave him the details of *salah*.
- It is also believed that this was the night when Moses died, when Joshua died and when Jesus was taken to heaven.
- Those who believe it is the Night of Destiny believe it is hugely important because God will decide everything to happen in the coming year.

Activity

Do you think your future has been decided or is your destiny in your own hands?

Section 2a: Practices

- It is particularly important for Shi'a Muslims because there is a hadith from Ali which says that this is the night when God decreed that Ali and his descendants would be the Imams:

    Imam Ali ibn Abu Talib said, 'The Messenger of Allah asked me once, "O Ali! Do you know the implication of Lailatul-Qadr?" I said, "No, indeed, O Messenger of Allah!" He said, "Allah, the Praised One, the Most Glorified, decreed in it what will take place till the Day of Judgement, and among what He, the most Exalted, the Most Great, decreed was your own Imamate and the Imamate of your offspring till the Day of Resurrection."'

Practice questions

c Explain two reasons why Muslims fast in Ramadan. In your answer you must refer to a source of wisdom and authority.

d 'One night in Ramadan is no more important than another.' Evaluate this statement considering arguments for and against. In your answer you should:
- refer to Muslim points of view
- reach a justified conclusion.

Summary

Sawm is the fourth pillar. It means fasting and is used to refer to the month-long fast during Ramadan. Adult Muslims do not eat or drink during daylight hours and say extra prayers. It is commanded in the Qur'an and Muslims believe it is a way of thanking God for the Qur'an, which was given in Ramadan on the Night of Power. On this night special prayers are said. Muslims believe that fasting in Ramadan forgives sins.

Topic 2.2a.5 *Zakah* and *khums*

Zakah

Zakah is the third pillar of Islam and is an annual tax on wealth. It is often known as the charity tax.

The Qur'an does not specify exactly how much *zakah* should be paid:

> *O ye who believe spend out of the bounties We have provided for you.* (Surah 2:254)

> *They ask thee what they should spend in charity. Say, 'Whatever ye spend, that is good'.* (Surah 2:215)

Consequently, Sunni Muslims follow the Shari'ah based on the *sunnah* of the Prophet to know what to give.

Clearly, poor people should not have to pay *zakah* and the Shari'ah sets down a **nisab** which sets out the minimum people need to have before they have to pay *zakah*. If what you have left over has been in your possession for a lunar year and is more than the UK *nisab* (£2220 for 2015) then you must pay 2½ per cent of that amount as *zakah* (more details can be found at http://zakatcalculator.co.uk).

Many Muslims pay their *zakah* direct to Muslim charities such as Islamic Relief and Muslim Aid. Every mosque also has a *zakah* committee which collects *zakah* and distributes it according to the wishes of the mosque committee.

Special *zakahs* are paid on Id-ul-Fitr (currently £4 per family member) and on Id-ul-Adha, when a donation is often given to charity rather than sharing meat with the poor.

Thinking points

In this topic you need to:
- think about the nature, history, purpose and benefits of both *zakah* and *khums*
- be able to explain why *zakah* is important for Sunni Muslims and why *khums* is important for Shi'a Muslims.

Useful words

Nisab – the amount of income or wealth a Muslim needs to have before they are liable for *zakah*

Activity

Explain why *zakah* is important for Sunni Muslims.

Muslims paying *zakah* at a mosque in Singapore.

Section 2a: Practices

> **Useful words**
> **Alms** – charitable giving to the poor
> **Sadaqah** – voluntary giving to the poor

The purpose of zakah

Surah 9:60 says,

> *Alms are for the poor and the needy, and those employed to administer the funds; for those whose hearts have been recently reconciled to the truth; for those in bondage and debt; in the cause of God and for the wayfarer.*

On the basis of this verse, *zakah* is used for orphans, widows, poor people, homeless people and tax collectors, and for religious purposes. Many Muslims give their *zakah* to charities helping the poor in less developed countries as they think this is the spirit of *zakah*.

Why Muslims give zakah

- It is the third pillar of Islam, which all Muslims must fulfil.
- Paying *zakah* is a sign of a Muslim's submission to God and worship of God.
- *Zakah* means purification. Islam teaches that wealth can be evil and cut people off from God, but if Muslims pays *zakah* they purify the wealth that they keep.
- There are Muslim teachings that connect *salah* and *zakah*; both are associated with purifying. Some scholars teach that God is more likely to accept prayers if the person praying pays *zakah*.

Sadaqah

Islam also has the idea of voluntary giving to charity. This is known as **sadaqah** because it is voluntary, whereas *zakah* is compulsory. *Zakah* aims to reduce the gap between the rich and the poor and so Muslims should give voluntary *sadaqah* above *zakah* to help the poor:

> *Seest thou one who denies the judgement to come? Then such is the man who repulses the orphan and encourages not the feeding of the indigent. (Surah 107:1–3)*

> *Those who in charity spend of their goods by night and by day, in secret and in public, have their reward with their Lord. (Surah 2:274)*

> *Protect your property by giving zakat, and help your relatives to recover from disease by giving charity. (Hadith)*

> *He who eats and drinks whilst his brother goes hungry is not one of us. (Hadith quoted by al-Bukhari)*

Khums

Shi'a Muslims also have a special *khums* tax.

Khums (one fifth of a gain) is based on this verse:

> *Know that whatever of a thing you acquire, a fifth of it is for Allah, for the Messenger, for the near relative, and the orphans and the needy and the wayfarer. (Surah 8:41)*

Activity

What are the similarities and differences between *zakah* and *khums*?

Topic 2.2a.5 *Zakah* and *khums*

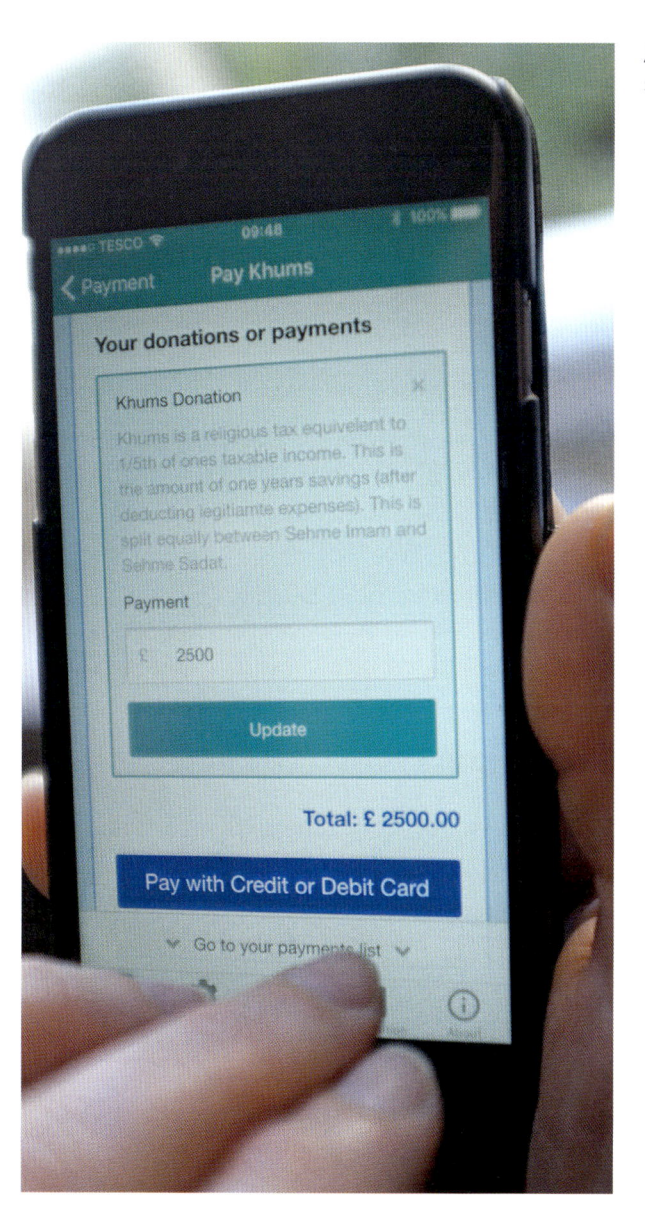

A business proprietor calculating her *khums* payment using a smartphone app.

(Sunni translations of the Qur'an read 'out of all the booty that ye may acquire a fifth share is assigned to God, and to the Apostle, and to near relatives, orphans, the needy, and to the wayfarer' and so Sunni Muslims teach that *khums* applies only to proceeds from war.)

Khums, in the Shi'a tradition, is applied to the business profit, or surplus, of a business income. It is payable at the beginning of the financial year. Shi'a lawyers say that twenty per cent of surplus of income (the difference between assets and outgoings), any proceeds from mines and minerals (this would include most jewellery), precious stones obtained from the sea by diving, treasures and proceeds from land sold to non-Muslims must be paid as *khums*.

Of the *khums* money, 50 per cent goes to religious causes and poor descendants of the Prophet, and 50 per cent goes to the poor, the orphans and the homeless. This means that ten per cent of income goes to religious lawyers and scholars. This has been a major source of income and financial independence for religious leaders in Shi'a areas.

Shi'as pay *zakah* if they are farmers or have gold or silver coins. They also pay *sadaqah* to the poor and needy.

Activities

1. Look at the photo above. How do you know this phone app is for a Shi'a Muslim?
2. Why do you think Shi'as feel it is important that religious leaders are properly cared for and are independent of state control or influence?
3. What do you think are the benefits of *khums* to: a) the community, b) those receiving *khums*, c) those giving *khums*?

207

Section 2a: Practices

The purpose of khums

- To ensure that the descendants of the Prophet are properly cared for.
- To make sure that religious leaders are properly cared for and are independent of state control or influence.
- To provide and support religious institutions such as school, colleges and mosques.
- To provide security for the poor, the homeless and orphans.

Why Shi'as pay khums

- It is commanded by the Qur'an.
- It is a way of supporting the descendants of the Prophet, who are given special reverence by Shi'a Muslims.
- It is commanded by Shi'a religious lawyers.
- It is a way of supporting and spreading Shi'a Islam.
- It helps the poor and needy.

The benefits of receiving zakah and khums

Rewards go not only to those who give *zakah* and *khums*, but also to the people who receive *zakah* and *khums*. Apart from receiving the benefit of money to relieve their poverty, they also receive the spiritual benefits of:

- knowing they have helped a fellow Muslim to purify their money
- knowing they have helped a fellow Muslim to have their sins forgiven
- knowing they have been part of God's plan to redistribute wealth from the rich to the poor.

> **Practice questions**
>
> **c** Explain two reasons why paying *zakah* is important for Muslims. In your answer you must refer to a source of wisdom and authority
>
> **d** '*Zakah* and *khums* alone will never solve the problems of poverty.' Evaluate this statement considering arguments for and against. In your answer you should:
> - refer to Muslim points of view
> - refer to different Muslim points of view
> - reach a justified conclusion.

> **Summary**
>
> *Zakah* is the third pillar and is an annual tax of 2½ per cent on wealth, which is paid to help the poor as commanded in the Qur'an. Special *zakahs* are paid on the *ids* and Muslims make voluntary donations called *sadaqah*. Shi'a Muslims pay a special *khums* tax of twenty per cent of business surplus which is how Shi'as interpret Surah 8:41, but Sunnis think it is twenty per cent of profits from war.

Topic 2.2a.6 *Hajj*

The nature of *hajj*

Hajj is the fifth of the Five Pillars and is the only one that is not compulsory. *Hajj* starts on the eighth day of the month of **Dhu al-Hijjah** and lasts until the thirteenth. Although all Muslims should try to go on *hajj*, they are only allowed to go if:

- They have sufficient money to provide for their dependants while they are away from home.
- They are physically and mentally fit and prepared for the physical demands of *hajj*.

While on *hajj* men must wear the **ihram** (two pieces of unsewn cloth, one around the waist and one over the shoulder); women wear a white garment covering the whole body except for the face and feet (no veils on *hajj*).

Hajj is now highly organised by the Saudi government, which is responsible for the holy sites and has carried out extensive building works so the area can cope with over 2 million pilgrims on *hajj*. Pilgrims are divided into groups (often called a caravan) with a group guide who will be a Saudi.

Most events take place in the Great Mosque of Makkah, which contains:

- the **Ka'aba**
- the **Zamzam well**
- the **Ma'sa**.

On the first day of *hajj* pilgrims circuit the Ka'aba seven times while saying the **talbiya** prayer (this is called a **tawaf**). Then they do seven circuits of the Ma'sa and return to the main courtyard for midday prayer, after which a sermon is preached outlining the events of *hajj* and giving advice to the pilgrims.

The next day the pilgrims are given water from the Zamzam well and then walk ten kilometres to **Mina**, where they stay until night prayers, and then walk overnight the eight kilometres to **Arafat**.

The next day is the Waquf of Arafat, when pilgrims stand on the plain in front of the hill of Arafat and confess their sins (it is believed that any sins confessed here are immediately forgiven). Then the pilgrims jog to Muzdalifah for a torchlight **waquf** before walking back to Mina. On the way to Mina they should collect 49 stones ready for the next day. Any pilgrims who miss the Waquf of Arafat must repeat *hajj*.

On the 10th of Dhu al-Hijjah the pilgrims throw stones at the stoning pillars (the pillars represent Satan and remind the pilgrims of Satan tempting Ibrahim to disobey God). Then the pilgrims offer a sacrifice to God remembering how God provided a sacrifice for Ibrahim after he obeyed God by being prepared to sacrifice his son. There are slaughterhouses around Mina and groups of pilgrims usually get together to buy an animal and appoint a slaughterer to make the sacrifice for them. Pilgrims should then eat some of the meat and give the rest to the poor. Nowadays, the Saudi government puts the meat on to refrigerator ships and sends it to poor

Thinking points

In this topic you need to:
- think about the nature, role, origins and significance of *hajj*, including Surah 2:124–130 and 22:25–30
- understand how *hajj* is performed and why *hajj* is important for Muslims
- be able to explain and evaluate the benefits and challenges from attending *hajj*.

Useful words

Dhu al-Hijjah – the twelfth month of the Islamic calendar, when *hajj* takes place
Ihram – pilgrim dress
Ka'aba – (or Ka'ba) the House of God in Makkah containing the black stone
Zamzam well – the well in the courtyard of the Great Mosque given by God for Hagar and Ismail
Ma'sa – the covered passageway between the hills Marwa and Safa, which pilgrims run between
Talbiya – the *hajj* prayer which pilgrims say constantly
Tawaf – seven circuits of the Ka'aba
Mina – the place ten kilometres from Makkah where pilgrims throw stones at Satan and make the sacrifice
Arafat – the plain and hill eighteen kilometres from Makkah where the central part of *hajj* takes place
Waquf – a standing prayer during *hajj*

Section 2a: Practices

countries. This is the part of *hajj* that all Muslims throughout the world join in as the festival of Id-ul-Adha.

For the next two days, pilgrims stone the pillars and then on the 12th of Dhu al-Hijjah the *hajj* regulations are over and pilgrims can dress ordinarily and have their hair cut. The next day, pilgrims walk to Makkah and perform a final *tawaf* and circuit of the Ma'sa. *Hajj* is then completed, although many Muslims go on to visit Madinah and the Mosque of Muhammad.

Anyone who completes *hajj* is known as a **hajji** and often colours their hair or beard with henna as a sign of their status. *Hajjis* receive special respect from the Muslim community, although there are many more of them nowadays thanks to the growth of package holidays.

> *Here I am O my God. Here I am. No partner hast thou, here am I. Truly the praise and the grace are thine and the empire. No partner hast thou, here am I. (The talbiya prayer which is said throughout* hajj*)*

The history of *hajj*

Hajj celebrates many historic events, from the founding of the Ka'aba by Adam to rebuilding by Ibrahim, and Ibrahim's relationship with his son Ismail and with God.

> *And remember that Abraham was tried by his Lord with certain commands, which he fulfilled: He said: 'I will make thee an Imam to the Nations.' He pleaded: 'And also (Imams) from my offspring!' He answered: 'But My Promise is not within the reach of evil-doers. Remember We made the House a place of assembly for men and a place of safety; and take ye the station of Abraham as a place of prayer; and We covenanted with Abraham and Isma'il, that they should sanctify My House for those who compass it round, or use it as a retreat, or bow, or prostrate themselves (therein in prayer). And remember Abraham said: 'My Lord, make this a City of Peace, and feed its people with fruits, such of them as believe in Allah and the Last Day.' He said: '(Yea), and such as reject Faith, for a while will I grant them their pleasure, but will soon drive them to the torment of Fire, an evil destination (indeed)! And remember Abraham and Isma'il raised the foundations of the House (With this prayer): 'Our Lord! Accept (this service) from us: For Thou art the All-Hearing, the All-Knowing'. (Surah 2:124–127)*

There were pilgrimages when Makkah was a non-Muslim state, but in 628CE Muhammad was given a vision from God of going on pilgrimage and the events of *hajj* were revealed to him in what is now Surah 22. Thereafter, Makkah became Muslim and Muhammad went on pilgrimage five times. On his final *hajj* in 632CE, Muhammad set out the pattern for all subsequent *hajj* and preached his final sermon at Arafat just a few weeks before he died.

> *Oh people listen carefully! All the believers are brothers ... none is higher than the other unless he is higher in obedience to Allah. No Arab is superior to a non-Arab except in piety. (From Muhammad's final sermon)*

Using an online travel agent to search for *hajj* travel packages from the UK.

Useful words

Hajji – one who has completed the *hajj*

Activities

1. What is pilgrim dress?
2. What happens at Arafat?
3. What happens at Mina?
4. Look at the quotations from the Qur'an opposite. What features of *hajj* are based on these verses?
5. Look at the photo above. How have websites like this changed the *hajj*?

Behold We gave the site to Abraham, of the Sacred House, saying: 'Associate not anything in worship with Me; and sanctify My House for those who compass it round, or stand up, or bow, or prostrate themselves therein in prayer.' And proclaim the Pilgrimage among men: they will come to thee on foot and (mounted) on every kind of camel, lean on account of journeys through deep and distant mountain highways; That they may witness the benefits (provided) for them, and celebrate the name of Allah, through the Days appointed, over the cattle which He has provided for them (for sacrifice): then eat ye thereof and feed the distressed ones in want. Then let them complete the rites prescribed for them, perform their vows, and (again) **circumambulate** *the Ancient House. (Surah 22:27–29)*

> **Activity**
>
> Look at the quotation from Muhammad's last sermon on page 210. Do you think this is shown during *hajj*?

Useful words

Circumambulate – walk round, make a circuit

The purpose of *hajj*

The main reasons for going on *hajj* are as follows:

- to fulfil the final pillar of the Five Pillars and so live a full Muslim life
- to follow the example of Muhammad in performing the actions he carried out in the places he did them
- to visit the holiest sites of Islam and feel part of their holiness
- to remember the ancient nature of Islam which began with Adam on Arafat and with Ibrahim and Ismail in Makkah and Mina
- for Muslims to prepare themselves for the Day of Judgement when they will next appear at Arafat (see Topic 2.1a.8, page 185) and to make sure that the sins they have committed will not count against them on that day
- to stone the devil within themselves at Mina and to show God they are prepared to sacrifice for him.

The benefits of *hajj*

- The pilgrim has fulfilled the requirements of the fifth pillar.
- The pilgrim has followed the example and actions of the Prophet.
- The pilgrim has taken part in the holiest event in the Muslim calendar and has come as close to God as is possible in this life – the contact with God which lasts for a short time in *salah* lasts for a week during *hajj*.
- The pilgrim has shown their devotion to God by taking part in a very expensive and physically demanding event.
- If a pilgrim dies on *hajj*, they will go straight to heaven without having to wait in the grave or face Judgement Day.
- The pilgrim has been made aware of the power of God to unite different races and languages into a common language, a common ritual and a common brotherhood (*ummah*) in Islam – many races, colours and languages come on *hajj*, but they all use the same words and perform the same actions, showing the unifying force of Islam.
- The pilgrim receives the respect and status of becoming a *hajji*.

Section 2a: Practices

The Ka'aba at the centre of the Great Mosque during *hajj*.

> **Activity**
>
> What happens in the Great Mosque during *hajj*?

The challenges of *hajj*

We have already seen, the two biggest challenges of *hajj* are the financial cost, even with a package trip, and the physical effort of walking, running and standing in one of the hottest places in the world (Makkah's average daytime temperature is more than 40°C for nine months of the year and *hajj* is based on a lunar calendar and so moves round the year). However, there are other challenges:

- Coping with the huge crowds (over 1800 people were crushed to death in a stampede at the 2015 *hajj*).

- Coping with the language problems (many of the people killed in 2015 would not have been able to understand the Arabic of the Saudi controllers).

- Coping with the hypocrisy of the rich and powerful getting preferential treatment on the holy *hajj* where everyone is supposed to be equal.

> *This obscenity reaches its peak around the Ka'ba itself when one of the heads of state performs the tawaf. The Ka'ba suffers the indignity of being surrounded by uniformed soldiers carrying arms and wearing boots. An area around the Ka'ba is cleared to allow the rulers of these nation states protection ... in the House of Allah!'*
> (Z. Khan, Hajj in Focus, *Open Press, 1986*)

The significance of *hajj*

Hajj has great significance for Muslims because a pilgrim:

- has fulfilled the fifth pillar as set down in Surah 22 and so can die happy
- has followed the example and actions of the Prophet in the very places the Prophet himself performed them
- has shown great devotion to God by fulfilling this expensive, dangerous (many pilgrims die or are injured during *hajj*) and time-consuming pillar
- has taken part in the holiest event in Islam and has come as close to God as is possible in this life; the sacred presence experienced momentarily during *salah* is believed to be present for the whole duration of *hajj*
- is made aware of the power of God to unite different races and languages into a common language, a common ritual and a common brotherhood in Islam
- can be called *hajji* when they return home; this is a title of honour and means they will be highly regarded in the community
- has their sins forgiven so they now live life as a perfect Muslim.

Practice questions

c Explain two reasons why *hajj* is important for Muslims. In your answer you must refer to a source of wisdom and authority.

d '*Hajj* has more benefits than drawbacks.' Evaluate this statement considering arguments for and against. In your answer you should:
- refer to Muslim points of view
- reach a justified conclusion.

Summary

Hajj is the fifth pillar and is the annual pilgrimage to Makkah which copies the ones Muhammad made. All Muslims should try to perform *hajj* once in their life, but they can only go if it will not cause their family financial hardship. Pilgrims perform special ceremonies at the Ka'aba in Makkah and on the plain of Arafat. The highlight is the sacrifice at the village of Mina which all Muslims join in as Id-ul-Adha.

Section 2a: Practices

Topic 2.2a.7 *Jihad*

Thinking points

In this topic you need to:
- think about the origins, meaning and significance of *jihad*
- understand the difference between lesser and greater *jihad*
- consider the conditions for the declaration of lesser *jihad*, including Surah 2:190–194, 22:39
- think about the different understandings of *jihad*
- be able to explain the importance of *jihad* in the life of Muslims today.

What is *jihad*?

The word *jihad* means 'to strive, to apply oneself, to struggle, to persevere'. However, it has come to be connected with struggling 'in the way of religion' or striving in the cause of God.

The origins of *jihad*

The belief in *jihad* is based on what the Qur'an says about *jihad* (which is translated as strive or striving, not fighting):

Those who believe, and suffer exile and strive with might and main in God's cause with their goods and their persons, have the highest rank in the sight of God. These are the people who will achieve salvation. (Surah 9:20)

And strive in His cause as ye ought to strive. (Surah 22:78)

Listen not to the unbelievers, but strive against them. (Surah 25:52)

That ye believe in God and His Apostle, and that ye strive your utmost in the cause of God, with your property and your persons; that will be best for you if ye but knew! (Surah 61:11)

Activity

What does the Qur'an say about *jihad*?

An advertisement for the #MyJihad campaign in an underground train station in the USA. The advertising campaign aims to reclaim *jihad* from Muslim and anti-Muslim extremists.

It seems clear from these verses that *jihad* means to strive with one's self and one's money in the cause of God. It is determining exactly what is meant by the cause of God which has led to there being two ideas about *jihad*: greater *jihad* and lesser *jihad*.

Greater *jihad*

Most Muslims believe that the greater *jihad* is the struggle to make oneself a perfect Muslim. This certainly requires 'striving with might and main', whether living in a Muslim or non-Muslim society:

- There is the struggle to perform all of the Five Pillars properly.
- There is the struggle to follow the Shari'ah exactly.
- There is the struggle to both discover and follow the perfect example of the Prophet Muhammad.
- There is the struggle to be 'pleasing to Allah' so that one will be allowed into paradise.

Most Muslim lawyers teach that the greater *jihad* is striving to uphold all of God's commandments and striving to avoid all of God's prohibitions. It is concerned with establishing right and removing evil from oneself before one can embark on removing evil from the world. It is the greater *jihad* which stops a Muslim from being a hypocrite – something which is condemned in the Qur'an – 'Why say ye that which ye do not? Grievously odious is it in the sight of God that ye say that which ye do not' (Surah 61:2).

By their greater *jihad* Muslims make sure that they practise Islam rather than just talking about how good it is.

Lesser *jihad*

Having removed the evil from themselves, Muslims can then begin the work of the lesser *jihad* and remove the evil from society.

Muslim scholars teach that Muslim societies should be the first target of the lesser *jihad*. Those Muslims who have completed the greater *jihad* should target such injustices as:

- underdevelopment
- unfair trading
- lack of education
- lack of a welfare state
- the gap between rich and poor.

Muslims aim to produce a perfect Muslim society before they are in a position to target non-Muslim societies and bring them into Islam.

Islam teaches that it is Islamic teaching and God's law which can bring world peace. The Islamic **ummah** is the 'abode of peace' and the world outside Islam is the 'abode of war'. The aim of the lesser *jihad* is to bring the whole world into Islam and so into the abode of peace.

Activities

1. What is the greater *jihad*?
2. What is the lesser *jihad*?

Useful words

Ummah – the Muslim community (brotherhood of Islam)

Section 2a: Practices

Useful words

Muslim Law Schools – the four schools which interpret the Shari'ah for Sunni Muslims

Jihadi – one fighting in a Holy War

Activity

What would make it difficult for a war to be called a Muslim Holy War?

Different understandings of *jihad* in Islam

Some Muslims feel that the lesser *jihad* prescribes a Holy War against non-Muslims to bring them into Islam. However, the **Muslim Law Schools** say that a Holy War can only be fought in the following conditions:

- in self-defence:

  Fight in the cause of God those who fight you, but do not transgress the limits; for God loveth not the transgressor. (Surah 2:190)

  To those against whom war is made, permission is given to fight because they are wronged; – and verily God is most powerful, for their aid. (Surah 22:39)

- if it is led by a religious leader well known for piety and chosen by the whole community
- if all the soldiers are good faithful Muslims well versed in the Qur'an
- if there is a good chance of the war being successful
- as long as the war does not harm the innocent (women, children or the elderly)
- after the enemies have been invited to join Islam peaceably.

Other Muslims feel that they are entitled to wage a Holy War against non-Muslims and they even call themselves *jihadi*. They believe that because Muhammad was forced to fight to defend Islam when attacked by Makkah (and there are verses in the Qur'an about this) they have the right to fight for the faith, especially as the Qur'an says that those who die fighting a Holy War will go straight to paradise:

Think not of those who are slain in God's way as dead. Nay they live finding their sustenance in the presence of their Lord. (Surah 3:169)

Those who kill innocent people in the name of Islam or in the name of God, and who think of themselves as martyrs, should think twice. Their act is categorically condemned by God ... in the Quran. These people are disobeying God's commandments and instead upholding the fabricated claims of their teachers/leaders! (True Islam, www.quran-islam.org)

The importance of *jihad* in the life of Muslims

Jihad is important in the life of a Muslim because being a good Muslim involves a great deal of struggle, especially for Muslims living in a non-Muslim country.

A Muslim living in a non-Muslim country faces a considerable struggle to avoid being involved in the payment of interest, which is banned in the Qur'an. For example, a good Muslim should not use a credit card, even if they pay off their bill every month and so never pay interest themselves, as they are relying on other people paying interest to finance the credit card system (there is argument in Islam as to whether such bank accounts as the Lloyds Bank Islamic current account can be used when the bank itself is involved in interest even though the Islamic account is not).

Muslims in non-Muslim countries can also struggle to ensure that they keep to the *halal* (permitted) and avoid the *haram* (banned). This can be a particular struggle in regard to food: the Qur'an says that Muslims must not eat pork and that they should only eat meat slaughtered in the *halal* way, by slitting the throat and draining the blood. Some Muslims become vegetarian to make sure they avoid the *haram*. Alcohol and gambling are also *haram* and Muslims can often struggle to avoid these in their daily life.

Keeping the Five Pillars is also a struggle, especially if living in a non-Muslim country. Praying five times a day and performing *wudu* before each prayer can be a major problem, especially when working for a non-Muslim employer. Fasting during Ramadan is difficult when working with people who are eating (and even worse drinking) during daylight hours. It is even more of a struggle for Muslims living well north or south of the equator when Ramadan falls in midsummer.

So *jihad* is important because everyday life is a *jihad* to be a good Muslim.

Useful words

Halal – that which is permitted
Haram – that which is not permitted

Activity

Look at the picture on page 214. Do you think it is hard to conquer yourself?

Practice questions

c Explain two reasons why there are different understandings of *jihad* among Muslims. In your answer you must refer to a source of wisdom and authority.

d '*Jihad* is about making yourself a good Muslim, not fighting wars.' Evaluate this statement considering arguments for and against. In your answer you should:
- refer to Muslim points of view
- refer to different Muslim points of view
- reach a justified conclusion.

Summary

Jihad is struggling for religion. Muslims divide *jihad* into greater and lesser. Most Muslims believe that the greater *jihad* is the struggle to make oneself a perfect Muslim and only then can the lesser *jihad* of making the world Muslim begin. Most Muslims believe that lesser *jihad* should be peaceful, but some Muslims think that lesser *jihad* involves war against non-Muslims and some even think that this is the greater *jihad*.

Section 2a: Practices

Topic 2.2a.8 The celebration/commemoration of Id-ul-Adha

Thinking points

In this topic you need to:
- think about the nature, meaning and significance of the celebration/commemoration of the festivals of Id-ul-Adha and Id-ul-Fitr in Sunni and Shi'a Islam, and Id-ul-Ghadeer and Ashura in Shi'a and Sunni Islam
- be able to explain and evaluate the importance of these celebrations/commemorations for Muslims today.

Useful words

Al-Hijra – 1 Muharram, Islamic New Year's Day
Mawlid al-Nabi – the birthday of the Prophet Muhammad
Lailat al-Miraj – the Prophet's night journey to Jerusalem and then to heaven
Shirk – the sin of associating other things with God; it is the worst sin
Hajj – pilgrimage to Makkah, the fifth pillar
Zakah – charity tax, the third pillar

The nature and importance of festivals and commemorations

Many Muslims and scholars believe that Islam is the only major world religion which does not have any real festivals. Most religions have festivals which are important in themselves, such as Christmas and Easter in Christianity and Diwali in Hinduism. But Islam has only two official festivals: Id-ul-Adha and Id-ul-Fitr, and they are not festivals in themselves, they are simply a part of the celebration of the pillar of *hajj* and the pillar of *sawm*.

There is much discussion among Muslims lawyers and scholars about the nature of festivals. Some believe that festivals should be celebrated in a similar fashion to other religions, connecting the celebration to parties and gifts. Others believe that in Islam there only two festivals and they are about worshippers coming close to God, not celebrating.

Many Sunni Muslims celebrate:

- **Al-Hijra** (1 Muharram), which is the Islamic New Year's Day and commemorates the Hijra in 622CE when the Prophet Muhammad moved from Makkah to Madinah.
- **Mawlid al-Nabi**, which celebrates the birthday of the Prophet Muhammad.
- **Lailat al-Miraj**, which celebrates the night journey when Muhammad was taken up to heaven and shown how to perform *salah*.

However, Salafi-type Muslims regard these celebrations as very wrong because they are dangerously close to worshipping Muhammad, which is the great sin of **shirk**.

Shi'a Muslims have many more festivals (the two greatest ones are explored below), but Sunni Muslims regard all of these as wrong because they verge on idolatry.

The festival of Id-ul-Adha

On Id-ul-Adha, Muslims dress in their best clothes and go to the mosque for a special congregational prayer during which there is a special *khutba* (sermon) when the people are reminded of the origins of the festival and united with the pilgrims in Makkah performing **hajj**. At the conclusion of the prayers and sermon, Muslims embrace and exchange greetings with one other (they wish each other 'Eid Mubarak'), give gifts to children and visit one another.

Families in rural communities sacrifice an animal and give a third to the poor, a third to relatives and a third to the close family. In urban communities, a special **zakah** is given to the poor and a special meal is held (although some families club together and buy an animal to be slaughtered by the *halal* butcher so that they take part in the sacrifice of *hajj*).

Activity

How and why do Muslims celebrate Id-ul-Adha?

Topic 2.2a.8 The celebration/commemoration of Id-ul-Adha

This festival originates in God testing Ibrahim by telling him to sacrifice his son Ismail. When God saw that Ibrahim was prepared to obey him, God sent an animal sacrifice instead:

> *Then when the son reached the age of serious work with him, he said, 'O my son, I see in vision that I offer thee in sacrifice.' ... So when they had both submitted their wills to God. We called out to him, 'O Abraha! Thou hast already fulfilled thy vision ...' And we ransomed him with a momentous sacrifice ... Thus indeed do We reward those who do right for he (Ibrahim) was one of Our believing servants. (Surah 37:102–111)*

It receives its meaning from the way it was incorporated into the *hajj* so that during Id-ul-Adha Muslims feel that they are:

- following in the footsteps of both prophet Ibrahim and Prophet Muhammad
- sharing in the *hajj*
- symbolically sacrificing themselves to God
- sharing the good things of life with the poor
- uniting the family, as the *id* is a great family celebration.

Activity
How and why do Muslims celebrate Id-ul-Fitr?

The festival of Id-ul-Fitr

Id-ul-Fitr is celebrated on the 1st of Shawwal, which is signalled by the sighting of the new moon in the same way as the beginning of Ramadan. It is the festival of breaking the fast. It is a joyful day when cards and gifts are exchanged and new clothes are bought for children. Special services are held in the mosque or in the open air if there are likely to be too many people. There are special prayers thanking God for the benefits of Ramadan and a *khutba* reminding Muslims of the meaning of Ramadan. Some Muslim families visit the cemetery to remember their dead relatives. A special meal is shared – the first daylight meal for a month.

The festival originates in the month-long fast of Ramadan and the need to celebrate not only the end of the fast, but also the successful completion of the fast. The first Id-ul-Fitr was celebrated by the Prophet Muhammad and so Muslims feel they are copying the Prophet and becoming close to him while they celebrate.

Id-ul-Fitr gains its meaning from the pillar of **sawm** and the Qur'anic instruction to fast during the month of Ramadan. Muslims celebrate Id-ul-Fitr because it means:

- Ramadan has ended and they have completed a great religious feat and will gain many benefits.
- They have completed the fourth pillar of Islam.
- Their sins have been forgiven.
- They have become close to God.
- The fast is over and they can eat and drink in daylight again.

Shi'a Muslims go on *hajj* and fast during Ramadan so they celebrate Id-ul-Adha and Id-ul-Fitr just like Sunnis, although there may be some cultural differences in the way they celebrate.

> *The religious duties of the first ten days of Ramadan gain the mercy of God, those of the second ten merit his pardon, while those of the last ten save those who do them from the punishment of hell. (Part of the Id-ul-Fitr khutba)*

Useful words
Sawm – fasting, the fourth pillar

Section 2a: Practices

The commemoration of Id-ul-Ghadeer

For Shi'a Muslims the 18th of **Dhu al-Hijjah** is the Id-ul-Ghadeer, when they celebrate the occasion of Muhammad appointing Ali as his successor. They celebrate by fasting, ritual bathing and having a special service when a sermon is preached on the event and special prayers called *du'a nudba* are said. Food is given to poor Muslims after the service.

The commemoration has its origins in an event towards the end of Muhammad's life which Shi'as claim is referred to in Surah 5:3, but Sunnis dispute this. Shi'as claim that on his way back to Madinah from his final pilgrimage, Muhammad met Ali (who was returning from missionary work in Yemen) at the Pool (Ghadeer) of Khum, about halfway between Makkah and Madinah. Muhammad ordered a tent to be set up in which Ali could sit to receive the allegiance oath of Muslims. Thousands of Muslims saluted and congratulated Ali as **Amir al-Mu'minin**, commander of the faithful.

This event is very important to Shi'a Muslims because it means that:

- Ali should have been the first Caliph.
- Shi'a beliefs about the importance of Ali are correct.
- Shi'as are the true followers of Muhammad because they have followed his request to regard Ali as Muhammad's true successor.

Sunni Muslims reject this view and argue that it would have made no sense for Muhammad to have done this at **Ghadeer Khum**, when few Muslims were there, when he could have done it in his final sermon at the end of *hajj* in Makkah. They claim the Shi'as have misinterpreted Muhammad defending Ali at Ghadeer after Ali had been slandered.

The commemoration of Ashura

Ashura is very much a remembrance rather than a celebration. On the 10th of **Muharram** 680CE, Muhammad's grandson, **Husayn**, who is regarded as the third imam by Shi'as, was killed (Shi'as say murdered) by **Yazid**, the leader of an Umayyad army, at the Battle of **Karbala**. This is remembered by Shi'a Muslims every year on Ashura Day.

On this day, Shi'a Muslims wear mourning attire, refrain from music, fast and treat it as a time for self-reflection as they commit themselves to the mourning of Husayn. Participants congregate in public processions for ceremonial chest beating as a display of their devotion to Husayn, in remembrance of his suffering. Many Shi'as also whip themselves and cut themselves as a sign of their devotion, although this has been banned in Iran and the Lebanon, where Shi'as often donate blood on Ashura as a sign of their identification with Husayn's martyrdom. In some Shi'a areas passion plays are performed, re-enacting the events of the martyrdom at Karbala.

The remembrance began as a ten-day commemoration, but can last for up to a month, and mosques, and some people, provide free meals on certain nights of the month. People also donate food and Middle Eastern sweets to the mosque. These meals are viewed as being special and holy, as they have been consecrated in the name of Husayn, and eating them is considered an act of communion with God and Husayn.

Husayn's grave at Karbala became a pilgrimage site among Shi'as only a few years after his death. A tradition of pilgrimage to the Imam Husayn Shrine and the other Karbala martyrs quickly developed, and from these came the public rites of remembrance now known as Ashura.

The Pool of Khum today.

Useful words

Dhu al-Hijjah – twelfth and final month of the Islamic calendar
Amir al-Mu'minin – commander of the faithful, a title given by Shi'as to Ali and his descendants
Ghadeer Khum – the Pool of Khum halfway between Makkah and Madinah
Muharram – the first month of the Islamic calendar
Husayn – Muhammad's grandson and the third imam of Shi'a Islam
Yazid – the sixth caliph of Sunni Islam
Karbala – site of the battle where Husayn was killed by Caliph Yazid (100 km southwest of Baghdad)

Activity

Look at the photo of Ghadeer Khum above. Why is this place important for Shi'a Muslims?

Topic 2.2a.8 The celebration/commemoration of Id-ul-Adha

Meanings of Ashura

Shi'as regard Husayn's martyrdom as a symbol of the struggle against injustice, tyranny and oppression. They believe the Battle of Karbala was a fight between the forces of good represented by Husayn and the forces of evil represented by Yazid. Shi'as also believe the Battle of Karbala was fought to keep the Muslim religion free from corruption and they believe that Yazid was directing Islam to a wrong, evil path.

Ashura is important to Shi'as because:

- It gives Shi'as a chance to remember the great betrayal of Islam by the Sunnis.
- It allows Shi'as to show their devotion to the imams.
- It gives Shi'as a chance to grieve for the imam.
- It is a time when Shi'as can show they stand for the forces of good and are opposed to the forces of evil.
- Many Shi'as believe that taking part in Ashura washes away their sins; a popular Shi'a saying has it that, 'a single tear shed for Husayn washes away a hundred sins'.

Clearly, Sunni Muslims do not accept the Shi'a view of Ashura since Yazid was the leader of the Sunnis.

Dozens of people were killed and hundreds injured (including both Shi'a and Sunni commemorators) during the Ashura procession on 28 December 2009 when a massive bomb exploded at the procession in Karachi, Pakistan. Thirty Shi'a pilgrims participating in Ashura processions were killed by a series of bomb attacks in Hilla and Baghdad, Iraq on 5 December 2011. A suicide attack on 6 December 2011 killed 63 people and critically wounded 160 at a shrine in Kabul, Afghanistan where a crowd of hundreds had gathered for the day of Ashura observation. (Compiled from news reports)

People on their way to the Husayn Mosque in Karbala, Iraq.

Activities

1. Look at the photo of the shrine at Karbala above. Why is this place important for Shi'a Muslims?
2. Look at the reports above about troubles at Ashura commemorations. Why do you think these events cause problems between Shi'as and Sunnis?

Practice questions

c) Explain two reasons why Muslims celebrate Id-ul-Fitr. In your answer you must refer to a source of wisdom and authority.

d) 'Religious celebrations cause nothing but trouble.' Evaluate this statement considering arguments for and against. In your answer you should:
   - refer to Muslim points of view
   - refer to different Muslim points of view
   - reach a justified conclusion.

Summary

All Muslims celebrate Id-ul-Adha to join in the *hajj* sacrifice at Mina so that all Muslims are part of the *hajj*. They also celebrate Id-ul-Fitr at the end of the month-long fast of Ramadan, rejoicing in the benefits *sawm* brings to Muslims. Only Shi'a Muslims celebrate Id-ul-Ghadeer as this remembers Muhammad choosing Ali as his successor, which Sunnis do not think happened. Also only Shi'as celebrate Ashura since that remembers the Sunni army killing Ali's grandson in battle.

Section 2a: Practices

How to answer questions

a) Describe two differences between Muslim forms of worship and forms of worship in the main religious tradition of Britain. [3]

The main religious tradition of Britain is Christianity. One difference is that Muslims must perform *wudu* before worship, but Christians do not, though some sprinkle themselves with holy water as they enter church. Another difference is that Muslims must face Makkah for *salah* whereas Christians can worship facing any direction (although most Catholic, Orthodox and Anglican churches face the east).

A high mark answer because Christianity is identified as the main religious tradition and two differences are clearly described.

b) Explain two reasons why the festival of Id-ul-Adha is celebrated by Muslims. [4]

Muslims celebrate the festival of Id-ul-Adha to remember the testing of Ibrahim when God told him to sacrifice his son Ismail and Ibrahim was rewarded for his obedience. They also celebrate it as a way of joining in the annual *hajj* as the festival occurs at the same time as the pilgrims are sacrificing animals in Mina.

A high mark answer because two correct reasons are given and each reason is developed.

c) Explain two reasons why *khums* is important for Shi'a Muslims. In your answer you must refer to a source of wisdom and authority. [5]

Khums is important for Shi'a Muslims as they believe it is commanded by the Qur'an: 'Know that whatever of a thing you acquire, a fifth of it is for Allah, for the Messenger, for the near relative, and the orphans and the needy and the wayfarer' (Surah 8:41).

It is commanded by Shi'a lawyers and is a way of supporting the descendants of the Prophet who are given special reverence by Shi'a Muslims.

A high mark answer because two correct reasons are given and each reason is developed with a reference to the Qur'an, Shi'a lawyers and descendants of the prophet as sources of authority.

d) 'Hajj is essential for all Muslims.' Evaluate this statement considering arguments for and against. In your response you should:
- **refer to Muslim points of view**
- **refer to different Muslim points of view**
- **reach a justified conclusion. [12]**

Many Muslims would agree with this because *hajj* is the final pillar and so fulfilling it completes a Muslim's life. It also provides Muslims with the opportunity to follow the example of Muhammad in doing the actions that he performed in the places where he performed them, the holiest sites of Islam. It is also essential because it gives Muslims a chance to prepare themselves for the Day of Judgement at Arafat and to make sure that the sins they have committed will not count against them on that day.

However, Islam does teach that *hajj* is not compulsory since Muslims are only allowed to go on *hajj* if they have sufficient money to provide for their dependants while they are away from home, and they are physically and mentally fit enough for the physical demands of *hajj*. Also, some Muslims might not want to risk travelling through war zones to get there.

I think it is essential for most Muslims to go on *hajj* because it is the fifth pillar, but I do not think it is essential for all Muslims because the Qur'an itself excuses certain groups of Muslims from going.

*A high mark answer because it gives three clear developed Muslim reasons for thinking that *hajj* is essential. It then gives two Muslim reasons for disagreeing and then reaches a fully justified conclusion.*

1b Beliefs and teachings

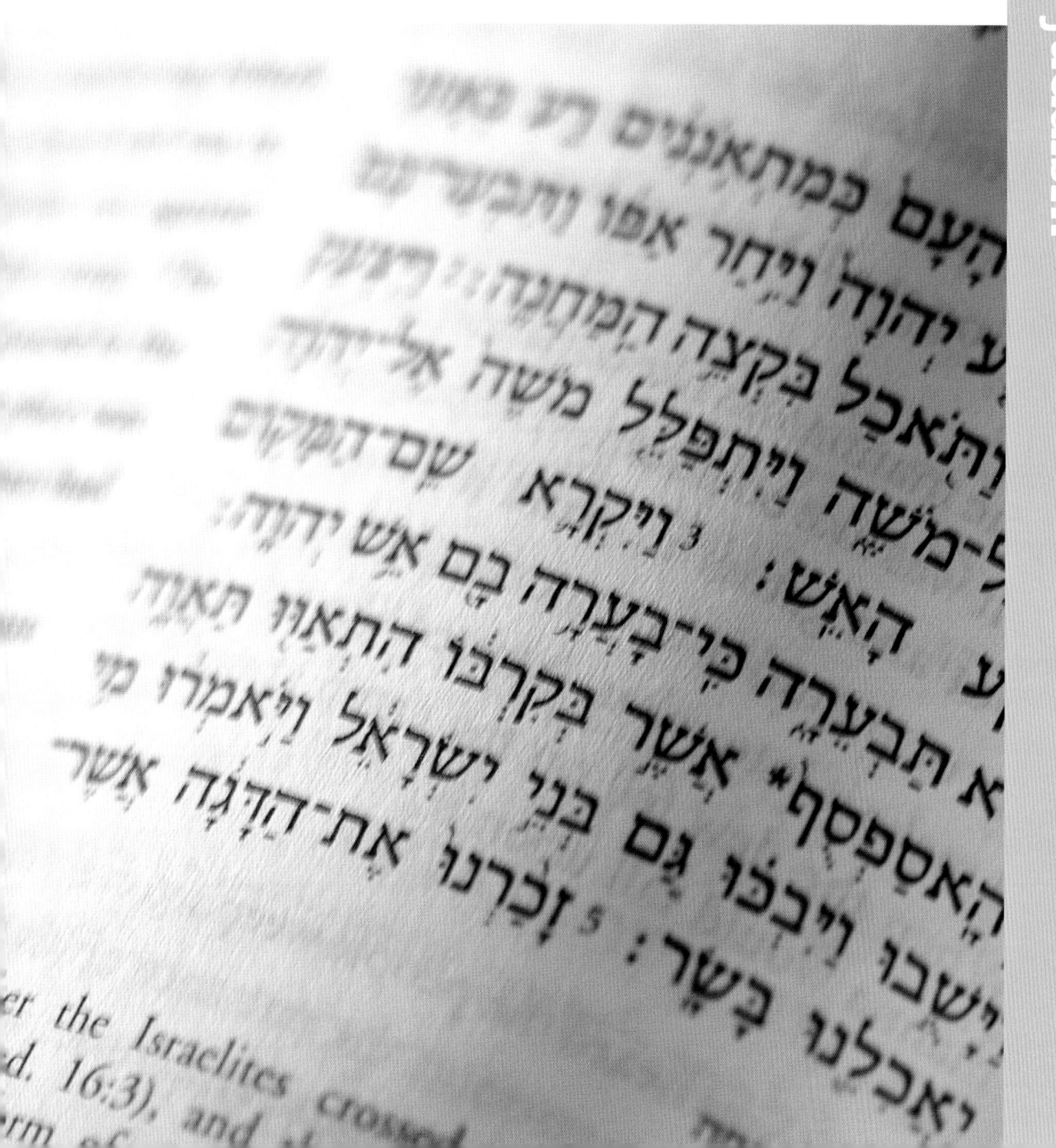

Area of study 2: Study of second religion, either Islam or Judaism

Section 1b: Beliefs and teachings

Area of study 2: Introduction (Judaism)

For those of you studying this area based on Judaism, it is important that you should understand some of the different groups within Judaism. This will allow you to understand Jewish beliefs and attitudes.

Five hundred years ago the major division in Judaism was between the Sephardic Jews and the Ashkenazi Jews. The Sephardi are the Jews from Spain, Portugal and the Middle East; the Ashkenazi are Jews from Germany and Eastern Europe whose separate language is Yiddish (a mix of German and Hebrew). However, the differences between these groups are mainly cultural, although the Sephardi have always believed in integrating within the community in which they live.

Hasidic Jews in London.

In modern Judaism, the main division is between Orthodox and Reform.

The Judaism most non-Jews think of as Judaism is Orthodox Judaism. The Orthodox regard the Torah as the infallible Word of God and therefore follow all of its commandments (*mitzvot*). But there are many differences within the Orthodox. The modern Orthodox teach that Jewish people should follow all the laws of the Torah (*halakhah*) but should otherwise integrate into modern life and the community in which they live.

However, there are other Orthodox groups such as the Hasidim who teach that Jewish people should maintain a separate culture and identity (as evidenced by their dress – a long black coat, white shirt, big black hat – and use of Yiddish). A development from the Hasidim is Lubavich or Chabad Judaism, which was led until 1994 by Rebbe Menachem Mendel. The Lubavich have many Hasidic practices, but believe that Judaism must relate to the modern world (they use the latest technology to spread their beliefs), and must be joyful (their worship involves music and dancing) and mystical (they are very connected to the *kabbalah*).

Reform Judaism resulted from nineteenth-century attempts to 'modernise' Judaism by bringing the findings of science and biblical criticism into Judaism. Reform Jews do not believe that the Torah is the Word of God, but rather that it was written by people inspired by God. They feel that it is the moral commands of the law which must be followed and believe that the ritual laws, such as keeping *kosher*, can be ignored. They are committed to working for social justice, which they call *Tikkun Olan* (the repair of the world), and have complete equality of the sexes including having women rabbis. Reform Judaism is the most popular group in American Judaism, but in British Judaism, the liberal and progressive synagogues are the ones closest to American Reform while the British Reform synagogues tend to be more traditional in observance of *Shabbat* and *kosher*.

It is important to be aware that the main religion in Britain is Christianity.

Section 1b: Beliefs and teachings

Topic 2.1b.1 The nature of the Almighty

Thinking points

In this topic you need to:
- think about how the characteristics of God are shown in the scriptures:
  - oneness
  - creator
  - law-giver
  - judge
- be able to evaluate the importance of these characteristics in Jewish life today.

Useful words

Tenakh – the Jewish scriptures
Torah – the law book or books of Moses
Nevi'im – the books of the prophets
Ketuvim – the books of the writings
Shema – statement of God's oneness

Jewish scriptures

The Jewish scriptures are known as the **Tenakh**, from the three divisions of the Jewish scriptures:

- **Torah** (the five books of Moses, initial letter *Te* in Hebrew)
- **Nevi'im** (the prophets, initial letter *Na*) and
- **Ketuvim** (the writings, initial letter *Kh*).

The Tenakh has the same books as the Protestant Christian Old Testament, although in a different order, and some of the books in the Tenakh have been separated into two or three books by the Christians (the Tenakh has 24 books, the Old Testament has 39; but remember the Tenakh came first!).

The Torah is the holiest and most important part of the Tenakh for Jewish people because they believe that it came directly from God to Moses. The Torah has always been written on scrolls and every synagogue has a Torah scroll kept in a special place.

God is one

It is the clear teaching of the Jewish scriptures that the most important characteristic of God is his oneness.

The Torah teaches that God is one:

> *The Lord is God in heaven above and on earth below. There is no other.* (Deuteronomy 4:39)

> *See now that I myself am He! There is no god besides me.* (Deuteronomy 32:39)

The most basic teaching of Judaism from the Torah is known as the **shema** and it begins with the words,

> *Hear, O Israel! The Lord our God, the Lord is one. Love the Lord your God with all your heart and with all your soul and with all your strength.* (Deuteronomy 6:4–5)

Judaism teaches strict monotheism (belief in only one God), just the same as Islam.

The *shema*

> *Hear, O Israel! The Lord our God, the Lord is one. Love the Lord your God with all your heart and with all your soul and with all your strength. These commandments that I give you today are to be upon your hearts. Impress them on your children. Talk about them when you sit at home and when you walk along the road, when you lie down and when you get up. 'Tie them as symbols on your hands and bind them on your foreheads. Write them on the doorframes of your houses and on your gates.'* (Deuteronomy 6:4–9)

Activities

1. What is the Tenakh?
2. What is the holiest part of the Tenakh and why?

Topic 2.1b.1 The nature of the Almighty

The importance of belief in God's oneness

Belief in God's oneness can be seen in the following ways:

- Jewish people have a container holding the *shema* on their gates and doorframes of each room in the house other than bathrooms and toilets (this is known as a **mezuzah**, even though technically a *mezuzah* is the parchment with the *shema* on it). Every time a Jew passes through a door with an affixed *mezuzah*, he or she should kiss their fingers and touch them to the *mezuzah*, expressing their love and respect for God and his commandments and reminding themselves of his oneness.
- Jewish men bind **tefillin** (leather boxes containing the *shema*) to their foreheads and arms when they pray every morning.
- Jewish people think of people, plants, animals, rock formations and so on as unified because they are the creation of the one God. In this way, belief in God's unity means that all of God's creation is an opportunity to come face to face with God.
- Judaism teaches the unity of creation and the need for people to try to bring unity to society.

Someone touching a *mezuzah* on a doorframe.

God the creator

The very first words of the Torah are:

> In the beginning God created the heaven and the earth (Genesis 1:1)

showing that another key characteristic of God is his creativity. God the creator is the one who can breathe life into inanimate objects – he is a life-giving force:

> Then the Lord God formed a man from the dust of the ground and breathed into his nostrils the breath of life, and the man became a living being. (Genesis 2:7)

As well as the Torah beginning by referring to God the creator, the concept of God the Creator is first of the **Thirteen Principles of Faith** set out by **Maimonides**, which are regarded as a summary of the Jewish faith: 'I believe with perfect faith that God is the Creator and Ruler of all things. He alone has made, does make, and will make all things'.

The Torah teaches that because God is the creator everything belongs to him: the universe and everything in it comes from God and therefore depends on God. However, the key teaching of the Torah is that God's creation is good. Genesis 1 states after each day of creation, 'and God saw that it was good', and at the completion of creation,

> God saw all he had made and indeed it was very good. (Genesis 1:31)

It also teaches that God gave humans control of the earth,

> God blessed them and said to them, 'Be fruitful and increase in number; fill the earth and subdue it. Rule over the fish … and the birds … and over every living creature'. (Genesis 1:28)

Useful words

Mezuzah – a container for the *shema* scroll put on doorposts
Tefillin – a container for the *shema* scroll to put on the arms and head
Thirteen Principles of Faith – a summary of Jewish beliefs written by Maimonides
Maimonides – medieval rabbi and philosopher (1135–1204) who wrote the Thirteen Principles

Activities

1. Why do you think the *shema* is so important for Jewish people?
2. How do Jewish people remind themselves of God's oneness every day?

Section 1b: Beliefs and teachings

Activity

Look at the picture opposite. Do you think Jewish people would think this is a good way of showing God creating?

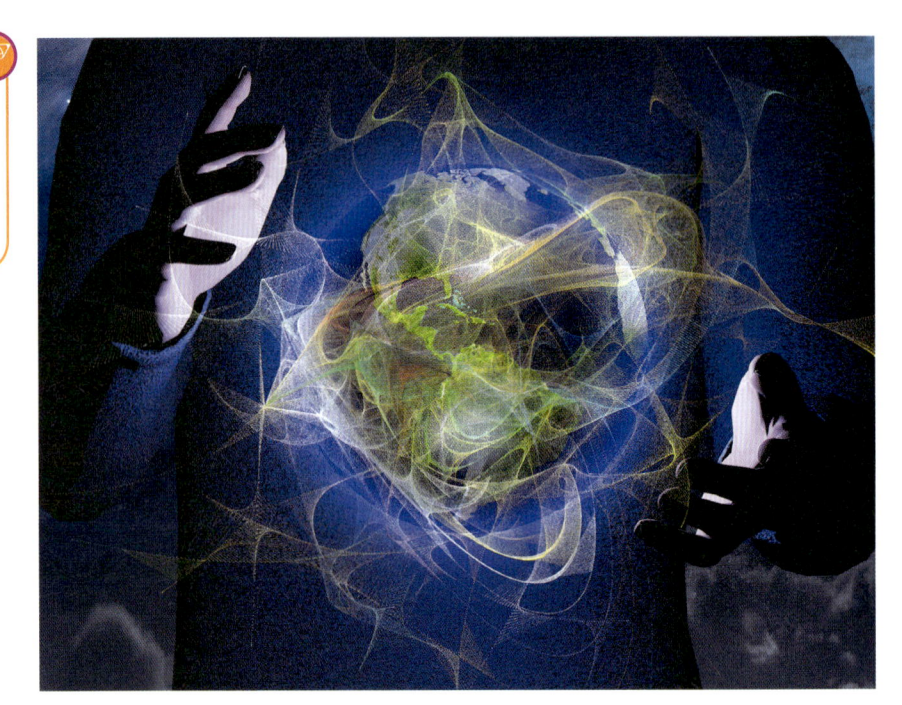

The Torah teaches that God is the creator.

The importance of belief in God as Creator

Belief that God created the universe and that his creation is good is important for Jews because it means that:

- Creation is a gift from God and Jews must therefore look after the earth in the way in which God intended.

- Since God created the universe and all the things in it, life has a meaning and purpose given to it by God.

- God's work of creation did not stop at the end of Genesis 1. God the creator continues to be the creator. In their prayer every day, Jewish people praise God who 'in His goodness renews the work of creation each day continually'.

- God's creation is good and so should be respected, which is why Jewish people care for the environment.

God the law-giver

The Torah teaches that as well as being the Creator and the One, God is the great law-giver.

God did not simply create the universe and leave humanity to get on with things. The Torah teaches that God gave laws to help people look after the earth in the way he wanted.

Some of these laws were given to Noah as part of God's **covenant** with Noah; others were given to Abraham as part of God's covenant with him (see Topic 2.1b.5, page 240). God then gave all 613 commands (*mitzvot*) of the Jewish law to Moses for him to give to the people. The laws were to help the people keep their side of the agreement:

> Take to heart all the words I have solemnly declared to you this day, so that you may command your children to obey carefully all the words of this law. They are not just idle words for you – they are your life. By them you will live long in the land. (Deuteronomy 32:46–47)

Useful words

Covenant – a binding agreement between two parties; usually refers to God and Israel
Mitzvot – commandments/laws (the singular of *mitzvot* is *mitzvah*)

Topic 2.1b.1 The nature of the Almighty

All 613 *mitzvot* are to be found in the Torah (the first five books – Genesis, Exodus, Leviticus, Numbers, Deuteronomy – which Orthodox Jews believe were given to Moses directly by God). By keeping the *mitzvot* Jewish people believe they are connecting with God in a deep and special way, and so can bring holiness into the world and prepare the world for the time when God's plan for the world will be fulfilled. By keeping the *mitzvot* they become God's people.

The importance of belief in God as law-giver

Believing that God is the law-giver is important in Judaism today because:

- God's laws (the *mitzvot*) form the **halakhah**, which is the basis of how Jews live their lives today.
- Following God's laws gives meaning and purpose to Jewish people's lives today.
- The laws of the Torah are part of the covenant with Moses, which is the basis of Judaism.
- The fact that God is a law-giver means that he cares about his creation and so cares about humans, which gives Jews security and helps them in their relationship with creation.

> *I believe with perfect faith that the entire Torah that we now have is that which was given to Moses. (Principle 8 of the Thirteen Principles)*
>
> *I believe with perfect faith that this Torah will not be changed, and that there will never be another given by God. (Principle 9 of the Thirteen Principles)*

Useful words

Halakhah – the holy law of Judaism

God the judge

The law of the Torah as set out in the *mitzvot* is known in Judaism as the *halakhah*, which literally means 'the path that one walks'. This is the divine law of Judaism, and any divine law requires a divine judge. The Tenakh has many references to God acting as judge for his creation:

> *For the Lord is our judge, The Lord is our lawgiver, The Lord is our king; He will save us. (Isaiah 33:22)*

The Tenakh teaches that God as judge will ensure that the good are rewarded and the evil punished. The dictionary defines justice as 'the exercise of authority in the maintenance of right', and the Tenakh shows that this is what God the Judge does:

> *And He will judge the world in righteousness; He will execute judgement for the peoples with equity. (Psalm 9:8)*

God is a just judge who will treat everyone fairly, making sure that justice reigns. However, the time when God the judge will make justice reign is in the future:

> *Before the Lord, for He is coming to judge the earth. (Psalm 98:9)*
>
> *For the Lord will vindicate His people, and will have compassion on His servants. (Deuteronomy 32:36)*

The Tenakh seems to connect this time of justice and judgement with the coming of the Messianic Age (see Topic 2.1b.3, page 234):

> *He will not judge by what he sees with his eyes or decide by what he hears with his ears; but with righteousness he will judge the needy, with justice he will give decisions for the poor of the earth. (Isaiah 11:3)*

Activity

Read Principles 8 and 9 above. How do they show the importance of Torah law?

Section 1b: Beliefs and teachings

The scales of justice.

The importance of belief in God as judge

The belief that God is judge is important for Jewish life today because it ensures that:

- The good are rewarded and the evil punished.
- The world is protected from the chaos that would come if there was no way of making sure that people keep God's laws.
- People know there will be punishments for those who do not keep God's laws.
- There will be rewards for those who do keep God's laws.

Principle 11 says, 'I believe with perfect faith that God rewards those who keep His commandments, and punishes those who transgress Him.'

Activity

Look at the picture of the scales of justice. Why is it important that God is both law-giver and judge?

Summary

The fundamental Jewish belief about God is that God is one as the Torah teaches in the *shema*. The Torah also teaches from its very first verse that God is the creator of everything and that God's creation is good. The Torah says God is the law-giver and it contains all 613 of God's *mitzvot*. God's laws require a judge and the Tenakh shows God as the one who judges everyone.

Practice questions

c Explain two reasons why it is important for Jews that God is a law-giver. In your answer you must refer to a source of wisdom and authority.

d 'God's oneness is his most important characteristic.' Evaluate this statement considering arguments for and against. In your answer you should:
- refer to Jewish points of view
- reach a justified conclusion.

Topic 2.1b.2 *Shekhinah*

What *shekhinah* is

The Hebrew word *shekhinah* is deliberately difficult to define because it is a way of describing the Almighty's presence in the world.

If you think of the characteristics of God outlined in Topic 2.1b.1, you can begin to realise why *shekhinah* is difficult to define because any definition is going to be an attempt to use finite words to describe the infinite – something which could never be accurate.

Jewish scholars sometimes define *shekhinah* as 'the majestic presence or manifestation of God which has descended to dwell among men'. Others translate this 'majestic presence' more simply as 'the glory of God'.

The **rabbis** always used the term *shekhinah* when they were referring to any form of contact humans may have with God. Humans cannot have contact with God's immensity (the finite cannot comprehend the infinite), they can only have contact with God's presence – that part of God which 'has descended to dwell among men'.

How *shekhinah* is shown in the Torah

The Torah speaks of God's presence (*shekhinah*) going with Moses to guide him through the wilderness to the promised land:

> My presence will go with you and I will give you rest. (Exodus 33:14)

The divine presence is associated with clouds,

> When Moses went up on the mountain, the cloud covered it, and the glory of the Lord settled on Mount Sinai. (Exodus 24:15)

It is also associated with smoke and fire:

> Mount Sinai was covered with smoke, because the Lord descended on it in fire. (Exodus 19:18)

The Torah also speaks of God choosing a place 'as a dwelling for His name' (Deuteronomy 12:11) and calls it the **tabernacle**. God instructed Moses to have the Israelites build this for God's presence to be: 'I will dwell among the Israelites and be their God' (Exodus 29:45). So the Torah makes plain that the *shekhinah* is the presence of God closely connected with the tabernacle, holy and untouchable:

> Then have them make a **sanctuary** for me, and I will dwell among them. (Exodus 25:8)

Activity

State four things the Torah says about *shekhinah*.

Thinking points

In this topic you need to:
- explore what *shekhinah* is and how it is shown in Jewish scriptures, including how it is shown in the Torah and 2 Chronicles 7:1–3
- be aware of the different understandings of *shekhinah* for Jews today
- be able to explain why *shekhinah* is important for Judaism and why the different understandings of it are important for Jews today.

Useful words

Rabbis – ordained Jewish religious leaders or teachers
Tabernacle – the holy place containing the Ark of the Covenant
Sanctuary – the most holy part of a religious building (can also mean a place of safety)

> When Moses came into contact with the divine presence when he received the commandments on Mount Sinai, his face shone and the people were afraid of how he looked. (Exodus 34:29–35)

Section 1b: Beliefs and teachings

Useful words
Temple – the centre of worship built by Solomon in Jerusalem and destroyed in 70CE
Mount Zion – the holy hill in Jerusalem where the Temple was
Talmud – writings explaining the Torah
Kabbalah – Jewish mysticism

The tabernacle became the **Temple** in Jerusalem when the Israelites reached the promised land, and when King Solomon dedicated the Temple the *shekhinah* came to dwell there:

> When Solomon finished praying, fire came down from heaven and consumed the burnt offering and the sacrifices, and the glory of the Lord filled the temple. The priests could not enter the temple of the Lord because the glory of the Lord filled it. When all the Israelites saw the fire coming down and the glory of the Lord above the temple, they knelt on the pavement with their faces to the ground, and they worshipped and gave thanks to the Lord, saying, 'He is good; his love endures forever.' (2 Chronicles 7:1–3)

The Nevi'im and Ketuvim make many references to the *shekhinah* being in Jerusalem and on **Mount Zion** (the hill in Jerusalem on which the Temple was built), for example:

> The Lord Almighty who dwells on Mount Zion. (Isaiah 8:18)

There are also many references to the prophets having visions of the presence of God, which are regarded as the presence of the *shekhinah*. For example, Isaiah said,

> I saw the Lord seated on a throne, high and exalted and the train of his robe filled the temple. (Isaiah 6:1)

In the **Talmud** (the writings explaining the Torah) and the writings of later rabbis, *shekhinah* begins to be used for the presence of God in the world.

Different understandings of *shekhinah* for Jews today

- Some Orthodox Jews base themselves on the teachings of Maimonides, who described the *shekhinah* as a light created to be a link between God and the world.

- Others regard the *shekhinah* as an expression for the various ways in which God is related to the world, especially such things as the dwelling of God in the midst of Israel and his personal presence.

- Others believe that *shekhinah* simply means God. They feel that *shekhinah* and God are interchangeable words.

- *Shekhinah* is held by some modern (especially Reform) Jews to represent the feminine attributes of the presence of God because *shekhinah* is a feminine word in Hebrew.

- In the **kabbalah** (Jewish mysticism which tries to define the nature of the universe and the nature and purpose of existence, and provide ways for people to gain their spiritual goal) *shekhinah* is called the tenth *sephira*, which is the gateway to higher consciousness, that brings followers into God's presence.

- Some Jews who have been influenced by Christian ideas claim that *shekhinah* is simply the Jewish word for the Holy Spirit – God's presence at work in the world.

Activities
1. Look at the painting of *shekhinah* on page 233. Do you think this is a good representation of Jewish belief?
2. What does 2 Chronicles 7:1–3 tell us about the *shekhinah*?

Why *shekhinah* is important for Judaism

- The idea of *shekhinah* shows that however close Jews may feel to God, God's presence is so holy and awesome that they must always maintain a deep sense of respect for God. This sense of respect is shown by Jews only referring to God's name in worship. Jews otherwise refer to God as the Almighty or, more often, **Hashem** (the name, the one whose name must be treated respectfully and not pronounced unnecessarily). When writing they will often use G–d to express this idea.
- The Tenakh references to the *shekhinah* being at the Temple, Mount Zion and Jerusalem are what makes those places so special for some Jews.
- The teaching that Moses was surrounded by the *shekhinah* when he received the Torah means that Moses received the *mitzvot* directly from God, so they are God's words.
- The *shekhinah* teaches that God's presence is in the world and that believers might therefore come across the *shekhinah* at any time.
- The *shekhinah* shows that the prophets of the Tenakh were truly inspired by God and so their message must be true.

Why the different understandings of *shekhinah* are important for Jews today

The fact that there are different understandings of the word *shekhinah* is important:

- The different meanings show that God is far beyond human thought. He is the eternal **immutable** and so there are many ways of understanding his presence.
- This allows Judaism to relate God to the ideas of the modern world such as feminism and the theological debates about whether God is masculine.
- It makes it easier for Jews and Christians to come together in their search for God.
- The concept of *shekhinah* in the *kabbalah* brought together different religions, making it easier to break down religious hatred; there are Christian, Sunni Muslim and Shi'a Muslim kabbalists.

'The Shekinah Glory Enters the Tabernacle', an illustration from 1908.

Useful words

Hashem – the Name, a word used to refer to God without mentioning his name

Immutable – unable to be changed and unchanging over time

Practice questions

c Explain two reasons why different understandings of *shekhinah* are important for Jews today.

d 'The concept of *shekhinah* is not important for understanding Judaism.' Evaluate this statement considering arguments for and against. In your answer you should:
- refer to Jewish points of view
- refer to different Jewish points of view
- reach a justified conclusion.

Summary

Shekinah refers to the presence of God on earth and is used in the Torah to describe God's presence in the Tabernacle, Temple and Jerusalem. It is difficult to understand and is interpreted in different ways by different rabbis, but it is the basis of the belief that God's name reflects his presence and is so holy that it should only be used in worship.

Section 1b: Beliefs and teachings

Topic 2.1b.3 Messiah

Thinking points

In this topic you need to:
- think about the nature and purpose of the Messiah
- consider how messiahship is shown in the scriptures
- understand the nature and significance of the Messianic Age
- think about the different understandings of the Messiah
- be able to explain the importance of the Messiah for Jews today.

Useful words

Messianic Age – a time when all nations will live at peace and there will be justice in the world
Inspired – stimulated by God to do things

The nature and purpose of the Messiah

The word Messiah means 'anointed one' and was used to refer to the kings of Israel who were anointed.

When the Israelite kingdom was captured by the Babylonians and the monarchy ended (586BCE), Jewish people began to refer to the purpose of the Messiah as the one who will:

- rebuild the Temple in Jerusalem
- unite all the peoples of the world
- make all the peoples of the world aware of the presence of God
- bring in the **Messianic Age**, when all will live at peace
- establish God's kingdom.

Most Jews believe that the nature of the Messiah will be to be:

- a descendant of King David
- a human, not a divine being
- a man of great piety and close to God
- a man of great learning
- a man with great leadership qualities.

How messiahship is shown in the scriptures

There are no references to the Messiah in the Torah, but the Nevi'im say that:

- The Messiah will be a descendant of David:

    'The days are coming,' declares the Lord, 'when I will raise up for David a righteous Branch, a King who will reign wisely and do what is just and right in the land. In his days Judah will be saved and Israel will live in safety. This is the name by which he will be called: The Lord Our Righteous Saviour.' 'So then, the days are coming,' declares the Lord, 'when people will no longer say, "As surely as the Lord lives, who brought the Israelites up out of Egypt," but they will say, "As surely as the Lord lives, who brought the descendants of Israel up out of the land of the north and out of all the countries where he had banished them." Then they will live in their own land.' (Jeremiah 23:5–8)

- The Messiah will be **inspired** by God:

    The Spirit of the Lord will rest upon him. (Isaiah 11:2).

    The Messiah will rule wisely and justly and ensure the poor are treated fairly. (Isaiah 11:3–5)

- The Messiah will rebuild the Temple in Jerusalem.

Topic 2.1b.3 Messiah

The Messianic Age

The time when the Messiah comes is known as the Messianic Age or *Olam Ha-Ba* (the 'world to come') and the Nevi'im say that during this time:

- There will be peace among all nations (Isaiah 2:4; Micah 4:3).
- There will be justice and prosperity throughout the world (Isaiah 11:6–9).
- All the Jewish people will return from **exile** to Israel (Jeremiah 23:8; Hosea 3:4–5).
- The Temple will be rebuilt in Jerusalem (Ezekiel 37:26–27).
- The whole world will accept the Jewish God and Jewish religion (Isaiah 2:3; Zechariah 14:9).
- There will be no sin or evil as everyone will obey all the commandments (Zephaniah 3:13).

Different understandings of the Messiah

Belief in the Messiah is basic to Judaism as it is one of the Thirteen Principles,

I believe with perfect faith in the coming of the Messiah. However long it takes, I will await His coming every day (the twelfth of Maimonides' Thirteen Principles).

However, exactly what this means is a matter of dispute:

- Some Orthodox rabbis have taught that there are a finite number of souls destined to enter the world and live within human bodies. When all these souls have arrived on earth, the Messiah will come and bring in the Messianic Age.
- Other Orthodox rabbis have taught that the Messiah will not come until all Jewish people observe all the *mitzvot* fully, with no Jew breaking a command.
- Some Kabbalistic Jews believe that the Messiah (Messiah ben David) will be preceded by Messiah ben Joseph, who will lead the Children of Israel to Jerusalem and re-establish Temple worship and set up his own dominion. Then the forces of evil will wage war against Messiah ben Joseph and kill him. After this, the Messiah ben David will appear, defeat the forces of evil, resurrect Messiah ben Joseph and bring in the Messianic Age.
- Some Orthodox Jewish thinkers believe that the Messianic Age will be similar to the current age except that the Jewish people will have returned to Jerusalem and Temple worship will have been restored.
- Other Orthodox Jewish thinkers believe that the coming of the Messiah will result in the resurrection of the dead and everyone being given a spiritual body to live in a spiritual world.

'I believe with complete faith in the coming of the Messiah and even though he may delay, nevertheless I anticipate every day that he will come.'

Useful words

Exile – when the Jewish people had to leave their homeland and live elsewhere
Sanctuary – God's holy place

My servant David will be king over them; and they will all have one shepherd. They will follow my laws and be careful to keep my decrees. They will live in the land I gave to my servant Jacob, the land where your fathers lived. They and their children and their children's children will live there for ever, and David my servant will be their Prince for ever. I will make a covenant of peace with them; it will be an everlasting covenant. I will establish them and increase their numbers, and I will put my **sanctuary** *among them for ever. My dwelling place will be with them; I will be their God, and they will be my people. Then the nations will know that I the Lord make Israel holy when my sanctuary is among them for ever. (Ezekiel 37:24–28)*

Activities

1. Read the passage from Ezekiel 37 opposite. Make a list of the features of messiahship and the Messianic Age in this passage and a list of those features which are not in the passage.
2. Do you think the Messianic Age will ever happen?

Section 1b: Beliefs and teachings

> **Activity**
>
> Do you think all Jews have the same ideas about the Messiah?

- Some Jewish rabbis have believed they know when the Messiah will arrive. This is particularly so among Ultra-Orthodox Jewish groups such as the Haredi.
- Most Orthodox rabbis have followed the teaching of Maimonides that no one can know when the Messiah will come other than God himself.
- Many Reform Jews no longer believe in the idea of an individual Messiah who will make the world perfect. They think that was an idea which arose out of the need for Jewish people to have a hope of returning to their homeland after being driven out by the Babylonians and then by the Romans. These Reform Jews believe that it is up to individual Jewish people to change this world, bringing the nations together and establishing justice and peace just as the Tenakh predicts the Messianic Age will do.

The importance of ideas about the Messiah for Jews today

Belief in the coming of the Messiah is one the Thirteen Principles of the Faith and so it has to be important since these are regarded as the minimum requirements of Jewish belief.

The importance can also be seen in the fact that in the prayer which Jews recite three times a day, they pray for the coming of the Messiah, as well as the return of the exiles, reward to the righteous, the rebuilding of Jerusalem, the restoration of the line of King David and the restoration of the Temple service.

The way the idea of the Messianic Age (especially the Reform view) has attracted Jewish people to liberal and left-wing political causes shows another importance. Many think that the Messianic ideal of peace and justice for the poor is the reason why so many left-wing thinkers were Jewish (for example, Karl Marx and Leon Trotsky).

Summary

Jews believe that the Messiah will be sent by God to bring in the Messianic Age, when everyone will live in peace and worship the one true God. There are different ideas among Jews about when the Messiah will come and how the Messianic Age will be bought in.

Practice questions

c Explain two reasons why beliefs about the Messiah are important for Jews today. You must refer to a source of wisdom and authority in your answer.

d 'All Jews should have the same beliefs about the Messiah.' Evaluate this statement, considering arguments for and against. In your answer you should:
- refer to Jewish points of view
- refer to different Jewish points of view
- reach a justified conclusion.

Topic 2.1b.4 The covenant at Sinai

The nature and history of the covenant at Sinai

Moses is the great teacher of Judaism. The Jewish people were in captivity in Egypt, working as slaves for the Egyptian pharaoh (probably Rameses II), when Moses was called by God to lead his people out of Egypt to the Promised Land of Canaan. This is known as the **Exodus** and the most famous event was when God opened up the Red Sea to let the Israelites cross on dry land, but then brought back the waters to trap the Egyptian army.

Moses then spent 40 years wandering in the Sinai wilderness preparing the people to enter and possess the promised land, where they would set up their own country based on God's laws. It was during this time that God appeared to Moses on Mount Sinai to make the **covenant**.

A covenant is a binding agreement between two parties with certain conditions and promises. The Mosaic Covenant was an agreement between God and the Jewish people given to Moses. God gave Moses his laws on two tablets of stone. These were to be kept in the **Ark of the Covenant**, which had to be kept in the tabernacle. The agreement was that if the people kept God's laws, then

> *out of all the nations, you will be my treasured possession ... you will be for me a kingdom of priests and a holy nation. (Exodus 19:5–6)*

The importance of the Mosaic Covenant for Jews today

- The Mosaic Covenant has become the very basis of Judaism. Moses was given 613 *mitzvot* by God in the Torah which provide the way of life for Jewish people and which separate them from **Gentiles** (see Topic 2.1b.7, page 246).
- The covenant God made with Moses means that Jewish people have a duty to keep the *mitzvot* as part of their side of the covenant to make them God's people.
- The Tenakh teaches that by keeping the Mosaic Covenant, the Jewish people will fulfil their destiny of bringing the whole world to worship God:

  > *I will also make you a light for the Gentiles, that you may bring salvation to the whole earth. (Isaiah 49:6)*

- The laws given to Moses are so important for modern Jews that the divisions into Reform and Orthodox, Hasidic and Ultra-Orthodox and so on are all based on interpretations of how Jewish people should obey the Mosaic Covenant.

The role of Moses in the covenant

Moses was crucial to the covenant. He met the *shekhinah* on Mount Sinai and received the laws directly from God. God made the covenant with Moses and Moses then delivered it to the Jewish people, and explained it to them so that they then took the covenant on themselves.

Thinking points

In this topic you need to:
- think about the nature and history of the covenant at Sinai (the Ten Commandments), including Exodus 20:2–17
- understand the role of Moses in the covenant
- be able to explain and evaluate the importance of the covenant and the Ten Commandments for Jews today.

Useful words

Exodus – the Israelites' escape from slavery in Egypt
Covenant – an agreement between God and his people
Ark of the Covenant – the holy container for the tablets of the commandments
Gentiles – non-Jews

> *You are standing here in order to enter into covenant with the Lord your God, a covenant the Lord is entering into with you this day and sealing with an oath, to confirm you this day as his people that he may be your God as he promised you and as he swore to your fathers, Abraham, Isaac and Jacob. I am making this covenant, with its oath, not only with you who are standing here with us today in the presence of the Lord our God, but also with those who are not here today.*
> *(Deuteronomy 29:12–15)*

Activity

What is the Mosaic Covenant?

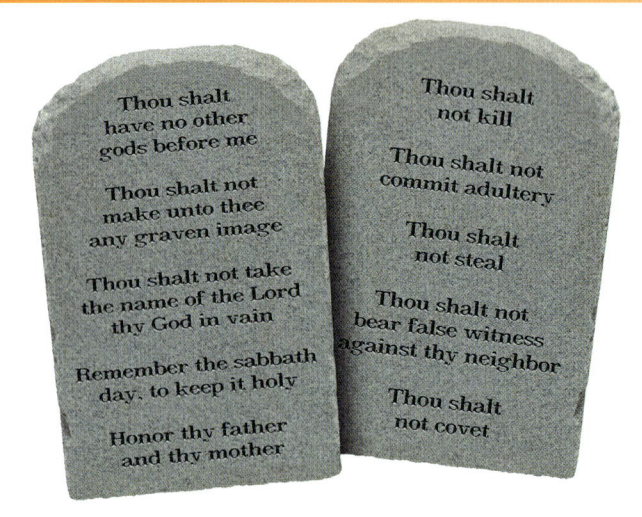

Section 1b: Beliefs and teachings

The Ten Commandments.

The Ten Commandments

Although Moses was given 613 commandments from God, Jews regard the Ten Commandments as special because they are commandments to be kept by all Jews, women as well as men, children as well as adults. This makes them different from the 613 *mitzvot* because some of the *mitzvot* are only to be kept by men, some are only to be kept by women and some are not to be kept by children. English-speaking Jews often refer to the Ten Commandments as the **Decalogue** (Exodus 20:2–17).

Why the Decalogue is important in Jewish life today

The first commandment is important because Jewish people:

- Touch the *mezuzah* when they go in and out to remind themselves of the *shema*, which tells them they worship one God only.
- Pray three times a day (morning, afternoon, evening) to the one true God, when males wear the *tefillin* containing the *shema* to remind them that they believe in one God only.
- Say grace to the one God before and after food.
- Have frequent reference in daily prayers and synagogue worship to the fact that Jewish people worship one God only.

The second commandment is important because Jewish people prohibit having any form of statue in the synagogue or their home. Most Jewish people would not make or have in the home anything that might look like an idol. They would allow paintings as long as they were somehow incomplete (for example, only the top half, no face, no human with an animal head). There is much debate about what art is permitted in Judaism, showing how seriously the second commandment is taken.

The third commandment is important because Jewish people would not use God's name in any form of swearing and, indeed, most Jewish people say, 'the Almighty' rather than speaking the word God or Lord or so on, which will always be written as G-d, L-rd and so on. The name which God told Moses was his name (Jahweh) in Exodus is never pronounced and only appears as JHWH.

The fourth commandment is very important in modern Jewish life. The commandment makes plain that the Sabbath is the seventh day of the week – Saturday – and on that day Orthodox Jews do no work. **Shabbat** begins at sunset on Friday and ends when the stars appear on Saturday. Orthodox Jews are very strict about what constitutes work. See Topic 2.1b.6 (page 244).

Useful words

Decalogue – the Ten Commandments
Shabbat – the Jewish holy day on Saturday, the seventh day of the week

Activity

Look at the abbreviation above. Do you think Jewish people would use this in a mobile message?

Topic 2.1b.4 The covenant at Sinai

'[Moses] took the calf which they had made and burned it with fire, and ground it to powder, and scattered it over the surface of the water and made the sons of Israel drink it.'

The fifth commandment to honour parents is important as it helps Jewish people in their family life and parents in their task of bringing their children up to be good Jews. As part of keeping the commandment, Jewish people in the UK support Jewish Care, a charity which provides community centres and care homes for elderly or disabled relatives.

Jewish people find the last five commandments very important when they are making moral decisions as they give very clear moral guidance:

- do not kill
- do not commit adultery
- do not steal
- do not lie
- do not desire other people's things.

If Jewish people follow these commandments, they will have a good relationship with their neighbours. By not killing and not stealing, they will be rejecting violence. By not committing adultery or desiring other people's partners, they will promote marriage and family life.

Following the Ten Commandments means Jewish people will not lie or cheat people, nor will they covet or desire other people's possessions. Applying the Ten Commandments means Jewish people should act against all forms of greed and materialism.

Activities

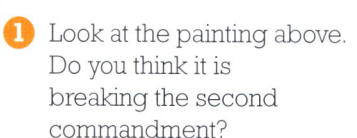

1. Look at the painting above. Do you think it is breaking the second commandment?
2. How would the last six of the Ten Commandments help Jewish people to make moral decisions?

Practice questions

c. Explain two ways in which Moses is important for the Jewish people. In your answer you must refer to a source of wisdom and authority.

d. 'The Mosaic Covenant is not relevant for Jewish life today.' Evaluate this statement considering arguments for and against. In your answer you should:
- refer to Jewish points of view
- refer to different Jewish points of view
- reach a justified conclusion.

Summary

The covenant with Moses is the agreement between God and the Jewish people that the people would keep the 613 *mitzvot* God gave to Moses and God would make them his holy people. The Ten Commandments (Decalogue) are part of the covenant which God gave to Moses on Mount Sinai. The Ten Commandments sum up the worship and morality of the covenant.

Section 1b: Beliefs and teachings

Topic 2.1b.5 The covenant with Abraham

Thinking points

In this topic you need to:
- think about what the Abrahamic Covenant is, including the role of Abraham in Genesis 17:1–12, and how it has developed
- be able to explain and evaluate the importance of this covenant for Jews today.

Useful words

Canaan – ancient name for the land of Israel
Ishmael – Abraham's son through Hagar, ancestor of Arab people
Isaac – Abraham's son through Sarah, ancestor of Jewish people
Brit Milah – covenant of circumcision

The nature and history of the Abrahamic Covenant

A thousand years before Moses, the Torah says that God called Abraham to leave his family in Iraq and travel to Canaan to worship the one true God. God said to him:

> *I will make you a great nation and I will bless you ... and all peoples on earth will be blessed through you.* (Genesis 12:2–3)

In a second appearance, God promised to give the land of **Canaan** to Abraham's descendants. Abraham had no children and so his wife, Sarah, offered him her maid, Hagar, to have a surrogate child who was named Ishmael, but Sarah found it difficult to accept **Ishmael**. Then God told Abraham that Sarah would have a child in her old age – **Isaac**. The couple found this difficult to believe, but it happened and their son Isaac became the heir to the promises. God promised that Ishmael would be the father of a great nation (both Jews and Muslims believe that Ishmael was the ancestor of the Arabs). However, it was with Abraham and Isaac that God made his covenant of circumcision (**Brit Milah**).

The Abrahamic Covenant

> *When Abram was ninety-nine years old, the Lord appeared to him and said, 'I am God Almighty; walk before me faithfully and be blameless. Then I will make my covenant between me and you and will greatly increase your numbers.' Abram fell facedown, and God said to him, 'As for me, this is my covenant with you: You will be the father of many nations. No longer will you be called Abram; your name will be Abraham, for I have made you a father of many nations. I will make you very fruitful; I will make nations of you, and kings will come from you. I will establish my covenant as an everlasting covenant between me and you and your descendants after you for the generations to come, to be your God and the God of your descendants after you. The whole land of Canaan, where you now reside as a foreigner, I will give as an everlasting possession to you and your descendants after you; and I will be their God.' Then God said to Abraham, 'As for you, you must keep my covenant, you and your descendants after you for the generations to come. This is my covenant with you and your descendants after you, the covenant you are to keep: Every male among you shall be circumcised. You are to undergo circumcision, and it will be the sign of the covenant between me and you. For the generations to come every male among you who is eight days old must be circumcised.'* (Genesis 17:1–12)

Activity

Read the passage from Genesis chapter 17 and make a list of what God's side of the agreement was and what Abraham's side was.

Topic 2.1b.5 The covenant with Abraham

'"Look up at the heavens and count the stars – if indeed you can count them." Then he said to him, "So shall your offspring be"' (Genesis 15:5).

Genesis 17:13–27 goes on to say that Abraham and Sarah would have a son Isaac with whom God would establish an everlasting covenant for his descendants. Then Abraham circumcised himself and his son Ishmael and all the male members of his household.

The Torah has many references to the importance of circumcision, but gives no reason why this should have been such a major part of the covenant with Abraham. Two suggestions made by the rabbis are:

- It is appropriate that a bodily sign of Israel's commitment to God throughout the generations should be on that part of the male anatomy which will create the future generations.
- Man should not be satisfied with his imperfect condition. Circumcision makes a perfect male without the useless foreskin and Jewish men should try to perfect themselves and serve God with every part of their body.

However, some modern Jews feel that it is the Mosaic Covenant that is important for Jewish people, not the Abrahamic one. They do not circumcise their children because the Torah prohibits marking or altering the human body:

> You shall not make any cuttings in your flesh on account of the dead or tattoo any marks upon you: I am the Lord. *(Leviticus 19:28)*

They also insist that the Torah does not allow another person to be harmed (Exodus 21:18–27). Added to this, growing awareness of infant pain has brought the ethics of circumcision into question. They also refer to the statement in the *Encyclopedia Judaica*: 'Any child born of a Jewish mother is a Jew, whether circumcised or not.'

Activities

1. Look at the photo above. Has the prediction come true?
2. Who are the Children of Israel?
3. What is the difference between an Israelite and an Israeli?

Section 1b: Beliefs and teachings

History of the Abrahamic Covenant

The promise God made to Abraham was that he would be the father of a great nation. Abraham's grandson, Jacob, was renamed by God and his new name was Israel:

> *Your name is Jacob, but you will no longer be called Jacob, your name will be Israel ... A nation and a community of nations will come from your body. The land I gave to Abraham and Isaac I will also give to you, and I will give this land to your descendants after you.* (Genesis 35:10–12)

Jacob had twelve sons, the Children of Israel. These twelve were the ancestors of the twelve tribes of Israel, from which any Jewish person can claim descent. In the Torah, the Children of Israel are the heirs to the promises made to Abraham and are the ones who are part of the Mosaic Covenant: 'Moses said to the whole Israelite community,

> *This is what the Lord has commanded.'* (Exodus 35:4)

In later Jewish history, the Jewish kingdom split into two: the ten northern tribes formed the Kingdom of Israel, which was conquered by the Assyrians in 721 BCE, and the two southern tribes formed the Kingdom of Judah, which was not conquered until 586 BCE. It is from this kingdom that the words Judaism and Jew originate. However, it is the Children of Israel who are the Jewish people.

When the modern Jewish state was established, it was called Israel; nowadays an Israelite is used to refer to an ethnic Jew who follows the Jewish religion whereas an Israeli is a citizen of the state of Israel.

Why the Abrahamic Covenant is important for Jews today

The covenant is important for Jews today for the following reasons:

- Most Jewish baby boys are circumcised, usually at eight days old. This often entails a special Brit Milah ceremony when a **mohel** circumcises the boy, and the father promises to bring the boy up in the Jewish faith and thanks God for circumcision,

    > *by which our sons enter into the covenant of Abraham our father.*

- Some Reform and Liberal Jews choose not to circumcise their sons, often because they are concerned about medical issues. However, the covenant is still important to them and some Reform rabbis have developed a welcoming ceremony that they call the **Brit Shalom** (covenant of peace), which claims the child as an heir of the Abrahamic covenant.

- The importance of the Abrahamic covenant can be seen in the increasing popularity of the **Brit Chayim** (covenant of life) ceremony for Jewish baby girls among Reform and Liberal Jews. This ceremony welcomes girls into the Jewish faith and claims them as heirs to the Abrahamic Covenant.

- The covenant gave rise to the idea that Jewish people had a right to live in the area that was the ancient Kingdom of Israel, which has led to the importance of the land of Israel to Jewish people. The state of Israel was established in 1947 as a place of security for all Jews, and Jewish people living anywhere in the world have the right to live in Israel and become a citizen. In 2015 there were 6.3 million Children of

Useful words

Mohel – expert circumciser
Brit Shalom – covenant of peace (ceremony welcoming uncircumcised male babies)
Brit Chayim – covenant of life ceremony for Reform girl babies

Activities

1. Do you think the Abrahamic Covenant is important for Jews today?
2. Look at the Pew Research Center data on page 243. Why do you think more American Christians than American Jews believe that God gave the Jewish people the land of Israel?

Israel living in Israel, making up 75 per cent of the population of Israel (worldwide there are 13.9 million Jews, of whom 5.7 million live in the USA).

There is a major debate in the Jewish communities outside Israel about the idea of the state of Israel being a fulfilment of God's promise to Abraham to give the Children of Israel the Promised Land. Ultra-Orthodox groups outside Israel teach that the return to the Promised Land will only come with the coming of the Messiah and that rather than supporting Israel, good Jews should be following all the *mitzvot* and praying for the coming of the Messiah.

> *Only 40 percent of American Jews believe the land that is now Israel was given to the Jewish people by God. However, 55 percent of American Christians believe this, and 64 percent of Protestant Christians in the USA believe it. (Pew Research Center, Survey of US Jews, 2013)*

Practice questions

c Explain two reasons why male Jewish babies are circumcised. In your answer you must refer to a source of wisdom and authority.

d 'The covenant with Moses is more important than the covenant with Abraham.' Evaluate this statement considering arguments for and against. In your answer you should:
- refer to Jewish points of view
- reach a justified conclusion.

Summary

The Abrahamic Covenant is God's agreement with Abraham that God would make a great nation from Abraham's descendants and give them the Promised Land as their own if all their male children were circumcised and they worshipped God alone. The covenant is so important that many Reform and Liberal Jews have a ceremony for girls to welcome them into Abraham's covenant.

Section 1b: Beliefs and teachings

Topic 2.1b.6 Sanctity of life

Thinking points

In this topic you need to:
- think about the nature and importance of *pikuach nefesh* (saving a life)
- think about why human life is holy and how life is shown as special and as taking precedence over everything (Talmud *Yoma*)
- be able to explain and evaluate Jewish ideas about the sanctity of life and its importance for Jews today.

Useful words

Talmud – collection of Mishneh and other writing on the Jewish law
Desecrate – violate a sacred place or law
Yom Kippur – the Day of Atonement when religious Jews fast for the whole day
Kashrut – keeping Jewish food laws

Activities

1. How do the scriptures show the sanctity of life?
2. What is the principle of *pikuach nefesh* based on?

The nature and importance of *pikuach nefesh*

Judaism teaches that life is sacred – life is a gift from God. It follows that as God is the author of life, life itself is holy and must be valued and preserved. As the Torah says:

> *See now that I myself am He! There is no god beside me. I put to death, and I bring to life. (Deuteronomy 32:39)*

> *You shall not murder. (Exodus 20:13)*

> *If anyone takes the life of a human being, he must be put to death. Anyone who takes the life of someone's animal must make restitution – life for life. (Leviticus 24:17–18)*

Jewish people believe that God is in control of his creation and that whatever comes to life or dies is caused to do so by God. Humans have to respect all human life. It is up to God to say when life will begin or end. As the Tenakh says,

> *Naked I came from my mother's womb, and naked I shall depart. The Lord gave and the Lord has taken away; may the name of the Lord be blessed. (Job 1:21)*

The sacredness and importance of human life is shown in the concept of *pikuach nefesh*, which is the principle in Jewish law that the preservation of human life overrides almost all other religious considerations.

The **Talmud** explains this principle of *pikuach nefesh* using the verse,

> *Keep my decrees and laws, for the person who obeys them will live by them. I am the Lord (Leviticus 18:5)*

to which the rabbis added:

> *That he shall live by them, and not that he shall die by them. (Babylonian Talmud, Yoma 85b)*

When life is involved, all Sabbath laws may be suspended to safeguard the health of the individual. A Jew is not merely permitted but is actually required to disregard a law that conflicts with life or health.

> *It is a religious precept to **desecrate** the Sabbath for any person afflicted with an illness that may prove dangerous; he who is zealous is praiseworthy while he who asks questions sheds blood. (Shulhan Arukh, Orah Hayyim 328:2)*

Pikuach nefesh is also derived from the Torah verse,

> *Do not do anything that endangers your neighbour's life. (Leviticus 19:16)*

According to *pikuach nefesh*, a person must do everything in their power to save the life of another, so it is permissible to break the **Yom Kippur** fast, break the **kashrut** rules and so on. The Talmud contains several instances where the laws of the Sabbath are to be broken to save the life of another; these occasions include rescuing a child from the sea, breaking apart a

244

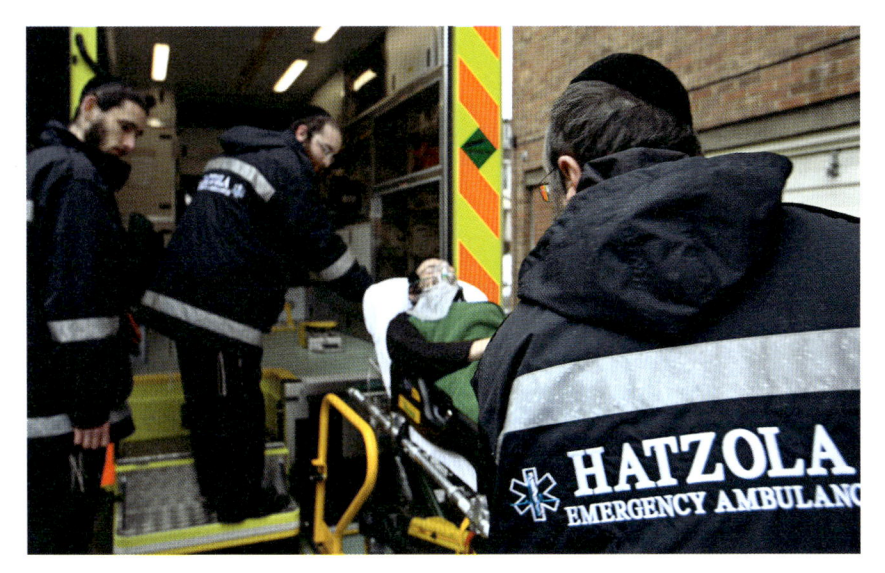

Topic 2.1b.6 Sanctity of life

Hatzola is a voluntary medical emergency service that provides care to the Orthodox Jewish community of north London. A Jew reluctant to violate Sabbath rules when receiving medical attention may be more at ease and easily convinced of the medical urgency when the paramedic is a fellow Orthodox Jew.

wall that has collapsed on a child, breaking down a door about to close on an infant, and extinguishing a fire (*Yoma* 84b).

Clearly the concept of *pikuach nefesh* is based on the **sanctity of life** and shows how important the belief in sanctity of life is to Judaism.

Why the concept of *pikuach nefesh* is important for Jews today

Pikuach nefesh is particularly important in areas of medical ethics such as:

- Abortion: some Jews believe that abortion can never be allowed because of the belief in the sanctity of life, but *pikuach nefesh* means that if the mother's life is at risk, then it should be allowed.
- Contraception: Orthodox Judaism does not allow the use of condoms because the Torah teaches that the male seed is sacred, but the Jewish Aids Trust promotes the use of condoms to prevent HIV transmission because this *mitzvah* can be broken to save the lives of people who may become infected with HIV.
- Transplant surgery should not be allowed because there is a *mitzvah* which says dead bodies must not be interfered with, but *pikuach nefesh* means that this *mitzvah* can be broken to transplant on organ from a dead person to save the life of a living person.

Pikuach nefesh is also an important principle for Jews living in the complex world of today. It is a means of deciding when and where the *mitzvot* take priority.

Useful words

Sanctity of life – the belief that life is holy and belongs to God

Activities

1. Look at the photo above. How does this photo explain the concept of *pikuach nefesh*?
2. Can you think of a situation where *pikuach nefesh* could be used to justify breaking a *mitzvah*?

Practice questions

c Explain two reasons why Jews believe in the sanctity of life. In your answer you must refer to a source of wisdom and authority.

d 'Orthodox Jews should always obey the *mitzvot*.' Evaluate this statement considering arguments for and against. In your answer you should:
- refer to Jewish points of view
- refer to different Jewish points of view
- reach a justified conclusion.

Summary

Jewish people believe in the sanctity of life because they believe that life is a gift from God which makes life itself holy. This is taught in the Torah. The importance of the sanctity of life is seen in the teaching of *pikuach nefesh*, which says that a Jew must do everything in their power to save a life even if it involves breaking the *mitzvot*.

Section 1b: Beliefs and teachings

Topic 2.1b.7 Moral principles and the *mitzvot*

Thinking points

In this topic you will need to:
- think about the nature of the *mitzvot*, including the Mishneh Torah of Maimonides
- consider the relationship between keeping the *mitzvot* and free will
- understand the *mitzvot* between the Almighty and humans
- be able to explain why the *mitzvot* are important for Jewish life today.

Useful words

Mitzvot – commandments (plural)
Oral Torah – the unwritten Torah given to Moses by God
Halakhah – Jewish law from the Written and Oral Torah
Mishneh – the Oral Torah

This day ... I have set before you life and death, blessings and curses. Now choose life so that you and your children may live. (Deuteronomy 30:19)

Activity

Look at the quotation from Deuteronomy above. What choice do you think is being referred to?

The nature of the *mitzvot*

As we have seen, Moses received 613 **mitzvot** on Mount Sinai. These are recorded in the Torah and the Jewish people are to observe them as their part of the Mosaic Covenant.

However, the *mitzvot* in the Torah are stated very briefly, and needed some explanation. For example, the fourth of the Ten Commandments says that Jewish people should do no work on the Sabbath, but it does not explain what is meant by work. According to Jewish tradition, this explanation was given to Moses by God in the form of the '**Oral Torah**' which was passed on by priests, judges and later by rabbis. The Oral and Written Torah made up the **halakhah** (the Jewish law).

The Oral Torah was written down in the Talmud during the second century CE, but the **Mishneh** Torah compiled by Maimonides between 1170 and 1180 (especially the five books of the Sefer Madda) is regarded by many Jews as the major code of Jewish law. Maimonides intended to provide a complete statement of the oral law, so that a Jew who mastered first the Written Torah and then the Mishneh Torah would be in no need of any other book. Many rabbis believe that the Mishneh Torah gives the correct meaning of the Oral Torah and so no decisions on the *halakhah* can be accepted if they disagree with Maimonides.

Although the *mitzvot* cannot change because they were given to Moses by God, the understanding of them and the interpretation of them for life today are always changing. New discoveries and new social conditions mean that people's ways of living have changed and the *halakhah* has to be adapted. As an example, can automated machinery be used on *Shabbat*? So new commentaries on the *mitzvot* are continually being added.

For most Jewish people the *mitzvot* and *halakhah* are one and the same thing because by following the Jewish law (*halakhah*) they are keeping the *mitzvot*.

Keeping the *mitzvot* and free will

The *mitzvot* are commandments and therefore not optional. Judaism teaches that each Jew must decide whether or not to follow the *mitzvot* of their own free will. The first book of the Torah (Genesis) teaches that God created humans in his own image:

So God created man in his own image, in the image of God he created him; male and female he created them. (Genesis 1:27)

Judaism understands this to mean that God has created humans with free will, every person is free to choose whether to do good or evil. In particular, they are free to choose whether to obey the *mitzvot* or ignore them.

This is important because it means that following the *mitzvot* is not something originating from people's nature as human beings. Humans have no choice about breathing, it is just something that happens; but humans do have a choice about following the *mitzvot*, and because it is a choice, it is something about which they can be judged (see Topic 2.1b.1, page 226).

Why the *mitzvot* are important for understanding the relationship between humans and the Almighty

The *mitzvot* should be understood at a much deeper spiritual level than simply keeping them day by day.

The word *mitzvah* means commandment, but it is closely related to the Hebrew word for 'connection' and Jewish people believe that the *mitzvot* are a way for individuals to connect with God. By keeping the *mitzvot*, Jewish people communicate with God.

The *mitzvot* are God's way of reaching out to human beings and helping them to live in the correct way. By obeying the *mitzvot*, humans are reaching back to God and so becoming in a true way, 'the people of God'. This, of course, is the meaning of the Mosaic Covenant – God has agreed to be the Jewish people's God, and look after them, if they keep his *mitzvot*.

The importance of the *mitzvot* for relationships between people

It is important for Jewish people to understand the *mitzvot* because it is only if a Jewish person really understands the *mitzvot* that he or she will keep them properly. Judaism teaches that through understanding the *mitzvot* will come better behaviour, and it is the aim of Judaism to help people behave in the best way possible. As the Talmud says, 'The *mitzvot* were given for the purpose of refining people'.

Activity
Do you think following the *mitzvot* will improve relationships between people?

A *kosher* McDonald's restaurant in Buenos Aires, Argentina.

Section 1b: Beliefs and teachings

Useful words

Mitzvah – commandment (singular)
Chukim – *mitzvot* with no reason given for them
Kosher – food which a Jew is allowed to eat

American Jews consider the most essential elements of being Jewish to be: Remembering the Holocaust, leading an ethical and moral life, working for justice/equality, being intellectually curious. (Pew Research Center, Survey of US Jews, 2013)

Each **mitzvah** (this is the singular, *mitzvot* is plural) has something to teach. For example, the laws about borrowing and lending teach compassion for those less well-off than oneself; the laws on damages and compensation teach the need for personal responsibility; the laws on the punishment of criminals teach the need to respect human dignity. Consequently, it is important to understand these *mitzvot* in order to understand what they teach.

However, there are some *mitzvot* (known as **chukim**) which have no reason given for them, for example the *mitzvot* on keeping **kosher**. Jewish scholars say it is important to understand that these *mitzvot* were given by God as a test of faith and that observing these *mitzvot* strengthens a Jew's faith in the Almighty.

Why there are different views in Judaism about the importance of the *mitzvot*

The Orthodox view

The *mitzvot* are particularly important for Orthodox Jews because they cover the whole of life. No feature of life is unaffected by the *mitzvot*. For the Orthodox Jew there is a right and a wrong way of doing everything. For example, there are *mitzvot* which tell people how to organise the kitchen, how to dress, what to eat, how to grow crops, who they can marry, how to divorce, when they can work, which jobs they cannot do, paying wages and ownership of property and business.

The Liberal/Reform view

The *mitzvot* are not as important for Liberal Jews as they do not regard the *mitzvot* as coming to Moses directly from God, and so they believe that observing the *mitzvot* is a matter of personal choice. For example, some Liberal Jews keep *kashrut*, some just eat *kosher* food, others ignore the food laws altogether. This attitude to the *mitzvot* means that they are not considered as important to Liberal Jews as to the Orthodox.

Summary

The *mitzvot* are the 613 commands/laws Moses received from God on Sinai. They are the Written Torah which are explained by the Oral Torahs written in the Talmud and Mishneh Torah. These make up the Jewish law (*halakhah*). They affect the whole of a Jew's life, but only the Orthodox follow all of them because for Liberal/Reform Jews the *mitzvot* are optional.

Practice questions

c Explain two reasons why Jews need the *halakhah* as well as the Written Torah. In your answer you must refer to a source of wisdom and authority.

d 'The *mitzvot* are no longer relevant to modern life.' Evaluate this statement considering arguments for and against. In your answer you should:
- refer to Jewish points of view
- refer to different Jewish points of view
- reach a justified conclusion.

Topic 2.1b.8 Jewish beliefs about life after death

Scriptural teachings about life after death

There is clear evidence in the Torah of belief in existence after death. The Torah indicates in several places that the righteous will be reunited with their loved ones after death, while the wicked will be excluded from this reunion. The Torah speaks of the **patriarchs** being 'gathered to their people':

There on the mountain that you [Moses] have climbed, you will die and be gathered to your people. (Deuteronomy 32:50)

Being gathered to your people after death is believed by Jews to mean that there will be an afterlife which will involve meeting with their dead family.

The Tenakh has many references to life after death. The Tenakh says that God will end the world, raise the dead and create a new world by rebuilding Jerusalem and the Temple. God will decide what happens to people in the afterlife on the basis of how they have lived their lives and what they have believed:

But your dead will live; their bodies will rise. You who dwell in the dust, wake up and shout for joy. Your dew is like the dew of the morning; the earth will give birth to her dead. (Isaiah 26:19)

At that time Michael, the great prince who protects your people, will arise. And there will be a time of distress, such as has not happened from the beginning of nations until then. But at that time your people – everyone whose name shall be found written in the book – will be delivered. Multitudes who sleep in the dust of the earth will awake, some to everlasting life, others to shame and everlasting contempt. (Daniel 12:1–13)

Different Jewish understandings of life after death

There is disagreement in Judaism about how the scriptural evidence for the afterlife should be interpreted.

Resurrection

The Thirteen Principles of Faith (written by Maimonides and described as 'Articles of the Jewish Creed' in the Jewish Daily Prayer Book) state,

I believe with perfect faith that there will be a resurrection of the dead at a time that will please the Creator, blessed be his name.

However, there are disagreements about resurrection, making it unclear exactly who will be resurrected, when it will happen and what will take place:

- Some sources imply that the resurrection of the dead will occur during the Messianic Age.
- Others indicate that resurrection will follow the Messianic Age.
- According to some, only the righteous will be resurrected.

Thinking points

In this topic you need to:
- think about Jewish teachings about life after death; the nature of resurrection and judgement; heaven and hell
- consider different Jewish understandings about life after death, including interpretations of Ecclesiastes 12:7
- similarities and differences between Christian and Jewish beliefs
- be able to evaluate different Jewish understandings about life after death and explain why life after death may be important for Jews today.

Useful words

Patriarchs – the fathers of Judaism (Abraham, Isaac, Jacob, Moses)

And the dust returns to the ground it came from, and the spirit returns to God who gave it. (Ecclesiastes 12:7)

Fear God and keep his commandments for this is the whole duty of man. For God will bring every deed into judgement, including every hidden thing whether it is good or evil. (Ecclesiastes 12:13–14)

Activity

Read the quotations from Ecclesiastes chapter 12. What do you think they mean?

Section 1b: Beliefs and teachings

Activities

1. Explain three different Jewish interpretations of judgement.
2. Outline three different Jewish ideas about what happens after judgement.

Useful words

Gan Eden – heaven
Gehinnom – hell
Mishneh Torah – the code of law written by Maimonides
Tosefta – rabbinic opinions extra to the Mishneh

- Other rabbis say that everyone will be resurrected and – as implied in Daniel – a day of judgement will follow.
- Other rabbis have argued for the immortality of the soul, the idea that the soul lives on after death as a spiritual being in the spiritual 'world to come' (*olam haba*), meaning there will be no resurrection.

The 'world to come' (*olam haba*) is another unclear idea. According to Maimonides, the 'world to come' refers to a time even beyond the world of the resurrected. He believed that the resurrected will eventually die a second death, at which point the souls of the righteous will enjoy a spiritual, bodiless existence in the presence of God. In other sources, the 'world to come' refers to the world inhabited by the righteous immediately following death, that is heaven (*Gan Eden*). In this view, the 'world to come' exists now, in some parallel universe.

Judgement

There are differences about the nature of judgement:

- Some rabbis have taught that judgement will be based purely on behaviour, for example Rabbi Hanina is recorded in the Babylonian Talmud, tractate Baba Metzia 58b, as saying that,

    *all who go down to **Gehinnom** will go up again, except adulterers, those who put their fellows to shame in public, and those who call their fellows by an obnoxious name.*

- The great Jewish scholar Maimonides went so far as to say that all good people will go to heaven, as can be seen in this quotation from **Mishneh Torah**, Repentance 3:5,

    *Moses Maimonides, echoing the **Tosefta** to Sanhedrin, maintained that the pious of all the nations of the world have a portion in the world-to-come.*

- Others have suggested that judgement will be based on a combination of belief and behaviour, as can be seen in this quotation from the Talmud (Sanhedrin 10:1),

    All Israelites have a share in the world-to-come ... [However], these are they that have no share in the world-to-come: one who says there is no resurrection of the dead prescribed in the Torah, and that the Torah is not from Heaven, and an Epicurean.

- Many modern rabbis prefer to concentrate on this life rather than worrying about the details of an afterlife about which no one can be certain. However, Jewish thinkers seem to be agreed that God will judge people on the basis of how they have lived their lives as much as, if not more than, on what they have believed.

Heaven and hell

There is disagreement about what happens after judgement. Indeed, the notion of heaven and hell has lots of different understandings. The earliest reference to *Gan Eden* (heaven) and *Gehinnom* (hell) as a pair is the first-century rabbinic statement: 'There are two paths before me, one leading to *Gan Eden* and the other to *Gehinnom*.' However, who goes to which and what they are like is unclear:

- Many rabbis have taught that the souls of the totally righteous ascend to heaven (*Gan Eden*) whereas the souls of ordinary people go to a

Topic 2.1b.8 Jewish beliefs about life after death

place of punishment known as *Gehinnom* (referred to in the Christian New Testament as *gehenna* or hell).

- Some rabbis have taught that *Gehinnom* is more like the Catholic **purgatory** and that souls are purified of their sins through punishment and fire.
- Other rabbis have taught that *Gehinnom* is a place where souls have a chance to review what they have done with their lives on earth and repent for their wrong actions. However, this period in *Gehinnom* will only last for twelve months, after which souls will rise to heaven to await the resurrection.
- Some rabbis teach that totally evil souls are eternally damned and so are punished in *Gehinnom* forever.
- Others teach that the souls of the truly wicked are destroyed by God and so cease to exist.

Why belief in life after death is important for Jews today

Belief in life after death is important because:

- It is the teaching of the Tenakh. Jews believe that the first five books of the Tenakh (the Torah) are a direct communication from God which must be believed. The other books of the Tenakh are inspired by God. Therefore, Jews should believe what the Tenakh says.
- It is the teaching of the Talmud. The Talmud is a collection of the Oral Torah, discussions by rabbis about the laws of the Torah, which most Jews try to follow.
- It is one of the Thirteen Principles of Faith which are described in the Daily Prayer Book as 'Articles of the Jewish Creed'. As part of the creed, Jews would feel they should believe it.
- Many Jews find that belief in life after death gives their lives meaning and purpose. They feel that for life to end at death does not make sense. A life after death, in which people will be judged on how they live this life, with the good rewarded and the evil punished, makes sense of this life. If the purpose of life is to live your life in such a way that you spend eternity in heaven, then that gives life meaning.
- Believing that God will decide what happens to people on the basis of how they have lived their lives is important for Jewish people because it means they must try to live good Jewish lives if they are to have a good life after death. This is a reason for them to observe the Torah and *halakhah*, making their beliefs about life after death have a big effect on their lives.

Christian and Jewish beliefs about life after death

Major differences:

- Most Jews believe that the Messiah will come and bring in the Messianic Age at the Last Day, whereas Conservative Christians believe that Jesus will return, and Liberal Christians do not believe in the Last Day.
- Many Jews believe that at the end of the world the Jewish people will bring all the non-Jews to worship God.

A Jewish cemetery in Southgate, London.

Useful words

Purgatory – a place where Catholic Christians believe souls go after death to be purified

Activity

Look at the photo of the cemetery above. Why do you think Jews call this the House of Life?

Section 1b: Beliefs and teachings

Activity

Explain why believing in life after death is important for Jewish people.

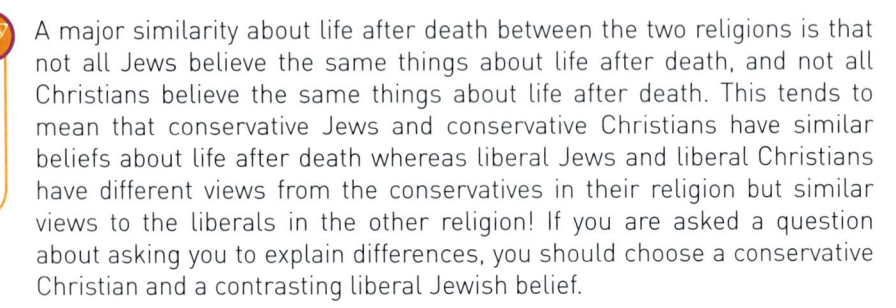

A major similarity about life after death between the two religions is that not all Jews believe the same things about life after death, and not all Christians believe the same things about life after death. This tends to mean that conservative Jews and conservative Christians have similar beliefs about life after death whereas liberal Jews and liberal Christians have different views from the conservatives in their religion but similar views to the liberals in the other religion! If you are asked a question about asking you to explain differences, you should choose a conservative Christian and a contrasting liberal Jewish belief.

Conservatives' beliefs:

- Some Jews and some Christians believe in resurrection of the body.
- Some Jews and some Christians believe that the dead will be raised on the Last Day.
- Some Jews and some Christians believe that the Last Day will bring the world as we know it to an end.
- Some Jews and some Christians believe that people will be judged on what they have believed as well as how they have behaved.
- Some Jews and some Christians believe in hell as well as heaven and that bad people and people with the wrong beliefs will go to hell.

Liberals' beliefs:

- Some Jews and some Christians believe in immortality of the soul not resurrection of the body.
- Some Jews and some Christians do not believe in the Last Day and believe judgement will take place as soon as people die.
- Some Jews and some Christians do not believe in hell and believe that eventually everyone will go to heaven.

Major similarities:

- Both Christians and Jews believe this life is not all there is and that there will be life after death.
- Both Christians and Jews believe there will be some form of judgement after death based on how people have lived on earth.
- Both Christians and Jews believe in heaven as a place of paradise with God.
- Both Christians and Jews believe that good people will go to heaven.
- Both Christians and Jews believe that life after death is important because it makes sense of this life because it makes sure that the good are rewarded.

Summary

Based on the teachings of the Tenakh, Jews believe that there will be life after death. Most Jews believe that the dead will be raised (resurrection) and judged by God, but there are lots of different Jewish ideas about life after death. Some Jews think judgement will be just about behaviour, others that it will also be about religion. Some think everyone will eventually go to heaven, others that the very evil will spend eternity in hell.

Practice questions

c Explain two reasons why believing in life after death is important for Jews. In your answer you must refer to a source of wisdom and authority.

d 'When you're dead, you're dead and that's the end of you.' Evaluate this statement considering arguments for and against. In your answer you should:
- refer to Jewish points of view
- refer to different Jewish points of view
- reach a justified conclusion.

How to answer questions

a) **Describe two similarities between Jewish beliefs about life after death and the beliefs of the main religious tradition of Britain. [3]**

Christianity is the main religious tradition of Britain. One similarity is that both Christians and Jews believe that this life is not all there is and that there will be life after death. Another similarity is that both Christians and Jews believe that there will be some form of judgement after death based on how people have lived on earth.

A high mark answer because Christianity is identified as the main religious tradition of Britain and two similarities are clearly described.

b) **Explain two reasons why the covenant with Abraham is important for Jews today. [4]**

The covenant with Abraham is important because it is the reason why Jewish boys are still circumcised at eight days old as a sign of their Jewishness. It is also important because many Jews believe that they have been given the state of Israel by God for keeping the covenant.

A high mark answer because two correct reasons are given and each reason is developed.

c) **Explain two reasons why it is important for Jewish people to keep all the *mitzvot*. In your answer you must refer to a source of wisdom and authority. [5]**

The covenant which God made with Moses on Sinai means that Jewish people have a duty to keep the *mitzvot* as part of their side of the covenant to make them God's people. The Tenakh teaches that by keeping the *mitzvot*, the Jewish people will fulfil their destiny of bringing the whole world to worship God – 'I will also make you a light for the Gentiles, that you may bring salvation to the whole earth' (Isaiah 49:6).

A high mark answer because two correct reasons are given and each reason is developed with a reference to the covenant, the Tenakh and Isaiah as sources of authority.

d) **'Only the Almighty should judge.' Evaluate this statement considering arguments for and against. In your response you should:**
- refer to Jewish points of view
- refer to different Jewish points of view
- reach a justified conclusion. [12 marks + 3 spelling, punctuation and grammar (SPaG) marks]

Many Jews would agree with this because the Tenakh is full of references to God acting as judge, for example, 'For the Lord is our judge, The Lord is our lawgiver, The Lord is our king; He will save us' (Isaiah 33:22). The Tenakh teaches that God as judge will ensure that the good are rewarded and the evil punished. 'And He will judge the world in righteousness; He will execute judgement for the peoples with equity' (Psalm 9:8).

However, the time when God the judge will make justice reign is in the future and so many Jews would say that although God is the perfect judge and will ensure that justice is done in the future, society needs judges other than God in order to function. Judaism has the Bet Din to make judgements about the *halakhah* and Jews accept the need for English courts and judges to ensure that the law is upheld here and now.

[Continued]

Section 1b: Beliefs and teachings

It seems to me that if you believe in the Jewish God, you will believe he is the only perfect judge for what happens at the end of the world, but for life to function properly, we need judges and a legal system operating in society in the present.

A high mark answer because it gives three clear developed Jewish reasons for thinking that God should be the only God. It then gives three reasons for disagreeing and then reaches a fully justified conclusion.

The answer would reach full marks for SPaG as spelling, punctuation and grammar are correct and a wide range of specialist vocabulary (Tenakh, Isaiah, Psalm, Bet Din, *halakhah*, legal system) is used appropriately.

SPaG

A high mark answer because the answer spells, punctuates and uses the rules of grammar with consistent accuracy and effective control of meaning. A wide range of specialist terms is used adeptly and with precision.

2b Practices

Area of study 2: Study of second religion, either Islam or Judaism

Section 2b: Practices

Topic 2.2b.1 Public acts of worship

Thinking points

In this topic you need to:
- think about the nature, features and purpose of public worship, including synagogue services
- be able to explain and evaluate the importance of synagogue services for the Jewish community and the individual.

Useful words

Homage – acknowledgement of superiority
Reverence – an act showing religious respect
Deity – god
Minyan – the required number of adult male Jews needed for certain prayers to be said in the synagogue
Shabbat – the Sabbath (from sunset on Friday to sunset on Saturday)
Rabbis – spiritual leaders of a Jewish community
Kiddush – a prayer said over wine to sanctify Shabbat
Sefer Torah – the scroll of the Torah
Ark – large cupboard at the front of the synagogue where the Torah scrolls are kept
Bimah – raised platform in front of the Ark from which the scriptures are read
Sidra – the portion of the Torah read at Shabbat morning service

Activity

What is public worship?

The nature of public worship

Worship is either **homage** or **reverence** paid to a **deity**. Jewish public worship is where this worship happens in a synagogue with a congregation of Jewish worshippers (the Orthodox would say with at least ten adult male Jewish worshippers forming a **minyan**).

The purpose of public worship

Public worship in Judaism has several purposes. Worshipping with others in the synagogue:

- Gives a Jewish person a sense of belonging to a whole community of Jewish believers.
- Gives an opportunity to feel the strength of the faith.
- Gives an opportunity to make friends with others in the faith.
- Provides the opportunity to take part in those prayers which can only be said in a congregation (*Shabbat* prayers and festival prayers in particular).
- Is important because the **rabbis** taught that there is more merit in praying with a group than there is in praying alone.
- Fulfils the requirement to worship publicly in the Temple. The rabbis take,

> How can I repay the Lord for all his goodness to me? I will lift up the cup of salvation and call on the name of the Lord. I will fulfil my vows to the Lord in the presence of all his people … I will sacrifice a thank-offering to you and call on the name of the Lord. I will fulfil my vows to the Lord in the presence of all his people, in the courts of the house of the Lord. (Psalm 116:12–19)

to mean that Jewish people are required to worship God in public as well as in the home.

Features of Jewish public worship

Each Friday after the welcoming of *Shabbat*, synagogues should hold *Shabbat* evening prayers when *Shabbat* is greeted like a bride coming to meet her husband – the Jewish people. After the service ends the rabbi takes a cup of wine and recites **Kiddush** to thank God for giving *Shabbat* to the Jewish people.

On *Shabbat* morning (Saturday), families go to synagogue for the morning prayer, which is the main service of the week. The high point of the service is when the **Sefer Torah** is taken out of the **Ark** and carried to the **bimah** for the rabbi to read the **sidra** (over the course of a year the whole Torah will be read). In an Orthodox synagogue, men are called from the congregation to recite a blessing at certain points of the reading, and at the end a man is called to read from one of the books of the prophets. After the Sefer Torah has been put back in the Ark, the rabbi gives a sermon.

Topic 2.2b.1 Public acts of worship

On *Shabbat* afternoon, synagogues have afternoon prayers, when the Sefer Torah is again taken out of the Ark and a short part of the following week's *sidra* is read.

Public worship also takes place for various festivals. In preparation for **Rosh Hashanah**, Jews should worship in the synagogue each day of the month of **Ellul** for the blowing of the *shofar*. **Yom Kippur** is the holiest day of the Jewish year and there are five prayer services in the synagogue during this day. The great festival of **Simchat Torah** must be celebrated in the synagogue to parade the sacred Sefer Torah around the congregation. The rabbinic festivals such as **Purim** also have special worship services in the synagogue.

Orthodox and Liberal/Reform synagogues have differences in their services. In Liberal synagogues:

- prayers are said mainly in English, not Hebrew
- women attend all the services and sit with the men
- the rabbi may well be a woman
- there are some different prayers.

The importance of synagogue worship

Worship is important for Jewish people because the Torah tells them

> *to love the Lord your God, and to serve him with all your heart and with all your soul. (Deuteronomy 11:13)*

Worship in the synagogue is important for the Jewish community because:

- To worship God with all your heart and all your soul requires people to be able to worship in community with other people who share the same beliefs and values.
- It is needed for the Jewish community to enhance *Shabbat* properly.
- It provides the community with the opportunity to share in family celebrations such as Brit Milah, Bar Mitzvah and weddings.
- It is required for the community to celebrate the great festivals such as Pesach, Rosh Hashanah, Yom Kippur and Simchat Torah.

Worship in the synagogue is important for a Jewish individual because:

- Worshipping with others in the synagogue gives a sense of belonging to a whole community of Jewish believers and an opportunity to feel the strength of the faith and make friends with others in the faith.
- It gives order and purpose to people's religious life.
- It also gives an individual the opportunity to reflect on the serious side of life, especially when worship gives an opportunity to think about the meaning of life at times such as Rosh Hashanah and Yom Kippur and at sad times like death.
- It gives an opportunity to listen to the reading of the Torah and the rest of the Tenakh.
- It also has sermons from the rabbi, which provide the individual with the opportunity to discover more about what it means to be a Jew, and how to live as a Jew in the twenty-first century.

Worship at the Western Wall of the Temple in Jerusalem, the holiest site for Jewish people.

Useful words

Rosh Hashanah – Jewish New Year
Ellul – the final month of the Jewish year
Shofar – ram's horn
Yom Kippur – Jewish holy day, also known as the Day of Atonement
Simchat Torah – the festival celebrating the giving of the Torah
Purim – Jewish holy day to celebrate the saving of the Jewish people from Haman, who was trying to kill all the Jews in Persia

Activities

1. Outline the main features of synagogue worship.
2. Why does Judaism regard public worship as important?

Section 2b: Practices

Activity

Look at the photos of worship on page 257 and here. Can you identify which is Orthodox and which is Liberal/Reform?

A synagogue in Paris, France.

Why Jewish people worship in different ways

- Liberal/Reform Jews allow the use of musical instruments in worship (banned on *Shabbat* by the Orthodox because it involves work) because of their belief that *Shabbat* rules can be interpreted to fit in with modern life.
- Orthodox women place much more importance on private worship as they do not attend daily prayers in the synagogue.
- Orthodox synagogues keep men and women separated because of the teachings of rabbis, whereas Liberal/Reform synagogues allow mixed seating.
- Liberal/Reform Jews often do not wear *tefillin* and *tallit* for worship, many of them do not keep *kosher*, and they have complete equality of the sexes, including having women rabbis. They do not believe that the Torah is the Word of God, but rather that it was written by people inspired by God. They feel it is the moral commands of the law which must be followed and believe the ritual laws can be ignored.
- There are slight variations in the words of the services. For example, Jews of Ashkenazi ancestry, Jews of Sephardic ancestry and Hasidic Jews have slightly different prayers because of their origins.

Summary

Jewish public worship takes place in the synagogue every day, but most Jews worship there on the evening and morning of *Shabbat* each week and on all the festivals. Public worship strengthens the Jewish community and gives individual Jews a sense of belonging and an opportunity to learn more about the faith. Orthodox Jews worship differently from Liberal/Reform Jews.

Practice questions

c Explain two reasons why Jewish people worship in different ways. In your answer you must refer to a source of wisdom and authority.

d 'You can worship God just as well at home as in the synagogue.' Evaluate this statement considering arguments for and against. In your answer you should:
- refer to Jewish points of view
- refer to different Jewish or non-religious points of view
- reach a justified conclusion.

Topic 2.2b.2 The Tenakh and Talmud

The purpose and history of the Tenakh

The Tenakh is the Jewish Bible. Its name comes from the initial letters (in Hebrew) of:

- **Torah** (the five books of Moses)
- **Nevi'im** (the books of the prophets)
- **Ketuvim** (holy writings).

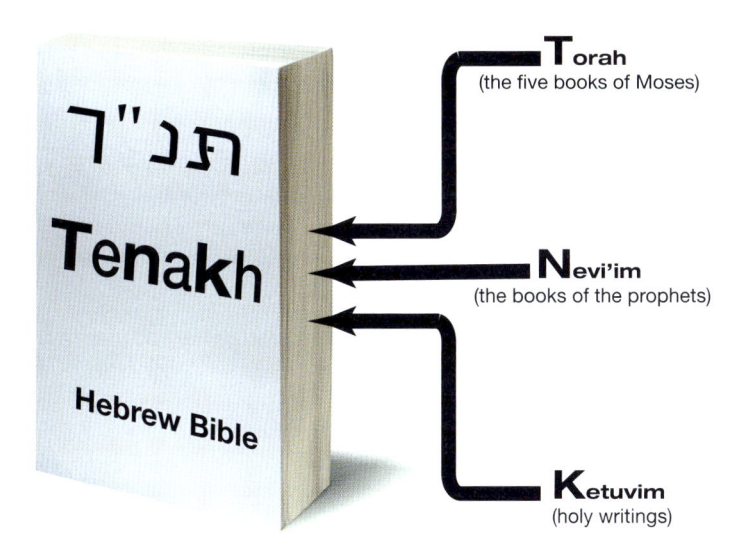

What the Tenakh consists of.

Torah

The Five Books of Moses contain the laws and moral ideas of Judaism set in the context of the history of the Jewish people (Israelites) from the creation of the world through the Exodus to the death of Moses. They contain the stories of the **patriarchs**, the Egyptian slavery, the Exodus, the long journey to the Promised Land, God's covenants with Abraham and Moses, and, of course, the giving of the Law to Moses.

They are regarded as the holiest part of the Tenakh because they contain the 613 *mitzvot* which are the basis of Jewish life. Their purpose is to tell the Jews who they are and how they must live to fulfil their part of the covenant and truly be God's chosen people.

Nevi'im

The first prophet books (Joshua, Judges, 1 & 2 Samuel, 1 & 2 Kings) are history books telling the story of Israel from the death of Moses, through the establishment of the monarchy by Saul and David, to the end of the kingdom and the exile of the Jewish people to Babylon. However, their main purpose is to teach the Jewish people how the covenant God made with Moses worked its way out through the Jewish people.

The other fifteen books are prophet books, starting with the huge works of Isaiah, Jeremiah and Ezekiel. Their purpose is to teach faith in the one God and to proclaim God's message of justice and compassion.

Thinking points

In this topic you need to:
- think about the purpose and history of the Tenakh and Talmud and the nature and purpose of Jewish food laws, including reference to Deuteronomy chapter 14
- be able to explain and evaluate the importance of the Tenakh and Talmud for daily life and the divergent implications of *kashrut* for Jewish people today.

Useful words

Torah – the five books of Moses
Nevi'im – the books of the prophets
Ketuvim – holy writings
Patriarchs – the fathers of Israel (Abraham, Isaac, Jacob and Moses)

Rabban Gamaliel the son of Rabbi Judah the Prince said: Great is study of the Torah when combined with a worldly occupation, for toil in them both puts sin out of mind. All study of the Torah which is not supplemented by work is destined to prove futile and causes sin. (Pirkei Avot 2:2)

Activity

Why do you think most Jews regard the Torah as the most important part of the Tenakh?

Section 2b: Practices

Ketuvim

The writings are about many things. There are history books (1 & 2 Chronicles, Ezra, Nehemiah, Esther), poetry books (Psalms, Lamentations, Song of Songs), philosophical books (Job, Proverbs, Ecclesiastes) and Daniel, which is a mix of history and prophecy. Their purpose is to show how the way the Jews behaved towards God affected their history, to express the ups and downs of living as God's people, to express thoughts on the ultimate questions of suffering and death, and to give advice on how to live a moral life.

The purpose and history of the Talmud

According to Jewish tradition, when God gave Moses the Torah, he also gave him the Oral Torah to explain how the laws were to be obeyed. The Written Torah and the Oral Torah together make up the **halakhah**. As time went on, people wanted explanations of these and also wanted to know how they applied to new situations. Decisions were given by priests, judges and later rabbis and added to the *halakhah*.

After the Temple was destroyed by the Romans and many Jews started to leave the Holy Land, Rabbi Judah the Prince saw that different versions of the *halakhah* were likely to develop in different countries and so he organised the writing down of the Oral Torah. This is known as the **Mishneh** and was completed in about 200CE.

From this time, the Mishneh was studied by rabbis and their students in academies in Israel and Babylon and their discussions on controversial points in the Mishneh were written down and filed into archives. In about 500CE, two Babylonian rabbis sorted out these archives and wrote down each paragraph of the Mishneh with the discussions that had gone on around it.

Why the Tenakh and Talmud are important to Jews today

The Tenakh is important because:

- The Psalms are an essential part of daily prayers and of much synagogue worship.
- The Torah is particularly important in synagogue worship and daily living.
- Portions of the Nevi'im are read at the end of the Torah readings in synagogue. These readings are known as the **haftarot**.
- Portions of the Ketuvim form an important part of the festivals of Yom Kippur (Book of Jonah) and Purim (Book of Esther).
- Jewish people study and meditate on the books of the Tenakh to help their understanding of, and their relationship with, God.

The Talmud is important because:

- It explains the meaning of the 613 *mitzvot*.
- It explains how the *mitzvot* should be applied in the daily lives of Jews.
- It is so important that commentaries relating the Talmud to life in the twenty-first century are still being written (for example, *Understanding the Talmud* by Rabbi Yitzchok Feigenbaum, 2012).

Useful words

Halakhah – Jewish law
Mishneh – commentaries on the Torah written about 200CE
Haftarot – portions of the Nevi'im read after the Torah in services

> *Anyone whose good deeds are more than his wisdom, his wisdom will endure. Anyone whose wisdom is more than his good deeds, his wisdom will not endure.*
> (Saying from a first-century CE rabbi)

> *Rabban Yochanan ben Zakkai received the Torah from Hillel and from Shammai. He used to say: If you have learnt much Torah do not claim for yourself moral excellence, for to this end you were created.*
> (Pirkei Avot 2:9)

Activities

1. Look at the saying by the first-century rabbi above. What do you think it means?
2. Explain why the Talmud is important for Jewish people.
3. Read the two quotations from Pirkei Avot (above and page 259). What do you think they mean for the study of the Torah?

- It is the basis of the *halakhah*, which is the foundation of Orthodox Jewish life today.
- It is the main subject studied in the *yeshivot* (Jewish academies for post-A-level Jewish studies).

The nature and purpose of Jewish food laws

The purpose of Jewish food laws is to obey these *mitzvot* about food which God gave to Moses:

> *These are the animals you may eat: the ox, the sheep, the goat, the deer, the gazelle, the roe deer, the wild goat, the ibex, the antelope and the mountain sheep. You may eat any animal that has a divided hoof and that chews the cud. (Deuteronomy 14:4–6)*

However, there are animals that are forbidden:

> *You may not eat the camel, the rabbit or the hyrax. Although they chew the cud, they do not have a divided hoof ... The pig is also unclean; although it has a divided hoof, it does not chew the cud. You are not to eat their meat. (Deuteronomy 14:7–8)*

Fish are allowed, but not shellfish, calamari and eels because:

> *Of all the creatures living in the water, you may eat any that has fins and scales. But anything that does not have fins and scales you may not eat; for you it is unclean. (Deuteronomy 14:9–10)*

Clean birds are allowed but Deuteronomy chapter 14 has a long list of birds which are not allowed (mainly birds of prey and birds that eat dead animals; perhaps because Deuteronomy 14:21 says, 'Do not eat anything you find already dead'). This is followed by 'Do not cook a young goat in its mother's milk' (Deuteronomy 14:21).

Leviticus 17:13 adds this restriction: 'Any Israelite or any alien living among you who hunts any animal or bird that may be eaten must drain out the blood.'

As a result of the *mitzvot*, Judaism developed quite complicated food laws known as **kosher** (fitting or correct), which leads to the term **kashrut** (the state of being *kosher*) for keeping the laws. The main points are:

- Cows, sheep, goats, deer, chicken, turkey, duck and all fish (with fins and scales) can be eaten.
- Pigs, camels and shellfish must not be eaten (any such foods and anything that is not *kosher* is called **treifah**).
- Animals must be slaughtered by the **shechitah** method of slitting the throat with a razor-sharp knife and draining out the blood (this is done by a specially trained slaughterer called a **shochet**, who must also be learned in the Torah).
- When meat is brought home it must be soaked in salt water for 30 minutes, then rubbed in salt and drained before washing in cold water (nowadays this is often done by the butcher before the meat is sold).
- Kitchens should be in two halves, one for meat and one for dairy, with separate crockery, pans and utensils for each – many will have two sinks.

A McDonald's restaurant in Israel.

Activity

Look at the photo of a McDonald's above. Would a non-Jew be able to eat here? Would an Orthodox Jew be able to eat in an ordinary McDonald's?

Useful words

Kosher – fitting; food a Jew is permitted to eat
Kashrut – the state of being *kosher*
Treifah – not *kosher*
Shechitah – Jewish method of slaughtering animals
Shochet – a Jewish butcher

Section 2b: Practices

> **Activity**
> Look at the photo opposite. How do you know this is an Orthodox Jewish kitchen?

A double sink in a Jewish home: the red side is for meat and the green side is for dairy.

Divergent implications of the food laws

Keeping *kashrut* is very important for Orthodox Jews because:

- By eating non-*kosher* foods or not keeping a *kosher* kitchen they have broken many of the *mitzvot*. This importance can be seen on supermarket shelves where many items now have a label (called a **hechsher**) showing that the food is *kosher*.
- It gives a sense of Jewish identity.
- It gives a bond with fellow Jews.
- It makes them think about God every time they decide to eat because they have to think about what God wants them to eat and how God wants them to prepare it.

Keeping *kashrut* is not as important for Liberal/Reform Jews because they believe that the laws of Moses are not God's direct commands, but rather they are a means for people to lead a holy life. Some will always eat *kosher* meat, but will not bother with the laws about meat and dairy and will not bother about eating non-*kosher* in the homes of non-Jews or in restaurants. Indeed, some Liberal Jews reject the whole concept of *kashrut* because they believe it is harmful for good relations between religions.

> **Useful words**
> *Hechsher* – a label certifying that a food is *kosher*

> **Summary**
> The Tenakh is the Jewish Bible: Torah, Nevi'm and Ketuvim. The Torah is the most important part as it contains the 613 commands (*mitzvot*) of the Law that Moses received from God. The Talmud contains the Oral Law explaining the Torah. The Torah contains the food laws which determine what can be eaten (*kosher*) and what cannot be eaten (*treifah*). The Orthodox Jews are much stricter about the food laws than the Liberal/Reform Jews.

> **Practice questions**
> **c** Explain two reasons why the Talmud is important for Jewish people. In your answer you must refer to a source of wisdom and authority.
>
> **d** 'It's more important to get on well with people of other religions than to follow religious food laws that divide people.' Evaluate this statement considering arguments for and against. In your answer you should:
> - refer to Jewish points of view
> - refer to different Jewish or non-religious points of view
> - reach a justified conclusion.

Topic 2.2b.3 Prayer

Purpose of Jewish prayer

Prayer is an attempt by humans to communicate with God.

Jewish people believe that prayer is very important because they believe that when they pray, they not only build up their relationship with God, but also believe they are serving God with their heart, so obeying God's commandment:

> to love the Lord your God and to serve him with all your heart and with all your soul. (Deuteronomy 11:13)

The Talmud tells Jewish people, 'What is service of the heart? That is prayer.'

Judaism teaches that through prayer, people have the opportunity to speak directly to God and that God will listen and respond to their prayers.

In a sense, there are only two types of prayer: formal prayers, where a set form of prayer is used; and informal prayers, where a person makes up their own spontaneous prayer to express their feelings to God.

The formal prayers of Judaism are contained in the **Siddur** (prayer book; there are different ones for Orthodox and Reform Jews) and are said in Hebrew by Orthodox Jews.

Prayer in the home

Much of Jewish worship and prayer is centred on the home. Some prayers at home are said as private prayers:

- When a Jew wakes up in the morning, they thank God for waking them before pouring water on their hands to purify themselves for the coming day.
- The day should end, as it should begin, by praising God – the *shema* is said followed by these words,

> may it be Your will that You should lay me down in peace and raise me up to good life and peace. Blessed are You God who lights up the whole world with His glory.

- The **mezuzah** on each door of the house is a constant reminder of God's presence and God's blessing:

> You will be blessed when you come in and blessed when you go out. (Deuteronomy 28:6)

– so Jewish people touch the *mezuzah* and thank God whenever they pass it.

- Eating food requires prayers as Jewish people bless God before food:

> Blessed are you Lord our God, King of the universe who brings food out of the ground

and bless him again when they have finished eating.

Thinking points

In this topic you need to:
- think about the nature and purpose of prayer in the home, private prayer, prayer three times a day and the importance of having different forms of prayer, including prayer in Psalm 55:16–23
- be able to explain and evaluate the importance of having different types of prayer.

Useful words

Siddur – the daily prayer book
Mezuzah – small scroll of the *shema* fixed to the doorpost of the rooms in a Jewish house

Activities

1. Why do you think people pray?
2. Do you think it is a good idea to wear special things when you pray?

Section 2b: Practices

> *For me, I call to God, and the Lord saves me. Evening, morning and noon I cry out in distress, and he hears my voice. He rescues me unharmed from the battle waged against me, even though many oppose me ... Cast your cares on the Lord and he will sustain you; he will never let the righteous fall. (Psalm 55:16–22)*

Useful words

Shacharit – morning prayer
Minchah – afternoon prayer
Arvit – evening prayer
Tefillin – leather boxes containing parts of the Torah strapped on the arms and head for prayers
Tallit – prayer shawl
Amidah – the standing prayer
Minyan – the number of men needed for synagogue services (usually ten)

The three daily prayers

During the day a Jew should pray a set formal prayer three times:

- **shacharit** is morning prayer
- **minchah** is afternoon prayer and
- **arvit** is evening prayer.

These prayers take place in an Orthodox synagogue but many Jews say the prayers at home. Orthodox men wear their **tefillin** and **tallit** for the *shacharit* prayers and will pray as a family group.

The format of the prayers is set out in the Siddur (daily prayer book) and each prayer includes the *shema*, and the **amidah**, and readings from the Torah and the Nevi'im.

In Orthodox families, the prayers are said in Hebrew, but in Liberal/Reform families the prayers will be said in English. In Liberal/Reform synagogues women can make up a **minyan**.

Private prayers

Judaism teaches that people should develop a relationship with God and that when they reach out to God, God listens and answers. In such a relationship prayers are not restricted to set forms and set times.

Jewish people pray whenever they feel the need to communicate with God, and obviously when they say these prayers, they use their own words. In private prayer, people can contact God when they want and can express their own thoughts and feelings rather than using other people's words. In such prayers they can ask for God's help for other people, and they can ask for God's help for themselves.

The importance of having different forms of prayer

Saying prayers in a set form, which have been used in this form for centuries, and at set times has many advantages:

- It stops prayer being focused on selfish concerns.
- It gives the worshipper a sense of being part of Jewish history.
- It gives the prayer a sense of community with Jews all over the world.
- It gives order and purpose to people's religious life.
- It helps people to pray who might find it difficult to know what to say.
- It gives people a feeling of stability and security by repeating familiar phrases in a familiar place.

Activity

Look at Psalm 55:16–22. How do you think these verses affect Jewish attitudes to prayer?

Saying prayers in your own words whenever you want to is important because people can only have a relationship with God if:

- they can contact God when they want
- they can express their own thoughts and feelings rather than other people's
- they can use their own words, so that they are saying what they want to say rather than using other people's words
- they can ask for God's help for other people
- they can ask for God's help for themselves.

Prayer in the home is important because the home is the heart of people's lives and praying as a family brings the family together.

Private prayer is important because people need to be able to pray to God in private so they can communicate with God one to one and express emotions they cannot express in front of others.

Public prayer is also important because praying with others in the synagogue gives a sense of belonging to a whole community of believers and an opportunity to feel the strength of the faith and make friends with others in the faith.

Practice questions

c) Explain two reasons why it is important for Jewish people to have different forms of prayer.

d) 'God doesn't need people to pray to him.' Evaluate this statement considering arguments for and against. In your answer you should:
- refer to Jewish points of view
- refer to different Jewish or non-religious points of view
- reach a justified conclusion.

Summary

Prayer is communicating with God, and Jews believe this is very important because it is obeying the *mitzvot* to love and serve God. There are set prayers for morning, afternoon and evening, and Jews also pray when they wake up, when they eat and when they go to bed. They believe it is important to have different forms of prayer so that prayer does not become a set ritual, but a search for God.

Section 2b: Practices

Topic 2.2b.4 *Shema* and *amidah*

Thinking points
In this topic you need to:
- think about the nature and importance of the *shema* and the *amidah*, when and how they are used and why, including Deuteronomy 6:4 and the *mezuzah*
- think about the similarities and differences between Christian and Jewish worship
- be able to explain the importance of the *shema* and *amidah* for Jews today.

Useful words
Shema – the declaration of Jewish belief in one God

Shema

Shema is known as the fundamental declaration of Judaism. Its main elements are:

> Hear, O Israel, the L–rd is our G–d, the L–rd is One.
>
> Blessed be the name of the glory of His kingdom forever and ever.
>
> You shall love the L–rd your G–d with all your heart, with all your soul, and with all your might. And these words which I command you today shall be upon your heart. You shall teach them thoroughly to your children, and you shall speak of them when you sit in your house and when you walk on the road, when you lie down and when you rise. You shall bind them as a sign upon your hand, and they shall be for a reminder between your eyes. And you shall write them upon the doorposts of your house and upon your gates.
>
> The L–rd spoke to Moses, saying: Speak to the children of Israel and tell them to make for themselves fringes on the corners of their garments throughout their generations, and to attach a thread of blue on the fringe of each corner. They shall be to you as tzizit, and you shall look upon them and remember all the commandments of the L–rd and fulfil them, and you will not follow after your heart and after your eyes by which you go astray – so that you may remember and fulfil all My commandments and be holy to your G–d. I am the L–rd your G–d who brought you out of the land of Egypt to be your G–d; I, the L–rd, am your G–d. Amen.

When the *shema* is said

The *shema* is said three times every day:
- once in the morning prayer
- once in the evening prayer and
- once before a Jewish person goes to sleep.

The first two paragraphs are written on the *mezuzah* scroll and so they are remembered, and sometimes spoken, every time a Jew goes into the house and from room to room. The first sentence is said whenever the Torah scroll is taken from the Ark.

Why the *shema* is said

The *shema* is important because it is also a declaration of the main points of the Jewish faith:
- There is only one God.
- People should love God and follow his commands.
- Those who serve God will receive blessings.
- The aim of Judaism is to become holy by fulfilling God's commands.

Activities
1. Look at the *shema*. How can you tell it comes from a Jewish prayer book?
2. Write a summary of the *shema*.

Topic 2.3b.4 *Shema* and *amidah*

This belief that there is only one God who demands moral obedience is often called '**ethical monotheism**' and is the basis of Judaism.

> *Hear, O Israel: The Lord our God, the Lord is one. Love the Lord your God with all your heart and with all your soul and with all your strength. These commandments that I give you today are to be on your hearts. Impress them on your children. Talk about them when you sit at home and when you walk along the road, when you lie down and when you get up. Tie them as symbols on your hands and bind them on your foreheads. Write them on the doorframes of your houses and on your gates. (Deuteronomy 6:4–9)*

Useful words

Ethical monotheism – belief in one God who demands moral obedience
Amidah – the standing prayer

Mezuzah

A *mezuzah* has a parchment scroll on which is written Deuteronomy 6:4–9 and Deuteronomy 11:13–21 (God's promises for the Jews if they keep the *mitzvot*). The *mezuzah* is the scroll but it is usually kept in a container and these are fixed to the doorposts of the house and every room in the house except the bathroom. Jews are expected to touch the *mezuzah* every time they pass it to remind themselves of the Mosaic Covenant. The *mezuzah* reminds Jews that they are dedicated to God. Every time they touch it they remind themselves of the covenant God made with Moses and how they need to keep the *mitzvot*. It also reminds them of God's promise: 'You will be blessed when you come in and blessed when you go out' (Deuteronomy 28:6).

Amidah

Amidah is the second most important prayer and is sometimes known as 'the prayer'. It contains nineteen blessings, each of which ends with the words:

> *Blessed are you, O Lord.*

The first three blessings praise God:
- for being the God of Abraham, Isaac and Jacob
- for his power and might
- for his holiness.

The next six are personal requests for God:
- to grant wisdom and understanding
- to help Jews to return to a life based on the Torah
- for forgiveness for all sins
- to heal the sick
- to bless the produce of the earth
- to allow the ingathering of the Jewish exiles back to the land of Israel.

The next six are requests for the people of Israel. They ask God:
- to restore righteous judges as in the days of old
- to punish those who slander Jews
- to have mercy on all who trust in him
- to support the righteous
- to rebuild Jerusalem and to restore the Kingdom of David
- to bring the descendant of King David, who will be the Messiah.

Someone touching a *mezuzah* on a doorframe.

Section 2b: Practices

The final three blessings:

- ask God to accept the prayers
- ask God to have mercy and be compassionate
- thank God for the opportunity to serve the Lord.

The last prayer is the one for peace, goodness, blessings, kindness and compassion.

When and how the *amidah* should be said

Amidah means standing and the prayer should be said standing facing Jerusalem. The whole prayer is said for weekday daily prayers, with slight amendments on *Shabbat* and festivals.

Every *amidah* is divided into three central sections: praise, petitions and thanks. Immediately before reciting the *amidah*, it is traditional to take three steps backward and then forward again to symbolise entering into God's presence.

If the *amidah* is prayed in the synagogue, it is repeated aloud by the cantor, with the congregation reciting 'Amen' to each blessing, which will end (as it began) with a formal bow. In the middle section, after making a request to God, the congregation say, 'Holy, holy, holy is the Lord of Hosts, the whole world is filled with His glory' and rock up on the balls of their feet three times, for each word 'holy', symbolising the fluttering of the angels who recited this line of praise. Several more biblical verses are also recited, ending in the blessing, 'Praised are You, Adonai, the holy God.'

The final section of every *amidah* concludes with blessings of thanksgiving to God requesting him to grant peace, goodness, blessings and compassion upon everyone.

Why the *amidah* is said

The *amidah* is 'the prayer' because it fulfils all the requirements of a prayer which had been determined by the great rabbis. They declared that a worshipper should come before the Almighty first with words of praise, then should ask one's petitions, and finally should withdraw with words of thanks, which is exactly what the *amidah* does. As well as this, people have two needs, the spiritual and the physical, and the *amidah* asks God to fulfil spiritual needs such as forgiveness and physical needs such as food.

Why the *amidah* is important

The *amidah* is important for Jews because:

- It fulfils the prayer requirements set out by the great rabbis: praise, requests, thanks.
- It asks God to fulfil their spiritual needs.
- It asks God to fulfil their physical needs.
- It is the major prayer in the Siddur and so must be the major prayer for Jews.
- It helps Jews to fulfil their service to God.

Some Jewish pilgrims pray at the historic Ghriba synagogue in Djerba.

Activity

Look at the photo. What prayer do you think is being said?

Topic 2.3b.4 *Shema* and *amidah*

Christian and Jewish worship

The main differences are between Orthodox Jewish worship and Christian worship. Worship in Liberal/Reform synagogues is very similar to Christian worship.

Differences:

- Jews should face Jerusalem for worship, whereas Christians can worship facing any direction (although most Catholic, Orthodox and Anglican churches face the east).
- Orthodox Jews worship in Hebrew, whereas Christians worship in their native language.
- Men and women worship separately in Orthodox Judaism, whereas the sexes worship together in Christianity.
- The Jewish special day for worship is Saturday, whereas the Christian special day is Sunday.
- Jews should worship three times a day at set times, whereas Christians are only required to go to church on Sunday, but are expected to pray every morning and evening.
- Christian worship usually has musical accompaniment and often has hymns, Orthodox Jewish worship does not.
- Christian worship often has visual stimuli (crosses, stained-glass windows, statues of Mary and the saints), Jewish worship does not

Similarities:

- Worship involves readings from the scriptures in both faiths.
- Weekly worship includes a sermon in both faiths.
- Worship involves the whole congregation saying a prayer together (even non-liturgical Christian worship includes saying the Lord's Prayer).
- Both worships involve praying for the needs of others.

Activity

Do you think all the rituals associated with the *amidah* are a good idea for prayers to God?

Practice questions

c Explain two reasons why the *shema* is important for Jewish people. In your answer you must refer to a source of wisdom and authority.

d 'Prayer should just be a private matter between the individual and God.' Evaluate this statement considering arguments for and against. In your answer you should:
- refer to Jewish points of view
- refer to different Jewish or non-religious points of view
- reach a justified conclusion.

Summary

The *shema* is the most important prayer for Jews as it reminds them of the oneness of God and the need for Jewish people to obey God's commands to receive his blessings. Jews remind themselves of the *shema* by touching the *mezuzah* every time they enter or leave a room. The *amidah* (standing prayer) is the second most important prayer and is said for the three daily prayers.

Section 2b: Practices

Topic 2.2b.5 Rituals and ceremonies

Thinking points

In this topic you need to:
- think about the importance of ritual; the nature, features and purpose of birth, marriage, Bar Mitzvah and Bat Mitzvah ceremonies, including Genesis 17, Genesis 21:1–8 and Leviticus 12
- consider the nature and importance of mourning ceremonies
- be able to evaluate and explain the importance of these rituals for Jews today and be aware of the different Jewish understandings of these.

Useful words

Brit Milah – the covenant of circumcision
Kvatters – people who carry the baby to Brit Milah
Sandek – person who holds the baby for Brit Milah
Mohel – person trained to perform Brit Milah

Jewish ritual

Rituals celebrating and marking important stages of life (birth, coming of age, marriage and death) are known as rites of passage. All societies seem to have such rites and in any society with its own religion, these rituals are religious. The rituals are important because they help both the person going through the ritual and the wider community hosting the ritual to come to terms with a changed status.

Birth ceremonies

Children are a great blessing in Judaism, indeed the very first *mitzvah* says Jews should have children:

> Be fruitful and increase in number. (Genesis 1:28)

Ceremonies for boys

Male children are circumcised eight days after their birth in a ceremony known as **Brit Milah**. This ceremony can take place in hospital, in the home or in the synagogue. If celebrated at home, there will often be ten adult males present to make a *minyan*.

The mother brings the baby in and hands him to the **kvatters** (bearers) – usually a married couple – who carry the child on a cushion to the *sandek*, who holds the child for the procedure. The *sandek* is often the grandfather or a respected member of the congregation and it is a great honour to be chosen as a *sandek*. The **mohel** (circumciser) then carries out the procedure and dresses the wound. The father recites a blessing which remembers that God commanded circumcision so that children can enter the covenant. The *mohel* then blesses the child and names him before handing him back to the *kvatters*. Then there is a celebratory meal to welcome the child into the covenant.

Circumcision is a 'sign in the flesh' of the covenant God made with Abraham:

> *This is my covenant with you and your descendants after you, the covenant you are to keep. Every male among you shall be circumcised. You are to undergo circumcision, and it will be the sign of the covenant between me and you. For the generations to come every male among you who is eight days old must be circumcised.* (Genesis 17:10–12)
>
> *When his son Isaac was eight days old, Abraham circumcised him, as God commanded him.* (Genesis 21:4)

These verses mean circumcision is a *mitzvah* which marks the entry of Jewish males into the covenant. They also make a link with Jewish history reaching all the way back to Abraham. Circumcision has been important in Jewish history as both the Greeks and the Romans tried to ban it as a way of ending the Jewish nation, but the Jews were martyred rather than giving up the practice. The Tenakh gives no reason for circumcision other than to fulfil God's command.

Activity

Why do you think the Brit Milah is important for most Jews?

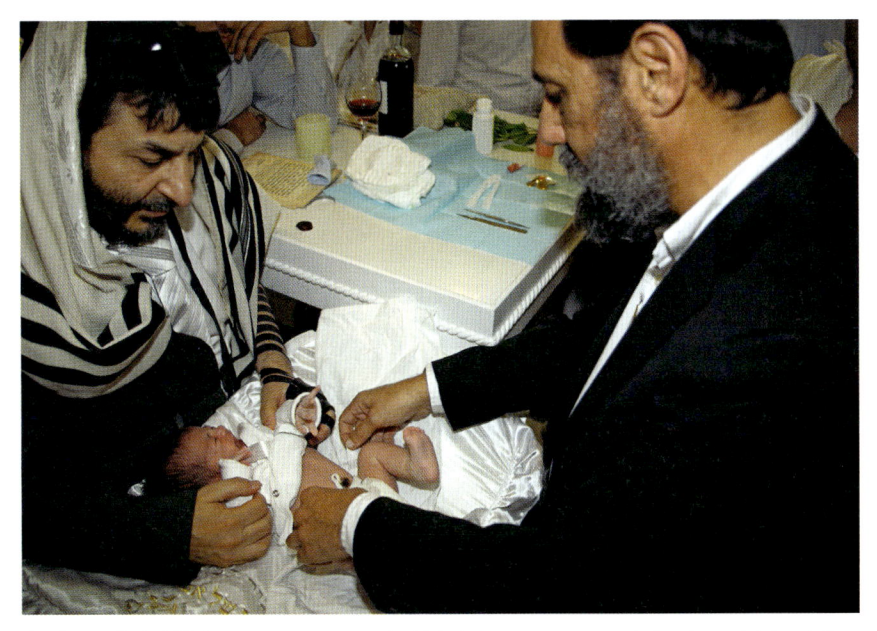

During a Brit Milah ceremony, a *mohel* (right) prepares an eight-day-old Jewish boy for circumcision. The infant is held in the lap of a *sandek*.

Although any adult male wanting to convert to Judaism must be circumcised, the **halakhah** makes clear that any male child born Jewish but not circumcised is still a Jew. Some very liberal Reform Jews do not circumcise their sons as they believe the covenant with Abraham was purely spiritual and so there is no need for a physical sign.

Ceremonies for girls

Female children of Orthodox Jews have a special naming ceremony in the synagogue on the *Shabbat* following the birth. The rabbi blesses and names the child and there is a celebratory meal. Many Reform/Liberal synagogues have a special welcoming ceremony for girls. The ceremony is usually led by a rabbi who gives a blessing of welcome:

> *Blessed be the child whom we now welcome. We praise you, Eternal God, Sovereign of the universe: You hallow us with Your Mitzvot, and command us to bring our daughters into the Covenant of Life.*

The rabbi then names the child and after Kiddush over the wine, a few drops may be given to the child, after which the cup might be shared by the parents and family before the festive meal. This ceremony is known as Brit Bat.

Marriage ceremonies

All Jews are expected to marry and have children because of the *mitzvah* that humans should be fruitful and increase the number of humans on earth.

Jewish marriage is based on these verses from the Torah:

> *The man said, 'This is now bone from my bones, flesh of my flesh; she shall be called woman for she was taken out of man.' For this reason a man will leave his father and mother and be united to his wife and they will become one flesh.* (Genesis 2:23–24)

Useful words

Halakhah – the holy law of Judaism

Activities

1. Do you think the Brit Bat will ever be as important as the Brit Milah?
2. Look at the photo of the Brit Milah above. Who is carrying out the circumcision?

Section 2b: Practices

> *Your wife has been given to you in order that you may realise with her life's great plan. A man who has no wife is doomed to an existence without joy, without blessing, without experiencing life's true goodness, without Torah, without protection and without peace. (Talmud)*

Marriage is regarded as essential for people to become complete. The Talmud says that,

> *A man without a wife is incomplete. An unmarried woman is an unfinished vessel.*

The purposes of Jewish marriage are:

- to obey the *mitzvah* and have children
- for a man and woman to share a life of love and companionship
- for a man and woman to share sex with each other in the way God intended
- to establish a Jewish home so that children can be brought up as Jews and continue the Jewish faith.

The marriage ceremony usually has the following features, although there can be many variations between Orthodox and Reform, and Sephardi and Ashkenazi:

- The couple fast before the wedding as repentance for their past sins, as the wedding (*kiddushin* in Hebrew) will **sanctify** them and forgive their sins.
- The ceremony takes place under a canopy called a **huppah**, which symbolises the couple's new home and unites them under one roof. The fact that it is closed on top and open at the sides symbolises how marriage needs both privacy and openness to friends and community.
- The bride and groom meet under the *huppah*.
- The rabbi blesses a glass of wine and thanks God for sanctifying Israel by his commands about marriage, and the bride and groom drink from the same glass.
- The groom puts a ring on the bride's finger with the words,

> *Behold you are consecrated to me with this ring according to the Law of Moses and Israel.*

This is what legalises the marriage according to the *halakhah* (Liberal Jews often have an exchange of vows and rings using the words 'with this ring I thee wed ...').

- The **ketubah** is read in which the groom promises to provide for his wife and specifies what she will receive in the event of his death or a divorce (marriage is a contract in Judaism so divorce is allowed).
- The rabbi recites seven blessings over a glass of wine; they include blessing God for wine, creation, making humans, making marriage, making children, and making the bride and groom rejoice.
- The bride and groom drink from the glass to show they will share everything together now they are man and wife.
- The bridegroom then stamps on the glass to remind everyone of the destruction of the Temple and that in the midst of joy some people are suffering and sorrowing.

A Jewish wedding ceremony can only take place between two Jews and so, if a non-Jew wishes to marry a Jew in a religious ceremony, they need to convert. However, some Liberal/Reform synagogues have special ceremonies for mixed (interfaith) marriages.

Useful words

Sanctify – to make holy
Huppah – wedding canopy
Ketubah – marriage contract

Activities

1. Read the Talmud passage about marriage above. What does it tell us about the Jewish attitude to marriage?
2. Outline the main features of a Jewish wedding ceremony.
3. Explain why marriage is important for Jewish people.

Bar Mitzvah

Bar Mitzvah (son of the commandment) is the term used for when a boy becomes responsible for his own actions and is regarded as an adult as far as religion is concerned. This means that after a boy's Bar Mitzvah he must put on *tefillin* for morning prayers, he can make up a *minyan*, he has to observe the fast days in full and he may be called up to read the *sidra* in synagogue services.

Bar Mitzvah is not about being a full adult in every sense of the word, ready to marry, go out on your own, earn a living and raise children. In Pirkei Avot in the Talmud, it says that while thirteen is the proper age for fulfilment of the Commandments, eighteen is the proper age for marriage and twenty is the proper age for earning a living.

A boy becomes Bar Mitzvah at the age of thirteen whether there is a special ceremony or not, but most Jewish families make sure their sons have a special ceremony. Before the ceremony a boy attends special Hebrew classes at the synagogue so that he can read the scriptures. The ceremony takes place on the first *Shabbat* after the boy's thirteenth birthday.

The main features of the ceremony are:

- The boy recites the blessing before the Torah reading.
- If possible, he reads the whole Torah passage for that day.
- The boy's father says, 'Blessed be he who hath freed me from the responsibility for this child'.
- The rabbi talks about the responsibilities of adult Jews and the joys of fulfilling the *mitzvot*.
- There is a celebratory meal.

There are no references to Bar Mitzvah in the Tenakh. The term first appears in the Talmud, which also refers to observing this rite of passage with a religious ceremony. The most complete references to Bar Mitzvah are in **Midrash** from the Middle Ages, for example:

> *The heathen when he begets a son consecrates him to idolatrous practices; the Israelite has his son circumcised ... and as soon as he becomes of age he brings him into the synagogue and school in order that he may praise the name of God, reciting the 'Brachu' (blessing) preceding the reading from the Law.* **(Midrash Hashkem)**

However, the nature and importance of Bar Mitzvah in modern Judaism mainly developed in the early twentieth century.

Bat Mitzvah

Bat Mitzvah (Daughter of the Commandment) ceremonies are very different in Orthodox Judaism from those in Liberal/Reform Judaism.

In Orthodox Judaism, girls attain their Bat Mitzvah at the age of twelve. However, they do not assume the same duties as boys (they cannot make up a *minyan*, wear *tefillin* or read the Torah in synagogue) so the ceremony is very different. Often a group of girls who have reached twelve years of age during the previous year are jointly addressed by the rabbi and each then reads a passage they have chosen from the Tenakh. This ceremony is sometimes called **Bat Chayil** (daughter of worth).

Useful words

Bar Mitzvah – son of the commandment; a Jewish boy's coming of age

Tefillin – a container for the *shema* scroll to put on the arms and head

Midrash – collection of rabbinic commentaries on the Tenakh

Bat Chayil – Daughter of worth; name used by some Orthodox synagogues instead of Bat Mitzvah

Activity

Do you think there should be a difference between girls' and boys' Bar Mitzvahs?

Section 2b: Practices

> **Activity**
>
> Look at the photo. How do you know this is not an Orthodox synagogue?

A girl at her Bat Mitzvah ceremony reading from the Torah.

In Liberal/Reform Judaism, girls are treated exactly the same as boys and have exactly the same responsibilities, and so their Bat Mitzvah is just the same as a boy's. It happens at the age of thirteen and they are called up to read the Torah.

Death and mourning rituals

Death is obviously a major issue for everyone as it marks the end of someone's life and causes grief for family and friends. Judaism deals with death in four stages:

At the point of death

If it is known someone is dying, family should gather to help the person die as a Jew. The prayer book contains a special prayer. It begins,

> 'I acknowledge unto thee, O Lord my God and God of my fathers, that both my cure and my death are in thy hands', and ends, 'Hear O Israel: the Lord is our God, the Lord is one.'

Ideally, every Jew dies with the last sentence of the prayer on their lips.

From death to the funeral

As soon as they hear of a death, close relatives make a tear in their clothes to fulfil the *mitzvah* which is the basis of much of the mourning ritual. The Torah records that when Jacob heard that his favourite son, Joseph, was dead,

> Then Jacob tore his clothes, put on sackcloth and mourned for his son many days. (Genesis 37:34)

Synagogues usually have a burial society (**chevra kaddisha**) which helps the family at their time of grief. They are in charge of the ritual washing of the body, after which it is wrapped in a plain linen shroud covered with the dead person's **tallit** and then placed into a plain coffin. The funeral takes place as soon after death as possible; the Orthodox do not allow cremation. This is based on the verse about criminals who have been hanged,

Useful words

Chevra kaddisha – burial society
Tallit – a fringed garment worn by Jews

Topic 2.2b.5 Rituals and ceremonies

A burial ceremony in Israel.

> you must not leave his body on the tree overnight. Be sure to bury him the same day ... you must not desecrate the land the Lord your God is giving you (Deuteronomy 21:23)

and God's warning to Adam,

> until you return to the ground, since from it you were taken, for dust you are and to dust you will return. (Genesis 3:19)

It is considered disrespectful to leave the dead person alone and someone stays with the body all the time until the funeral. During the time before the burial, mourners are exempt from the positive *mitzvot* as they will be too grief-stricken to think what they have to do.

The funeral itself is a very simple affair: some Psalms are read before a short prayer praising God for giving life and for taking it away. The rabbi usually gives a short speech about the dead person.

Everybody then accompanies the body to the grave, where prayers are said. It is customary for the family mourners to place a shovelful of earth into the grave, with all those attending the funeral then taking a turn. It is a *mitzvah* to help bury the dead. The family of the deceased may then be comforted by other mourners with the words: '**The Omnipresent** will comfort you among the mourners of Zion and Jerusalem.'

Everyone then washes their hands before leaving the cemetery as contact with the dead is considered unclean. At this point the family mourners move into the second stage of mourning – *avelut*.

Useful words

The Omnipresent – a title used of God during mourning to remind that Jews that God is with the living and the dead
Avelut – the mourning period

Section 2b: Practices

Activities

1. Look at the photo. Outline what is involved in sitting *shiva*.
2. Do you think the Jewish mourning customs would help close relatives to cope with their loss?
3. Why do you think people often find it difficult to talk to someone who has lost a close relative or friend?

Jewish mourners.

Useful words

Shiva – the seven days of intense mourning
Kaddish – the prayer recited publicly by mourners
Yarzheit – the anniversary day of someone's death

Avelut: the period of mourning

On returning home, the mourners are served a meal of hard-boiled eggs, symbolising the idea that just as an egg has no opening so the mourners will be too grief-stricken to speak. *Avelut* has three stages:

- *Shiva*: the first seven days are extreme mourning. Mourners stay in their homes except for going to synagogue on *Shabbat*, and do not cut their hair or nails; they sit on low chairs and do not listen to music, wear leather shoes or have sex. All mirrors are covered so that the mourners cannot pay attention to their appearance. They sit on low chairs because of this part of the story of Job:

   then they sat on the ground with him for seven days and seven nights. No one said a word to him because they saw how great his suffering was. (Job 2:13)

   A candle is kept burning day and night because of the verse in Proverbs 20:27:

   the candle of the Lord searches the soul of man.

   During the week, friends (and people from the synagogue) visit and bring food for the mourners. At the end of the week the mourners can return to normal life.

- For the next three weeks male mourners go to synagogue every day to pray **kaddish**. During this time a headstone should be set up in the cemetery which must be simple, both to avoid idolatry and to show the equality of everyone in death.

- Those mourning a parent or a child observe a twelve-month period of mourning counting from the day of death. During this period most activity returns to normal, although male mourners continue to recite the mourner's *kaddish* as part of synagogue services and do not listen to or play music unless it is part of their job.

Yarzheit

This is the anniversary of the death and as long as mourners live they keep *yarzheit* on the anniversary of relatives' deaths. A candle is kept burning for a night and a day and *kaddish* is said.

How the Liberal and Reform Jews differ from Orthodox

Many Liberal/Reform Jews think that some of the Orthodox customs are out of place in the modern world. So they:

- allow more time to elapse before the funeral so all family members can attend
- allow cremation
- put on a black ribbon rather than tearing their clothes
- sit *shiva* only for one day or at most three days and do not use low chairs
- do not cover the mirrors
- do not stay in the house for seven days
- allow the playing of music.

The importance of rituals for Jews

This topic is all about Jewish rites of passage. A rite of passage is a ceremony which marks the transition from one phase of life to another (births and beginnings, reaching adulthood, partnerings, and endings or death). All religions and cultures mark and celebrate these passages in life, both because they are occasions which require marking and because they provide an opportunity for strengthening the society or religion concerned.

The Brit Milah and **Bat Brit** bring a child into the community of Judaism and are important in providing the parents with the promise of support in bringing up this new life in the Jewish faith.

The Bar and Bat Mitzvah are important because they give a young person the opportunity to take upon themselves the responsibility of being a Jew and ensure the continuity of the Jewish faith.

Jewish marriage ceremonies are important because they bring two people together in the Jewish faith and provide the opportunity for a new Jewish family to develop and continue the faith.

The death and funeral rituals are important because the death of a family member is a time of great grief but the rituals provide the comfort and hope for the future which help people to cope with this terrible time.

Useful words

Bat Brit – ceremony for female babies in Liberal/Reform synagogues

Practice questions

c Explain two reasons why the Bar Mitzvah is important for Jewish boys. In your answer you must refer to a source of wisdom and authority.

d 'We don't need rites of passage rituals nowadays.' Evaluate this statement considering arguments for and against. In your answer you should:
- refer to Jewish points of view
- refer to different Jewish or non-religious points of view
- reach a justified conclusion.

Summary

Rites of passage are rituals celebrating important stages in life. Birth ceremonies for Jews are Brit Milah (circumcision) but Liberal Jews also have a Brit Bat for girls. All Jews should marry because the *mitzvot* say they should. Jewish boys have a Bar Mitzvah ceremony at the age of thirteen when they can be part of the *minyan*. Girls have a Bat Mitzvah. Synagogues have a *chevra kaddisha* to help with death. Orthodox Jews do not allow cremation. *Avelut* is the period of mourning, the first seven days of which are keeping *shiva*. Jews keep *yarzheit* on the anniversary of a family member's death.

Section 2b: Practices

Topic 2.2b.6 *Shabbat*

Thinking points

In this topic you need to:
- think about the nature, history and purpose of celebrating *Shabbat* and how it is celebrated in the home and in the synagogue, including Exodus 31:12–18
- be able to explain why *Shabbat* is important for Jews today.

Nature, history and purpose of celebrating *Shabbat*

Shabbat means ceasing from work. In the Genesis account of creation, God created the universe, the earth, vegetation, animals and humans in six days and on the seventh day he rested. In celebration of this, God instructed that on the seventh day of the week Jewish people should rest from work:

> *Remember the Sabbath day by keeping it holy. Six days you shall labour and do all your work, but the seventh day is a Sabbath to the Lord your God. On it you shall not do any work, neither you, nor your son or daughter, nor your manservant or maidservant, nor your animals, nor the alien within your gates. For in six days the Lord made the heavens and the earth, the sea, and all that is in them, but he rested on the seventh day. Therefore the Lord blessed the Sabbath day and made it holy. (Exodus 20:8–11)*

The seventh day of the week is Saturday, but Genesis chapter 1 says that the day begins and ends with sunset and so *Shabbat* begins at sunset on Friday and ends at sunset on Saturday. As the timing of sunset varies, Jews in the UK discover the times from the synagogue, from a paper like the *Jewish Chronicle* or from a phone app.

Shabbat has been celebrated by Jewish people throughout their history, but the regulations as to what work is – and therefore what must be avoided on *Shabbat* – are set out as 39 categories in the **Mishneh *Shabbat*** in the Talmud. These have been interpreted for the modern world by the rabbis, for example one of the categories is lighting fire, so Orthodox Jews do not switch on lights because that is interpreted as lighting fire. This means that in an Orthodox home lights are switched on at sunset on Friday and stay on until sunset on Saturday unless on a timer. They do not cook on *Shabbat* and have special slow cookers so meals can be prepared before *Shabbat* begins. There are complex rules as to how to keep water hot and make tea and coffee from it. The Orthodox believe it is wrong to drive cars on *Shabbat* and so they usually live within walking distance of synagogue.

Liberal/Reform Jews take a much more relaxed attitude to *Shabbat* observance, although they would normally celebrate the Friday evening meal as a family and go to synagogue for the Saturday morning service. Most would not go to their job on *Shabbat* (although some would if it was part of their contract), but they would switch on lights and televisions, cook meals and drive to synagogue.

Jewish people celebrate *Shabbat* to:

- proclaim their belief that God created the world and then rested
- fulfil the *mitzvot* about *Shabbat*
- obey the fourth of the Ten Commandments
- spend time as a family

Activities

1. How do Jewish people welcome *Shabbat*?
2. Look at the photo below. Why might you need an app to find out when *Shabbat* begins and ends?

Useful words

Mishneh *Shabbat* – the part of the Talmud which contains all the regulations for *Shabbat*

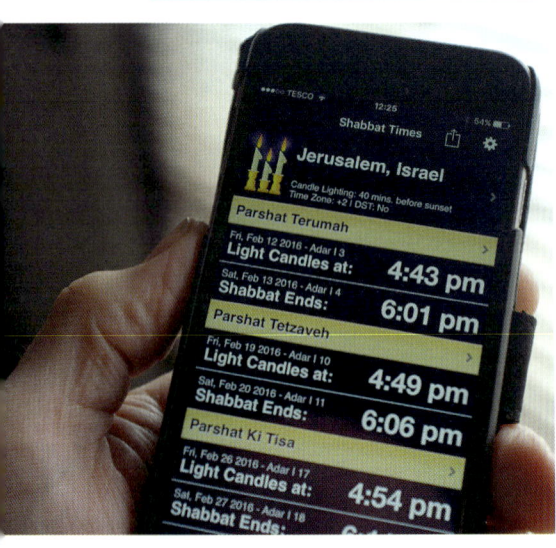

Checking *Shabbat* times using a smartphone app.

- spend time in worship, prayer and study
- think about what God intends life to be like and how they can fulfil God's wishes.

How *Shabbat* is celebrated in the home

Shabbat begins when the woman of the home lights the *Shabbat* candles and beckons with her arms to welcome *Shabbat* into the home. She covers her eyes and recites a blessing for the commandments, lights the candles and recites another blessing for her family before they go to service at the synagogue.

When the family return from the synagogue service, *Shabbat* worship continues at home with the *Shabbat* meal:

- The father of the household blesses the children and then recites Kiddush over the wine. The first part of Kiddush is reading the Genesis account of God resting on the seventh day. Wine is used to symbolise the sweetness and joy of the day. All the family join in the Amens, showing that they agree.
- There is a ritual cleansing of the hands before the father says the blessing over the bread. This is two specially plaited loaves called **challot**, reminding the family of the time in the wilderness when God sent two lots of manna on *Shabbat*.
- After the blessing, the father cuts the bread, then dips a little in salt to recall the sacrifices at the Temple which were dipped in salt.
- Then the meal begins and between courses the parents tell Bible stories and the family sing songs.

Shabbat morning is spent at synagogue. The family then spend time together at home before the afternoon service in the synagogue.

When night falls the **havdalah** ceremony takes place to mark the end of *Shabbat*. Havdalah means separation and is a ceremony to mark the end of a holy day. At the end of *Shabbat* the father says a blessing over a cup of wine, then another over the *havdalah* spice box and a final one over a lighted candle. *Shabbat* begins and ends with wine and lighted candles. The spice box is passed round the family so that the memory of *Shabbat* lingers into the week. *Shabbat* is now over, the separation of the holy from the ordinary is ended and the new week begins.

How *Shabbat* is celebrated in the synagogue

Each Friday after the welcoming of *Shabbat*, synagogues should hold *Shabbat* evening prayers when *Shabbat* is greeted as a bride coming to meet her husband, the Jewish people. At the end of the service the rabbi takes a cup of wine and recites Kiddush to thank God for giving *Shabbat* to the Jewish people.

On *Shabbat* morning (Saturday) families go to synagogue for the morning prayer. The high point of the service is when the **Sefer Torah** (scroll of the Torah) is taken out of the Ark and carried to the *bimah* for the rabbi to read the **sidra** (section of the Torah so chosen that over a year the whole Torah will be read). Men are called from the congregation to recite a blessing at certain points of the reading, and at the end a man is called to read from one of the books of the prophets. After the Sefer Torah has been put back in the Ark, the rabbi gives a sermon.

This shop is closed for the *Shabbat*.

Useful words

Challot – plaited loaves used on *Shabbat* and festivals
Havdalah – ceremony marking the ending of *Shabbat*
Sefer Torah – the Torah scroll kept in the Ark
Sidra – a passage from the Torah

Activities

1. Outline what happens at the *Shabbat* meal.
2. How do Jewish people mark the ending of *Shabbat*?
3. Write an outline of the synagogue services for *Shabbat*.
4. Read the quotation from Exodus 31 on page 280. Does it help to explain why Orthodox Jews are so serious about keeping *Shabbat*?

Section 2b: Practices

> *Then the Lord said to Moses, 'Say to the Israelites, You must observe my Sabbaths. This is a sign between me and you for the generations to come, so that you may know that I am the Lord, who makes you holy. Observe the Sabbath, because it is holy to you. Anyone who desecrates it is to be put to death; those who do any work on that day must be cut off from their people. For six days work is to be done, but the seventh day is a day of sabbath rest, holy to the Lord. Whoever does any work on the Sabbath day is to be put to death. The Israelites are to observe the Sabbath, celebrating it for the generations to come as a lasting covenant. It will be a sign between me and the Israelites forever, for in six days the Lord made the heavens and the earth, and on the seventh day he rested and was refreshed.' (Exodus 31:12–17)*

On *Shabbat* afternoon, prayers take place. These are shorter than the daily afternoon prayer, but the Sefer Torah is again taken out of the Ark and a short part of the next week's *sidra* is read.

Liberal/Reform synagogues have differences in the services. Prayers are said in English, not Hebrew, women attend all the services and sit with the men, the rabbi may well be a woman, and some of the prayers may be missed out.

Why *Shabbat* is important for Jewish people (the individual) today

- *Shabbat* offers Jewish people a chance to renew themselves both physically and spiritually as they rest from work and concentrate on religion.
- *Shabbat* gives a person time to think about what matters most to them and what they want life to be about.
- *Shabbat* provides time for a person to think about God and find out more about their faith.
- *Shabbat* provides an opportunity to socialise outside the demands and pressures of work. Friendships can be developed because of what people are, without any thought of how they might bring benefits.

Why *Shabbat* is important for the Jewish community

- *Shabbat* has been celebrated since the creation of the world and so is the oldest Jewish festival, making it important for the community to keep it going.
- *Shabbat* is God's gift to the Jewish people which binds them together – only Jews celebrate *Shabbat*.
- It reminds Jews of when they were slaves in Egypt:

> *remember that you were slaves in Egypt and that the Lord your God brought you out with a mighty arm ... Therefore the Lord your God has commanded you to observe the Sabbath day (Deuteronomy 5:15)*

and refraining from work is a sign of freedom.

- *Shabbat* gives families time to spend together and provides an opportunity for families to grow together in their Jewish faith.

Summary

There are many *mitzvot* commanding Jews to rest on *Shabbat*, both as a sign of God's creation taking six days and because of God's covenant with Moses. *Shabbat* lasts from sunset on Friday to sunset on Saturday and there are special ceremonies in the home to welcome *Shabbat* and synagogue services on Friday evening and Saturday morning. No work should be done on *Shabbat*, but Orthodox and Liberal/Reform Jews have different ideas on this.

Practice questions

c Explain two reasons why *Shabbat* is important for Jewish people. In your answer you must refer to a source of wisdom and authority.

d '*Shabbat* should be about worshipping God, not keeping rules.' Evaluate this statement considering arguments for and against. In your answer you should:
- refer to Jewish points of view
- refer to different Jewish or non-religious points of view
- reach a justified conclusion.

Topic 2.2b.7 Festivals

Jewish festivals

Judaism has many festivals during the year, but these do not have exact dates in the Western calendar. The Jewish calendar has twelve months, but the months are determined by the moon and only have 29 days. This means that the lunar calendar goes out of sync with the solar calendar and so an extra month is added to the Jewish calendar every few years to keep it in line with the seasons of the year. Consequently, the timing of Jewish festivals varies from year to year, but stays in the same season. Jewish New Year, for example, is the first two days of the month of Tisri, but this can fall any time between early September and early October.

The main festivals are:

- New Year – Rosh Hashanah (September/October)
- Day of Atonement – Yom Kippur (September/October)
- Tabernacles – Sukkot (October)
- Rejoicing of the Law – Simchat Torah (October)
- Dedication – Hanukkah (December)
- Purim – (February/March)
- Passover – Pesach (March/April)
- Weeks – Shavuot (May/June).

All of these festivals have been celebrated since biblical times and they are important for Jews because:

- They celebrate important events in Jewish history:
  - Pesach celebrates how God saved the Jews from slavery in the Exodus
  - Sukkot celebrates the time the Jews were in the wilderness after escaping from Egypt
  - Hanukkah celebrates the preservation of the Jewish religion when the Greeks tried to destroy it
  - Purim celebrates the saving of the Jews in Persia as recorded in the Book of Esther
  - Shavuot celebrates the giving of the Law to Moses.
- They celebrate the special relationship the Jewish people have with God, for example Simchat Torah celebrates the Torah and the *mitzvot*, which are the basis of Jewish life. Rosh Hashanah celebrates God's kingship and his willingness to forgive his people's sins.
- They celebrate God being the creator and sustainer of nature, as Shavuot and Sukkot have connections with harvest.
- They give an opportunity for Jewish people to turn over a new leaf by repenting of their sins and determining a new start at festivals like Yom Kippur.

Thinking points

In this topic you need to:
- think about the nature, history and purpose of festivals, and the origins and meaning of Rosh Hashanah, Yom Kippur, Pesach, Shavuot and Sukkot, including interpretations of Leviticus 23
- be able to explain why these festivals are important for Jews today.

Activity

Why are festivals important in Judaism?

Section 2b: Practices

> **Activity**
>
> Do you think the way Jews celebrate New Year is better than the way the UK celebrates New Year?

Rosh Hashanah

Rosh Hashanah marks the beginning of the Jewish New Year. This is one of the holiest times of the year for Jewish people.

Origins

The celebration is one of the *mitzvot* as it is commanded in the Torah:

> *The Lord said to Moses, 'Say to the Israelites: "On the first day of the seventh month you are to have a day of sabbath rest, a sacred assembly commemorated with trumpet blasts. Do no regular work, but present a food offering to the Lord".' (Leviticus 23:23–25)*

Rosh Hashanah has been celebrated since biblical times, but the Talmud says it is to be celebrated as the day when God created the earth and created the human race.

The Torah says that on the 1st of Elul (the month before Rosh Hashanah), Moses went up Mount Sinai to receive new tablets of stone with the Ten Commandments written on them to replace the ones Moses had smashed when he found the Israelites worshipping the golden calf. Forty days later (the day now celebrated as Yom Kippur) he returned with the new tablets, showing that God had forgiven the people because they had repented.

Features

During the month of Elul the **shofar** is blown every day in the synagogue. People think about their sins and their relationship with God so that they cast off their sins with feeling and have really thought about their resolutions for the new year.

Making New Year resolutions is not an optional extra for Jews, it is a requirement. New Year cards are exchanged and friends are greeted with the words, 'May you be inscribed for a good year'. This reflects the idea that God has a **Book of Life** in which he records the quality of people's lives and what he will record for the next year depends on what resolutions for improvement people make between Rosh Hashanah and Yom Kippur.

Rosh Hashanah is welcomed in the home by a Kiddush over foods containing honey in the hope that the New Year will be a sweet one; and the hope that there will be plenty of good deeds is expressed by eating fish which are found in shoals or pomegranates which have lots of seeds.

At the morning service, 100 notes of the *shofar* are blown to express the crying of the souls about past sins and the yearning of the soul to be reunited with God. After the service, families go to a river and in the ceremony of *tashlich* symbolically throw their sins into the water:

> *and you will cast all their sins into the depths of the sea. (Micah 7:19)*

> **Useful words**
>
> *Shofar* – a musical instrument
> **Book of Life** – the book where one's quality of life for the coming year is recorded
> *Tashlich* – casting away sins into running water

A *shofar* with pomegranate and honey.

Meaning and importance

After thinking about their sins during the month of Elul, on Rosh Hashanah people should consider their relationship with God and with each other, and decide how they are going to make both of these better in the coming year.

Rosh Hashanah is the day when the Book of Life is opened and when God writes down the quality of people's lives:

> *See I have set before you this day life and good, death and evil ... choose life. (Deuteronomy 30:1)*

The book is open until the end of Yom Kippur, after which it is sealed and cannot be altered, so what people decide on Rosh Hashanah and confirm on Yom Kippur is what will be in the book for the coming year.

Choosing to be good can be a real struggle and when people fail and do things wrong they feel guilty. Rosh Hashanah is a chance to come before God, acknowledge what they have done wrong and show how they are going to do good in the coming year.

Yom Kippur

Yom Kippur (Day of Atonement) occurs ten days after Rosh Hashanah. These ten days are known as the '**Days of Awe**', when people reflect on what they promised at Rosh Hashanah and make sure that they put things right with anyone they have wronged.

Origins

Yom Kippur is commanded in the Torah:

> *The Lord said to Moses, the tenth day of the seventh month is the Day of Atonement. Hold a sacred assembly and deny yourselves, and present an offering made to the Lord by fire. Do no work on that day, because it is the Day of Atonement, when atonement is made for you before the Lord your God. Anyone who does not deny himself on that day must be cut off from his people. (Leviticus 23:26–29)*

During the days of the Temple the priest sacrificed a bull as a sin offering to atone for sins he may have committed unintentionally throughout the year. Then he took two goats and presented them at the door of the tabernacle. Two goats were chosen by lot: one to be 'for the Lord', which was offered as a sacrifice, the other to be the scapegoat to be sent away into the wilderness. The high priest confessed the intentional sins of the Israelites to God, placing them symbolically on the head of the other goat, the scapegoat, who would symbolically take them away into the wilderness.

Yom Kippur involves a 25-hour fast, reflection of past sins, confession of sins and prayers for forgiveness. People wear simpler clothes and do not wear jewellery or leather shoes as they are forbidden in Leviticus.

On the eve of Yom Kippur, families have a special meal and make a family donation to the poor rather than sacrificing a chicken. Then they go to synagogue for a special evening service. This begins with the **Kol Nidrei** prayer, which used to be said by Jews at the time of the Spanish Inquisition to forgive them for pretending to be Christians so they would not be persecuted. This is followed by a confession of sins.

Useful words

Days of Awe – the ten days between Rosh Hashanah and Yom Kippur

Kol Nidrei – annulment of vows made before Yom Kippur

Activity

What happens on Yom Kippur and how might this help a Jewish person to make a new start?

Section 2b: Practices

There are prayers of general confession, but people are expected to make their own confession in silence to God because confession should be personal to the sinner and God.

At home there is a *havdalah* ceremony just as at *Shabbat* to show that Yom Kippur is over.

Meaning and importance

- The *mitzvah* that Jews who do not deny themselves on Yom Kippur must be cut off means that this is regarded as the most important festival. Many Jews who never obey the *mitzvot* during the rest of the year fast and go to synagogue on Yom Kippur.
- Atonement has two meanings: reconciling God and man, and reparation for a wrong or an injury.
- Yom Kippur releases people from the guilt felt about the sins of the past.
- Yom Kippur makes people feel free to make a new start.
- The fasting takes people's minds off their physical needs so they can concentrate on the spiritual.
- Fasting encourages the self-discipline needed to keep the resolutions made at Rosh Hashanah.
- Fasting helps people to feel compassion for the poor who fast through necessity, not choice.

Sukkot (Tabernacles)

Sukkot begins just five days after Yom Kippur and many families start building the family *sukkah* (*sukkot* is the plural) as soon as they finish the family meal at the end of Yom Kippur.

Origins

After the Israelites escaped from Egypt in the Exodus, they spent 40 years living as nomads in the wilderness, in temporary huts (*sukkot*) roofed with palm leaves. This festival takes Jewish people back to those times.

The festival is commanded in Torah *mitzvot*:

> On the fifteenth day of the seventh month the Lord's Festival of Tabernacles begins, and lasts for seven days. The first day is a sacred assembly; do no regular work ... So beginning with the fifteenth day of the seventh month, after you have gathered the crops of the land, celebrate to the Lord ... take a choice fruit from the trees, and palm fronds, leafy branches and poplars and rejoice before the Lord your God for seven days ... live in booths for seven days ... so that your descendants will know that I made the Israelites live in booths when I brought them out of Egypt. (Leviticus 23:33–43)

Sukkot begins at the end of the fruit harvest in Israel. Families, and often the synagogues, make an outdoor *sukkah* with at least three walls and a covering of leafy branches. Depending on the climate, people either live in their *sukkah* for seven days or just eat their meals in it.

On each day of the festival people meet in the synagogue carrying an **etrog** (a fruit that looks like a lemon) in one hand and a **lulav** (palm branch), myrtle and willow, as commanded in the *mitzvah*. They wave the *lulav* in all directions and there is much rejoicing since Sukkot is called 'the season

Useful words

Etrog – a citron fruit
Lulav – palm branch

A *sukkah*.

of our rejoicing'. On the last day of Sukkot people process round the *bimah* seven times waving the *lulav* and carrying the *etrog*.

Meaning and importance

- It symbolises and encourages harmony, with families living in their *sukkah* as a unit.
- It is a link with the ancestors, reinforcing the idea that Jews belong to an ancient people.
- The four species symbolise God's presence everywhere and the blessings he showers on his people.
- The four species also symbolise four different types of people:
  - the *etrog* stands for people who both know the Torah and do good deeds
  - the *lulav* stands for those who are learned in Torah but do no good deeds
  - the myrtle stands for those who do good deeds but do not know the Torah and
  - the willow stands for those who are both ignorant of the Torah and selfish.

Pesach

Pesach is a seven-day festival at the beginning of spring. In the days before Pesach, houses are cleaned to remove all traces of leaven (yeast). Any food containing leaven is called **chametz** and children have special games hunting for any *chametz* in the house, which is all burnt before Pesach begins.

> **Activity**
>
> Look at the photo above. Why do Jews build one of these for Sukkot?

> **Useful words**
>
> *Chametz* – any food containing yeast/leaven

Section 2b: Practices

Origins

Pesach began with Moses, and the Torah recounts how, after Joseph had brought the Israelites into Egypt to escape famine, they were enslaved by the Pharaoh and made to work as slaves on building projects. Moses was called by God to bring the people out of Egypt. The Pharaoh refused and so God sent plagues on the Egyptians and after each plague the Pharaoh said the Israelites could go, but then changed his mind.

Before the tenth plague, the Israelites were told to sacrifice a lamb and spread its blood on their doorposts so the angel of death would pass over their houses, but when it came to Egyptian houses it killed the firstborn in each house. After this, the Pharaoh agreed to let the Israelites go and Moses led them out, but again the Pharaoh changed his mind and led his army in a chase after the Israelites.

When they came to the Red Sea, God parted the sea so that the Israelites could cross, but when the Egyptians followed, the waves came back and destroyed the army. So God saved Israel and gave the people their freedom, which is why Pesach is sometimes called the freedom festival.

There are Pesach *mitzvot* about the festival:

> *The Lord's Passover begins at twilight on the fourteenth day of the first month. On the fifteenth day of that month the Lord's feast of Unleavened Bread begins; for seven days you must eat bread made without yeast.* (Leviticus 23:5–7)
>
> *For seven days no yeast is to be found in your houses. And whoever eats anything made with yeast in it must be cut off from the community of Israel.* (Exodus 12:19)
>
> *Sacrifice as the Passover to the Lord your God an animal from your flock or herd.* (Deuteronomy 16:2)

Activity

Why do Jewish people celebrate Pesach?

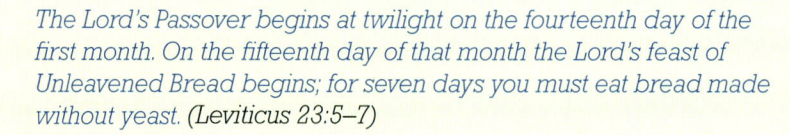

Pesach has been celebrated by Jews ever since these events, which probably took place about 1250 BCE.

Pesach begins an hour before nightfall, when the candles are lit and the festival is welcomed into the home. There is then a synagogue service where special prayers are said thanking God for freeing their ancestors from slavery in Egypt. Then the family return for the great meal of Pesach, which is called **seder**. *Seder* means order and there is a special order to be followed in the meal as set out in the **hagadah** book. There are special foods on the *seder* plate which are only tasted, and there are a whole series of questions asked by the youngest family member and answered by the father. Then they have a proper meal featuring lamb. They sing songs about the Exodus and at the end of the meal they eat a piece of unleavened bread known as the *afikomen*.

Unleavened bread is eaten for seven days, then there is a *havdalah* ceremony after which those families who have been using special Pesach crockery wash it and put it away.

Useful words

Seder – the Passover meal
Hagadah – book telling the story of the first Passover

Meaning of the *seder* plate foods

Food	Meaning
Charoset	Paste made with nuts, fruit and spices to represent the mud bricks the Israelite slaves had to make in Egypt, and when eaten it gives the sweet taste of freedom
Bitter herbs (horseradish)	Represent the pain of slavery
Shank bone	A reminder of the lamb sacrificed at Passover
Burnt boiled egg	A reminder of the sacrifices offered in the Temple
Green herbs (parsley)	Green parsley represents freedom; it is dipped in salt water to represent the tears of the slaves and the sea they crossed to freedom
Lettuce	The leaves symbolise freedom and the bitter stalk slavery

A *seder* plate.

Meaning and importance

- Pesach is the freedom festival and is a great celebration of freedom and condemnation of slavery.
- It is also a celebration of God's power and God's control of history, for without the Passover and Exodus there would be no Jewish people.
- It is celebrated as the birthday of the Jewish nation and the *seder* meal is like a birthday party for the nation.
- It is a celebration of Jewish history and of the way God has preserved his chosen people.

Shavuot (also known as Pentecost or Weeks)

Shavuot is the Feast of Weeks. It is celebrated seven weeks after Passover, meaning that the first day of Shavuot is 50 days after Passover, hence the name Pentecost (Greek for the number 50).

Origins

Shavuot began as a harvest festival, marking the beginning of the wheat harvest. The Torah commands the Jews to offer the first fruits of the harvest to God:

> When you have entered the land the Lord your God is giving you as an inheritance and have taken possession of it and settled in it, take some of the first fruits of all that you produce from the soil of the land that the Lord your God is giving you and put them in a basket … Place the basket before the Lord your God and bow down before him. (Deuteronomy 26:1–11)

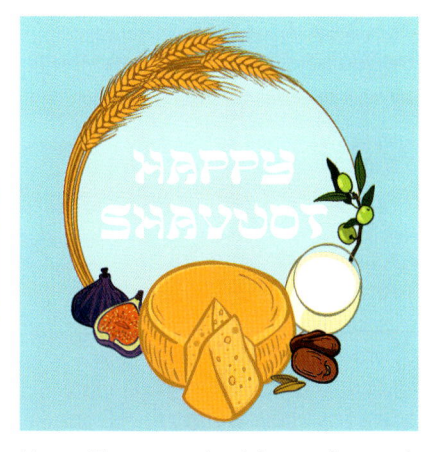

Seven weeks after the events of the Exodus celebrated at Pesach, Moses was given the Torah on Mount Sinai, and this is now the main element of the festival – thanking God for the gift of the Torah.

Activities

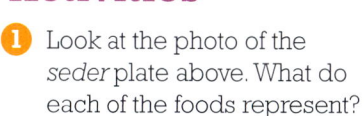

1. Look at the photo of the *seder* plate above. What do each of the foods represent?
2. Why might some people think Shavuot is the most important Jewish festival?

Happy Shavuot: a Jewish greeting card for this holiday.

Section 2b: Practices

Shavuot is the only festival without a specific *mitzvah* ordering its celebration. This is because the giving of the Torah is so important to the Jewish people that celebrating the giving of it is required by all 613 of the *mitzvot*.

Shavuot is a two-day festival and, as a festival, no work is done. The main things that happen at Shavuot are:

- Candles are lit to bring in the festival, on both the first and second evenings.
- Many people stay up to read the Torah on the first night of Shavuot.
- Everyone goes to synagogue on the first day of Shavuot to hear the reading of the Ten Commandments.
- People eat dairy foods rather than meat.
- On the second day of Shavuot, a special prayer for those who have died is recited in the synagogue.
- The Book of Ruth is read, as she was an ancestor of King David who was born on Shavuot and died 70 years later on Shavuot.
- Flowers and greenery are placed all around the synagogue, as Mount Sinai blossomed after God gave the Torah to the Israelites.

Meaning and importance

- The gift of the Torah is the most important thing in Jewish history. Following the 613 *mitzvot* of the Torah gives Jewish people their identity.
- It is thought that Shavuot completes Pesach, as Pesach was about the Israelites gaining physical freedom, but Shavuot celebrates the spiritual freedom brought by the *mitzvot*.
- Studying the Torah on the first night represents an attempt to put the past right and show people's eagerness to be given the Torah, as many of the Jews went to sleep the night before Moses brought them the Torah.
- Dairy produce is eaten rather than meat because people did not know what the laws about meat would be and so they made sure they did not break the laws by eating dairy products instead.
- The fruit and greenery represent not only the flowering of Sinai after the giving of the law, but also the *mitzvah* to present the first fruits to God.

Summary

Judaism has many festivals to celebrate the great events in Jewish history. The main ones are: Rosh Hashanah, celebrating the New Year; ten days later comes Yom Kippur, a whole-day fast giving people a chance to put things right for the New Year; Sukkot, remembering the 40 years in the wilderness; Pesach, remembering the Israelites' escape from Egypt; and Shavuot, celebrating the giving of the Torah to Moses.

Practice questions

c Explain two reasons why Pesach is important for Jewish people. In your answer you must refer to a source of wisdom and authority.

d 'You can't be considered a Jew if you don't fast and attend synagogue on Yom Kippur.' Evaluate this statement considering arguments for and against. In your answer you should:
- refer to Jewish points of view
- refer to different Jewish or non-religious points of view
- reach a justified conclusion.

Topic 2.2b.8 Features of the synagogue

The Jewish synagogue

A Jewish place of worship is called a synagogue, which is a Greek word meaning to gather together, or the place where people gather together.

It seems that synagogues began in the sixth century BCE when most Jews were in exile in Babylon and could not go to worship in the Temple in Jerusalem. In this situation, they had to develop places where they could meet for prayer, worship and study, and they became known as synagogues. However, most Jewish people refer to the synagogue either as 'temple' or '*shul*'.

Synagogues have features based on the layout of the Jerusalem Temple, especially the Ark of the Covenant, which was a precious box containing the tablets of the law received by Moses, lost when the first Temple was destroyed by the Babylonians (as featured in films such as *Raiders of the Lost Ark*).

After the destruction of the second Jerusalem Temple in 70CE, synagogues became more and more important. Some of the daily prayers such as *kaddish* can only be said when there is *a minyan* and so needed a synagogue. Young people needed to be taught the Hebrew language and the basics of the faith, and the synagogue was used for this. Finally, the synagogue became a community centre of the local Jewish community, providing socialising facilities for local Jews.

Nowadays the synagogue is a place of worship, an education centre and a community centre. Most synagogues run Hebrew classes for children, and have a hall which can be used for weddings, Bar Mitzvahs, mother and toddler groups, study groups, youth clubs, scouts, guides and so on.

Exterior synagogue design

A synagogue can be in any type of building and so the exterior can be of any design, except that it should:

- have either a Star of David or a *menorah* to show that it is Jewish
- have windows letting the light in so that worship is not a retreat from the world and to pour light as a sign of God's strength and guidance
- be built facing Jerusalem, where the Temple stood.

Interior synagogue design

All synagogues should have the following features:

- They should have a sink at the entrance for worshippers to ceremonially cleanse themselves before prayer.
- They have a Holy Ark (**Aron Hakodesh**), which is a cupboard fixed to the front wall, making it the focal centre of the synagogue. Sometimes it has an embroidered black and gold curtain in front, while others are painted black and have two gold lions on the doors representing the tribe of Judah from which will come the Messiah.

Thinking points

In this topic you need to:
- think about the nature, history and purpose of the design of the synagogue; how and why objects of devotion are used within the synagogue and how the synagogue is used by different communities, including reference to Exodus 27:20–21
- be able to explain the importance of the synagogue in Judaism.

Useful words

Shul – the name used for the synagogue by many Jews
Menorah – seven-branched candlestick
Aron Hakodesh – the Ark

Activities

1. Why did synagogues develop?
2. How would you know a building was a synagogue?
3. What compass direction should UK synagogues face?

Section 2b: Practices

> Command the Israelites to bring you clear oil of pressed olives for the light so that the lamps may be kept burning. In the tent of meeting, outside the curtain that shields the ark of the covenant law, Aaron and his sons are to keep the lamps burning before the Lord from evening till morning. This is to be a lasting ordinance among the Israelites for the generations to come.
> (Exodus 27:20–21)

A man holding a Torah scroll in a British synagogue.

- Inside the Ark are the Torah scrolls (Sefer Torah). A Torah scroll is about 60 metres long and is stitched at each end to a wooden pole so it can be wound and kept ready at the point of the next reading. The scroll is wound in a black and gold silk or velvet wrapping with a crown and bell on top of the poles, so that the congregation hear the bells when the scroll is removed from the Ark. Usually a shield decorated with the first two words of each of the Ten Commandments is placed on the front of the wrapped scroll.

- When reading the scroll the reader uses a **yad** (a pointer stick) to keep his place. This is important because the holy words of the Sefer Torah must not be stained or damaged by being touched by dirty fingers.

- They have a **bimah** (raised platform) with a desk for reading the Torah, a chair on one side for the rabbi and one on the other side for the **chazzan** or cantor who leads the prayers, and sometimes a pulpit for the rabbi to give the sermon. The *bimah* can be in the middle of the synagogue or in front of the Ark.

- Above the Ark is the **ner tamid** or everlasting light. This light is never put out and represents the *menorah* in the Jerusalem Temple, whose seven wicks were never allowed to go out.

- Many synagogues also have an actual *menorah* on a lampstand, but the *menorah* in the synagogue will generally have six or eight branches instead of the Temple *menorah*'s seven, because exact duplication of the Temple's ritual items is thought to be improper by the Orthodox.

- On the wall next to or above the Ark there is usually a plaque with the words of the Ten Commandments on it.

Useful words

Yad – pointer for reading the Sefer Torah
Bimah – the raised platform for Torah readings
Chazzan – the leader of worship who chants the prayers (also called a cantor)
Ner tamid – the everlasting light

How the synagogue is used by the different communities

The reason for the differences can be found in the introduction about Orthodox and Liberal/Reform Jews and Topic 2.2a.1 (page 254).

- In Orthodox synagogues there will be separate seating for women, sometimes with a screen between the men's and women's sections. In Liberal/Reform synagogues men and women sit together.
- In Orthodox synagogues the rabbi and cantor will always be men. In Liberal/Reform synagogues the rabbi and/or cantor may be women.
- In Orthodox synagogues there will be no musical instruments played on *Shabbat* because that would be work. In Liberal/Reform synagogues there may be an organ or a piano or a band for *Shabbat* worship.
- In Orthodox synagogues only males would be asked up to read. In Liberal/Reform synagogues both men and women can be asked up to read.
- In Orthodox synagogues prayers will be in Hebrew. In Liberal/Reform synagogues many of the prayers will be in English.
- In Orthodox synagogues there are prayers for the rebuilding of the Temple and the return of all Jewish people to the Holy Land. In Liberal/Reform synagogues these payers are not said.
- In Orthodox synagogues only men carry the Torah scrolls. In Liberal/Reform synagogues women or girls may be invited to carry the Torah scrolls.
- In Orthodox synagogues people will have walked to synagogue. In Liberal/Reform synagogues people will often come to synagogue by car.

Schedule of events and services at a synagogue in New York, USA.

Activity

Do you think it matters what a synagogue looks like? Remember to read Exodus 27:20–21.

How else the synagogue is used

Most synagogues have classrooms for learning Hebrew, lessons preparing for Bat or Bar Mitzvahs, and for meetings and lectures to learn more about the faith.

Many synagogues have a hall for wedding and Bar or Bat Mitzvah celebrations. It is also used for mother and toddler groups, senior citizens' clubs and other community activities.

Most synagogues also hold youth activities such as youth clubs, scouts and guides. They also run day camps during school holidays.

Practice questions

c Explain two reasons why the synagogue is used differently by different communities. In your answer you must refer to a source of wisdom and authority.

d 'The synagogue is the centre of Jewish life.' Evaluate this statement considering arguments for and against. In your answer you should:
- refer to Jewish points of view
- refer to different Jewish or non-religious points of view
- reach a justified conclusion.

Summary

The synagogue took the place of the Temple in Jewish worship and acts as a school and social centre for the Jewish community. Synagogues are built facing Jerusalem. The Torah scrolls are kept in the Holy Ark at the front of the synagogue where there is a *bimah* to read the Torah scroll from. All synagogues have a *ner tamid* or everlasting light to fulfil the *mitzvah* of Exodus 27. There are differences between Orthodox and Liberal/Reform synagogues.

Section 2b: Practices

How to answer questions

a) Describe two differences between Jewish forms of worship and forms of worship in the main religious tradition of Britain. [3]

The main religious tradition of Britain is Christianity. One difference is that Orthodox Jews worship in Hebrew, whereas Christians worship in their native language. Another difference is that men and women worship separately in Orthodox Judaism whereas the sexes worship together in Christianity.

A high mark answer because Christianity is identified as the main religious tradition and two differences are clearly described.

b) Explain two differences between Jewish and Christian forms of worship. [4]

One difference is that in Orthodox Jewish worship all the prayers are said in Hebrew, whereas in Christian worship everything is in the language of the country. In Jewish worship there are no images, but in Catholic and Orthodox worship there are likely to be crucifixes and statues of the Virgin Mary.

A high mark answer because two correct differences are given and each difference is developed.

c) Explain two reasons why circumcision is important for Jews. In your answer you must refer to a source of wisdom and authority. [5]

Circumcision is important because it is a 'sign in the flesh' of the covenant God made with Abraham in Genesis chapter 16. This made circumcision a *mitzvah* which marks the entry of Jewish males into the covenant. It has been particularly important in Jewish history as both the Greeks and the Romans tried to ban circumcision as a way of ending the Jewish nation, but many Jews were martyred rather than give up the practice.

A high mark answer because two correct reasons are given and each reason is developed with a reference to covenant, Genesis and *mitzvah* as sources of authority.

d) 'The Bar Mitzvah is where a Jewish boy becomes an adult.' Evaluate this statement considering arguments for and against. [12 marks + 3 spelling, punctuation and grammar (SPaG) marks]

Some people may think that Bar Mitzvah is where a Jewish boy becomes an adult because it is the term used for when a boy becomes responsible for his own actions and is regarded as an adult as far as religion is concerned. Certainly, after his Bar Mitzvah, a Jewish boy must put on *tephilin* for morning prayers; he can make up a *minyan*; he has to observe the fast days in full and he may be called up to read the *sidra* in synagogue services. All of these show him being an adult.

However, others may disagree because Judaism does not regard a thirteen-year-old boy as an adult because he has had his Bar Mitzvah. In Pirkei Avot in the Talmud, it says that while thirteen is the proper age for fulfilment of the Commandments, eighteen is the proper age for marriage and twenty is the proper age for earning a living. Nowadays, most Jews would regard the Bar Mitzvah as making a Jewish boy responsible for his actions and for his religion but not a full adult.

It seems to me that few Jewish people would regard the Bar Mitzvah as making a boy an adult. I do not think anyone can be regarded as an adult at the age of thirteen and so I think that Bar Mitzvah makes a boy an adult for religion, but not for life.

A high mark answer because it gives three clear developed reasons for thinking that a boy becomes an adult at Bar Mitzvah. It then gives three reasons for disagreeing and then reaches a fully justified conclusion.

The answer would reach full marks for SPaG as spelling, punctuation and grammar are correct and a wide range of specialist vocabulary (*tephilin*, *sidra*, synagogue, Pirkei Avot, Talmud) is used appropriately.

SPaG

A high mark answer because the answer spells, punctuates and uses the rules of grammar with consistent accuracy and effective control of meaning. A wide range of specialist terms is used adeptly and with precision.

1 Arguments for the existence of God

Area of study 3: Philosophy and ethics based on Catholic Christianity

Section 1: Arguments for the existence of God

Topic 3.1.1 Revelation as proof of the existence of God

Thinking points

In this topic you need to:
- think about revelation as proof of the existence of God
- understand the significance of Jesus Christ as the culmination of God's revelation
- consider what the revelation of Jesus Christ shows about the nature of God for Catholics, including reference to Hebrews 1:1–4
- be able to evaluate the importance of revelation as a proof of God's existence.

What is revelation?

The word 'revelation' comes from a Greek term meaning to unveil. It is used in religion to describe God's unveiling of himself to humanity.

Catholics believe that God has gradually unveiled aspects of his being and his commandments through **natural revelation** and **special revelation**.

Natural revelation

Believers see all sorts of clues around them in the world suggesting to them that God exists. These are thing such as aspects of nature that are complex and beautiful, as well as the love between people and the wonder of our personality and our consciousness. These sorts of things cannot be reduced to chemicals and atoms and placed in a test tube or under a microscope. They are more personal, moral, emotional and **spiritual**.

Think about how you might answer the question, 'can you weigh a sentence?' One way is to write the words and then weigh the ink and the paper but this is not what the question really asks. Can you weigh the speech, the idea, the thought? Religious believers think that life, just like the sentence, is more than atoms, electrical forces and chemicals; it is also spiritual and evokes a sense of **awe** at the vastness of the universe and the beauty of nature.

The way believers use natural revelation to prove that God exists is covered in Topic 3.1.5 (page 310) by the design argument.

Useful words

Natural revelation – the revealing of God in the nature of the universe
Special revelation – the revealing of God in such things as holy books, for example the Bible
Spiritual – the non-material element of life, such as religion, feelings and values
Awe – a sense of overwhelming wonder at the vastness, mystery or beauty of something

Human beings look around them at the beauty of nature with a sense of awe, and of the vastness of space. On a smaller scale, human life and its beginning is also a cause for wonder.

Special revelation

However, natural revelation gives only a vague awareness of the nature of God. Christians believe that God has revealed some more of his nature to humanity in what they call special revelation or the Bible (the holy book of Christianity). The first part of the Bible, the Old Testament, contains God's laws for the Jews, prophecies about the coming of Jesus, and the history of the Jewish people before Jesus. The second part of the Bible, the New Testament, contains the four Gospels about the life, death and resurrection of Jesus. Christians believe that the Bible proves the existence of God because:

- It is inspired by the Holy Spirit, which means it comes from God and reveals God.

- The Church teaches that God speaks through both the Old Testament and New Testament, showing his character and commands.

- The Bible contains God's laws on how to behave, such as the Ten Commandments; these rules are there to help people to live as God intends, so it has authority by showing them how God wants them to live.

- The Bible can bring people into a closer relationship with God by learning about what God wants and how God cares for them.

> *To compose the sacred books, God chose certain men who, all the while he employed them in this task, made full use of their own faculties and powers so that, though he acted in them and by them, it was as true authors that they consigned to writing whatever he wanted written, and no more.* (Catechism of the Catholic Church 106)

Activities

1. How do you think we can find out what God is like?
2. Do you think the Bible proves that God exists?

The significance of Jesus Christ as the culmination of revelation

Catholics believe that God's revelation culminated in the incarnation (God becoming flesh in Jesus). This means that all of the small revelations in the Old Testament are not only summed up in the life of Jesus but also made even clearer and fuller:

> *It pleased God, in his goodness and wisdom to reveal himself, and to make known the mystery of his will. His will was that men should have access to the Father through Christ, the Word made flesh, in the Holy Spirit and thus become sharers in the divine nature.* (Catechism of the Catholic Church 51)

The Catholic Church teaches that there can be no further and fuller revelation of God after Jesus, as God's message to humanity reached its highest point in him:

> *The Christian economy, therefore, since it is the new and definitive Covenant, will never pass away; and no new public revelation is to be expected before the glorious manifestation of our Lord Jesus Christ.* (Catechism of the Catholic Church 66)

This means that although there were religions formed after the time of Jesus, such as Islam and Sikhism, Catholics cannot agree with all that they teach because, even if there is much in these religions that they can respect, God's final truth came in Jesus.

Section 1: Arguments for the existence of God

Activities

1. Look at the icon of Christ. What do you think it means to say that Christ is the culmination of God's revelation?
2. Look at the quotation from Hebrews 1:1–4. What does it tell us about Jesus?

'The Word became flesh' (John 1:14).

What the revelation in Jesus Christ shows Catholics about God's nature

For Catholics, Jesus shows them what God is like: their God is Christ-like. God, who is beyond the universe and created the stars, cannot be grasped by human beings on one level, but in Jesus people see God as:

- one who is love
- one who forgives
- one who meets people where they are
- Jesus on the cross showed an ultimate act of self-giving love and forgiveness for the sins of the world.

This significance of Jesus Christ is summed up in the opening of the letter to the Hebrews:

> In the past God spoke to our ancestors through the prophets at many times and in various ways, but in these last days he has spoken to us by his Son, whom he appointed heir of all things, and through whom also he made the universe. The Son is the radiance of God's glory and the exact representation of his being, sustaining all things by his powerful word. After he had provided purification for sins, he sat down at the right hand of the Majesty in heaven. So he became as much superior to the angels as the name he has inherited is superior to theirs. (Hebrews 1:1–4)

Yet, there is much that believers do not fully understand that will only become clear in heaven. Even what has been revealed takes time to unfold and be taken on board:

> Yet if Revelation is already complete, it has not been made completely explicit; it remains for Christian faith gradually to grasp its full significance over the course of the centuries. (Catechism of the Catholic Church 66)

Practice questions

c) Explain two reasons why Catholics believe that Jesus is the culmination of God's revelation. In your answer you must refer to a source of wisdom and authority.

d) 'The Bible proves that God exists.' Evaluate this statement considering arguments for and against. In your answer you should:
- refer to Catholic points of view
- refer to different Christian or non-religious points of view
- reach a justified conclusion.

Summary

Catholics believe that the nature of the universe and humanity reveals a certain amount about God's nature and prove that God exists (natural revelation). Special revelation in such things as the Bible reveals much more about God and proves that God exists. However, the full revelation of God came in Jesus himself as the Son or Word of God. The Church today is the guardian of that revelation.

Section 1: Arguments for the existence of God

Topic 3.1.2 Visions

Thinking points

In this topic you need to:
- think about the nature and importance of visions for Catholics
- be aware of biblical and non-biblical examples of visions, including Joan of Arc, Genesis 15 and Matthew 17:1–13
- consider reasons why visions might lead to belief in God and Catholic responses to non-religious arguments (including atheist and Humanist) that visions provide no proof that God exists
- be able to evaluate the importance of visions.

Useful words

Vision – something seen in a dream, trance or religious ecstasy, which gives a religious message

Apparitions – visionary experiences that have a physical effect on people around the visionary

Auditory vision – a vision which is only a voice with no images

The nature and importance of visions for Catholics

A **vision** is something seen in a dream, trance or religious ecstasy, especially an appearance of a divine messenger, which gives a religious message to the person having the vision.

Catholics believe that God can use our mental faculties to communicate truths and messages to us. Catholics, especially the saints, have had visions or **apparitions** of the risen Christ, or of an angel, or a saint, but most particularly of the Virgin Mary, which have given them messages for the Church.

Visions that have been authenticated by the Church are important for Catholics because:

- They show that God cares for and can intervene in the world.
- They authenticate some aspect of the Christian message.
- They prove that Christ, or the Virgin Mary, or the saints have a continuing and active presence in the life of the Church.
- They show that it is worthwhile to pray to Christ and the Virgin Mary and to pray through the saints.

Biblical examples of visions

There are many visions mentioned in the Old Testament, one of which is that of Abraham in Genesis:

> After this, the word of the Lord came to Abram in a vision: 'Do not be afraid, Abram. I am your shield, your very great reward.' But Abram said, 'Sovereign Lord, what can you give me since I remain childless and the one who will inherit my estate is Eliezer of Damascus?' And Abram said, 'You have given me no children; so a servant in my household will be my heir.' Then the word of the Lord came to him: 'This man will not be your heir, but a son who is your own flesh and blood will be your heir.' He took him outside and said, 'Look up at the sky and count the stars – if indeed you can count them.' Then he said to him, 'So shall your offspring be.' (Genesis 15:1–5)

This is what is known as an **auditory vision** as Abraham does not see God, he only hears his voice. But, like all classic visions, the vision gives Abraham a message: a) he will have a son, even though he is childless and has had to appoint a servant as his heir; b) Abraham's own flesh and blood will be his son and his heir; and c) Abraham will have numerous descendants.

The prophet Ezekiel had symbolic visions such as the four-faced living creatures and the moving wheels.

The New Testament records several visions, one of the most famous of which is St Paul's vision of the risen Christ on the road to Damascus, which changed Paul from a persecutor of Christians to the fist great Christian missionary. Another significant vision recorded in the New Testament is the vision given to the apostles, Peter, James and John, at the transfiguration:

> *After six days Jesus took with him Peter, James and John the brother of James, and led them up a high mountain by themselves. There he was transfigured before them. His face shone like the sun, and his clothes became as white as the light. Just then there appeared before them Moses and Elijah, talking with Jesus. Peter said to Jesus, 'Lord, it is good for us to be here. If you wish, I will put up three shelters – one for you, one for Moses and one for Elijah.' While he was still speaking, a bright cloud covered them, and a voice from the cloud said, 'This is my Son, whom I love; with him I am well pleased. Listen to him!' When the disciples heard this, they fell facedown to the ground, terrified. But Jesus came and touched them. 'Get up,' he said. 'Don't be afraid.' When they looked up, they saw no one except Jesus. As they were coming down the mountain, Jesus instructed them, 'Don't tell anyone what you have seen, until the Son of Man has been raised from the dead.'* (Matthew 17:1–9)

This is both a visual and an auditory vision. Visually, the apostles see Moses and Elijah talking to Jesus, a bright cloud covers them and they hear a voice which they take to be God. The voice gives them this message: Jesus is God's Son; God is pleased with what Jesus has done; the apostles are to listen to what Jesus tells them.

Non-biblical visions

There have been many examples of visions since biblical times, such as St Catherine of Sienna and St Bernadette of Lourdes. Another one is St Joan of Arc.

Section 1: Arguments for the existence of God

St Joan of Arc (1412–31) was a peasant girl from Domremy in France during the time of the Hundred Years' War between England and France. At the age of nineteen, she claimed to have had a vision of the Archangel Michael, and Saints Margaret and Catherine, who told her to drive the English out of France. The voices continued throughout her life and she managed to convince the French royal court of their truth. She inspired the French armies by her words and by carrying her banner in battle. Joan led the French to several victories before being captured by the English, tried as a heretic and burned at the stake in 1431. This trial was overturned by the Pope in 1456, and she was declared a martyr for the faith, but was only **canonised** in 1920 by Pope Benedict XV.

Joan believed that she saw reality in her visions and that the voices she heard actually came from the saints. Catholics also believe this because her claims have been investigated three times by the Vatican: once when her trial was overturned and she was declared a martyr, once when she was **beatified** and once when she was canonised. Many also feel that it must have been almost impossible for an illiterate peasant girl to convince royalty and rally battle-hardened soldiers to her cause without divine help.

Joan of Arc at prayer.

Useful words

Canonised – a person being declared a saint by the Church
Beatified – the first stage in being declared a saint; the declaration that a deceased person is counted among the blessed

Why visions might lead some people to believe in God

Visions might lead people to believe in God because:

- They might know enough about the person having the vision to know that they must be telling the truth, and if they are, then the vision could only come from God.
- The changes to the behaviour of the person having the vision (for example, St Joan of Arc) make them think that the vision must have come from God.
- The details of the vision (for example, that of St Bernadette in the next topic) make them think it must have come from God.
- The message in the vision makes them think it must have come from God.

What visions show about the nature of God

For Catholics, visions show that:

- God is still at work in the world.
- God is love because he is concerned about his world.
- God is still communicating his revelation to humans.
- God can change people's lives for the good through visions.

Atheist and Humanist attitudes to visions

Atheists and Humanists do not believe in God and so, as far as they are concerned, visions cannot be communicating anything real. They believe that visions can be explained by scientific enquiry of the people having the vision and the details of what they have seen. Atheists and Humanists claim that people suffering from mental illness or stress or taking certain types of medication experience hallucinations very similar to the visions reported by the saints. They have also looked at the details of visions and claim that the identification of the people in the vision, such as the Virgin Mary, is based on images which the visionary has already seen and associated with the saint.

These images are often different from what they would actually have looked like as a historical person, for example the Virgin Mary was most probably brown-skinned and dark-haired like most Middle Eastern Jews of the time. Therefore, atheists and Humanists believe that visions only exist in the mind of the person experiencing them and so prove nothing.

Catholic responses

Catholics disagree with the atheist and Humanist attitude because the Church has investigated reported visions on a case-by-case basis. Their investigations make sure that:

- the visionary was not suffering from mental or physical illness at the time
- the visionary was not on medication or drugs
- the visionary had a good moral nature
- the meaning of the vision agrees with the teaching of the Bible and the Church
- the vision has had a good effect on the visionary, and on Catholics in general.

So, if the Church approves a vision, it must have been genuine.

Visions remind Catholics that God and heaven are mysterious. They are spiritual and **transcendent** and cannot be reduced to the material.

Activities

1. What do you think visions show us about God?
2. Look at the vision of Abraham in Genesis 15 on page 298. What did Abraham see in this vision? What did he hear?
3. Look at the vision the apostles had at the transfiguration on page 299. What did they see and hear?
4. Do you think St Joan of Arc had genuine visions?
5. What do you think about the Humanist attitude to visions?

Useful words

Transcendent – the 'beyond', that which is more than the physical

Practice questions

c) Explain two reasons why Catholics believe visions are important. In your answer you must refer to a source of wisdom and authority.

d) 'Visions prove that God exists.' Evaluate this statement considering arguments for and against. In your answer you should:
- refer to Catholic points of view
- refer to different Christian or non-religious points of view
- reach a justified conclusion.

Summary

Catholics believe that God can communicate with humans through visions. Visions show that God cares for the world and can intervene to help people. There are accounts of visions in the Bible, such as Abraham being told of the birth of his son and the apostles seeing Moses and Elijah at the transfiguration. Visions have continued, such as those of St Joan of Arc and St Bernadette. Visions cause some people to believe in God, but atheists and Humanists think they are just a product of people's imaginations.

Section 1: Arguments for the existence of God

Topic 3.1.3 Miracles as proof of the existence of God

Thinking points

In this topic you need to:
- think about the nature and importance of miracles for Catholics
- consider biblical and non-biblical examples of miracles, including those at Lourdes and John 4:43–54
- understand the reasons why miracles might lead to a belief in God and Catholic responses to non-religious arguments (including atheist and Humanist) which maintain that miracles can be scientifically explained and provide no proof that God exists
- be able to evaluate the importance of miracles and what miracles show about the nature of God for Catholics.

Useful words

Nature miracle – a miracle involving a change in natural objects or forces

What is a miracle?

A miracle is an event which seems to break a law of science and the only explanation for which seems to be God. Miracles are often divided into healing miracles (where someone is healed from an incurable disease, for example Jesus giving a blind man sight) and **nature miracles** (where things like the weather are changed, for example, Jesus walking on water).

Jesus performs a healing miracle.

Biblical miracles

Miracles are recorded in most religions and the Bible records many miracles, such as Moses leading the Israelites across the Red Sea and Jesus restoring sight to the blind, or feeding 5000 people with five loaves and two fishes. Miracles are a major part of Catholic belief. The process of declaring someone a new saint (canonisation) depends on being able to establish two miracles connected with the proposed saint. In the Bible, miracles are linked to people's faith and help faith to grow. As the Catechism says:

> The signs worked by Jesus attest that the Father has sent him. They invite belief in him ... they are not intended to satisfy people's curiosity or desire for magic. (Catechism of the Catholic Church 548)

This Catholic teaching is made plain in St John's account of Jesus healing a royal official's son:

> After the two days he left for Galilee. (Now Jesus himself had pointed out that a prophet has no honour in his own country.) When he arrived in Galilee, the Galileans welcomed him. They had seen all that he had done in Jerusalem at the Passover Festival, for they also had been there.
>
> Once more he visited Cana in Galilee, where he had turned the water into wine. And there was a certain royal official whose son lay sick at Capernaum.
>
> When this man heard that Jesus had arrived in Galilee from Judea, he went to him and begged him to come and heal his son, who was close to death.
>
> 'Unless you people see signs and wonders,' Jesus told him, 'you will never believe.' The royal official said, 'Sir, come down before my child dies.' 'Go,' Jesus replied, 'your son will live.' The man took Jesus at his word and departed. While he was still on the way, his servants met him with the news that his boy was living. When he enquired as to the time when his son got better, they said to him, 'Yesterday, at one in the afternoon, the fever left him.' Then the father realised that this was the exact time at which Jesus had said to him, 'Your son will live.' So he and his whole household believed. This was the second sign Jesus performed after coming from Judea to Galilee. (John 4:43–54)

This miracle shows that:

- Jesus had the power to heal at a distance.
- Miracles lead people to believe – the official and his whole household believed in Jesus because of the miracle.
- Jesus performed miracles as a sign of his true nature (God's Son).

Non-biblical miracles

Catholics believe that God still performs miracles.

On Thursday 11 February 1858, fourteen-year-old Bernadette Soubirous saw a beautiful girl in a niche at a rocky outcrop called Massabielle near Lourdes in France. The apparition beckoned to her, but Bernadette did not move and the girl smiled at her before disappearing. Bernadette later described how she had seen a girl of about her own age and height, clothed in a brilliant and unearthly white robe, with a blue girdle round her waist and a white veil on her head. This was the beginning of eighteen apparitions

Activities

1. How would you define a miracle?
2. If someone told you that they had witnessed a miracle, how would you react?
3. What does the healing of the official's son show about Jesus?

The rocky outcrop in Lourdes as it looks today.

Section 1: Arguments for the existence of God

during the spring and early summer of 1858. During one of these, Bernadette asked the girl her name and she said, 'I am the **immaculate conception**.' During another apparition, the girl led Bernadette to a grotto where a miraculous spring appeared. Since these miraculous appearances of the Virgin Mary, Lourdes has become a great place of pilgrimage for Catholics and many healing miracles have taken place there.

Only a small number of healings are classed as miracles by the authorities at Lourdes. A medical board investigates reported cases and it has to be convinced that the illness could not have improved naturally or by the medication the pilgrims were taking. The cure also has to be complete and not a partial cure. Many more pilgrims report partial cures, an improvement in health, but not complete cures.

The case of Danila Castelli is an example of a certified cure. Mrs Castelli had been receiving repeated surgery and treatment for spontaneously high blood pressure as well as removal of tumours. She entered baths in Lourdes which are fed by spring water in 1989 and felt an incredible sense of well-being afterwards. Mrs Castelli reported a complete cure and the medical board examined her case five times, in 1989, 1992, 1994, 1997 and 2010, certifying the cure.

Many Catholics claim that while not all people who go to Lourdes are cured, the religious experiences they have there give them great inner strength to cope with their illnesses and other problems of life.

Why miracles can lead to a belief in God

Miracles can lead to a belief in God because:

- If a miracle has really happened, it means that God has acted on the earth and that the people witnessing it have had direct contact with God, so he must exist.
- If a miracle has happened, God must have performed the miracle and to perform it, he must exist.
- If an atheist or agnostic witnesses a miracle, their first reaction will be to look for a natural explanation. However, if they cannot find one, they will be led to believe in God.

Atheist and Humanist attitudes to miracles

Atheists and Humanists are very doubtful about whether any miracles have ever happened. They argue that:

- Miracles are supposed to break the laws of nature, but the laws of nature are based on our whole experience of life, so the evidence for a miracle would have to be stronger than our whole experience of life, but it never is.
- The evidence for miracles is always based on the evidence of witnesses, but we know that witnesses can be mistaken about things they think they have seen, or even tell lies about things.
- Any miracles from the past must be suspect because people in the past did not know enough about science to be able to investigate natural explanations for the events they thought had no explanation other than God.
- Many miracles from the past can now be explained, for example the crossing of the Red Sea can be explained by tectonic activity in the Great Rift Valley where it occurred.

A priest at the head of the **Blessed Sacrament procession** to bless the people. Healings when the Blessed Sacrament is present are often reported at Lourdes.

Useful words

Immaculate conception – the Catholic belief that God preserved Mary from original sin from the moment she was conceived

Blessed Sacrament procession – the consecrated host is carried through the streets in a special container, a monstrance

Topic 3.1.3 Miracles as proof of the existence of God

- If God really performed miracles, he would surely use them to help remove hunger and poverty, rather than just helping the odd sick person?
- All religions claim to have miracles, especially Hinduism and Buddhism, so miracles cannot prove anything about any one religion.

Catholic responses

Catholics do not agree with the atheist and Humanist attitudes. They believe that:

- We can rely on the truth of biblical miracles because they are in the Bible, which is authenticated by God,
- We can believe miracles authenticated by the Church such as those used in the process of canonisation because they have been examined scientifically and proven to be true,
- If God used miracles to end hunger and stop war, life would be totally different; God uses miracles as signs of his presence in the world and to strengthen people's faith.

Some Catholics are not sure about stories and claims of miracles. They have a very ordinary and simple faith in a God who is quietly present with people and guides them through life. They believe in biblical miracles, especially the resurrection of Jesus, but are wary of ideas that God constantly suspends the laws of nature to perform miracles.

What miracles show about the nature of God for Catholics

Miracles are important for Catholics because they believe that miracles show them a lot about what God is like. Catholics believe that miracles show them that:

- God is active in the world he has made, as shown in the feeding of the 5000 and the stilling of the storm miracles performed by Jesus.
- God cares for the people in his world and uses miracles to help strengthen people's faith, as seen when the father of an epileptic boy said to Jesus, 'Lord I do believe, help me overcome my unbelief' (Mark 9:24) and Jesus answered by healing his son.
- God's nature is love and so he sends miracles out of love, as Jesus did in the raising of Lazarus because when the people saw the miracle they said, 'See how he [Jesus] loved him [Lazarus]' (John 11:36).

Activities

1. Why do you think Lourdes is important for Catholics?
2. What do you think about the atheist and Humanist attitudes to miracles?
3. Why do you think miracles are important for Catholics?

Practice questions

c) Explain two beliefs about God's nature which Catholics believe are shown by miracles. In your answer you must refer to a source of wisdom and authority.

d) 'Miracles prove that God exists.' Evaluate this statement considering arguments for and against. In your answer you should:
- refer to Catholic points of view
- refer to different Christian or non-religious points of view
- reach a justified conclusion.

Summary

A miracle is an event that breaks a law of science and can only be explained by God. There are many miracles recorded in the Bible, but the Church sees the miracles of Jesus (such as the healing of an official's son) as signs that Jesus came from the Father. There are also non-biblical miracles such as those which have occurred at Lourdes in the place where St Bernadette was visited by the Virgin Mary. Miracles can lead people to believe in God, but atheists and Humanists would say that miracles cannot prove anything because no one can prove they have happened.

Section 1: Arguments for the existence of God

Topic 3.1.4 Catholic attitudes to religious experience

Thinking points

In this topic you need to:
- think about the nature of religious experience and why not all religious experiences are approved by the Church, including reference to Catechism of the Catholic Church 66–67
- understand the use of religious experience to prove God's existence
- consider non-religious (including atheist and Humanist) arguments that religious experiences do not provide proof that God exists and Catholic responses to them
- be able to evaluate different attitudes to religious experience.

What is religious experience?

Religious experience is an event that people feel gives them direct contact with God. The clearest types of religious experience are visions and miracles, but these are given to very few people (although you can use them for answering exam questions about religious experience). Other types of religious experience are:

Conversion

Conversion is the word used to describe an experience of God which is so great that the person experiencing it wants to change their life and commit themselves to God in a special way. It can also be used to describe an experience which causes someone to change their religion or change from agnosticism or atheism to belief in God. It is sometimes called a **regenerative experience** because it gives a feeling of being 'born again'.

If someone has a conversion experience, that will lead them to believe in God because they will feel that God is calling them to do something for him. When St Paul was on the road to Damascus (Acts 9:1–19) and Jesus spoke to him from a bright light in the sky, telling him to become a Christian, the experience was so powerful that Paul decided to convert to Christianity. Many Evangelical Protestants and Pentecostals have a conversion experience before they decide to be baptised as adults.

A good example of a conversion experience happened during the Civil War in Lebanon. Raymond Nader was a commander in the Christian militia who led the fighting against Muslim militias. On a cold November night in 1994, Mr Nader went to pray at the shrine of St Charbel. Suddenly, the night became warmer and Mr Nader felt surrounded by a great light. He reached out to touch the light and his arm was burned by what he, and the Church authorities, believed was the presence of St Charbel. The vision made him give up his work in the militia to work for Télé Lumière, the only Christian television station in the Middle East. Télé Lumière and Mr Nader are now dedicated to spiritual peace, the defence of human rights and dignity as a way of challenging the violence and horror of conflict in the Middle East.

Useful words

Conversion – an experience which changes a person's life or religion

Regenerative experience – a conversion experience giving the feeling of being 'born again'

Activities

1. Look at the conversion experience of Raymond Nader. Do you think he could have been an atheist after this experience?
2. Look at the photo of prayer. Why might prayer be considered a religious experience?

Prayer is a religious experience for many Catholics.

Topic 3.1.4 Catholic attitudes to religious experience

Numinous experience

The most common religious experience is known as the **numinous**. This is the name given to a feeling of the presence of God. When people are in a religious building, in a beautiful place or looking up at the stars on a clear night, they may be filled with the awareness that there is something greater than them, which they feel to be God. It is often described as an experience of the **transcendent** (something going beyond human experience and existing outside the material world).

If someone has a numinous experience, it may lead them to believe in God because the experience will make them feel that God is real. For example, Father Yves Dubois has had numinous experiences while praying before a statue of Our Lady:

> Twice I have experienced the certainty of the presence of the Mother of God, which was an awareness of purity, holiness and love unlike anything I have ever known. Her holiness would have been frightening, but for the strong feeling of love and compassion. (Yves Dubois, quoted in Denise Crush, Carol Miles and Margaret Stylianides, Christians in Britain Today, Hodder, 1991)

Prayer

Prayer is a religious experience for many Catholics. The Church teaches that human beings are born searching for God and that prayer is a way to complete the search. Prayer is the way to encounter God; it is a gift from God because God is waiting to hear human prayers. Although people may not always know how to pray properly, the Church teaches that if prayers come from the heart they are acceptable to God and allow communion with God. The importance of prayer for Catholics can be seen in the fact that one quarter of the Catechism is about Christian prayer. There are many different types of prayer, from the formal prayers offered in worship, such as the prayers said during Mass, to the very informal prayers where a believer makes their own prayer to God in their own private place or as they go about their daily activities.

If the person praying to God feels that God is listening to the prayer, then they have a religious experience through prayer and are sure that God exists. Perhaps the biggest religious experience anyone can have is when their private prayer is answered, for example when someone prays for a sick loved one to get better and they recover. During prayer, a person may experience a sense of joy and peace or the closeness of God, or not feel anything in particular. The desire to pray is in itself a religious experience. Christians believe no prayer is ever wasted, although prayer is answered in God's time and on God's terms. As Jesus prayed, 'thy will be done'.

The teaching of the Church on religious experience

Although religious experiences are important for Catholics, the Catholic Church teaches that such experiences can only be regarded as genuine as long as they do not contradict the beliefs of the Church. Religious experiences strengthen people's faith and prove the existence of God for Catholics, but if they are used to make any other claims about the faith, they need to be confirmed as genuine by the Church.

Activity

Look at the religious experiences of Father Dubois. Do you think he could have doubted God's existence after these experiences?

Useful words

Numinous – the feeling of the presence of something greater than you

Transcendent – something going beyond human experience and existing outside the material world

> The Christian economy, therefore, since it is the new and definitive Covenant, will never pass away; and no new public revelation is to be expected before the glorious manifestation of our Lord Jesus Christ ... Throughout the ages, there have been so-called 'private' revelations, some of which have been recognised by the authority of the Church. They do not belong, however, to the deposit of faith. It is not their role to improve or complete Christ's definitive Revelation, but to help live more fully by it in a certain period of history. Guided by the Magisterium of the Church, the sensus fidelium [sense of faith] knows how to discern and welcome in these revelations whatever constitutes an authentic call of Christ or his saints to the Church. Christian faith cannot accept 'revelations' that claim to surpass or correct the Revelation of which Christ is the fulfilment, as is the case in certain non-Christian religions and also in certain recent sects which base themselves on such 'revelations'. (Catechism of the Catholic Church 66–67)

Section 1: Arguments for the existence of God

For Catholics, Jesus Christ is the fullest revelation of God.

Religious experience as a proof of God's existence

People who believe that religious experience is genuine also believe that it is a proof for God's existence because:

- For people to have a numinous experience, something must be causing the experience and the only possible cause of such an experience would be God, so God must exist.
- If a miracle happens, then all the laws of science have been broken (for example, someone feeding 5000 people with two loaves and five fishes), and the only explanation for such an event is God, so God must exist to cause the miracle.
- If a person has such a vivid religious experience that it converts them, and totally changes their life, then God must have caused the experience and so God must exist.
- If a person prays and their prayer is answered (for example, when someone prays for a sick loved one to get better and they recover), then God must have answered the prayer and so God must exist.

Atheist and Humanist attitudes to religious experience

Atheists and Humanists do not believe in God and so they do not believe that religious experiences come from God. They argue that religious experiences are just experiences that some people interpret as being religious. Other than miracles, religious experiences have no existence except in people's minds. That means they cannot be investigated scientifically because there is nothing to test. A religious experience might mean something to the person who experiences it, but can mean nothing to anyone else. If religious experiences were true, they argue, then everyone would have them. For example, everyone in the church where someone had a numinous experience would have the same numinous experience.

Activities

1. Read the extract from the Catechism of the Catholic Church 66–67 on page 307. How should Catholics decide whether a religious experience is genuine?
2. Look at the picture of Jesus teaching. Why must genuine religious experiences fit in with the teaching of Jesus?
3. 'It's all in the mind!' How would you try to answer an atheist or a Humanist who thinks that religious experience is imaginary or the result of mental disturbance?

Atheists and Humanists believe that religious experience does not prove God's existence because:

- A numinous experience is caused by people's surroundings, whether a church or the stars, or their own mental state. It may have nothing to do with God, but to prove God's existence everyone in the same place at the same time would have to have the same experience.
- They believe that all miracles can be explained, for example Jesus may not have been dead when he was taken down from the cross and so he just recovered rather than rising from the dead; and so they cannot prove anything.
- A conversion experience is only in that person's head and cannot prove anything to anyone else.
- There are more unanswered prayers than answered ones, so the unanswered prayers prove God does not exist.
- Followers of all religions claim to have religious experiences, so they cannot prove the truth of any one religion.

Catholic responses

The Catholic Church teaches that there is an innate spiritual sense in each person, and that even though a person does not believe in God, they will have some awareness of the mystery of life, and of humans being special and of value. The Church teaches that when non-believers seek peace, justice and meaning, they are seeking God without realising it:

> *The desire for God is written in the human heart, because man is created by God and for God; and God never ceases to draw man to himself.* (Catechism of the Catholic Church 27)

Based on this view, everyone has had some sort of religious experience, they have just interpreted it differently.

Many Catholics would agree that people's religious experiences do not prove the truth of their religion, that is the job of revelations, but they think religious experiences do prove the existence of God.

Prayer is often quiet, peaceful and still.

Practice questions

c Explain two beliefs about God's nature which Catholics believe are shown by miracles. In your answer you must refer to a source of wisdom and authority.

d 'Religious experiences prove that God exists.' Evaluate this statement considering arguments for and against. In your answer you should:
- refer to Catholic points of view
- refer to different Christian or non-religious points of view
- reach a justified conclusion.

Summary

Religious experiences are any events which give people direct contact with God. There are several types of religious experience, such as visions, miracles, conversion, the numinous (a feeling of the presence of something greater than you) and prayer. The Church teaches that religious experiences strengthen people's faith and prove that God exists, since if God contacts people he must therefore exist. Atheists and Humanists think that religious experiences are just a product of people's imagination or mental states and so cannot prove God's existence.

Section 1: Arguments for the existence of God

Topic 3.1.5 The design argument

Thinking points

In this topic you need to:
- think about the classical design argument for the existence of God
- understand its use by Catholics as a philosophical argument for the existence of God
- consider understandings about what the design argument shows about the nature of God for Catholics, including Romans 1:18–24
- think about Catholic responses to non-religious (including atheist and Humanist) arguments against the design argument as evidence for the existence of God
- be able to evaluate the design argument as evidence for the existence of God.

Useful words

Design – when things are connected and seem to have a purpose, for example the eye is designed for seeing

What is design?

Any complex mechanism is designed for a purpose. **Design** involves things working together according to a plan to produce something that was intended. If you look at a car, you can see that the fuel powers an engine, which turns a shaft, which turns the wheels, and so makes a self-propelling vehicle that allows people to travel further and more easily. A look at any part of the car makes you think that the car has been designed.

St Thomas Aquinas (1225–74) was a Dominican friar and a theologian. He worked out five ways to argue for the existence of God and the design argument was one of these.

Many philosophers, perhaps starting with the ancient Greek philosopher Plato, have used the idea that the universe seems to be designed and so must have a designer to prove God's existence. The great Catholic philosopher St Thomas Aquinas also used this idea, but its classic form is that put forward by William Paley in *Natural Theology*, published in 1802.

The classic design argument for God's existence

Paley argued that if you were walking in an uninhabited place and came across a watch, you could not say it had been put there by chance. The complexity of the watch's mechanism would make you say it must have had a designer. The universe is a far more complex mechanism than a watch; if a watch needs a designer then the universe must definitely need a designer. The only being that could design the universe would be God, so therefore God must exist.

Modern forms of the design argument

Many Catholic philosophers begin the design argument by pointing out the features of the world and arguing that they appear to have been designed:

- The universe works according to laws. The laws of gravity, electricity, magnetism, motion, bonding, gases, and so on, all involve complex things working together.
- DNA seems to be another piece of evidence of design in the world. DNA is a nucleic acid which forms the material of all living organisms. The structure of DNA and its formation of templates seem to indicate a design or blueprint for the structure of organisms.
- Some also see evidence of design in the process of **evolution**, where complex life forms develop from simple ones.
- They also see evidence of design in the beauties of nature, where sunsets, mountains and oceans appear to have beauty which an artist would have to spend a long time designing.

Having shown that there is plenty of evidence that the universe has been designed, they then argue that:

- Anything that has been designed needs a designer.
- If the world has been designed, the world must have a designer.
- The only possible designer of something as beautiful and complex as the world would be God.
- Therefore the appearance of design in the world proves that God exists.

This argument shows how the appearance of design in the world can lead people who are not sure about God's existence to believe that he exists; and how it will give extra reasons for believing in God to those who already believe.

Useful words

Evolution – the idea that life forms change over time (humans have developed from single-celled organisms)

Activities

1. Do you think a human eye needs a designer in the same way as a car?
2. Is there as much evidence for the universe being designed as there is for a watch being designed?

Section 1: Arguments for the existence of God

Roger Bacon was a thirteenth-century Franciscan friar who helped to build the scientific method based on observation and measurement. He argued that this was possible because God had created the universe and thus it had order.

Why the design argument is important for Catholic beliefs about the nature of God

Catholics believe that the design argument is important because it shows that:

- God's existence can be demonstrated by looking at his creation:

    the existence of God the Creator can be known with certainty through his works by the light of human reason. (Catechism of the Catholic Church 286)

    As St Paul said,

    Ever since the creation of the world his eternal power and divine nature, invisible though they are, have been understood and seen through the things he has made. (Romans 1:20)

- God wants humans to use their reason to understand the world as well as the revelation he has given to the Church:

    since what may be known about God is plain to them, because God has made it plain to them. (Romans 1:19)

- The universe works on fixed, logical principles designed by God which have enabled humans to make all the discoveries science has made.

- God is the Creator of the universe and keeps it in existence.

Atheist and Humanist rejection of the argument from design

Atheists and Humanists do not believe in God and they think that the design argument does not prove God's existence because:

- The argument ignores the evidence of lack of design in the universe, for example volcanoes, earthquakes, hurricanes, diseases.
- All the evidence for design can be explained by science without needing to consider God. Science says that matter is eternal and that the universe began when this matter exploded. The solar system came out of the explosion, and the nature of the earth allowed life to develop through evolution.
- The design argument does not refer to the existence of dinosaurs, which must have been a part of design, but no one thinks they could have been part of a design plan for the world.
- The argument only proves that the universe has a designer, but this is not necessarily God. The designer could be many gods, an evil creator, or a god who used this universe as a trial run so that he could create a better one.

Catholic responses

The Catholic Church believes that the arguments of atheists and Humanists are based on the belief that the universe has come about through chance combinations of particles, whereas the Church sees the order of the universe as a sign of a creator.

The Church argues that believing the universe came about by chance takes just as much, if not more faith than believing the universe came about through the design of God. In other words, it is far less likely that the universe came about through random chance than through the design of an almighty, loving God. Faith is about trust; trust in what cannot be absolutely proven. The Church accepts that there is no absolute proof of a creator, but also argues that there is no proof that there is not. Proof of God's existence is an open question and one which the Church feels comes down in favour of an intelligent creator.

> *Now faith is the assurance of things hoped for, the conviction of things not seen ... By faith we understand that the worlds were prepared by the word of God, so that what is seen was made from things that are not visible.* (Hebrews 11:1–3)

Practice questions

c Explain two reasons why Catholics believe the design argument is important. In your answer you must refer to a source of wisdom and authority.

d 'The design argument proves that God exists.' Evaluate this statement considering arguments for and against. In your answer you should:
- refer to Catholic points of view
- refer to different Christian or non-religious points of view
- reach a justified conclusion.

Activities

1. Why do dinosaurs cause problems for the design argument?
2. Do you think the universe could have come about by random chance?

Summary

The design argument claims that the universe seems to be designed, and that anything that is designed must have a designer. Therefore, God must exist because only God could have designed the universe. Atheists and Humanists claim the argument does not work because things like volcanoes and earthquakes show a lack of design, and the argument does not prove the existence of God, only there might be a designer who could possibly even be evil.

Section 1: Arguments for the existence of God

Topic 3.1.6 The cosmological argument

Thinking points

In this topic you need to:
- think about the cosmological argument for the existence of God (including Thomas Aquinas' First Three Ways) and its use by Catholics as a philosophical argument for the existence of God
- consider understandings of the nature and importance of what the cosmological argument shows about the nature of God for Catholics
- understand Catholic responses to non-religious (including atheist and Humanist) arguments against the cosmological argument
- be able to evaluate the cosmological argument as evidence for the existence of God.

What is a cosmological argument?

A cosmological argument is one which argues that God exists from a philosophical study of the origin and nature of the universe.

St Thomas Aquinas put forward the classic form of the argument in the first three of his ways to prove God's existence in his work **Summa Theologica**.

Way 1: the way of motion

Aquinas argued that things in the universe are in motion, but nothing can move unless it is moved by something else: 'But this cannot go on to infinity because then there would be no first mover, and, consequently, no other mover ... Therefore it is necessary to arrive at a first mover, moved by no other; and this everyone understands to be God.'

Way 2: the way of causation

Next, Aquinas argued that everything seems to have cause and there is no example of anything causing itself. However, there must be a 'first efficient cause' otherwise there could not be the effect of the universe; and this first efficient cause is given the name God.

Way 3: the way of contingency

All material things are **contingent**, that is their existence is not necessary and at one time they did not exist. However, if everything is contingent, then at one time nothing existed; but things do exist, therefore there must be a non-contingent being whose existence is necessary so it has always been in existence; and everyone would call this God.

Useful words

Summa Theologica – Thomas Aquinas' major book, written in 1265–74

Contingent – the fact that something does not have to exist, it could either be or not be

Activities

1. Which of Aquinas' Three Ways do you think is most convincing?
2. Look at the photo of the line of railway wagons. How do you think Aquinas could have related these trucks to the cosmological argument?

This line of railway wagons appears to be moving on its own.

Modern form of the cosmological argument

- Cause and effect seem to be a basic feature of the world. Whatever we do has an effect. If I do my homework, I will please my parents. If I do not do my homework, I will annoy my parents.

- Modern science developed through looking at causes and effects and, in particular, looking for single causes of an effect, for example increases in heart rate. Just as my parents' happiness may be caused by things other than my doing my homework, so the increase in someone's heart rate may be caused by things other than exercise. So, when scientists try to discover the cause of an increase in heart rate, they try to reduce all the variables so that a single cause can be identified. Science seems to show that when investigated sufficiently, any effect has a cause and any cause has an effect.

- Anything caused to exist must be caused to exist by something else. To cause your own existence, you would have to exist before you exist, which is nonsense.

- You cannot keep going back with causes because in any causal chain you have to have a beginning, for example you have to have water to produce ice. So, if the universe has no first cause, then there would be no universe, but as there is a universe, there must be a first cause.

- The only possible first cause of the universe is God, therefore God must exist.

> **Activity**
> What could explain someone's heart rate increasing other than exercise?

The importance of the cosmological argument for Catholic beliefs about the nature of God

The cosmological argument is important because it shows Catholics that:

- God is the origin of everything: he is the unmoved mover, the first cause, the non-contingent being.

- God is not another thing within the universe. He is both within and beyond it: a different order entirely. God is 'being', that which allows anything to be, and not floating around as a 'super thing' somewhere. God is the source of all being and so has no beginning or end. God is infinite and eternal. The laws of cause and effect stop with this material universe.

- God is a mystery, more a question than an answer. Human beings can only grasp so much about God's being and nature:

> *God is infinitely greater than all his works: 'You have set your glory above the heavens'. Indeed God's greatness is unsearchable.*
> (Catechism of the Catholic Church 300)

Atheistic and Humanist arguments against the cosmological argument

Atheists and Humanists think the argument from causation does not prove that God exists because:

- If everything needs a cause then God must also need a cause. Why should the process have to stop with God?

- It is possible that matter itself is eternal and so was never created. That would mean that there would be no need for a first cause because the process of causes could go back forever.

Section 1: Arguments for the existence of God

Activities

1. What makes God different from the universe?
2. What do you think of the atheist response to the cosmological argument?

Useful words

Big Bang – the beginning of the universe from a 'cosmic egg'

- Just because everything in the universe needs an explanation does not mean the universe itself needs an explanation. The universe could just have been there forever.
- Even if there was a first cause, unmoved mover or non-contingent being, it would not have to be the Christian God, it could be the God of any religion.
- There is no need for a first cause, unmoved mover or non-contingent being to be good. It could be evil, a mixture of good and evil, and so on.

Catholic responses

Although the Catholic Church recognises the atheist position, it believes:

- To say that the **Big Bang** and the entire universe 'just happened' is more unbelievable than to say that it was designed and created by God.
- The universe is too vast and complex, and works according to too many laws to have just appeared by chance. There must be a reason for the universe being here.
- Humans are preciously unique individuals with an immortal soul. The Church teaches that the immortal soul cannot be pinned down, observed or measured by science. The Church also teaches that our immortal soul is a sign that the universe is more than the material and that it is much deeper than physical laws, and it can only be explained by God.

Practice questions

c) Explain two reasons why Catholics believe the cosmological argument is important. In your answer you must refer to a source of wisdom and authority.

d) 'The cosmological argument proves that God exists.' Evaluate this statement considering arguments for and against. In your answer you should:
- refer to Catholic points of view
- refer to different Christian or non-religious points of view
- reach a justified conclusion.

Summary

Aquinas used the Way of Motion, the First Cause Way and the Way of Contingency as cosmological arguments to argue about the nature of the universe to prove the existence of God. Everything seeming to have a cause makes people think that the universe must also have a cause, and the only possible cause of the universe is God, so God must exist. Atheists and Humanists reject this argument because they think the sequence of cause and effect could go on forever. However, the argument shows to Catholics that God is greater than the universe he created.

Topic 3.1.7 The problem of evil and suffering

The nature of evil and suffering
The world is full of evil and suffering but these can take two forms.

Moral evil
Moral evil is suffering that is caused by humans misusing their free will (the human faculty of making choices). It is always possible to choose to do something good or something evil. Humans choosing to do evil usually cause moral suffering. War, rape, murder and burglary are clear examples of moral suffering. Catholics often call acts of moral evil sins because they are against what God wants humans to do (as revealed to them, for example, in the Ten Commandments).

Natural suffering
Natural suffering is suffering that has not been caused by humans. Earthquakes, floods, volcanoes, drought, tsunamis, hurricanes, tornadoes, cancers and so on are not actually caused by humans, but they result in massive amounts of human suffering.

A Japanese town two days after a powerful tsunami triggered by an earthquake hit the country's east coast in March 2011.

Thinking points
In this topic you need to:
- think about the issues raised by the existence of suffering and God as all-loving
- think about the issues it raises for Catholics about the nature of God, including Isaiah 45
- consider how the problem and its basis as a philosophical argument may lead some people to examine and others to reject their belief in God
- be able to evaluate the problems that evil and suffering cause for Catholic belief.

Useful words
Moral evil – suffering caused by actions done by humans
Natural suffering – suffering which is caused by nature and has nothing to do with humans

Activities
1. What reasons might a burglar have for his actions?
2. Look at the photo. Who could be blamed for the massive suffering caused by the Japanese tsunami?

Section 1: Arguments for the existence of God

Useful words

Omnipotent – the belief that God is all-powerful
Omni-benevolent – the belief that God is all-good
Omniscient – the belief that God knows everything that has happened and everything that is going to happen

Why evil and suffering raise problems for Catholic beliefs about the nature of God

Catholics believe that God is **omnipotent** (all-powerful):

We believe that his might is universal, for God who created everything also rules everything and can do everything. (Catechism of the Catholic Church 268)

But if God is all-powerful, he must be able to remove evil and suffering from the world.

Catholics believe that God is **omni-benevolent** (all-good):

God's very being is love. By sending his only Son … God has revealed his innermost secret. God himself is an eternal exchange of love. (Catechism of the Catholic Church 221)

So God must want to remove evil and suffering from the world because they cause so much unhappiness.

Catholics believe that God is **omniscient** (knows everything that is going to happen) and everything that happens is part of his divine plan:

By his providence, God protects and governs all things which he has made reaching mightily from one end of the earth to the other, and ordering all things well. (Catechism of the Catholic Church 302)

This means that God must have known all the evil and suffering which would come from creating the universe in the way he did. Therefore, he should have created the universe in a different way to avoid evil and suffering.

These beliefs are also seen in the Bible, especially in Isaiah chapter 45:

- which shows God's omnipotence:

    I will go before you and will level the mountains; I will break down gates of bronze and cut through bars of iron. (Isaiah 45:2)

    I form the light and create darkness, I bring prosperity and create disaster; I, the Lord, do all these things. (Isaiah 45:7)

    It is I who made the earth and created mankind on it. My own hands stretched out the heavens; I marshalled their starry hosts. (Isaiah 45:12)

- and God's omniscience:

    Declare what is to be, present it— let them take counsel together. Who foretold this long ago, who declared it from the distant past? Was it not I, the Lord? And there is no God apart from me, a righteous God and a Saviour; there is none but me. (Isaiah 45:21)

- and God's omni-benevolence:

    But Israel will be saved by the Lord with an everlasting salvation; you will never be put to shame or disgraced, to ages everlasting. (Isaiah 45:17)

It follows that, if God exists, with the nature Catholics believe he has, there should be no evil or suffering in the world. As there is evil and suffering in the world, either God is not omnipotent, or God is not omni-benevolent, or God is not omniscient, or God does not exist.

Activities

1. Find out about the Holocaust, then look at the photo on page 319 and explain why some of the soldiers might have lost their faith in God.
2. What problems do evil and suffering cause for Catholic beliefs about the nature of God?

Topic 3.1.7 The problem of evil and suffering

Why this leads some Christians to examine or reject their belief in God

Catholics believe that God is omnipotent, omni-benevolent and omniscient. So, the existence of evil and suffering challenges their beliefs about God, and as these beliefs come from the Bible and the magisterium it causes Catholics to examine their beliefs. This especially happens when Catholics come into contact with evil or suffering personally. So, if they experience the suffering caused by a natural disaster such as an earthquake, or if their child dies from a disease, they begin to think again about their beliefs.

Some people cannot believe that a good God would have designed a world that contained natural evils. They find it easier to believe that natural disasters are a result of the earth being formed by accident from the Big Bang and so they question or reject God's existence.

People find it hard to believe in a God who allows humans to cause so much evil and suffering when he could stop it if he wanted to. If God exists, he must have known what Adolf Hitler was going to do, so why not intervene before so many people suffered throughout the Second World War and the **Holocaust**? The existence of this suffering may mean that God does not exist.

However, Isaiah chapter 45 also warns that God has reasons for his actions which humans are not really in a position to challenge:

> *Woe to those who quarrel with their Maker, those who are nothing but potsherds [fragments of pottery] among the potsherds on the ground. Does the clay say to the potter, 'What are you making?' Does your work say, 'The potter has no hands'?* (Isaiah 45:9)

This is dealt with in the next topic.

A British soldier (left) guards Fritz Klein, the doctor of the Bergen-Belsen Nazi concentration camp, standing in front of a mass burial site for dead prisoners.

Useful words

Holocaust – the mass murder of Jews by the Nazis in the Second World War

Practice questions

c Explain two reasons why evil and suffering in the world cause problems for Catholic beliefs about the nature of God.

d 'Evil and suffering in the world are not the fault of God.' Evaluate this statement considering arguments for and against. In your response you should:
- refer to Christian teachings
- refer to non-religious points of view
- reach a justified conclusion.

Summary

Catholics believe that God is all-loving and all-powerful, so there should be no evil and suffering in the world that he made. A good God should not want evil and suffering to happen. A powerful God ought to be able to get rid of such things, yet they still exist. This causes some Catholics to examine their beliefs and might even make them wonder whether God exists.

Section 1: Arguments for the existence of God

Topic 3.1.8 Solutions to the problem of evil and suffering

Thinking points

In this topic you need to:
- think about how Christians respond to the problem of suffering biblically, theoretically and practically
- consider Psalms, including reference to Psalm 119, Job and free will (St Augustine) as a way for humans to develop (St Irenaeus)
- understand prayer and charity as solutions to the problem of evil and suffering
- be able to evaluate the success of these solutions.

Useful words

Holiness – the state of being very moral and spiritual
Psalms – a book of the Old Testament containing 150 sacred songs
Theodicy – a philosophical justification of God allowing evil and suffering
Free will – the idea that human beings are free to make their own choices

Activities

1. Make a list of the good and bad points of the biblical responses.
2. Do you think Psalm 119 answers the problem of why evil and suffering exist?

Biblical responses to the problem of evil and suffering

Many Christians believe that there is no point in worrying about the problem of evil because humans cannot understand God's reasons for doing things.

This view is based on the Book of Job in the Old Testament. Job was a sinless man who worshipped God faithfully. However, Satan argued with God that Job only worshipped him because God had given him a good life and that if his good life disappeared he would then stop worshipping God. God did not believe this and so allowed Satan to remove Job's good life and afflict him with terrible diseases. Job asked God why this was happening to him and demanded that God should speak to him directly. However, when Job came face to face with God and was presented with his greatness and **holiness**, he realised that God is so great, humans have no right to question him. God must have a reason for allowing evil and suffering, but people cannot understand the reason.

Christians often combine this response with the one shown in the Book of **Psalms** in the Old Testament. The Psalms show that suffering is intended to be a part of life and many of the Psalms tell of good religious people suffering, but the Psalms show that life is more than suffering. The other side of suffering is joy and in the Psalms suffering and joy go side by side. For example, the Psalms also show that suffering can bring believers to a deeper knowledge of God, as shown in this Psalm:

> Teach me knowledge and good judgement, for I trust your commands. Before I was afflicted I went astray, but now I obey your word. You are good, and what you do is good; teach me your decrees. Though the arrogant have smeared me with lies, I keep your precepts with all my heart. Their hearts are callous and unfeeling, but I delight in your law. It was good for me to be afflicted so that I might learn your decrees. (Psalm 119:66–71)

Having God's help and strength when suffering helps Catholics to cope with the problem.

Theoretical responses to evil and suffering

The term used for philosophical arguments about God and evil is **theodicy**, from the Greek words meaning 'to justify God'.

Many Catholics respond by using an argument from St Augustine. He claimed that evil and suffering are not God's fault because, according to Genesis 1, God created humans in his image, which means he created them with **free will**. Catholics believe that God wanted people to be free to decide whether to believe in him or not; he did not want to force them to worship him. However, to be free means to be free to do either good or evil. So, when God created free people, he could not create people who always did good because such people would not be free. Creating free people has brought evil and suffering into the world, but the evil and suffering are a problem caused by humans misusing their free will, and so not God's fault.

Topic 3.1.8 Solutions to the problem of evil and suffering

Another Catholic response is based on the teachings of St Irenaeus, who argued that the evil and suffering in this life are not a problem because they are part of a plan in which those who suffer will be rewarded by eternal paradise after they die. Most Christians claim that this life is a preparation for paradise. If people are to improve their souls they need to face evil and suffering in order to become good, kind and loving. They claim that the evil and suffering of this life are things that God cannot remove if he is going to give people the chance to become good people. But, in the end, he will show his omni-benevolence and omnipotence by rewarding them in heaven. This is often known as the '**vale of soul making**' response. God created this world as a place for people to develop their souls.

Catholics often connect this to the belief that good can come out of evil. For example, in the evil of the Holocaust, Maximilian Kolbe, a **Franciscan friar**, was arrested and sent to **Auschwitz**. Here, he continued his priestly ministry discreetly, hearing many confessions and smuggling in bread and wine for Mass. When a married man with children was to be executed, Maximilian offered to take his place. He was canonised in 1982, when the man whose life he saved was still living and able to attend the ceremony in Rome.

Maximilian Kolbe (1894–1941) celebrated in a stained-glass window of the Basilica of the Assumption of the Virgin Mary in Marija Bistrica, Croatia.

Practical responses to evil and suffering

Catholic Christians believe that they should respond to evil and suffering in practical ways. The life of Jesus in the Gospels shows that even God's own Son had to suffer, and that Jesus commanded his followers to respond to suffering by helping those who suffer. All Christians believe that they should respond to the problem by helping those who suffer and trusting in God for the answer to the problem. The New Testament teaches Christians that Jesus regarded evil and suffering as things to be fought against. Jesus healed the sick, fed the hungry, challenged those who were evil and even raised the dead. Christians feel that they should follow the example of Jesus and fight against evil and suffering by prayer and charity.

Prayer

Christians believe that prayer is a very powerful way of responding to the problem. They believe that by praying for those who suffer, God will ensure that they get the right type of relief for their suffering. Such prayers are called **intercessory prayers** and all Christian services include prayers of intercession asking God to help those who suffer from poverty, sickness, famine, war and so on. Christians believe that the power of prayer can be seen in its results. Catholic Christians would see this especially in the prayers offered during pilgrimage to Lourdes, and Protestant Christians in the healing services held in many churches.

Useful words

Vale of soul making – the idea that God gave people this life to make their souls good enough for heaven
Franciscan – a member of a religious order that follows the teachings and spiritual disciplines of St Francis of Assisi
Friar – a member of a religious order who does not own property and who has to either work or beg to earn their living
Auschwitz – a Nazi Second World War concentration camp in Poland where at least 1.1 million Jews died
Intercessory prayers – prayers asking God's help for other people

Activity

Do you think Maximilian Kolbe deserves to be a saint?

321

Section 1: Arguments for the existence of God

Activities

1. Make a list of the good and bad points of the theoretical responses.
2. Make a list of the good and bad points of the practical responses to evil and suffering.
3. Look at the photo of a food bank. Why do you think many food banks are run by churches?

Charity

Many Christians believe that the best way of responding to evil and suffering is to try to overcome them in practical ways. Jesus did not just pray and preach, he healed the sick, brought sight to the blind, fed the hungry. Christians believe that they should follow Jesus' example and respond to evil in a practical way. As a result, many Christians try to overcome evil and suffering by becoming doctors, nurses or social workers, so that they can help to reduce the amount of suffering in the world. Christians have also founded charities to help to eliminate suffering, such as Christian Aid and CAFOD to help to ease the suffering of those in less economically developed countries. In the UK, Christian churches organise food banks, campaigns to remove child poverty, charities to help refugees, groups promoting racial harmony and so on.

A church helping in collecting donated food for distribution by a food bank.

Summary

Catholics respond to the problem of evil and suffering by:

- accepting the teaching of the Bible in Job that God has a reason for suffering but humans cannot understand it
- accepting the Bible teaching in Psalms that suffering and joy are an essential part of life
- claiming that evil and suffering are the fault of humans misusing their free will (St Augustine)
- claiming that evil and suffering are part of a test to prepare people for heaven (St Irenaeus)
- praying for those who suffer
- helping those who suffer.

Practice questions

c) Explain two ways in which Catholics respond to the problem of evil and suffering. In your answer you must refer to a source of wisdom and authority.

d) 'Evil and suffering are not a problem for Catholics.' Evaluate this statement considering arguments for and against. In your response you should:
- refer to Catholic teachings
- refer to different Christian or non-religious points of view
- reach a justified conclusion.

How to answer questions

a) Outline three things the design argument shows about the nature of God for Catholics. [3]

One thing it shows is that God's existence can be demonstrated by looking at his creation. It also shows that God is a God of love who wants humans to use their reason to understand the world as well as the revelation he has given to the Church. Thirdly, it shows that God is the creator of the universe and keeps it in existence.

A high mark answer because three things the design argument shows about God's nature are clearly outlined.

b) Explain two ways Catholics respond to the problem of suffering. [4]

Catholic Christians believe that they should respond to evil and suffering in practical ways. Jesus commanded his followers to respond to suffering by helping those who suffer. Jesus healed the sick, fed the hungry, challenged those who were evil and even raised the dead, and Catholics should follow the example of Jesus.

Another response of Catholic Christians is to pray for those who suffer, so that God will ensure that they get the right type of relief for their suffering. Such prayers are called intercessory prayers and all Christian services include prayers of intercession.

A high mark answer because two correct ways of Catholics responding are clearly explained.

c) Explain two reasons why miracles are important for Catholics. In your answer you must refer to a source of wisdom and authority. [5]

Miracles are important for Catholics because they show Catholics a lot about what God is like. For example, they show that God cares for the people in his world and uses miracles to help strengthen people's faith, as seen when the father of an epileptic boy said to Jesus, 'Lord I do believe, help me overcome my unbelief' (Mark 9:24) and Jesus answered by healing his son.

They are also important because they prove that God exists. After all, if a miracle happens, then all the laws of science have been broken (for example, someone feeding 5000 people with two loaves and five fishes), and the only explanation for such an event is God, so God must exist to cause the miracle.

A high mark answer because two correct reasons are given and each reason is developed with a reference to the Bible and the actions of Jesus, which are both sources of authority for Catholics.

d) 'Visions prove the existence of God.' Evaluate this statement considering arguments for and against. In your response you should:
- refer to Christian points of view
- refer to different Christian points of view
- reach a justified conclusion. [12 marks + 3 spelling, punctuation and grammar (SPaG) marks]

Some people might agree with this because a vision like that of St Paul on the road to Damascus is in the Bible and they believe the Bible is the Word of God so it must be true. But if the vision is true it must have come from God and for that to happen, God must exist. They might also think that the results of a vision, such as St Joan of Arc, being able to lead an army mean the vision must have come from God and so God must exist. Or they might think that the details of the vision, such as St Bernadette and the immaculate conception, prove it came from God so God must exist.

[Continued]

Section 1: Arguments for the existence of God

Atheists and Humanists do not believe in God and so they think visions are not real. They believe that visions can be explained by mental illness, stress and so on. They quote people on certain types of medication who experience hallucinations very similar to the visions reported by the saints. They have also looked at the details of visions and claim that the identification of the people in the vision, such as the Virgin Mary, is based on images which the visionary has already seen and associated with the saint. They also claim that a vision simply proves someone has had a vision, not that anything outside the visionary's mind exists.

Looking at both sides, it seems to me that visions can give us ideas about religion and may well be true, but they cannot be used to prove things because they are too personal.

A high mark answer because it gives three clear developed reasons for thinking that visions prove God's existence. It then gives three reasons for disagreeing before reaching a fully justified conclusion.

Spelling, punctuation and grammar are correct and a wide range of specialist vocabulary (St Paul, road to Damascus, St Joan of Arc, St Bernadette, immaculate conception, atheists, Humanists, Virgin Mary) is used appropriately.

2 Religious teachings on relationships and families in the twenty-first century

Area of study 3: Philosophy and ethics based on Catholic Christianity

Section 2: Religious teachings on relationships and families in the twenty-first century

Topic 3.2.1 Marriage

Thinking points

In this topic you need to:
- think about the importance and purpose of marriage in Catholic life
- consider Catholic teachings about marriage including *Not Just Good, But Beautiful*
- understand the importance of marriage in society
- think about the different atheist and Humanist attitudes to marriage, including cohabitation, and the Catholic responses to them
- be able to explain and evaluate different Catholic and non-religious attitudes to marriage.

The importance and purpose of marriage in Catholic life

Marriage is very important in Catholic life because:

- Catholic Christians believe that marriage was created by God as the way of establishing and preserving society.
- Marriage is one of the seven sacraments of the Church which brings God's grace, strength and salvation.
- Catholic Christians believe that marriage is the only acceptable way for them to have a sexual relationship.
- Marriage is the only acceptable way for Catholic Christians to have children and raise a family, since a Christian family must be headed by a married man and woman.
- Christian families are brought about through marriage and are the way new life is brought into the Church as the children of Christian parents are baptised and confirmed.

Two different wedding ceremonies.

Activity

Look at the two wedding photos. Which do you think is a more accurate reflection of British society today?

Topic 3.2.1 Marriage

The purpose of marriage in the teaching of the Catholic Church is that God created marriage for man and woman:

- so that a couple can have a **lifelong relationship** of love, companionship and **faithfulness**
- so that a couple can have the support and comfort of each other and enjoy sex with each other in the way God intended
- for the **procreation** of children
- so that children can be brought up in a Christian family and become members of Christ's Church
- as a way for the couple to show their love for each other and to gain God's grace to help them in their married life.

Catholic teachings about marriage

The Catholic Church teaches the following:

- Marriage can only be between a man and a woman because this was how marriage was established by God when he created humans:

  But at the beginning of creation God made them male and female. For this reason a man will leave his father and mother and be united to his wife, and the two will become one flesh. (Mark 10:6–8)

- Marriage is a sacrament between the couple and God. In the sacrament of marriage God joins the couple together in a bond that humans have no right to break:

  So they are no longer two, but one flesh. Therefore what God has joined together, let no one separate. (Mark 10:9–10)

- The sacramental nature of marriage means that marriage is for life because God's bonds cannot be broken:

  Anyone who divorces his wife and marries another commits adultery. (Mark 10:11)

- Although marriage is particularly important it is not for everyone. The Church teaches that God calls some people to the celibate life so they can dedicate themselves to serving God as priests, monks or nuns.

In a book published in 2015 called *Not Just Good, But Beautiful*, Pope Francis expressed his worries about people giving up on marriage and causing a crisis in the social environment. He urged society to return to lifelong marriage because:

- 'the union of a man and woman in marriage is a unique, natural, fundamental good for persons, communities and whole societies'
- marriage is the basis of society: 'a family grounded in marriage is the first school where we learn to appreciate our own and others' gifts and where we begin to acquire the art of cooperative living'
- the family is the pillar which holds society together
- 'children have a right to grow up in a family with a father and a mother'.

Useful words

Lifelong relationship – the idea that marriage can only be ended by the death of a partner

Faithfulness – staying with your marriage partner and having sex only with them

Procreation – making a new life

Adultery – a sexual act between a married person and someone other than their marriage partner

Activities

1. Why do you think Catholic Christians believe that marriage is important?
2. Why do you think many young people cohabit before they marry?

Section 2: Religious teachings on relationships and families in the twenty-first century

Activity

Look at the civil wedding photo. Why do you think many people now have a civil rather than a religious wedding?

Atheist and Humanist attitudes to marriage

Humanists believe that sex and marriage are matters for individual decisions. It is up to individuals whether they live together without marrying or get married in a civil ceremony. However, Humanists expect sexual relations to be based on respect and trust. They believe that relationships should be exclusive (one partner at a time) and many believe that marriage is a good thing when raising a family.

Most atheists have a similar view to Humanists, although some would accept people having multiple sexual partners.

A civil wedding of a couple on a tropical beach.

Marriage is still important for the non-religious

In 2012, the number of marriages in England and Wales actually increased by 5.3 per cent to 262,240, from 249,133 in 2011. Although the Civil Partnerships Act 2004 provided same-sex couples with the same rights and treatment as opposite-sex couples who enter into a civil marriage, there was great pressure for this to become a proper marriage, pressure which led to the Marriage (Same Sex Couples) Act 2013 which allowed same-sex couples to marry in just the same way as heterosexual couples, but did not require religions to provide same-sex marriage ceremonies.

Research shows that most cohabiting couples would like to get married at some point because marriage provides:

- a stable legal and financial backing for a relationship (there can be major problems for a cohabiting **spouse** if their partner dies)
- more social acceptance of the relationship
- a more stable home for a family (many cohabiting couples decide to marry when they decide to start a family)
- a public ritual to declare and celebrate the couple's love.

Humanists and atheists are often classed as non-religious and the number of non-religious people in the UK is increasing. The Census of 2011 and more recent surveys indicate that less than half of the British public believe in God.

Useful words

Spouse – marriage or cohabitation partner

How Catholic Christians have responded to non-religious attitudes to marriage and cohabitation

The official response of the Catholic Church has been to disagree with the non-religious attitude and to insist that Christians should refrain from sex until they have had a Christian marriage.

- The teaching of the Catechism on sex before marriage has been reaffirmed:

    The sexual act must always take place exclusively within marriage. Outside marriage it always constitutes a grave sin and excludes one from sacramental communion ... Human love does not tolerate trial marriages [living together before marriage] it demands a total and definitive gift of persons to one another. (Catechism of the Catholic Church 2390–91)

- **Cohabitation** has been judged to be against God's will. The Church advises Catholic couples against cohabitation, as can be seen in this letter from the Catholic Bishops of Pennsylvania to engaged couples, published in 1999:

    ... one important area in which many priests and couples have shared their concerns with us is that of engaged couples living together before marriage. While many in our society may see no problem with this arrangement, living together and having sexual relations before marriage can never be reconciled with what God expects of us. In addition, countless studies have shown that couples who live together before marriage have higher rates of divorce and a poorer quality of marital relationship than those who do not. (Pennsylvania Catholic Conference)

Activity

Do you agree with the Catholic response to non-religious attitudes to marriage and cohabitation?

Useful words

Cohabitation – living as man and wife without being married

Practice questions

c Explain two reasons why Catholic Christians get married. In your answer you should refer to a source of wisdom and authority.

d 'Couples who live together are living in sin.' Evaluate this statement. In your response you should:
- refer to Catholic Christian teachings
- refer to other Christian or non-religious points of view
- reach a justified conclusion.

Summary

Catholics believe that marriage was established by God for a lifelong relationship of love and faithfulness and bringing up a Christian family. Marriage is important for Christians because it was created by God and taught by Jesus, and is the only recommended way for Christians to have sex and raise a family.

Sex before marriage and cohabitation (living together) are much more common as society becomes less religious, but even atheists and Humanists regard marriage as a good thing when bringing up a family. The Catholic Church still disagrees with sex before marriage and cohabitation.

Section 2: Religious teachings on relationships and families in the twenty-first century

Topic 3.2.2 Sexual relationships

Thinking points

In this topic you need to:
- think about Catholic teachings about the nature and importance of sexual relationships (marital, unitive and procreative, including Catechism 2360–2365)
- consider Catholic teachings on sexual relationships outside marriage and homosexuality
- understand different atheist and Humanist attitudes to sexual relationships and Catholic responses to them
- be able to explain and evaluate Catholic and non-religious attitudes to sexual relationships.

Useful words

Premarital sex – sex before marriage
Homosexuality – sexual attraction to a same-sex partner
Extramarital sex – sex outside marriage, usually refers to adultery
Procreative sex – sex which is open to the possibility of new life being formed

Catholic teachings about the nature and importance of sexual relationships

The nature of sexual relationships:

- **Premarital sex** is sex before marriage. Any sexual relationship between two people who are not married is classed as premarital sex.
- Cohabitation refers to two people who are living together in a sexual relationship without being married.
- Same-sex sexual relationships are classed as **homosexuality**, although they are usually known colloquially as gay relationships. Female same-sex relationships are known as lesbianism.
- **Extramarital sex** refers either to married people having a sexual relationship with someone other than their marriage partner or to an unmarried person having a sexual relationship with a married person.

The Catholic Church teaches that sex is important because:

- It is a gift from God to be enjoyed between one man and one woman who are married to each other (this is known as marital sex).
- Sex was given to humans by God for the joy, pleasure and bond of a married couple (this is known as unitive sex).
- Sex was given by God so that children could be brought into the world (this is known as **procreative sex**).
- The combination of marital, unitive and procreative sex in a marriage helps to fulfil God's purpose of a Christian family bringing up children in the Christian faith.

The Catechism of the Catholic Church 2360–2365 teaches that:

- Sex should not be simply biological; the sacrament and commitment of marriage make marital sex 'truly human'.
- Marital sex strengthens a marriage through its self-giving and the joy and pleasure it brings.
- Marital sex is both unitive and procreative, which is the 'twofold end of marriage'.
- Marital sex symbolises that in marriage two have become one.
- Marital sex not only keeps a couple together, it keeps them faithful to each other.

The conjugal love of man and woman thus stands under the twofold obligation of fidelity and fecundity. (Catechism of the Catholic Church 2363)

Topic 3.2.2 Sexual relationships

Catholic teachings on sexual relationships outside marriage

The Catholic Church teaches that any form of sexual relationship outside marriage is wrong:

- The Bible says that fornication (a word used in religion for both premarital sex and **promiscuity**) is sinful and Christians should follow the teachings of the Bible.
- The Catechism of the Catholic Church teaches that premarital sex is wrong because God intended sex to be restricted to marriage.
- Adultery is wrong because it breaks the wedding vows to be faithful to each other.
- Adultery is also wrong because it is prohibited in one of the Ten Commandments, and is condemned by Jesus in the Gospels.

> *The sexual act must always take place exclusively within marriage ... Human love does not tolerate 'trial marriages'. It demands a total and definitive gift of persons to one another.* (Catechism of the Catholic Church 2390–2391)

Useful words

Promiscuity – having sex with a number of partners without commitment

Celibate – living without sexual activity

Civil partnerships – legal ceremonies giving homosexual partners the same legal rights as husband and wife

Catholic attitude towards homosexuality

The Catholic attitude towards homosexuality is that being a homosexual is not a sin but that homosexual sexual relationships are a sin. The Catholic Church asks homosexuals to live without any sexual activity (that is, to be **celibate**). It believes that the sacraments of the Church will help them do this. The Church does not accept same-sex marriage or **civil partnerships**. The Church teaches this because:

- The Bible condemns homosexual sexual activity.
- It is the tradition of the Church that sexual activity should be creative as well as unitive (see Topic 3.2.5, page 342), and it is not possible for homosexuals to have procreative sex.
- The Catechism of the Catholic Church teaches that marriage is for a man and a woman to join as one and to raise a family.

However, the Church teaches that it is sinful to discriminate against anyone on the grounds of their sexuality or orientation because:

- People cannot help their sexual orientation (but they can control their sexual activity), therefore discriminating against people because of their sexual orientation is wrong.
- The Bible teaches that everyone has human dignity because they are made in the image of God and should be treated with respect.
- The Church does not refer to 'heterosexual' or 'homosexual' alone, but speaks about homosexual persons whose identity is as a child of God.

> *Every person, independently of their sexual tendencies, is respected in their dignity and should be received with sensibility and delicateness, both in the church and in society.* (Summary document from the Family Synod October 2015)

> *There are absolutely no grounds for considering homosexual unions to be in any way similar or even remotely analogous to God's plan for marriage and family.* ('The Joy of Love', Pope Francis, April 2016)

Activities

1. Look at the quotation from Catechism 2363 on page 330 and try to put it into your own words.
2. Do you think Catholic Christians should regard adultery as worse than premarital sex?

331

Section 2: Religious teachings on relationships and families in the twenty-first century

Mary Glasspool, Bishop of Los Angeles, was the first open lesbian to be elected an Anglican bishop.

Useful words

Consensual sex – when both parties freely agree to sex

Activity

Look at the photo of the bishop. Should gay people have equal rights in the Church?

Atheist and Humanist attitudes to sexual relationships

Although Humanists and many atheists do not condemn sex before marriage, premarital sex is acceptable only within certain limits:

- Sex must be **consensual sex**: rape in any form is seen as totally unacceptable.
- Sex must be between people 'of age'. Paedophilia is regarded as wrong regardless of religious teachings.
- A sexual partner ought ideally to be single or separated from their partner; non-religious people find cheating on a partner offensive.
- No payment should be involved in sex; there is still a stigma attached to prostitution.
- Sex should involve a degree of stability; high levels of promiscuity are frowned upon.
- Sex ought to be safe; given the risk of disease and pregnancy, barrier methods of contraception should be used.

Non-religious people believe there must be some limitations on sexual activity; what they object to are the limits Christianity places on premarital sex.

Atheist and Humanist attitudes to same-sex relationships

There have been many developments in the attitude of society to same-sex relationships:

- The various changes in the laws on homosexuality have made it easier to be openly homosexual and made society more aware and accepting of homosexuality.

- Medical research has shown that homosexuality is most probably genetic. As society began to realise that at least five per cent of the population is homosexual, people began to accept equal status and rights for homosexual couples.
- The increased openness of gay celebrities has led to a greater acceptance of all gay people.
- The work of such organisations as **Stonewall** changed many people's attitudes and led to a greater acceptance of equal rights for homosexuals.

Perhaps as a result of these changes, Humanists, and the vast majority of atheists, see no problems with same-sex sexual relationships. They regard people's sexuality as their own concern unless it interferes with other people's human rights. This could be because all the Christian arguments against same-sex relationships are based on religious reasons only, so that if people have no religion then the reasons for disapproving of homosexuality disappear.

Catholic responses

Some of the Catholic responses to the non-religious attitudes to sexual relationships have been dealt with in the previous topic.

The official response of the Catholic Church to non-religious attitudes to homosexuality has been to restate the teaching that Christian homosexuals should refrain from sex and that same-sex marriages should not be legal. This has been confirmed by Pope Francis in his Apostolic Exhortation, 'The Joy of Love' in April 2016.

Practice questions

c Explain two reasons why many Catholic Christians are against people having sex before they are married. In your answer, you must refer to a source of wisdom and authority.

d 'Sex should only take place in marriage.' Evaluate this statement. In your response you should:
- refer to Catholic Christian teachings
- refer to other Christian or non-religious points of view
- reach a justified conclusion.

Activity

Look at the statement by the Catholic bishops below. Do you think this is a valid reason for banning same-sex marriage?

Useful words

Stonewall – a group which campaigns for the equality of lesbian, gay, bisexual and transgender people across Britain

With this new legislation, marriage has now become an institution in which openness to children, and with it the responsibility on fathers and mothers to remain together to care for children born into their family unit, are no longer central. That is why we were opposed to this legislation on principle. (Statement by the president and vicepresident of the Catholic Bishops Conference of England and Wales, 17 July 2013, commenting on the passing of the Marriage (Same Sex Couples) Act 2013)

Summary

The Catholic Church teaches that sex before marriage is wrong. It also teaches that adultery is wrong because it breaks the marriage vows. Humanists and most atheists believe that sex is up to the people involved as long as they are of age and agree to it.

As far as homosexuality is concerned, the Church teaches that there is nothing wrong with homosexual feelings or relationships as long as there is no sexual activity. The Church is against same-sex marriage. Humanists and atheists believe in equal rights for homosexuals and approve of same-sex marriages, as do the vast majority of non-religious people.

Section 2: Religious teachings on relationships and families in the twenty-first century

Topic 3.2.3 Families

Thinking points

In this topic you need to:
- think about Catholic teachings about the purpose and importance of the family, including procreation, security and education of children
- consider Catholic and non-religious responses to the purpose of the family
- understand Catholic responses to different types of family within twenty-first century society: nuclear, single-parent, same-sex parents, extended and blended families, including *Familiaris Consortio* 77–85
- be able to explain Catholic and non-religious attitudes to families.

The purpose of the family in Catholic Christianity

The Church teaches the following:

- The family was created by God as the basic unit of society and as the only place in which children should be brought up. Therefore, it is the most important part of society and without the family society would collapse.
- The family has the basic task of bringing up children safely and securely until they are mature enough to look after themselves. This means that parents have a duty to ensure that the **physical needs** and **material needs** of the children are met.
- A Catholic family has a duty to instil **moral values** into their children so that they become good responsible citizens.
- A Catholic family should bring the children up in the Catholic faith and do their best to ensure that the children become good Catholic Christians as adults.
- In a Catholic family, children have a duty to care for their parents when their parents are too old or infirm to care for themselves. The Commandments tell Christians to honour their mother and father.

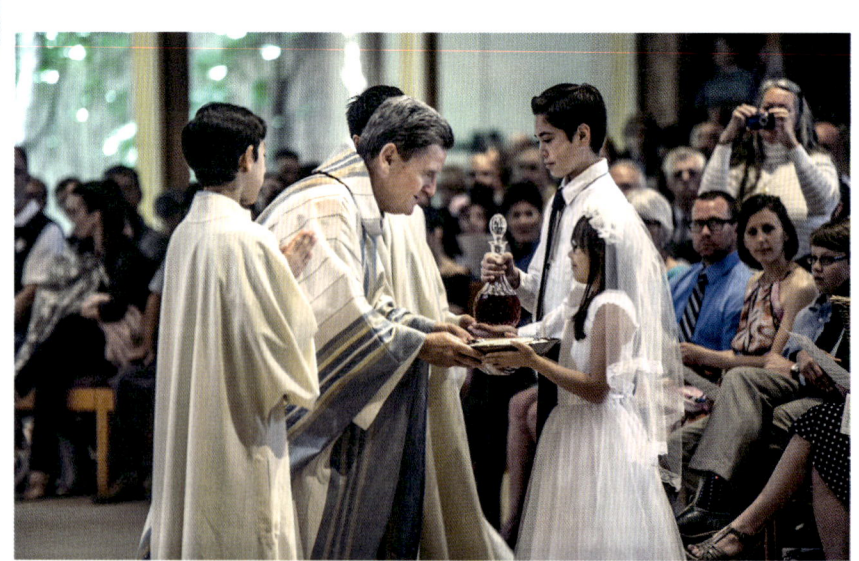

First Communion is a family occasion for Catholics.

Family life is important for Catholic Christians for the following reasons:

- One of the main purposes of a Catholic Christian marriage is to have children and bring them up in a secure and loving Christian environment so that they will come to love God and follow Jesus.
- The Church teaches that the family was created by God as the basic unit of society and as the only place in which children should be brought up.

Useful words

Physical needs – such things as housing and shelter from the elements
Material needs – such things as food, drink and clothing
Moral values – the standards of good and evil, which govern people's behaviour and choices

Activity

Look at the First Communion photo. Do you think sharing in Christian events such as this will help a family?

- Catholic teaching on divorce makes it clear that Catholic parents should stay together and bring up their children together because the family is so important.
- The family is the place where children learn the difference between right and wrong, so that without the family there would be much more evil in the world.
- The family is the place where children are introduced to the Catholic faith through baptism and then through being taken to church for worship, First Communion, festivals and so on. This means that the family is very important for the Church to continue and grow.

However, there is a tradition dating back to Jesus, which says that there are more important things than the family for Christians. Marriage is not compulsory for Christians and many Catholic Christians feel they can serve God best by remaining single, for example priests, nuns and monks leave their families to serve God.

Different types of family

Throughout history there have been many different types of family, from small clans (a large extended family) to families with **polygamous** parents (several spouses) to families with **monogamous** parents (husband and wife). Families have developed as children cannot survive on their own until adulthood. The main family types in the UK in the twenty-first century are:

- nuclear families
- single-parent families
- same-sex parent families
- extended families
- blended families.

Nuclear families

Although technically a nuclear family is one where mother, father and children are living together as a unit, most people, especially religious people, think of it as a married couple of opposite sexes living together with their children. Fifty years ago, such a nuclear family was regarded as the norm, and this is still the type of family portrayed in television adverts. However, of the 7.9 million families with dependent children in the UK in 2014, only 4.75 million were married couple families. This means that only 60 per cent of families are now nuclear families and that 40 per cent of families with children are no longer nuclear families. Nearly 2 million families consist of a single parent and dependent children and 1.17 million families are headed by cohabiting couples.

Activities

1. Why are there so many single-parent families?
2. Look at the photo of a nuclear family below. Do you think this family would be any different if the parents were cohabiting rather than married?

Useful words

Polygamous – having more than one spouse at a time
Monogamous – having only one spouse at a time

The cast of *Outnumbered*, an award-winning television comedy programme aired from 2007 to 2014.

Section 2: Religious teachings on relationships and families in the twenty-first century

Single-parent families

In 2013 there were 1.9 million families consisting of a single parent and dependent children, which meant that more than 3 million children were living in families headed by a lone parent. In fact, 25 per cent of all families with dependent children are now single-parent families.

The main cause of the large number of single-parent families has been the rising number of divorces and the increasing number of family breakdowns where couples are cohabiting.

However, the divorce rate has reduced over the past few years (see Figure 1). Overall, 42 per cent of marriages will end in divorce, inevitably producing many single-parent families. As far as cohabiting couples are concerned, on average, cohabitations last less than two years before breaking up or converting to marriage; indeed, less than four per cent of cohabitations last for ten years or more. Over 120,000 families with dependent children separated in 2013; about half were married couple families (1.3 per cent of 4.7 million married families) and half were from cohabiting couples (5.3 per cent of 1.2 million cohabiting families). See Figures 2 and 3.

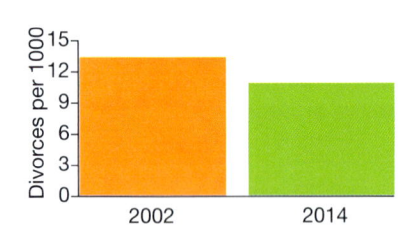

Figure 1 Divorces for every 1000 married couples for 2002 and 2014 in the UK. (Source: ONS.)

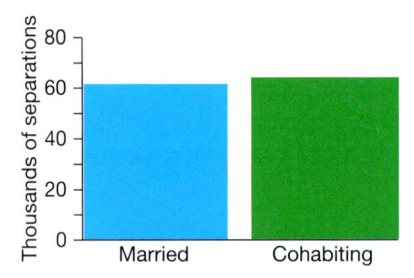

Figure 2 Families with married or cohabiting parents in the UK. (Source: ONS.)

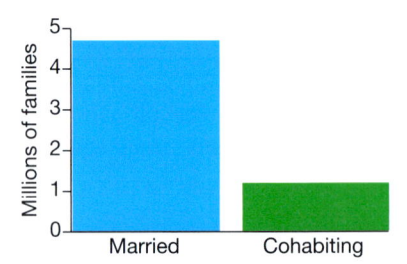

Figure 3 Separated families with married or cohabiting parents in the UK. (Source: ONS.)

Forty-one per cent of children living in one-parent families are living in poverty whereas only 23 per cent of children from two-parent households are living in poverty. Moreover, 91 per cent of lone parents in single-parent families are women, so many children in single-parent families lack a paternal role model.

Same-sex parent families

The Civil Partnerships Act 2004 provided same-sex couples with the same rights and treatment as opposite-sex couples who enter into a civil marriage. The Marriage (Same Sex Couples) Act 2013 allowed same-sex couples to marry in just the same way as **heterosexual** couples, but did not require religions to provide same-sex marriage ceremonies. The Equality Act 2010 made discriminating against same-sex couples illegal, so giving them equal adoption and fostering rights. In 2014 there were 21,000 families headed by a same-sex couple. Of these, 12,000 were in civil partnerships and 9000 were cohabiting. Many male same-sex partners have adopted hard-to-place children.

Extended families

An extended family is one where three generations (parents, children and grandparents – usually called multigeneration) are living in the same house or one where parents, children, grandparents, aunts and uncles live in close proximity and have frequent contact with and reliance on each other. According to the 2011 Census, only one per cent of families with

Useful words

Heterosexual – attracted to the opposite sex

dependent children were multigenerational, but research indicates that many more families live in close proximity and rely on grandparents and family members for childcare. More recent research indicates that there has been a big increase in multigenerational households since the Census because of the squeeze on incomes and jobs, and the increased cost of housing and both childcare and eldercare.

Blended families

A blended family is when two separate families are joined together when parents decide to marry or cohabit. The increase in divorce has led to an increase in **remarriage** (most people who divorce before the age of 50 remarry). This means that there are now many more blended families (sometimes called step-families or reconstituted families). The number of blended families with dependent children fell by fourteen per cent between the 2001 Census (631,000 blended families) and the 2011 Census (544,000 blended families). Estimates from the General Lifestyle Survey in 2011 for Great Britain show that 85 per cent of blended families with dependent children include children from the woman's previous relationship, but only eleven per cent include children from the man's previous relationship, with even fewer, four per cent, coming from both partners' previous relationships.

Singer-songwriter Sir Elton John (left) with husband David Furnish and their two children.

Useful words

Remarriage – marrying again after a divorce

The Catholic response to different types of family

Much of the Catholic response is found in *Familiaris Consortio*, an Apostolic Exhortation issued by Pope St John Paul II in 1981. Its English title is 'On the Role of the Christian Family in the Modern World'.

- The Catholic Church gives its blessing to both nuclear and extended families as both of these can live within Catholic law and fulfil all the needs and requirements of a Catholic Christian family.

- As far as single-parent families are concerned, Pope St John Paul II recommended that families with special needs should be given extra help and support by the local church. Although a single-parent family may have come about in a wrong way (cohabitation gone wrong, divorce and so on), the family itself is not living in sin and so deserves the help of the local church with the special needs which such families are likely to have.

- Same-sex families are considered inferior to a marriage between a man and a woman by the Church. The Catholic Church teaches that a family should be headed by a married man and woman, and that marriage can only be between a man and a woman. Also, Pope St John Paul II said that Catholics in civil marriages cannot receive the sacraments until the marriage is validated and same-sex parents can only have had a civil marriage.

- The Church also disapproves of blended families, unless they have come about through the marriage of a widow and a widower. Pope St John Paul II said that divorced or separated spouses who remarry or enter new relationships have chosen a way of life contrary to the Gospel and cannot be admitted to the sacraments.

- Pope St John Paul II also disapproved of families headed by cohabiting couples. He stated that trial marriages and cohabitation violated the dignity of both the man and the woman. However, he did realise that some young people cohabit through lack of money, and St John Paul II recommended that governments should do what is possible to make it possible and easier for cohabiting couples to marry.

A multigenerational family.

Activities

1. Look at the photo of Sir Elton John's family. Do you think it was a good idea to allow same-sex families?

2. Why do you think so many of the single parents in single-parent families are women?

Section 2: Religious teachings on relationships and families in the twenty-first century

Activities

1. What do you think would be the main differences between living in a Christian family and living in a non-religious family?
2. What do you think about the Catholic response to different types of family?

- St John Paul II also considered the problems of families where one of the parents is Catholic, but the other is either a non-Catholic Christian or a non-Christian. St John Paul II recommended that there should be special care from the Church for such families. St John Paul II recommended that such couples should make a joint decision to bring up any children as Catholics.

Non-religious ideas about the family

Most families in the UK are now non-religious. All recent surveys show that at least 60 per cent of people have little or no contact with religion. However, the family is very important to people regardless of religion.

Falling in love and having a family is a goal in life for most people, no doubt because raising a family is part of what is sometimes called the 'selfish gene'. That is, we want our genes to continue into future generations.

Non-religious people see that the purpose of family life is as follows:

- to bring up children safely and securely until they are mature enough to look after themselves, by making sure that the physical and material needs of the children are met
- to pass on moral values to the children so that they become good, responsible citizens
- to provide emotional and financial support throughout life.

The importance of family life to non-religious people can be seen in the way that family members will always come to the rescue in times of need regardless of religious commitment (according to the General Lifestyle Survey of 2011, 80 per cent of parents expect to help their adult children with housing costs). Non-religious families also come together at times like Christmas just as much as religious families.

Summary

Catholic Christians believe that the family was created by God as the basis of society. It is where children are safe and nurtured, learn moral values and are brought up as Christians.

Non-religious people think the family is important for safety, nurture and moral values.

There are lots of different types of families in the twenty-first century and the Church has reacted to them in different ways. The Catholic Church approves of nuclear and extended families and offers special help to single-parent families. However, the Church thinks there should be no families with same-sex parents and no blended families unless the blending has come from the death of a parent.

Practice questions

c. Explain two reasons why the family is important for Catholic Christians. In your answer you must refer to a source of wisdom and authority.

d. 'The family is more important for Catholics than for non-religious people.' Evaluate this statement considering arguments for and against. In your answer you should:
  - refer to Catholic points of view
  - refer to different Christian or non-religious points of view
  - reach a justified conclusion.

Topic 3.2.4 Support for the family in the local parish

What is the parish?

The Catholic Church in England and Wales is organised into parishes and **dioceses**. A diocese is a collection of parishes under the jurisdiction of a bishop. The Bishop of Middlesbrough, for example, is head of the Middlesbrough diocese and its 89 parishes. The Catholic Church in England and Wales has 22 dioceses divided into five provinces, each under the leadership of an archbishop. Each parish has a **parish priest** and is based in a parish church for the local area.

The Church of England is also organised into parishes and dioceses. Other Churches in England and Wales are not based on the parish system, but any local Baptist, Methodist or Pentecostal church will be organised similarly, although only the Church of England and the Catholic Church have large numbers of Church schools.

How the parish tries to help families

- Most parishes have a local Church primary and secondary school connected to them. These provide Christian teaching and worship in addition to the standard education. The school buildings are provided and maintained by the Church, and taxpayers pay for the teachers and equipment. This education helps parents because it teaches children right from wrong, teaches children about the Christian faith and helps parents to fulfil their marriage and baptism promises to bring their children up as Christians.

- Many churches are exploring new ways to be more family friendly, including new forms of family worship. Local parishes believe that having family-friendly worship helps family life because it can be strengthened by families worshipping together. Family worship helps to unite the family and gives families an opportunity to discover religion together. Often, children have their own **children's liturgy** especially geared to their needs before joining with the whole church family for the Liturgy of the Eucharist.

- Parishes also help families through rites of passage. When a child is brought for baptism, the priest meets the family before the sacrament and gives advice to the parents. He also gives advice to the church members about their duty to help the child and its family to come to the adult Christian life. Catholic parishes run classes to prepare children for first confession and **First Communion** and later for confirmation. These classes help parents with the Catholic Christian upbringing of their children as they bring children into full membership of the Church.

- Most parish **clergy** spend some time reminding parents of the importance of the family and of the importance of keeping their marriage vows. Clergy in the local church are available for help with counselling families on family or marital problems. There are also family-help services run by the Church, such as the Bishops' Committee for Marriage and Family Life, Catholic Marriage Care and the National Catholic Child Welfare Council.

Thinking points

In this topic you need to:
- think about how and why the local church community tries to support families, including through family worship, the sacraments, rites of passage, classes for parents, groups for children and counselling
- understand the importance of the support of the local parish for Christians today
- be able to explain and evaluate Christian support for the family.

Useful words

Dioceses – church areas under the direction of bishops
Parish priest – the clergy person responsible for a local church
Children's liturgy – a celebration and explanation of the readings at Mass especially for children
First Communion – the first time a person receives the sacrament of the Eucharist; children receive special lessons before this important occasion
Clergy – those ordained by the Church

Activity

Do you think it is important for Christian families to be given help by their local church?

Section 2: Religious teachings on relationships and families in the twenty-first century

- A recent initiative for local parishes has been the Family Group Movement. Family Groups are parish friendship groups drawn from the Catholic community and open to any parishioner. Family Groups are made up of young, elderly, single, widowed, married, separated and divorced parishioners who commit to spending time together once a month in low-cost activities. The groups bring people in the local parish together with a commitment to know, support and love each other as brothers and sisters in Christ.

> *Education in the faith by the parents should begin in the child's earliest years. This already happens when family members help one another to grow in faith by the witness of a Christian life in keeping with the Gospel. Family catechesis precedes, accompanies, and enriches other forms of instruction in the faith. Parents have the mission of teaching their children to pray and to discover their vocation as children of God. The parish is the Eucharistic community and the heart of the liturgical life of Christian families; it is a privileged place for the catechesis of children and parents.* (Catechism of the Catholic Church 2226)

Useful words

Catechesis – teaching about the faith

The Holy Trinity Rosehill Church of England School.

Why parishes try to help families

Parishes try to help families because they have a duty to help children baptised in the Church. In fact, in some churches the clergy and the congregation make promises to God that they will help the parents with the Christian upbringing of the children.

Also, the Church teaches that one of the main purposes of Christian marriage is to have children and bring them up in a secure and loving Christian environment. It is then that they will come to love God and follow Jesus, so it is the responsibility of the parish to assist in that task.

Christianity teaches that the family was created by God as the basic unit of society and as the only place in which children should be brought up. Therefore, it is the most important part of society. Without the family, society would collapse, so the parish has a social as well as a sacred duty to help parents with their family life.

Activities

1. Read Catechism 2226. Do you think most Catholic families follow its advice?
2. Why do you think the parish is important for Catholics?
3. Read the section on how the parish helps families. Can you think of anything churches near to you do to help families which is not on this list?
4. Look at the photo of a Church school. Make a list of arguments for and against having Church schools.

The parish also has a duty to make sure that the Church continues to grow. The family is the place where children are introduced to the faith through baptism and then through being taken to church for worship, festivals, first confession and communion. If the parish does not help the family, then Christianity will not grow and the Church will have failed the task God has given it.

Activity

'Families only need help from the family.' Evaluate this statement.

Why support from the Church is important for Christian families

Support from the Church is important for Christians who are trying to raise a Christian family because:

- Raising children as Christians means taking them to church regularly and that requires the Church to be helpful to children.
- Teaching children about Christianity requires knowledge and expertise in the faith that parents are not likely to have, so Church schools are vital.
- For Catholic families, taking part in the sacraments is essential and that requires the help of the Church.
- Knowing that they are part of the larger family of the Church which will give help if needed is a great source of comfort and strength for a family.
- Christians believe in the power of prayer, and knowing that the local parish is praying for families brings them God's strength.

Practice questions

c Explain two reasons why the local parish helps the families in the parish. In your answer you must refer to a source of wisdom and authority.

d 'The help of the local parish is what makes a successful family.' Evaluate this statement considering arguments for and against. In your answer you should:
- refer to Catholic points of view
- refer to different Christian or non-religious points of view
- reach a justified conclusion.

Summary

The parish is the local Catholic church. It helps families by supporting the local Catholic schools to provide a Catholic education. The parish provides family worship, rites of passage, counselling and family support. The parish provides these because it has a duty to make the Church grow and this can only happen through Catholic Christian families. Families find the parish's support a very important help for raising a good Catholic family.

Section 2: Religious teachings on relationships and families in the twenty-first century

Topic 3.2.5 Contraception

Thinking points

In this topic you need to:
- think about Catholic teaching on family planning, artificial contraception and natural family planning, including reference to *Humanae Vitae*
- understand different Christian, atheist and Humanist attitudes to family planning and Catholic responses to them
- be able to explain and evaluate different Christian and non-religious attitudes to contraception.

Useful words

Unitive purpose – sex as a source of joy and pleasure
Procreative purpose – sex as a means of creating a family
Abortifacient – bringing about a very early abortion
NFP – natural family planning

Catholics and family planning

The Catholic Church teaches that sexual intercourse is a gift from God as a source of joy and pleasure to married couples (the **unitive purpose**) as well as a means of creating a family (the **procreative purpose**). The Church also teaches that Christians should practise responsible parenthood. This means deciding on the number of children to have and when to have them; this is often known as the 'regulation of births'. However, the Catholic way to achieve this is through using natural methods of family planning (see below). The Church teaches that using artificial methods of contraception is going against God's intentions. Catholics believe this because of the following:

- In 1968, Pope Paul VI's encyclical *Humanae Vitae* ('Of Human Life') affirmed the teaching of Pope Pius XI which condemned all forms of artificial contraception, and the teaching of Pope Pius XII who declared that Catholics could use natural methods of family planning.

- *Humanae Vitae* declared that the only allowable forms of family planning for Catholics are natural methods because they do not separate the unitive and procreative purposes of sexual intercourse. This teaching has been confirmed in the Catechism of the Catholic Church.

- Artificial methods of birth control separate the unitive and creative aspects of sex, which the Catechism says is not what God intended.

- Some contraceptives have **abortifacient** effects in that they bring about a very early abortion and so are against the teaching of the Church.

- The Catholic Church regards contraception as a major cause of sexual promiscuity, broken families, the rise in the divorce rate and sexually transmitted diseases.

Natural methods of regulating births

Natural methods of regulating the number of births are the only ones permitted by the Catholic Church. The most common natural method is known as natural family planning (**NFP**), or fertility awareness. It involves reducing the chance of becoming pregnant by planning sex around the most infertile times during the woman's monthly cycle. To be as effective as possible, it should be taught by an experienced NFP teacher. Another method uses a device to measure hormone levels in the urine.

Natural methods require a couple to be in a loving, stable relationship as they require planning and sufficient love and concern for the partner to give up sex at certain times of the month. As they are natural, they do not involve any drugs or any risk of promoting an early abortion.

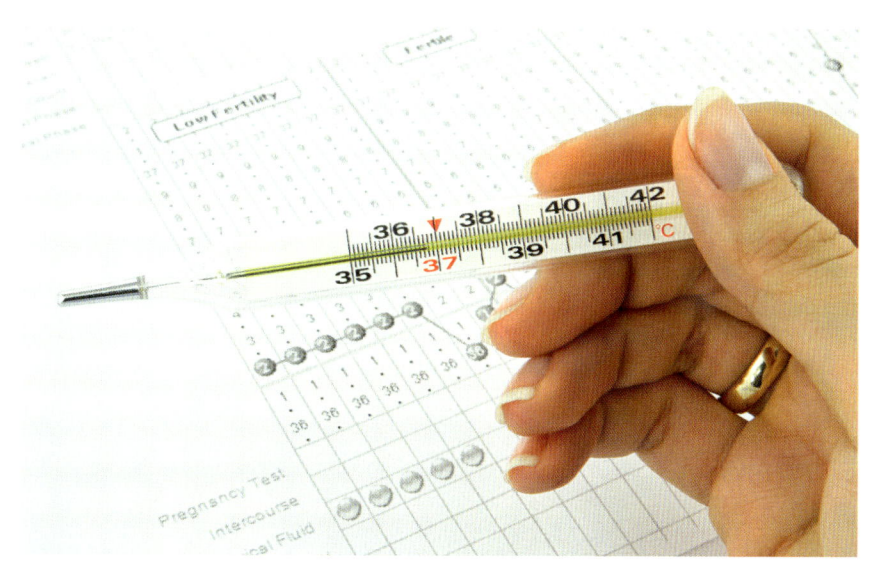

A fertility chart combining several indicators or signs of fertility.

Throughout history, people have tried to control the number of children that they have had, for a number of reasons:

- for the health of the mother
- to provide more food for the family unit
- to provide a better standard of living for the family unit.

Artificial contraception is something that allows sex to happen without conception occurring and so permits a couple to control the number of children they have. The use of artificial methods of contraception in the West has become very popular. It is now estimated that 90 per cent of the sexually active population of **childbearing age** in the UK use some form of artificial contraception.

Non-Catholic Christians and artificial methods of contraception

Almost all non-Catholic Christians believe that all forms of contraception are permissible as long as they are used to restrict the size of the family and not simply to stop having children altogether. They have this attitude because:

- Christianity is about love and justice, and contraception improves women's health and raises the standard of living of children as families are smaller.
- God created sex for enjoyment and to cement the bonds of marriage. Within marriage, contraception allows the role of sex to be separated from making children and this is not against God's will.
- There is nothing in the Bible that forbids the use of contraception.
- In 1930, the Lambeth Conference of the worldwide Anglican Communion (the Church of England) declared that it was legitimate for Christians to use contraception to limit family size. This has been followed by the major Protestant Churches and the Orthodox Churches.

Useful words

Childbearing age – the age when a woman is capable of having children

Section 2: Religious teachings on relationships and families in the twenty-first century

- They believe that it is better to combat HIV/AIDS by using condoms than by expecting everyone to follow Christian rules about sex and marriage.

Contraception is seen as a gift from medical science under God's sovereignty. Choosing not to have or space families is morally defensible, considering the needs of the world, population size and family responsibility. However, those contraceptives that have an abortifacient function (for example, IUD and various pills) are considered to take human life and should be avoided. (Statement by the Baptist Church in What the Churches Say*)*

Useful words

IUD – intrauterine device (the coil)

The methods of birth regulation based on self-observation and the use of infertile periods ... respect the bodies of the spouses, encourage tenderness between them ... In contrast, 'every action which, whether in anticipation of the conjugal act, or in its accomplishment, or in the development of its natural consequences, proposes, whether as an end or as a means, to render procreation impossible' is intrinsically evil. (Catechism of the Catholic Church 2370)

Atheist and Humanist attitudes to artificial methods of contraception

Non-religious people are in favour of artificial methods of contraception because they assess the rights and wrongs of birth control by looking at its consequences. They argue that as contraception prevents unwanted children from being born, improves the material and emotional standard of living in families, and prevents the spread of sexually transmitted diseases, it must be morally right to use it. Humanists argue that if contraception

Activities

1. Make a list of the similarities and differences between the Catholic and non-Catholic attitudes to contraception.
2. Read the statements by the Baptist Church and the Catholic Catechism and then put them into your own words. Which one would you agree with most?

results in every child being a wanted child, and in better, healthier lives for women, it must be a good thing. (British Humanist Association)

Most non-religious people think contraception should be used by people indulging in casual sex because it is important to avoid unwanted pregnancies and sexually transmitted diseases.

Humanists played a major part in promoting contraception in modern times. Charles Bradlaugh, leader of the National Secular Society, and his partner Annie Besant were given prison sentences in 1877 for publishing a book that advocated birth control because it was thought that contraception would lead to sexual immorality. However, their advocacy of contraception gradually led to its wider acceptance in society.

Catholic responses

The Catholic Church disagrees with the use of artificial contraception and so its response to other attitudes has been to issue statements to Catholic couples that they must only use natural methods of regulating births. The Church has reaffirmed the teachings of Pope Paul VI and the Catechism.

On board the papal plane in January 2015, Pope Francis backed Pope Paul VI's teaching against birth control and urged openness to life:

> *I believe that openness to life conditions the sacrament of matrimony. A man cannot give the sacrament to the woman, and the woman give it to him, if they are not in agreement on this point to be open to life. The key word ... and the one the Church always uses, and I do too, is 'responsible parenthood'.*

By 'responsible parenthood' the Pope meant that Catholics should use natural family planning.

The Church has also opposed the use of condoms to prevent the spread of HIV and sexually transmitted diseases, although Pope Benedict did say in 2010 that for some homosexual prostitutes the use of a condom may indicate an awakening of a moral sense. Pope Francis has confirmed that this limited use is acceptable, but not in heterosexual relations where procreation is possible.

Practice questions

c Explain two reasons why there are different attitudes to contraception in Christianity. In your answer you must refer to a source of wisdom and authority.

d 'The world would be a better place if everyone followed Catholic teachings on contraception.' Evaluate this statement considering arguments for and against. In your answer you should:
- refer to Catholic points of view
- refer to different Christian or non-religious points of view
- reach a justified conclusion.

Summary

Catholics believe that parents should plan the size of their families but that they should do this by only using natural methods of contraception. This is because the Church teaches that the unitive and creative aspects of sex should not be separated. Non-Catholic Christians, atheists and Humanists accept the use of artificial methods such as condoms and the Pill.

Section 2: Religious teachings on relationships and families in the twenty-first century

Topic 3.2.6 Divorce and remarriage

Thinking points

In this topic you need to:
- think about Catholic teachings about divorce, annulment and remarriage, including reference to Catechism 2382–2386
- consider different Christian, Humanist and atheist attitudes to divorce and remarriage, including the application of Situation Ethics, and Catholic responses to them
- be able to explain and evaluate Catholic and different Christian and non-religious attitudes to divorce and remarriage.

Useful words

Civil divorce – a divorce according to the law of the country but not the Church

Consummate – complete a marriage through sexual intercourse

Ending a marriage

In 1950 there were 30,870 divorces in the UK, in 1975 there were 120,522, in 2000 there were 141,135 and in 2012 there were 118,140 divorces. Clearly, attitudes to divorce changed greatly between 1950 and 1975. This is probably because:

- New laws made divorce much cheaper and easier to obtain for ordinary people.
- Increased equality for women meant that women were no longer prepared to accept unequal treatment from men.
- Equal rights legislation meant that many women were financially independent and could afford to live after a divorce.

Although there were 118,140 divorces in England and Wales in 2012, the divorce rate has actually gone down, with 10.8 divorcing people per 1000 married population in 2012 compared with 13.3 per 1000 in 2002. Fifty-eight per cent of marriages today will not end in divorce, and around ten per cent of married couples should reach their diamond anniversary of 60 years.

Until about 2000, most people who divorced remarried within ten years of their divorce, but the remarriage rate is declining as more divorced people decide to cohabit if they meet a new partner. However, religious people who divorce are far more likely to remarry.

Catholic teachings on divorce

The Catholic Church cannot allow religious divorce or remarriage. Catholic marriage is a sacrament and the exchange of vows means that the only way a marriage between baptised Catholics can be dissolved (religiously) is by the death of one of the partners or if the marriage is annulled.

However, the Catholic Church does allow for the legal separation of spouses if they find it impossible to live together, and even **civil divorce** if that will ensure the proper care of the children and the safety and security of the married partner. Neither of these routes, however, has ended the marriage: the couple are still married in the eyes of God and the Church and so cannot remarry. Catholics have this attitude because of the following reasons:

- Jesus taught that divorce is wrong and that marriage is for life:

    For this reason a man will leave his father and mother and be united to his wife, and the two will become one flesh. So they are no longer two, but one. Therefore what God has joined together, let man not separate. (Mark 10:7–9)

- The couple have made a covenant with God in the sacrament of marriage and that covenant cannot be broken by any earthly power:

    *a ratified and **consummated** marriage cannot be dissolved by any human power or for any reason other than death. (Catechism of the Catholic Church 2382)*

- The Church teaches very clearly in the Catechism that a marriage cannot be dissolved and so religious divorce is impossible:

  Thus the marriage bond has been established by God himself in such a way that a marriage concluded and consummated between baptised persons can never be dissolved. (Catechism of the Catholic Church 1640)

- The Catechism teaches that divorce is immoral because it

  introduces disorder into the family and into society. (Catechism of the Catholic Church 2385)

The Church also teaches that a spouse who has tried to keep the sanctity of marriage but has been divorced and abandoned by the other partner must be treated as totally innocent by the Church.

Catholic teachings on annulment

Annulment is a legal declaration that the marriage was never a true marriage and so the partners are free to marry someone else. The Catholic Church allows annulment if it can be proven to the Church's legal authorities that:

- the marriage was never consummated
- the marriage was not a true Christian marriage because one of the partners was not baptised
- the marriage was not a true Christian marriage because one of the couple was not fully aware of what marriage meant, for example, if they were too young, mentally unprepared or insufficiently prepared
- it was not a true Christian marriage because one of the couple can be shown to have not been willing or able to fully participate in the marriage, for example, unwilling to have children or being forced into marriage
- one of the spouses concealed important things such as they were infertile, they had a serious contagious disease, they had children from a previous relationship or they were not a believer at the time of the marriage.

The annulment process is a lengthy one, but is now local and goes through a special diocese committee and the local bishop is the final judge. If an annulment is granted, it is as if the marriage never existed and the partners are therefore free to marry.

Catholic teachings on remarriage

As there can be no religious divorce, there can be no remarriage because that would be the same as bigamy and adultery, both of which are very serious sins. Catholics who remarry are therefore in a state of sin unless they end their new relationship. They cannot be absolved of a sin unless they promise to stop sinning. As those with unabsolved sins should not take communion at Mass, it follows that remarried Catholics may be refused communion unless they end their new relationship.

The remarriage of persons divorced from a living, lawful spouse contravenes the plan and law of God as taught by Christ. (Catechism of the Catholic Church 1665)

Useful words

Annulment – a declaration by the Church that a marriage was never a true marriage and so the partners are free to marry

Activities

1. Why do you think many marriages end in divorce?
2. What is the difference between divorce and annulment?
3. Look at the photo on page 348. Why do you think divorce is sometimes regarded as the lesser of two evils?
4. Explain why there are different attitudes to divorce among Christians.
5. Do you think remarriage is a good idea?

Section 2: Religious teachings on relationships and families in the twenty-first century

A couple arguing in front of their children. Is it better to divorce than live in hatred and quarrel all the time?

Useful words

Repentance – feeling so sorry for a sin that you determine never to do it again

The attitude of non-Catholic Christians

Most non-Catholic Churches think that divorce is wrong, but allow it if the marriage has broken down. Non-Catholic Churches allow divorce because:

- Jesus allowed divorce in Matthew 19:9 for a partner's adultery, therefore Jesus showed that divorce can happen if the reasons for it are sufficiently severe.

- They believe that there are certain situations where Christians must choose 'the lesser of two evils'. If a marriage has really broken down then the effects of the couple not divorcing would be a greater evil than the evil of divorce itself.

- Christians are allowed forgiveness and a new chance if they confess their sins and are truly repentant. This belief in forgiveness should apply to divorce and remarriage as much as anything else. So a couple should have another chance at marriage as long as they are determined to make it work the second time.

- It is the teaching of these Churches that it is better to divorce than live in hatred and quarrel all the time.

Most of these Churches allow divorced people to remarry, but they usually require them to talk to the priest or minister about why their first marriages failed. They are sometimes asked to show **repentance** for the failure and required to promise that this time their marriage will be for life. There is no such thing as annulment in non-Catholic Christian Churches because they allow divorce. Non-Catholic Christians find it difficult to see any difference between annulment and divorce.

Atheist and Humanist attitudes to divorce and remarriage

Atheists do not believe in God and so they regard marriage as a purely human and legal institution. Some atheists do not believe in marriage and would cohabit and so would have no need to divorce. Many atheists have the same attitude to divorce and remarriage as Humanists (many of whom are atheists). The Humanist attitude is that:

- All married couples should have the right to divorce if they feel the marriage has failed.

- Divorce should make sure that the spouses are treated equally in the financial arrangements.

- Divorce should make sure that any children are well provided for.

- Any divorced person should be treated as a single person and so have the right to remarry if they so wish.

Atheists and Humanists see annulment as a legalistic way of allowing people to divorce without calling it divorce.

Catholic responses to non-Catholic responses to divorce and remarriage

The Catholic Church rejects non-Catholic criticism of the Catholic attitude and teaches that the non-Catholic attitudes are responsible for the breakdown of family life in modern society. However, Pope Francis has indicated that the Church should adopt a more loving approach to Catholics who have divorced and remarried.

Situation Ethics and divorce

Christians, Humanists and atheists often look at a problem like divorce and remarriage and apply an ethical theory to the problem. One such theory is Situation Ethics. This is an ethical theory which began with an American Christian thinker, Joseph Fletcher. He taught that although the rules of the Bible or the Church are important, they can be altered by a situation. For example, the Bible and the Church say that stealing is wrong, but if we found a madman who had gained possession of a nuclear weapon, it would surely be right to steal the weapon from him.

People who use Situation Ethics base their decisions on looking at the situation, deciding on the good and bad points of the possible choices and then determining what would be the best thing to do.

Using Situation Ethics they would look at the advantages of divorce:

- It brings domestic peace and emotional security as it removes the conflict between the spouses.
- It gives opportunities for the spouses to gain personal fulfilment as they are not being forced to stay in a relationship they hate.
- It ends children's exposure to damaging parental conflict since research shows it is unhealthy for children to be around parents who fight and criticise each other.
- It gives a chance for fresh starts for the spouses and opportunities for new, better relationships.

Then they would look at the disadvantages of divorce:

- It is expensive; apart from the legal costs, divorce usually means selling the family home as it is more expensive for two people to live separately than live together. The expense usually means that divorce reduces a family's living standards.
- It can hurt children as they are forced to choose between parents and choose which one to live with.
- It hurts family relatives as they can often lose contact with the children if their relation is not awarded **custody**.
- It causes stress as it forces new relationships and new living situations.

Then they would look at the people involved and try to work out the best and most loving choice. They would probably decide that, if a marriage has broken down and there are no children involved, divorce has more advantages than disadvantages. However, if children were involved the decision would be more difficult. Some research suggests that children suffer from a divorce, but other research suggest they don't, and may even benefit from their parents divorcing.

Activity
Do you think Situation Ethics is a good way of deciding about an issue like divorce?

Useful words
Custody – one parent being made responsible for the care of the children

Practice questions

c Explain two reasons why the Catholic Church does not allow divorce. In your answer you must refer to a source of wisdom and authority.

d 'Christians should never divorce.' Evaluate this statement considering arguments for and against. In your answer you should:
- refer to Catholic points of view
- refer to different Christian or non-religious points of view
- reach a justified conclusion.

Summary
Many marriages now end in divorce, but the Catholic Church does not permit divorce because the sacrament of marriage can only be ended by God. The Church does allow legal separation and the annulment of a marriage if it can be proved to have been invalid. Remarriage is not allowed unless the first marriage has been ended by the death of a spouse or annulment. Non-Catholic Christians, atheists and Humanists allow both divorce and remarriage.

Section 2: Religious teachings on relationships and families in the twenty-first century

Topic 3.2.7 Equality of men and women in the family

Thinking points

In this topic you need to:
- think about Catholic teachings about the equality and roles of men and women in the family, including reference to Catechism 2207
- understand different Christian, atheist and Humanist attitudes about the equality of men and women in the family and Christian responses to them
- be able to explain Catholic and different Christian and non-religious attitudes to the equality of men and women in the family.

Catholic attitudes to the equality and roles of men and women in the family

The Catholic Church teaches that men and women have equal status in the sight of God:

> So God created man in his own image, in the image of God he created them; male and female he created them. (Genesis 1:27)

In the new Catholic marriage service, the priest says: 'May her husband put his trust in her and recognise that she is his equal and the heir with him to the life of grace.'

However, in his 'Letter to the Bishops of the Catholic Church on the Collaboration of Men and Women in the Church and in the World' of 2004, Pope John Paul II clarified that equality does not mean sameness. The Catholic Church teaches that men and women are of equal status, but have different qualities since women are the ones with the biological capacity to bring new life into the world; they are also the ones with the caring capacity needed to bring up a Christian family and so women have a crucial role in family life.

This was confirmed by Pope Francis when addressing a national congress hosted by the Italian Women's Centre, a Catholic women's association promoting greater democracy, solidarity, human rights and human dignity, in January 2014. Pope Francis said that women should play a greater role in society and the Church, but without sacrificing their essential attention and contribution to their families. The Pope said that women have an irreplaceable role within the family, particularly in handing down to future generations 'solid moral principles' and the Christian faith. They should also have the right to equal roles with men in the world of work and politics. However, this is not easy for women as Pope Francis said, 'The critical question for each woman is to discern the right balance of work, community and family.'

Nevertheless, in most Catholic families husband and wife have equal roles.

> The family is the original cell of human life. It is the natural society in which husband and wife are called to give themselves in love and in the gift of life. Authority, stability and a life of relationships within the family constitute the foundations for freedom, security and fraternity within society. The family is the community in which, from childhood, one can learn moral values, begin to honour God and make good use of freedom. Family life is an initiation into life in society. (Catechism of the Catholic Church 2207)

Activities

1. What do you think it means to say that men and women have equal status but different qualities?
2. What do you think of Pope Francis's advice to Catholic women?
3. Read the statement from Catechism of the Catholic Church 2207. What do you think it means for the roles of men and women in the family?

Other Christian attitudes to the equality and roles of men and women in the family

Many Evangelical Protestants teach that men and women have separate and different roles. It is the role of women to bring up children and run a Christian home. Women should not speak in church and must submit to their husbands. It is the role of men to provide for the family and to lead the family in religion; it is the role of women to bring up the children. Traditional Evangelical Protestant Christians believe that women should grow their hair long and keep their heads covered in church as instructed in 1 Corinthians 11:3–10. Men must love their wives as themselves, but only men can be church leaders and teachers.

This attitude is based on the teachings of St Paul in his Letters to Timothy about women not being allowed to teach or speak in church, and his teaching in Ephesians 5:22–30 that wives should submit to their husband as the head of the wife in the same way that Christ is the Head of the Church. This implies that the wife should do as she is told by the husband, but St Paul tries to lessen this by saying that husbands should love their wives in the same way they love their own bodies. However, his words that a husband feeds and cares for his body imply that men should feed and care for women, reinforcing the superiority of men.

Most Protestant Churches now accept that men and women are equal, and should have totally equal roles in life and the family. Their attitude is based on:

- the teachings of Genesis 1 that male and female were created at the same time and equally
- the teaching of St Paul in Galatians that in Christ there is neither male nor female
- the evidence from the Gospels that Jesus treated women as his equals.

Women covering their heads with lace mantillas (veil or shawl) at an Evangelical service in Panajachel, Guatemala.

Atheist and Humanist attitudes to equal roles of men and women in the family

Atheists tend to have the same attitudes to equal roles as the general non-religious population. Their attitude to equal roles of women has changed considerably. In 1965, 85 per cent of men agreed that, 'a man's job is to earn money, a woman's job is to look after the home and family', but in 1989, only 32 per cent of men agreed, and by 2008 only seventeen per cent of men agreed with the statement. The effect of these changed attitudes can be seen in this table, based on research from British Social Attitudes.

Activity	Parent	Hours per week in 1965	Hours per week in 2011
Childcare	Mother	10	14
	Father	3	7
Housework	Mother	32	18
	Father	4	10
Paid employment	Mother	8	21
	Father	42	37

Activities

1. Look at the photo of women worshipping with their heads covered. Do you think women should dress differently from men in church?
2. Look at the table of parental activities (1965 and 2011). What conclusions can be drawn from this about differences in family attitudes between 1965 and 2011?

Section 2: Religious teachings on relationships and families in the twenty-first century

> ### Activity
> Select some different age groups and ask their reactions to the following statement: 'a man's job is to earn money, a woman's job is to look after the home and family'. Discuss your findings.

As can be seen from these changes, the most common non-religious attitude is that men and women are equal and should have equal roles in the family.

However, some non-religious people (in 2008 seventeen per cent of men) still believe that it is 'a man's job is to earn money, a woman's job is to look after the home and family', and a YouGov survey in 2014 showed that:

- married women of working age do three-quarters of the housework
- when women earn more than 65 per cent of family income, their housework hours increase rather than decrease
- men who earn more than their wives do little housework.

Humanists base their beliefs on science and reason and so most Humanists would say they are equalists; that is, they believe that men and women are equal and should have equal rights and therefore have totally equal roles in the family. Many of the suffragettes and early feminists were Humanists and modern Humanism teaches that men and women should have equal roles in the family.

Practice questions

c) Explain two reasons why Christians have different attitudes to equal roles of men and women in the family. In your answer you must refer to a source of wisdom and authority.

d) 'Men and women are totally equal and so should have completely equal roles in the family.' Evaluate this statement considering arguments for and against. In your answer you should:
- refer to Catholic points of view
- refer to different Christian or non-religious points of view
- reach a justified conclusion.

Summary

The Catholic Church teaches that men and women have equal status but different qualities. Women's biological childbearing capacity makes them carers, giving them a crucial role in the family, but with equal roles in the worlds of work and politics. Evangelical Protestants believe that men and women should have different roles and that men should be the head of the family. Liberal Protestants and Humanists believe that men and women are totally equal and should have totally equal roles.

Topic 3.2.8 Gender prejudice and discrimination

Sex discrimination

What is gender prejudice, gender discrimination and sexism?

- Gender prejudice is believing that one sex is superior to another based on feeling rather than an assessment of evidence.
- Gender discrimination is putting the prejudice into practice and treating people differently because of their sex.
- Sexism is discrimination, prejudice or stereotyping on the basis of gender. Sexism is most often expressed towards girls and women.

Catholic attitudes

The Catholic Church is against gender prejudice and discrimination. It teaches that men and women should have equal roles in life and equal rights in society because Genesis 1:27 teaches that God created men and women at the same time and both in the image of God. Furthermore, it is the teaching of the Catholic Catechism that men and women are equal, and should have equal rights in life and society, and so the Catechism opposes all forms of gender prejudice.

> *There exist also* **sinful inequalities** *that affect millions of men and women. These are in open contradiction of the Gospel: 'Their equal dignity as persons demands that we strive for fairer and more humane conditions. Excessive economic and social disparity between individuals and peoples of the one human race is a source of scandal and militates against social justice, equity, human dignity, as well as social and international peace.' (Catechism of the Catholic Church 1938)*

In its 'Theology of the Body', summarised in Pope Benedict's first encyclical, *Deus Caritas Est* ('God is Love'), the Church teaches that there should be no gender prejudice or discrimination because God gave humans their bodies and therefore the nature of male and female bodies. The differences in bodies should be celebrated as the means to the joys of family life, not used as an excuse for prejudice and discrimination.

> *There is neither Jew not Greek, slave nor free, male nor female, for you are all one in Christ Jesus. (Galatians 3:28)*

Examples of Catholic opposition to gender prejudice and discrimination

In the second half of the twentieth century the reforms instituted by the Second Vatican Council led to pressure from Catholic women for greater equality within the Church, which led to the Church changing the rules about women's roles in the Church.

Thinking points

In this topic you need to:
- think about Catholic teachings about gender prejudice and discrimination, including theology of the body
- consider examples of Catholic opposition to gender prejudice and discrimination, including Catechism 1938
- understand different Christian, atheist and Humanist attitudes to gender prejudice and discrimination, and Catholic responses to them
- be able to explain and evaluate different Catholic, other Christian and non-religious attitudes to gender prejudice and discrimination.

Activity

What is the difference between gender prejudice and gender discrimination?

Section 2: Religious teachings on relationships and families in the twenty-first century

Useful words

Extraordinary minister – a non-ordained man or woman who assists the work of priests

Lector – someone given the authority to read the Bible readings at Mass

Ordination – the act of conferring holy orders (making a priest)

Ordained – set down by God – or made a priest

As a result of this pressure, women are now able to:

- study and teach in theological colleges
- be **extraordinary ministers** of Holy Communion (people who give out the bread and wine which has been consecrated by a priest)
- visit the sick
- read the Bible readings at Mass (**lectors**)
- take funerals in certain circumstances.

Cynthia Stewart, in her 2008 book *The Catholic Church: A Brief Popular History*, claims that although the hierarchy of the Church is entirely male as a result of the restriction against **ordination** of women, the vast majority of Catholics that participate in lay ministry are women. She says that approximately 85 per cent of all Church roles that do not require ordination are performed by women.

The importance of women to the 'life and mission of the Church' was emphasised by Pope John Paul II, who wrote:

> The presence and the role of women in the life and mission of the Church, although not linked to the ministerial priesthood, remain absolutely necessary and irreplaceable. As the Declaration Inter Insigniores points out, 'The Church desires that Christian women should become fully aware of the greatness of their mission: today their role is of capital importance both for the renewal and humanization of society and for the rediscovery by believers of the true face of the Church'. (Ordonatio Sacerdotalis, *St John Paul II, 1994*)

Mary Robinson, president of Ireland 1990–7

Mary Robinson was born in County Mayo in 1944 and educated at Catholic schools and Trinity College Dublin. She became a civil rights lawyer and politician, in which role she campaigned for an end to the discrimination which women faced in Ireland at the time. Even in the 1970s, Irish women could not serve on juries, could not divorce (even if their husbands were cruel and violent) and had to resign their jobs in the civil service if they married. Mrs Robinson led campaigns against all of these and for legalising contraception and decriminalising homosexuality. In 1990, Mrs Robinson was elected president of Ireland, the first woman to hold that position. During her presidency, divorce, contraception and homosexuality were all legalised, her other campaigns having been successful before 1990. Mary Robinson resigned the presidency to become UN High Commissioner for Human Rights, working for equal rights for all.

Other Christians and gender prejudice

Evangelical Protestants

Evangelical Protestants teach that men and women have separate and different roles and so cannot have equal rights in religion. It is the role of women to bring up children and run a Christian home. They also believe that women should not speak in church, should not teach and must submit to their husbands. It is the role of men to provide for the family and to lead the family in religion. Men must love their wives as themselves, but only men can be church leaders and teachers. They do not see this as discrimination because it is what God **ordained** in the New Testament, which they believe

Activities

1. Outline the similarities and differences between the Evangelical Protestant and Catholic attitudes to gender prejudice and discrimination.

2. Look at the photo on page 355. Why do you think so many Christians were against having women bishops?

Topic 3.2.8 Gender prejudice and discrimination

is the final Word of God. St Paul teaches that women should not teach or speak in church. He also uses the story of Adam and Eve in Genesis to show that men have been given more rights by God because Adam was created first and it was the woman who was led astray by Satan and then led man astray.

Liberal Protestant Churches

Liberal Protestant Churches are totally opposed to any form of gender discrimination and believe that men and women should have totally equal rights in life and in the Church. Consequently, they have women ministers, priests and bishops because the creation story in Genesis 1 says that God created male and female at the same time and of equal status. St Paul taught that in Christ there is neither male nor female, and there is evidence in the Gospels that Jesus treated women as his equals.

Activities

1. Would your responses to the MTV survey have been the same?
2. Do you think men and women are treated equally in the Church?
3. Look at the photo on page 356. Do you think this ever could, or should, happen?

Pat Storey (left) became Britain and Ireland's first female bishop when she was consecrated by the Anglican Church in a ceremony in Dublin in November 2013.

Atheist and Humanist attitudes to gender prejudice and discrimination

Most atheists and all Humanists believe that men and women are equal and should have equal rights. The pressure for equal pay for women and to end **sex discrimination** came from non-religious politicians like Barbara Castle in the 1970s. Humanists are against any form of gender prejudice or discrimination and have been keen supporters of legislation to promote women's rights. Humanists believe that it is wrong for religion to be able to discriminate against women and that gender discrimination in religion should be banned. In particular, they believe that the Catholic Church's refusal to ordain women or have women leaders should be made illegal because it denies equal rights.

Useful words

Sex discrimination – treating people differently on the ground of their gender

Section 2: Religious teachings on relationships and families in the twenty-first century

Young people and gender prejudice

In a 2014, an MTV survey of young people's opinions found the following:

- An overwhelming 92 per cent of males and 94 per cent of females believe that nobody should be treated differently due to gender.
- More than three in four males (76 per cent) and eight in ten females say favouring one gender is unfair.
- Both genders (85 per cent of males, 90 per cent of females) believe that gender inequality can lead to big problems for society.
- Only two per cent of young people say that men and women are totally equal today and only 23 per cent say men and women are at least mostly equal.

Catholic responses

The opposition of the Catholic Church to gender prejudice and discrimination means that the only criticism it needs to respond to is the criticism that not allowing women to become priests amounts to gender discrimination.

The Church responds to this charge as follows:

- Only men being permitted to be priests is not discriminatory because women cannot fulfil a basic function of the priesthood. The priest stands in the place of Jesus during the Mass and women cannot stand in the place of a man.
- This is not a judgement on women's abilities or rights, it is a fact about the role of the priest in Catholicism – to represent Jesus in the Mass.
- Men and women are equal, but their sexuality is not interchangeable – people's gender is not an accident – a woman cannot represent Jesus in the Mass.
- Jesus chose twelve men – and no women – to be his **apostles**. This was a clear, deliberate choice which must apply to every age.
- People should not be surprised that the Church expects a man to stand 'in the person of Christ' as a priest, to represent Jesus in his humanity, because humanity is not sexually neutral.

Activists of the Women's Ordination Advocates organisation hold a banner during their vigil in St Peter's Square at the Vatican in 2010, calling on Pope Benedict XVI to ordain women.

Useful words

Apostles – men chosen by Jesus to preach his gospel (often used for the twelve disciples)

Summary

The Catholic Church opposes gender prejudice and discrimination, both of which are condemned in the Catechism. Women can have any job in the Church which does not require ordination, and up to 85 per cent of these jobs are held by women. Mary Robinson, the first female Irish president, is a Catholic who has spent much of her life working for equal rights. As far as other Christians are concerned, Evangelical Protestants believe in separate and different roles for men and women. However, Liberal Protestants believe in completely equal status and roles and have women priests and bishops. Humanists also believe in complete equality and object to the Catholic Church preventing women from being ordained.

Practice questions

c Explain two reasons why Catholic Christians are opposed to gender prejudice and discrimination. In your answer you must refer to a source of wisdom and authority.

d 'Christians should never treat women differently from men.' Evaluate this statement considering arguments for and against. In your answer you should:
- refer to Catholic points of view
- refer to different Christian or non-religious points of view
- reach a justified conclusion.

How to answer questions

a) Outline three purposes of the family for Catholics. [3]

Catholics believe the family has the basic task of bringing up children safely and securely until they are mature enough to look after themselves. Also, a Catholic family has a duty to instil moral values into their children so that they become good responsible citizens. Thirdly, a Catholic family should bring the children up in the Catholic faith and do their best to ensure that the children become good Catholic Christians as adults.

A high mark answer because three purposes of a Catholic family are clearly outlined.

b) Explain two ways a Catholic church helps the family. [4]

One way is by funding and supporting the local church primary and secondary schools, which provide Christian education and worship in addition to the standard education. This education helps the family because it teaches children right from wrong, teaches children about the Christian faith and helps parents to fulfil their marriage and baptism promises to bring their children up as Christians.

Another way is by having family-friendly worship which helps family life, because family life can be strengthened by families worshipping together. Family worship helps to unite the family and gives families an opportunity to discover religion together. Often children have their own Liturgy of the Word specially geared to their needs before joining with the whole church family for the Liturgy of the Eucharist.

A high mark answer because two correct ways of a Catholic church helping families are clearly explained.

c) Explain two reasons why marriage may be important for Catholics. In your answer you must refer to a source of wisdom and authority. [5]

Marriage is very important in Catholic life because Catholic Christians believe marriage was created by God as the way of establishing and preserving society. 'But at the beginning of creation God made them male and female. For this reason a man will leave his father and mother and be united to his wife, and the two will become one flesh' (Mark 10:6–8). Also, in 'Not Just Good, But Beautiful', Pope Francis showed the importance of marriage by expressing his worries about people giving up on marriage and causing a crisis in the social environment similar to the ecological crisis in the material environment. He urged society to return to lifelong marriage because 'the union of a man and woman in marriage is a unique, natural, fundamental good for persons, communities and whole societies'.

A high mark answer because two correct reasons are given and each reason is developed with a reference to the Bible and the teachings of the Pope, which are both sources of authority for Catholics.

d) 'The purpose of sex is to have children.' Evaluate this statement considering arguments for and against. In your response you should:
- refer to Catholic Christian points of view
- refer to different Christian or non-religious points of view
- reach a justified conclusion. [12 marks + 3 spelling, punctuation and grammar (SPaG) marks]

Many Catholics would agree with this because the Catechism teaches that sex should be both unitive and procreative, which is the 'twofold end of marriage'. They would also refer to

[Continued]

Section 2: Religious teachings on relationships and families in the twenty-first century

Pope Francis's statement that 'openness to life conditions the sacrament of matrimony'. The Catechism (2366) also states that 'each and every marriage act (sex) must remain open to the transmission of life', indicating that the purpose of sex is to have children.

Non-Catholic Christians and the non-religious would disagree. They believe that sex can be purely an expression of love between a couple. This is clearly seen in their acceptance of artificial methods of birth control which allow them to have sex without any purpose of procreation. In 1930, the Lambeth Conference of the worldwide Anglican Communion (Church of England) declared that it was legitimate for Christians to use contraception to limit family size. This has been followed by the major Protestant Churches and the Orthodox Churches.

Non-religious people are in favour of artificial methods of contraception and so they believe that sex does not have to involve procreation. They might also use ethical principles like Situation Ethics to assess whether sex should involve procreation and decide that sex without procreation has the most loving consequences. If they used utilitarianism they would argue that sex without procreation brings the greatest happiness to the greatest number of people.

So it appears that although having children is one of the purposes of sex, it is by no means the only purpose, and sex as an expression of love is accepted by Catholics, non-Catholic Christians and the non-religious as a major purpose of sex.

A high mark answer because it gives three clear developed Catholic reasons for thinking that the purpose of sex is to have children. It then gives three reasons for disagreeing before reaching a fully justified conclusion.

Spelling, punctuation and grammar are correct and a wide range of specialist vocabulary (unitive, procreative, Catechism, Pope Francis, twofold end of marriage, Lambeth Conference, Anglican Communion, Situation Ethics, utilitarianism) is used appropriately.

Glossary

Abortifacient Bringing about a very early abortion

Absolution Through the actions and words of a priest or minister pardon of sins is assured

Abu Bak'r Muhammad's friend and first Caliph, who ordered the first collection of the Qur'an

Acolyte A server who carries a candle

Adalat God's attribute of justice

Adhan The call to prayer

Adoptionism The heresy that the Son of God was adopted by God and not begotten of God

Adoration Praising or adoring God for what he is

Adultery A sexual act between a married person and someone other than their marriage partner

Aggiornamento The Italian for bringing something up to date

Ahmadiyya A Muslim sect founded in Pakistan by Yirza Ahmad

Akirah Belief in the Last Day and life after death

Al-Hijra 1 Muharram, Islamic New Year's Day

Al'Jannah Heaven

Alb A long white garment worn by a priest during the Mass

Allah The Arabic for God

Alms Charitable giving to the poor

Alpha A Christian course trying to convert non-churchgoers

Alpha and omega The first and the last, the start and end of the Greek alphabet

Altar The place where the bread and wine are consecrated; it is a place of sacrifice and a table of sharing

Ambo A raised platform where people read or speak from

Amidah The standing prayer

Amir al-Mu'minin Commander of the faithful, a title given by Shi'as to Ali and his descendants

Annulment A declaration by the Church that a marriage was never a true marriage and so the partners are free to marry

Annunciation The greeting of the Archangel Gabriel to the Virgin Mary when he announced that she was to have a son who would be the Christ

Anoint Apply oil to the head or body as part of a religious rite

Apocalyptic A style of writing that used symbols and codes to teach spiritual truths and to try to foretell the future

Apostles Prophets or messengers: the titles given to those who brought God's message

Apostolic Based on the teaching of the twelve apostles

Apostolic Succession The line of bishops going back to the apostles

Apostolic Tradition The faith taught by Jesus and the apostles

Apparitions Visionary experiences that have a physical effect on people around the visionary

Arafat The plain and hill eighteen kilometres from Makkah where the central part of *hajj* takes place

Arianism The heresy that the son of God was created by God after the creation

Ark A container; the Ark of the Covenant contained the Ten Commandments and was seen as being especially blessed

Ark of the Covenant The holy container for the tablets of the commandments

Aron Hakodesh The Ark

Arvit Evening prayer

As'r Afternoon prayer

Ascension The return of Christ to heaven

Assumption The belief that the Virgin Mary was taken into heaven body and soul

Auditory vision A vision which is only a voice with no images

Auschwitz A Nazi Second World War concentration camp in Poland where at least 1.1 million Jews died

Avelut The mourning period

Awe A sense of overwhelming wonder at the vastness, mystery or beauty of something

Ayatollah The highest ranking religious leader in Twelver Shi'ism

Bar Mitzvah Son of the commandment; a Jewish boy's coming of age

Baroque Elaborate style of church building and decoration from the seventeenth century onwards

Barzakh The period between death and the Last Day

359

Glossary

Basilicas Important church buildings and place of pilgrimage

Bat Brit Ceremony for female babies in Liberal/Reform synagogues

Bat Chayil Daughter of worth; name used by some Orthodox synagogues instead of Bat Mitzvah

Beatified The first stage in being declared a saint; the declaration that a deceased person is counted among the blessed

Benevolence Being all-good, all-loving

Berith The Hebrew for covenant

Biblia The Greek word that 'Bible' is derived from, meaning 'the books'

Big Bang The beginning of the universe from a 'cosmic egg'

Bimah The raised platform for Torah readings

Bismillah the words at the beginning of each surah, 'in the name of Allah, the Merciful, the Compassionate'

Blasphemy Speaking sacrilegiously about God or sacred things

Blessed Sacrament The consecrated bread and wine

Blessed Sacrament procession The consecrated host is carried through the streets in a special container, a monstrance

Book of Life The book where one's quality of life for the coming year is recorded

Brit Chayim Covenant of life ceremony for Reform girl babies

Brit Milah Covenant of circumcision

Brit Shalom Covenant of peace (ceremony welcoming uncircumcised male babies)

Caliph Leader of the Islamic community

Canaan Ancient name for the land of Israel

Canon A rule or list of approved books

Canonised A person being declared a saint by the Church

Cardinal virtues The major virtues: justice, prudence, fortitude and temperance

Catechesis Teaching about the faith

Catechetical programmes Religious instruction given in preparation for Christian baptism or confirmation

Catholic Means 'whole world' or 'universal'

Catholic Catechism A compendium of the official teaching of the Catholic Church

Celibate Living without sexual activity

Cenacle The Upper Room in Jerusalem where the Last Supper took place

Chalice A silver or gold cup for the wine to be consecrated at the Mass

Challot Plaited loaves used on *Shabbat* and festivals

Chametz Any food containing yeast/leaven

Charisms Special gifts or callings

Chasuble A colourful garment worn by a priest over the alb and stole

Chazzan The leader of worship who chants the prayers (also called a cantor)

Chevra kaddisha Burial society

Chi-Rho A sign made up of the first two letters for Christ in Greek

Childbearing age The age when a woman is capable of having children

Children's liturgy A celebration and explanation of the readings at Mass especially for children

Chrism The oil used in baptism, confirmation and ordination

Chukim *Mitzvot* with no reason given for them

Church Councils Assemblies of bishops authorised to make decisions on theological issues

Ciborium The silver or gold container for the hosts

Circumambulate Walk round, make a circuit

Civil divorce A divorce according to the law of the country but not the Church

Civil partnerships Legal ceremonies giving homosexual partners the same legal rights as husband and wife

Clergy Those ordained by the Church

Cohabitation Living as man and wife without being married

Committal The burial of a dead body

Common priesthood All the baptised who follow Christ and serve him

Concelebrate When priests join together in the consecratory prayers of the Eucharist

Conciliar The Church meeting and working as a Council of Bishops with the Pope

Confession Prayers saying sorry for sins and asking God's forgiveness

Conscience A reasoned approach to what is right and wrong using our innate moral faculty

Consecrated To be dedicated to a religious purpose

Consensual sex When both parties freely agree to sex

Consubstantial Of one substance

Consummate Complete a marriage through sexual intercourse

Contemplation Communion with God

Contingent The fact that something does not have to exist, it could either be or not be

Contrition Sorrow for the sin committed and deciding not to commit the sin again

Glossary

Conversion An experience which changes a person's life or religion

Council A meeting of the Pope and the bishops

Covenant A binding, sacred agreement

Creator Used with a capital C to describe God as the Creator of the universe

Creed Statement of Christian beliefs

Custody One parent being made responsible for the care of the children

Days of Awe The ten days between Rosh Hashanah and Yom Kippur

Dead Sea Scrolls Copies of Old Testament books discovered in the Holy Land in about 1947

Decades The ten Hail Marys said during the Rosary

Decalogue The Ten Commandments

Decree An official order from a high authority

Deity God

Desecrate Violate a sacred place or law

Design When things are connected and seem to have a purpose, for example the eye is designed for seeing

Destiny What has been set out to happen

Dhu al-Hijjah Twelfth and final month of the Islamic calendar

Dioceses Church areas under the direction of bishops

Dominion Power and authority over the earth

Doxology The praise of God in words, music or song

Eastern Rite Eastern customs and liturgy followed by Catholics who were once Orthodox

Ecumenical Working together for unity, from the word for 'the whole world'

Ellul The final month of the Jewish year

Encyclical A letter addressed by the Pope to all the bishops of the Church

Ethical monotheism Belief in one God who demands moral obedience

Etrog A citron fruit

Eucharist A sacrament commemorating the Last Supper

Eucharistic prayer The prayer of thanksgiving and consecration over the bread and wine

Evangelisation Proposing or spreading the faith through teaching about the religion helping others

Evangelist A Gospel writer

Evolution The idea that life forms change over time (humans have developed from single-celled organisms)

Ex cathedra 'From the chair'; from the throne of St Peter

Ex nihilo Latin words meaning from nothing

Exile When the Jewish people had to leave their homeland and live elsewhere

Exodus The Israelites' escape from slavery in Egypt

Extempore Spontaneous, personal prayers in a person's own words

Extramarital sex Sex outside marriage, usually refers to adultery

Extraordinary minister A non-ordained man or woman who assists the work of priests

Faithfulness Staying with your marriage partner and having sex only with them

Fajr Dawn prayer

Fatimid An Ismaili caliphate that ruled North Africa from 909CE to 1171CE

First Communion The first time a person receives the sacrament of the Eucharist; children receive special lessons before this important occasion

Foreknowledge Knowing what is going to happen long before it does

Form The words used in the sacrament

Franciscan A member of a religious order that follows the teachings and spiritual disciplines of St Francis of Assisi

Free will The idea that human beings are free to make their own choices

Fresco A painting rendered on fresh plaster

Friar A member of a religious order who does not own property and who has to either work or beg to earn their living

Fundamentalist One who believes the Bible is the literal word of God

Fundamentalist Protestants Those who believe that statements in the Bible are the literal truth

Gan Eden Heaven

Gehinnom Hell

Gentiles Non-Jews

Ghadeer Khum The Pool of Khum halfway between Makkah and Madinah

Golden rule Do to others what you would wish them do to you

Good Friday The day that Jesus died on the cross; called 'Good' by Catholics as Jesus is seen as dying to forgive sins

Gospel Literally 'Good News', telling the life and teachings of Jesus

Gothic Style of medieval church building with pointed arches

Grace Undeserved blessing from God

Great Commission Jesus' last command to his disciples to go out and convert the world

Glossary

Hadith Sayings of the Prophet Muhammad

Haftarot Portions of the Nevi'im read after the Torah in services

Hagadah Book telling the story of the first Passover

Hajj Pilgrimage to Makkah, the fifth pillar

Hajji One who has completed the *hajj*

Halakhah Jewish law from the Written and Oral Torah

Halakhah The holy law of Judaism

Halal That which is permitted

Halo The golden circle around Christ's or a saint's head to show that they are holy

Haram That which is not permitted

Harrowing of Hell A medieval play about the risen Christ freeing people from hell

Hashem The Name, a word used to refer to God without mentioning his name

Havdalah Ceremony marking the ending of *Shabbat*

Hawwa The first woman, Adam's wife (Eve)

Heaven A place of infinite peace in the presence of God

Hechsher A label certifying that a food is *kosher*

Hell A place of eternal separation from the love of God

Heresies Religious opinions which contradict official Church teaching

Heterosexual Attracted to the opposite sex

Hidden Imam The twelfth Imam who disappeared and is believed to be in contact with the ayatollahs

Holiness The state of being very moral and spiritual

Holocaust The mass murder of Jews by the Nazis in the Second World War

Holy Hour An hour spent in Eucharistic adoration

Holy of Holies The Holy Place in the ancient Jerusalem Temple

Homage Acknowledgement of superiority

Homosexuality Sexual attraction to a same-sex partner

Host Sacramental unleavened bread

Human dignity The belief that humans are persons, not things, and that they have self-knowledge and free will

Huppah Wedding canopy

Husayn Muhammad's grandson and the third imam of Shi'a Islam

Ibadah Worship

Ichthus Greek for fish; an early Christian symbol

Icon A devotional painting of Christ or other holy figures

Iconostasis The screen separating the sanctuary from the nave in Eastern churches, which is decorated with icons

Iftar The meal breaking the fast at night

Ihram Pilgrim dress

Imam Prayer leader

Imamah Belief in the successors of the Prophet Muhammad. For Shi'as, Imam is a successor, but 'imam' with a small 'i' is a prayer leader for Sunnis

Imamate The office of the Imam

Iman Faith

Immaculate conception The Catholic belief that God preserved Mary from original sin from the moment she was conceived

Immutable Unable to be changed and unchanging over time

Incarnation The belief that God became a human being as Jesus

Initiation A ritual action admitting someone into a group

Injil The Gospel given to Isa (Jesus)

Insh Allah If God wills

Inspired Stimulated by God to do things

Intercede To use your influence to persuade someone in authority to forgive another person

Intercessory prayers Prayers asking God's help for other people

Interiority Taking space and time for quiet, self-reflection

Interment Burial of a dead body

Isaac Abraham's son through Sarah, ancestor of Jewish people

Isha Night prayer

Ishaq Ibrahim's son Isaac, the father of the Jewish people

Ishmael Abraham's son through Hagar, ancestor of Arab people

Ismaili Shi'as who believe that the seventh Imam, Isma'il, was the final Imam

Israfil The angel who begins the Last Day by blowing his trumpet

IUD Intrauterine device (the coil)

Izra'il The angel of death

Jahannam Hell

Jami mosques Mosques appointed for Friday prayers

Jibril The archangel Gabriel

Jihadi One fighting in a Holy War

Jummah Friday midday prayers

Glossary

Ka'aba The House of God in Makkah containing the black stone (or Ka'ba)

Kabbalah Jewish mysticism

Kaddish The prayer recited publicly by mourners

Karbala Site of the battle where Husayn was killed by Caliph Yazid (100 km southwest of Baghdad)

Kashrut Keeping Jewish food laws

Ketubah Marriage contract

Ketuvim Holy writings

Keys of the kingdom The authority Catholics believe that St Peter (and then the popes) received from Christ

Khalifahs Allah's stewards or vicegerents

Khums An additional charity tax for Shi'a Muslims

Khutba Sermon

Kiddush A prayer said over wine to sanctify *Shabbat*

Kutub Holy books (singular *kitab*)

Kol Nidrei Annulment of vows made before Yom Kippur

Kosher Food which a Jew is allowed to eat

Kvatters People who carry the baby to Brit Milah

Lady Chapel A side chapel in a Catholic church reserved for devotion to the Blessed Virgin Mary

Lailat al-Miraj The Prophet's night journey to Jerusalem and then to heaven

Laylat al-Qadr The Night of Power (destiny)

Lectern Raised stand where the Bible is read from

Lectio Divina Sacred or divine reading; a way of praying and studying a passage from the Bible

Lectionary A list of Bible readings to be read at certain times of the year

Lector Someone given the authority to read the Bible readings at Mass

LEDCs Less economically developed countries

Liberal One who believes the Bible was written by humans inspired by God and so may need reinterpreting in light of the modern world

Lifelong relationship The idea that marriage can only be ended by the death of a partner

Liturgical year The year in the Church's calendar based on the special festivals from Advent to the Ordinary Sundays

Liturgy A set form of public worship

Lulav Palm branch

Ma'sa The covered passageway between the hills Marwa and Safa, which pilgrims run between

Madonna 'Mother of God', referring to how Mary carried God in Jesus in her womb. God as Spirit ultimately does not have or need a mother, but the incarnation of God in Christ did

Maghrib Sunset prayers

Magisterium The teaching office of the Church, from the Latin word *magister,* for 'teacher'

Maimonides Medieval rabbi and philosopher (1135–1204) who wrote the Thirteen Principles

Makkah The city in Arabia where Muhammad was born

Malaikah Angels

Maryam The Virgin Mary

Material needs Such things as food, drink and clothing

Matrimony Marriage

Matter The symbolic actions performed in the sacrament

Maundy Thursday The day before Good Friday

Mawlid al-Nabi The birthday of the Prophet Muhammad

MEDCs More economically developed countries

Meditation Thinking about religious matters

Menorah Seven-branched candlestick

Messiah The Hebrew word for Christ, meaning God's Anointed King, the coming deliverer

Messianic Age A time when all nations will live at peace and there will be justice in the world

Mezuzah Small scroll of the *shema* fixed to the doorpost of the rooms in a Jewish house

Midrash Collection of rabbinic commentaries on the Tenakh

Mihrab Alcove in mosques showing the direction of Makkah

Mika'il The angel Michael

Mina The place ten kilometres from Makkah where pilgrims throw stones at Satan and make the sacrifice

Minaret The tower beside the mosque from which the call to prayer is announced

Minchah Afternoon prayer

Ministry of Jesus The teaching and public activity of Jesus

Minyan The required number of adult male Jews needed for certain prayers to be said in the synagogue

Mishneh Commentaries on the Torah written about 200CE

Mishneh *Shabbat* The part of the Talmud which contains all the regulations for *Shabbat*

Mishneh Torah The code of law written by Maimonides

Mission Metropolis The Catholic mission to start the re-evangelisation of Europe from the cities

Mitzvah Commandment (singular)

Mitzvot Commandments (plural)

363

Glossary

Mohel Expert circumciser

Monogamous Having only one spouse at a time

Monotheism Belief that there is only one God

Monstrance Vessel used for the exhibition of the Blessed Sacrament

Moral evil Suffering caused by actions done by humans

Moral imperatives Things people feel they must do because they are the right things to do

Moral values The standards of good and evil, which govern people's behaviour and choices

Mount Zion The holy hill in Jerusalem where the Temple was

Mu'tazilites Eighth-century Muslim theologians regarded as non-Muslim by most Sunni Muslims today

Muezzin The prayer caller who announces the call to prayer five times a day

Muharram The first month of the Islamic calendar

Mujtahid A Shi'a scholar with sufficient training and knowledge to interpret the Shari'ah

Muslim Law Schools The four schools which interpret the Shari'ah for Sunni Muslims

Mystery play A medieval play about the great stories of the Bible

Narthex The porch area at the entrance of a church building

Natural law The inbuilt moral order to the universe

Natural revelation The revealing of God in the nature of the universe

Natural suffering Suffering which is caused by nature and has nothing to do with humans

Nature miracle A miracle involving a change in natural objects or forces

Nave The main part of a church building where the worshippers stand, sit or kneel

Ner tamid The everlasting light

Nevi'im The books of the prophets

NFP Natural family planning

Ninety-nine names The titles or characteristics given to Allah in the Qur'an

Nisab The amount of income or wealth a Muslim needs to have before they are liable for *zakah*

Nubuwwah Prophets of God

Numinous The feeling of the presence of something greater than you

Nuptial blessing A special blessing on the bride and groom

Omni-benevolent The belief that God is all-good

Omnipotence The quality of being all-powerful

Omnipotent The belief that God is all-powerful

Omniscience God's characteristic of being all-knowing

Omniscient The belief that God knows everything that has happened and everything that is going to happen

Oral Torah The unwritten Torah given to Moses by God

Ordained Set down by God – or made a priest

Ordination Making someone a priest, bishop or deacon by the sacrament of holy orders

Original sin The sin of the first humans (symbolised by Adam and Eve) inherited by humans as mortality and selfishness

Papal infallibility When the Pope speaks authoritatively on a disputed matter of doctrine

Parish priest The clergy person responsible for a local church

Paschal Relating to Easter: the death and resurrection of Jesus

Passion The journey of Jesus to the cross

Passion plays Plays retelling the story of the passion and resurrection

Paten A silver or gold plate that has the priest's host

Paten Small plate used to hold the Eucharistic bread

Patriarchs The fathers of Israel (Abraham, Isaac, Jacob and Moses)

Penance An action showing contrition

Penitential Rite The confession and absolution at the beginning of the Mass

People In the Bible, more than a collection of human beings; a special set, tribe, nation who were called and blessed by God for service, and who belonged to God

Physical needs Such things as housing and shelter from the elements

Pieta Lamentation, a scene of Mary holding the dead Christ

Piety Religious devotion

Pilgrim people The idea that Christians are pilgrims whose life is a pilgrimage to heaven

Plainchant A style of unaccompanied singing for monastic offices or the Mass

Polygamous Having more than one spouse at a time

Polytheism Worshipping many gods

Pontifical Relating to the office of the Pope as the Supreme Pontiff, the Head of the Church on earth

Popular piety Worship, respect and devotion shown to God and the saints

Precepts of the Church Rules Catholics are expected to follow

Glossary

Predestination The belief that everything that happens has already been decided

Premarital sex Sex before marriage

Procreation Making a new life

Procreative purpose Sex as a means of creating a family

Procreative sex Sex which is open to the possibility of new life being formed

Promiscuity Having sex with a number of partners without commitment

Prophecy Speaking the Word of God, either for the future or for the present

Prophesied Predicted events in the future

Proselytism Converting others, often through aggressive or coercive techniques, which are frowned upon by Catholics today

Prostrated To put oneself flat on the ground so as to be lying face downwards, especially in respect of submission

Psalm A prayer of praise, petition or lament in the Old Testament

Psalms A book of the Old Testament containing 150 sacred songs

Purgatory A place where Catholic Christians believe souls go after death to be purified

Purgatory A preparation for heaven, a place of purification and healing

Purim Jewish holy day to celebrate the saving of the Jewish people from Haman, who was trying to kill all the Jews in Persia

Qibla Direction of the Ka'aba in Makkah

Rabbis Spiritual leaders of a Jewish community

Raka The set actions in the prayer ritual (plural *rakat*)

Ramadan Ninth month of the Islamic year; the month of fasting

Reconciliation Bringing together people who were opposed to each other

Regenerative experience A conversion experience giving the feeling of being 'born again'

Relics Parts of a dead saint's body or belongings

Remarriage Marrying again after a divorce

Remembrance of Allah Thinking about God in a meditative way

Repentance Feeling so sorry for a sin that you determine never to do it again

Resurrection A belief that the body will be raised again to life but in a new, spiritual, transformed way

Reverence An act showing religious respect

Risalah Belief in Allah's angels, prophets and holy books

Rood screen A medieval, Western version of the Eastern iconostasis separating the sanctuary from the nave

Rosary The prayer beads used to help in saying the set series of prayers based on the rosary beads

Rosh Hashanah Jewish New Year

Rylands fragment The earliest definite fragment of a Gospel, the Gospel of John

Sacraments Outward signs of an inward blessing through which invisible grace is given to a person

Sacred Heart An image where the heart of Jesus is surrounded by thorns with a flame burning on top of it

Sadaqah Voluntary giving to the poor

Sahifa Ibrahim The holy book given to Ibrahim (Abraham)

Salah Ritual prayers to be said five times a day, the second pillar

Salvation Deliverance from sin and its consequences

Salvation history The plan and process of God's saving work on earth

Sanctify To make holy

Sanctity of life The belief that life is holy and belongs to God

Sanctuary God's holy place

Sanctuary The most holy part of a religious building (can also mean a place of safety)

Sandek Person who holds the baby for Brit Milah

Sanhedrin The supreme religious authority in Israel in biblical times

Sarcophagus A stone container for bones (plural: sarcophagi)

Sawm Fasting, the fourth pillar

Sects Group with different religious beliefs from those of a larger group to which they belong

Seder The Passover meal

Sefer Torah The scroll of the Torah

Self-knowledge Knowing who you are and why you are here

Self-subsistent Without dependence on or support from anything else

Seminaries Educational institutions which prepare pupils for ordination as clergy

Separated brethren Non-Catholic Christians

Sex discrimination Treating people differently on the ground of their gender

Shabbat The Jewish holy day on Saturday, the seventh day of the week

Shacharit Morning prayer

Shahadah The Muslim creed and first pillar

Shari'ah The holy law of Islam

365

Glossary

Shaytan The devil

Shechitah Jewish method of slaughtering animals

Shema The declaration of Jewish belief in one God

Shirk The sin of associating other things with God; it is the worst sin

Shiva The seven days of intense mourning

Shochet A Jewish butcher

Shofar A musical instrument

Shrine A place of worship holding the tomb or relic of a saint

Shroud Burial cloth

Shul The name used for the synagogue by many Jews

Siddur The daily prayer book

Sidra A passage from the Torah

Sidra The portion of the Torah read at *Shabbat* morning service

Simchat Torah The festival celebrating the giving of the Torah

Sin An act that is against God's will

Sirah A biography of the prophet Muhammad

Sister Churches The Eastern Orthodox Churches which have most of the Apostolic Tradition and Succession, although separate from the Pope

Sistrum Ethiopian musical instrument with small cymbals

Sola scriptura 'Scripture alone'; the Protestant idea that the Bible alone is the source of authority in the Church

Special revelation The revealing of God in such things as holy books, for example the Bible

Spiritual The non-material element of life, such as religion, feelings and values

Spouse Marriage or cohabitation partner

Stewardship Looking after something so it can be passed on to the next generation

Stole A colourful scarf worn by the priest beneath the chasuble

Stonewall A group which campaigns for the equality of lesbian, gay, bisexual and transgender people across Britain

Stoup A container on the wall to hold holy water

Suhur The meal just before fasting starts at dawn

Summa Theologica Thomas Aquinas' major book, written in 1265–74

Sunnah The example and way of life of the Prophet Muhammad

Supplication Prayers asking for God's help

Surah A chapter of the Qur'an (there are 114 surahs)

Synoptic The Gospels of Matthew, Mark and Luke that have similar styles

Tabernacle A safe place in which is kept the Blessed Sacrament

Talbiya The *hajj* prayer which pilgrims say constantly

Tallit A fringed garment worn by Jews

Talmud Collection of Mishneh and other writing on the Jewish law

Tashlich Casting away sins into running water

Tawaf Seven circuits of the Ka'aba

Tawhid Belief in Allah's unity

Tawrat The holy book given to Musa (Moses)

Tefillin Leather boxes containing parts of the Torah strapped on the arms and head for prayers

Temple The centre of worship built by Solomon in Jerusalem and destroyed in 70 CE

Tenakh The Jewish scriptures

Thanksgiving Prayers thanking God

The Omnipresent A title used of God during mourning to remind that Jews that God is with the living and the dead

Theodicy A philosophical justification of God allowing evil and suffering

Theotokos Greek for 'God bearer'

Thirteen Principles of Faith A summary of Jewish beliefs written by Maimonides

Tilma Simple tunic made of cactus fibres worn by ancient Mexicans

Tomb An underground burial place

Torah The five books of law which are the first five books of the Old Testament

Tosefta Rabbinic opinions extra to the Mishneh

Transcendent Something going beyond human experience and existing outside the material world

Transubstantiation The belief that during the Mass the bread and wine become the body and blood of Jesus through the power of the Holy Spirit

Treason Attempting to overthrow one's government or state

Treifah Not *kosher*

Ummah The Muslim community (brotherhood of Islam)

Unitive purpose Sex as a source of joy and pleasure

Usul ad-din The five roots of Shi'a Islam

Uthman The third caliph, who ordered the final official copy of the Qur'an

Vale of soul making The idea that God gave people this life to make their souls good enough for heaven

Veneration of the cross Kissing and honouring a cross on Good Friday

Glossary

Vernacular The language of the people

Via Dolorosa 'The way of tears', the route Jesus took from Pilate's court to Golgotha

Vicegerency Looking after something on behalf of someone else

Vicegerent A person appointed to look after things on behalf of a ruler

Vigil A period of devotional staying awake on the eve of a religious festival/funeral

Virgin birth The belief that Jesus was not conceived through sex

Vision Something seen in a dream, trance or religious ecstasy, which gives a religious message

Vocal prayer Prayer using words

Vocation The calling a person has to live their life in a certain way

Votive candles Candles that are lit as a prayer is offered

Waquf A standing prayer during *hajj*

Worship song A short, modern song with one or two verses

Wudu The ritual washing before prayers

Yad Pointer for reading the Sefer Torah

Yahya John the Baptist

Yarzheit The anniversary day of someone's death

Yazid The sixth caliph of Sunni Islam

Yom Kippur Jewish holy day, also known as the Day of Atonement

Yusuf The prophet Joseph (coat of many colours)

Zabur The holy book given to Dawud (David)

Zakah Charity tax, the third pillar

Zamzam well The well in the courtyard of the Great Mosque given by God for Hagar and Ismail

Zayd ibn Thabit Muhammad's chief secretary, who organised Uthman's Qur'an

Zuhr Midday prayers

Index

Abortion 119, 245, 342
Allah 158, 160, 161, 162, 165–9
Alpha course 78–9
Anglicans 53, 70, 98, 199, 269, 332, 343, *see also* Church of England; Protestant Christians
Annulment of marriage 347
Anointing of the sick 46–7
Apostolic Tradition 5, 97, 110
Atheists 103
    attitudes to miracles 304–5
    attitudes to religious experiences 306, 308–9
    attitudes to visions 300–1
    contraception 344
    cosmological argument 315–16
    creation of universe 18
    design argument 313
    divorce and remarriage 348, 349
    gender prejudice and discrimination 355
    marriage 328
    roles of men and women 351
    sexual relations 332–3
    view of life after death 188
Atonement 284

Baptism 43
Baptist Church 339
Bible 86–94
    Dei Verbum 101
    divergent interpretations 93
    implications of interpretation 94
    Lectio Divina 94
    origins 86, 88
    Protestant views 96, 98, 107
    source of guidance and teaching 93
    source of wisdom 86
    structure 87
Big Bang theory 13–14, 316, 319
Buddhism 305

CAFOD 75–6
Cardinal virtues 72
Catechism of the Catholic Church 2, 16
Catholic Church
    abortion 119, 342
    animal rights 17
    beliefs and teachings 1–40
    contraception and family planning 342–3
    divorce and remarriage 346–7
    environment 17, 73, 74
    evangelisation 77–82
    families 334–8, 350
    four marks of the Church 108–111
    funeral rites 54–6
    gender prejudice and discrimination 353–4, 356
    heaven and hell 33, 34–5
    homosexuality 331, 333
    life after death 33
    liturgical worship 50–3
    marriage 326–7
    Mass 4, 5, 32, 37, 48, 50–2, 56, 60, 78, 80, 86, 93, 101, 103, 106, 109, 116, 127, 129, 132, 154
    missionary and evangelical work 77–81
    pilgrimage 66–71
    popular piety 61–5
    prayer 57–60
    purgatory 33, 35, 37, 62, 188
    social teaching 72–6
    support for the family in the local parish 339–41
    sexual relationships 330–1
    Trinity 2–6
    see also Catholic churches; Sacraments
Catholic churches
    altar 128
    architecture and design 122–3, 124–6
    artworks 135
    cloths and vestments 133
    crucifix 129
    decoration 123, 124–6
    hunger cloths 133
    internal features 127–31
    lectern 127
    religious art 135–9
    sacred vessels 132
    sarcophagi 133
    sculptures and statues 140–2
    tabernacle 129
Census information on religion in Britain 328
Charity 192, 205, 206, 239, 322
Christian symbolism 143–6
    alpha and omega 144
    Chi-Rho 144
    cross 143
    crucifix 143
    dove 144
    eagle 144
    fish 143
Church of England 339, 343
Civil partnerships 328, 331, 336
Confirmation 45
Conflict, *see* Terrorism; Violence; War
Contraception 101, 245, 332, 342–5, 354
Cosmological argument 314–16

Creation 11–15

Decalogue 88, 238
Design argument 294, 310–13
Divorce and remarriage 48, 101, 116, 248, 272, 327, 329, 335, 336, 337, 340, 342, 346–9, 354
Drama 147–50

Equality 225, 258, 276, 346, 350–2, 353
Eschatology 33–8
Eucharist 44, 50
Evolution 12, 13, 14, 311, 313

Families 334–8, 339–41
    blended 337
    extended 336–7
    nuclear 335
    same sex 336
    single parent 336
Family planning, *see* Contraception; Natural family planning
Four marks of the Church 108–111

Grace 30, 31–2
Great Commission 77

Hinduism 81, 218, 305
Holy books
    Bible 2, 3, 4, 7, 13, 14, 15, 36, 42, 50, 86–94
    Catholic Catechism 2, 16
    creeds 2, 14, 108, 110
    gospels 21
    hadith 161, 163, 171, 182, 185, 192, 203
    Injil 173, 176
    Mishneh 246, 250, 260, 278
    Qur'an 159, 160, 161, 163, 165, 166–7, 170, 171, 174, 175–8, 179
    Talmud 232, 244, 246, 259–62
    Tenakh 90, 178, 226, 259–62
    see individual topics for quotations from holy books
Holy orders 48–9
Holy War 186, 216
Homosexuality 119, 330, 331, 332–3, 345, 354
Human rights 16, 103, 306, 333, 350
Humanists
    attitudes to miracles 304–5
    attitudes to religious experiences 306, 308–9
    attitudes to visions 300–1
    contraception 344
    cosmological argument 315–16

Index

creation of universe 18
design argument 313
divorce and remarriage 348, 349
gender prejudice and discrimination 355
marriage 328
roles of men and women 351
sexual relations 332–3
view of life after death 188
Humanity 16–18

Incarnation 19–22
Islam, see Muslim beliefs and practices (Islam)

Jesus
 ascension 27–8
 betrayal and arrest 24
 crucifixion 25
 fulfilment of the Law 115–16
 resurrection
 source of moral teaching 115
 trial 24
Jewish beliefs and practices (Judaism)
 acts of worship 256–8
 amidah 264, 266–9
 covenants 228, 229, 237, 240–3, 246, 247, 259, 267, 270
 festivals 281–8
 food laws 261–2
 God 226–30
 life after death 249–52
 Messiah 234–6
 mezuzah 227, 238, 263, 266, 267
 mitzvot 228, 229, 238, 246–8
 nature of the Almighty 226–30
 prayer 263–5
 rituals and ceremonies 270–7
 sanctity of life 244–5
 Shabbat 238, 256–7, 278–80
 shekhinah 231–3
 shema 266–7
 synagogues 151, 225, 279, 289–91
 Talmud 232, 244, 259–62
 Tenakh 90, 178, 226, 259–62
 see also Holy books

Last Supper 23
Liturgical worship 50–3
Lord's Prayer 58
Luther, Martin 71

Magisterium 2, 4, 95–9, 102, 319
Malaikah (angels) 180–2
Marriage 47–8, 326–9
Mary 62, 65, 66, 67, 68, 69, 70, 71, 112–14
Mass 4, 5, 32, 37, 48, 50–2, 56, 60, 78, 80, 86, 93, 101, 103, 106, 109, 116, 127, 129, 132, 154

Methodist Church 339
Miracles 8, 30, 69, 70, 113, 173, 302–5, 306, 308, 309
Mosques 197, 198
Music in worship 151–4
Muslim beliefs and practices (Islam)
 Allah 158, 165–9
 angels (*Malaikah*) 180–2
 fate (*al-Qadr*) 183–4
 festivals and commemorations 218–21
 hajj 209–13
 holy books 175–9
 jihad 214–17
 jummah prayer 197, 198
 khums 205–8
 life after death (*Akirah*) 161, 185–8
 Muhammad 158, 161
 Night of Power (*Laylat al-Qadr*) 202–4
 prophets (*Risalah*) 161, 170–4
 sadaqah 193, 206
 salah 169, 192, 196–9
 sawm 166, 169, 192, 200–4
 shahadah 165, 166, 192, 194–5
 Shi'a Islam 158, 159, 163–4, 183, 192, 193, 195, 198, 206, 207, 208, 219, 220, 221
 six beliefs of Islam 160–2
 Sunni Islam 158, 160, 161, 162, 163, 164, 184, 192, 193, 195, 198, 203, 205, 207, 218, 220
 Tawhid 161, 163, 164, 166, 168
 Ten Obligatory Acts 192–3, 195, 198
 zakah 205–8
 see also Holy books
Mystery plays, see Drama

Natural family planning 342–3
Nonconformist Churches 53

Orthodox Christians 10, 49, 53, 60, 90, 91, 107, 108, 110–11, 124, 152, 199, 343
Orthodox Judaism 88, 225, 29, 232, 237, 238, 243, 245, 248, 256, 257, 258, 261, 262, 263, 264, 269, 271, 272, 273, 274, 277, 278, 290, 291, see also Jewish beliefs and practices (Judaism)

Papal encyclicals 73, 342, 353
Papal infallibility 95, 100
Parishes 339–41
Paschal mystery 23–8
Passion plays, see Drama
Pentecost 100, 133, 287
Pentecostal Churches 49, 199, 306, 339
Pilgrimage
 Jerusalem 67

Lourdes 69
Rome 68
Walsingham 70
see also Muslim beliefs and practices (Islam), Hajj
Prayer
 Christian 57–60
 Islamic 196–9
 Jewish 263–5
'Preparing for my funeral' 56
Protestant Christians 10, 13–14, 32, 37, 49, 53, 65, 71, 77, 91, 94, 96, 97, 98, 104, 107, 108, 110–11, 117, 119, 152–3, 188, 199, 306, 321, 343, 351, 354–5
Public acts of worship 50, 58, 60, 256–8, 265

Quakers 49

Reconciliation 46
Religious Society of Friends, see Quakers
Risalah (prophets) 170–4

Sacraments 4, 5, 32, 42, 43–9
 anointing of the sick 46–7
 baptism 43
 confirmation 45
 Eucharist 44, 50
 holy orders 48–9
 marriage 47–8
 reconciliation 46
Salvation 29–30, 31–2
Salvation Army 49
Same-sex marriages 328, 331, 333, 336
Sanctity of life 244–5
Second Vatican Council 52, 87, 95, 100–4, 108, 353
Sexual relationships 330–3
Sikhism 295
Situation Ethics and divorce 349
Stations of the Cross 61, 63, 64, 65, 131, 151
Stewardship 16, 17
Suffering 13–14, 29, 317–19, 320–2
Synagogues 289–91

Ten Commandments 88, 238
Trinity 2–6, 7–10

Vatican II, see Second Vatican Council
Virgin Mary, see Mary
Visions 69, 70, 89, 140–1, 232, 237, 298–301, 306

World Council of Churches 107

Photo credits

Photo credits:

p1 Yotrak Butda/123rf; p3 sedmak/Thinkstock; p6 Photos 12/Alamy; p8 FineArt/Alamy; p9 Davezelenka/Creative Commons Attribution-Share Alike 3.0 Unported; p11 Granger, NYC./Alamy; p14 Stephen Dorey ABIPP/Alamy; p17 Nils Jorgensen/REX/Shutterstock; p19 rdonar/123rf; p20 INTERFOTO/Alamy; p22 IndiaPicture/Alamy; p23 North Wind Picture Archives/Alamy; p25 Michele Burgess/Alamy; p26 Lebrecht Music and Arts Photo Library/Alamy; p29 Stephen Barnes/Religion/Alamy; p30 Manor Photography/Alamy; p31 RIA Novosti/TopFoto; p34 The Art Archive/Alamy; p35 Wellcome Library, London/http://creativecommons.org/licenses/by/4.0/; p41 Diego Cervo/123rf; p42 Andriy Kravchenko/123rf; p44 Vojtech Vlk/123rf; p45 Friedrich Stark/Alamy; p46 Myrleen Pearson/Alamy; p47 Agencja Fotograficzna Caro/Alamy; p48 robertharding/Alamy; p54 Marmaduke St. John/Alamy; p55 Sally and Richard Greenhill/Alamy; p57 Glenda Powers/123rf; p60 Aleksandr Volkov/Alamy; p61 arsgera/123rf; p62 federicofoto/123rf; p63 Zvonimir Atletić/123rf; p64 Rangan Datta Wiki/Creative Commons Attribution-Share Alike 3.0 Unported; p66 DeAgostini/Getty Images; p67 Eldhorajan92/CC BY-SA 4.0; p68l Vandeville Eric/ABACA/PA Images; p68r Franco Origlia/Getty Images; p69 imageBROKER/Alamy; p70 CountrySideCollection-Homer Sykes/Alamy; p73 Pacific Press/Alamy; p75 Matthew Chattle/Alamy; p78 Borderlands/Alamy; p79 TopFoto.co.uk; p81 Friedrich Stark/Alamy; p85 RealyEasyStar/Riccardo Squillantini/Alamy; p86 Ihar Balaikin/123rf; p87 The Art Archive/Alamy; p88 World History Archive/Alamy; p89 Yadid Levy/Alamy; p91 www.BibleLandPictures.com/Alamy; p92 FineArt/Alamy; p95 Guido Dingemans/Alamy; p96t Everett Collection Historical/Alamy; p96b Benoit Chartron/123rf; p97 RealyEasyStar/Fotografia Felici/Alamy; p99 Pontino/Alamy; p100 dpa picture alliance archive/Alamy; p103 imageBROKER/Alamy; p104 Cathy Yeulet/123rf; p105 Friedrich Stark/Alamy; p106 Alexandr Chernyshov/123rf; p107 Sean Sprague/Alamy; p109 David Crausby/Alamy; p110 Franck Metois/Alamy; p111 joseasreyes/123rf; p112 Heritage Image Partnership Ltd/Alamy; p113 Peter Horree/Alamy; p114 World History Archive/Alamy; p116 Art Directors & TRIP/Alamy; p118 Ian Allenden/123rf; p121 Steve Speller/Alamy; p122t Hemis/Alamy; p122b marina99/123rf; p124 Timothy Budd/Alamy; p125 LOOK Die Bildagentur der Fotografen GmbH/Alamy; p127 Jim Pruitt/123rf; p128 robertharding/Alamy; p129 https://commons.wikimedia.org/wiki/File:Kruis_san_damiano.gif; p130 wanderworldimages/Alamy; p131 anyka/123rf; p132l VStock/Alamy; p132r ML Harris/Alamy; p133 Lanmas/Alamy; p134 Hemis/Alamy; p135 www.BibleLandPictures.com/Alamy; p136 Heritage Image Partnership Ltd/Alamy; p138 GL Archive/Alamy; p139 B Christopher/Alamy; p140l CountrySideCollection-Homer Sykes/Alamy; p140r FR Images/Alamy; p141t Timewatch Images/Alamy; p141bl nejron/123rf; p141br James Steidl/123rf; p143 Tilly Gops/123rf; p144t Claudio Ventrella/123rf; p144m Photononstop/Alamy; p144b Simon Balson/Alamy; p145 World History Archive/Alamy; p146 David Grossman/Alamy; p147 Falkensteinfoto/Alamy; p148t Artokoloro Quint Lox Limited/Alamy; p148b Marmaduke St. John/Alamy; p149 Kevin Galvin/Alamy; p150 Art Directors & TRIP/Alamy; p151l Sean Sprague/Alamy; p151r archive.org; p152 Eric Lafforgue/Alamy; p153 Godong/Alamy; p157 robertharding/Alamy; p159 Carlos Cazalis/Corbis; p160 Art Directors & TRIP/Alamy; p164 dbimages/Alamy; p165 Art Directors & TRIP/Alamy; p170 Zeynurbaba/Thinkstock; p172 United Archives GmbH/Alamy; p176 David Knopf/Alamy; p179 robertharding/Alamy; p180 Iulian Dragomir/Alamy; p181 ZUMA Press, Inc./Alamy; p185 epa european pressphoto agency b.v./Alamy; p186 Art Directors & TRIP/Alamy; p191 Oktober64/Thinkstock; p194 Art Directors & TRIP/Alamy; p197 Sally and Richard Greenhill/Alamy; p198 World Religions Photo Library/Alamy; p201 Louise Batalla Duran/Alamy; p202 sam garza/CC BY 2.0; p205 Suhaimi Abdullah/Getty Images; p207 Robert Gray; p210 Robert Gray; p212 prmustafa/Thinkstock; p214 Saul Loeb/AFP/Getty Images; p220 Still Works/arabianEye/Corbis; p221 World Religions Photo Library/Alamy; p223 Purestock/Thinkstock; p224 Alex Segre/Alamy; p227 tzahiV/Thinkstock; p228 bestdesigns/Thinkstock; p230 Image Source/Alamy; p233 Wikimedia Commons; p235 Debra Hershkowitz/Alamy; p238t Michael Burrell/Alamy; p238b Valeriy Kachaev/Thinkstock; p239 Lebrecht Music and Arts Photo Library/Alamy; p241 ESO/B. Tafreshi (twanight.org)/CC BY 4.0; p245 Andrew Aitchison/In Pictures/Corbis; p247 Geogast/CC BY-SA 3.0; p251 World Religions Photo Library/Alamy; p255 Mauro Matacchione/Thinkstock; p257 Yadid Levy/Alamy; p258 Godong/Alamy; p261 Paul Souders/Corbis; p262 Art Directors & TRIP/Alamy; p267 tzahiV/Thinkstock; p268 Fethi Belaid/AFP/Getty Images; p271 Dan Porges/Getty Images; p274 grahamandgraham/Thinkstock; p275 David Silverman/Getty Images; p276 Ira Berger/Alamy; p278 Robert Gray; p279 Robert Gray; p282 natushm/Thinkstock; p285 chameleonseye/Thinkstock; p287t blueenayim/Thinkstock; p287b museyushaya/Thinkstock; p290 67photo/Alamy; p291 Ira Berger/Alamy; p293 lightwise/123rf; p294 ymgerman/123rf; p296 Andreas Wahra/Creative Commons Attribution-Share Alike 3.0 Unported; p299 Mary Evans Picture Library/Alamy; p300 David Crossland/Alamy; p302 Zvonimir Atletić/123rf; p303 Jon Arnold Images Ltd/Alamy; p304 robertharding/Alamy; p306 Joshua Minso/123rf; p308 Artisticco LLC/123rf; p309 udra/123rf; p310 Jozef Sedmak/123rf; p312 Photo Researchers, Inc/Alamy; p314 Victor Watton; p317 yoshiyayo/123rf; p319 Prisma Bildagentur AG/Alamy; p321 Zvonimir Atletić/Alamy; p322 Rosemary Harris/Alamy; p325 Cathy Yeulet/123rf; p326t Victor Watton; p326b David Fisher/REX/Shutterstock; p328 Grant Rooney/Alamy; p332 Mark J. Terrill/AP/Press Association Images; p334 Marmaduke St. John/Alamy; p335 Brian J. Ritchie/Hotsauce/REX Shutterstock; p337t CPA/SIPA/REX/Shutterstock; p337b szeyuen/Thinkstock; p340 Victor Watton; p343 Piotr Adamowicz/Alamy; p348 wavebreakmedia/Thinkstock; p351 Philip Scalia Alamy; p355 Michael Debets/Alamy; p356 Alberto Pizzoli/AFP/Getty Images.

Every effort has been made to trace all copyright holders, but if any have been inadvertently overlooked, the Publishers will be pleased to make the necessary arrangements at the first opportunity.